Romane memento

Romane memento

Vergil in the Fourth Century

Edited by Roger Rees

Duckworth

First published in 2004 by
Gerald Duckworth & Co. Ltd.
90-93 Cowcross Street, London EC1M 6BF
Tel: 020 7490 7300
Fax: 020 7490 0080
inquiries@duckworth-publishers.co.uk
www.ducknet.co.uk

The contributors retain copyright in their individual chapters.
Editorial arrangement © 2004 by Roger Rees

All rights reserved. No part of this publication
may be reproduced, stored in a retrieval system, or
transmitted, in any form or by any means, electronic,
mechanical, photocopying, recording or otherwise,
without the prior permission of the publisher.

A catalogue record for this book is available
from the British Library

ISBN 0 7156 3242 6

Typeset by Ray Davies
Printed and bound in Great Britain by
Biddles Ltd, King's Lynn, Norfolk

Contents

Preface — vii
List of Contributors — viii
Timeline — x
Abbreviations — xii

Introduction
   Roger Rees — 1

1. Refinement and Reappraisal in Vergilian Pastoral
   Roger Green — 17

2. Praising in Prose: Vergil in the Panegyrics
   Roger Rees — 33

3. Vergil and the Gospels: The *Evangeliorum libri IV* of Juvencus
   Michael Roberts — 47

4. Vergil, Homer and Empire: The *Descriptio orbis terrae* of Avienus
   Roy Gibson — 62

5. Sex and Salvation in the Vergilian *Cento* of the Fourth Century
   Karla Pollmann — 79

6. Doing What Comes Naturally? Vergil and Ambrose
   Ivor Davidson — 97

7. Augustine, the Grammarians and the Cultural Authority of Vergil
   Richard Lim — 112

8. Recycled Words: Vergil, Prudentius and Saint Hippolytus
   Charles Witke   128

9. *sunt etiam Musis sua ludicra*: Vergil in Ausonius
   Gerard O'Daly   141

10. Claudian, Vergil and the Two Battles of Frigidus
    Catherine Ware   155

11. 'The Plato of Poets': Vergil in the *Historia Augusta*
    Daniel den Hengst   172

12. The Truth about Vergil's Commentators
    Charles Murgia   189

Epilogue
   Danuta Shanzer   201

Bibliography   215
Index Locorum   229
General Index   237

Preface

A former colleague told me that his objection to the spelling Vergil was not because it is a hypercorrection, but because it makes Rome's *summus poeta* sound like he came from England's West Midlands. I am perfectly happy with this appropriation of the bard – it was there as a schoolboy that I first met Vergil, introduced to me as the jewel in my Latin 'O' and 'A' level courses – and rightly so. For me, as for many others no doubt, the fourth century had to wait, until I was an undergraduate in fact. Then it was I first encountered Diocletian, Julian, Theodosius, Goths and the rest. This was a history course, with no room for poetry – I certainly don't recall Vergil's name cropping up – but it did fire me with an enthusiasm for late antiquity.

The main ambition of this volume is to be an original contribution to scholarly appreciation of Vergilian reception in a period of profound cultural change. At the same time, it might bring to those whose educational trajectory leaves them better informed about Vergil than the fourth century (and to any for whom the reverse prevails) a sense of the continuities, diversities, problems and poetics inherent in the literary culture of the late antique Latin world. The twelve chapters, commissioned from three continents, cover a broad range of texts and genres – poetry, prose, pagan, Christian, political, exegetical, and so on. The collection makes no claim to cover all important writers or texts from the 300s – I regret that Lactantius in particular, but also Jerome, Ammianus and others could not be included – but it can at least hope to illuminate the curious energy and scope of that century's literary output.

Some of my long-term debts will be apparent from the opening paragraph above; to those who have interested me in Vergil and the fourth century, my sincere thanks. For their help in various ways, thanks to Deborah Blake, Roy Gibson, Tom Harrison, Allan Hood, Susanna Morton Braund, Karla Pollmann, Danuta Shanzer and Claire Sotinel; to the contributors, for bearing my bullying with good cheer; and to Aileen, Halina, Logan, Tristan and George, who might reasonably feel this book has taken four centuries to write.

I have learned much in preparing this volume – about Vergil, the fourth century, reception, and editing. I hope it is not too obvious that the latter has been a particularly steep learning curve.

Edinburgh   R.R.

Contributors

Ivor J. Davidson is Senior Lecturer in Systematic Theology at the University of Otago, New Zealand. He has written on a number of topics in patristic Latin and early church history, especially Ambrose of Milan. He is the author of *Ambrose, De officiis*, edited with an introduction, translation and commentary, 2 vols (Oxford 2002).

Roy Gibson teaches Classics at the University of Manchester. He is the author of a commentary on *Ovid, Ars Amatoria 3* (Cambridge 2003), and the co-editor with Chris Kraus of *The Classical Commentary: Histories, Practices, Theory* (Leiden 2002), and, with Ruth Morello, of *Re-Imagining Pliny the Younger* (*Aretheusa* special number 2003).

Roger Green, Professor of Humanity in the University of Glasgow, includes among his late Latin interests the reception of Vergil, especially in epic and pastoral. He has published major works on Ausonius, Augustine, George Buchanan and medieval writers.

Daniel den Hengst is Professor of Latin at the University of Amsterdam. He is a specialist on late antique historiography. He has published on the *Historia Augusta* (*The Prefaces in the Historia Augusta*, Amsterdam 1981) and works with den Boeft, Drijvers and Teitler on a series of commentaries on Ammianus. The latest volume is the Commentary on Book 24 (Leiden 2002).

Richard Lim, Associate Professor of History at Smith College, focuses on the history and religions of late antiquity. He is now writing a book on public spectacles and civic transformation from the fourth to sixth century.

Charles Murgia is Professor of Classics Emeritus at the University of California, Berkeley. He is contracted to edit volume 5 of the Harvard Edition of Servius, and eventually Vergil for Teubner. Publications include studies in text, dating, or authenticity on Servius, Vergil, Tacitus, Quintilian, Ovid, Propertius, Lucretius and the *Carmina Priapea*.

Gerard O'Daly is Professor of Latin at University College London. He is the author of books on Plotinus, Augustine and Boethius, most recently *Augustine's City of God: A Reader's Guide*.

Contributors

Karla Pollmann is Professor of Classics at St Andrews University. Among her interests are patristics and the reception of classical thought in Christian writings. Her publications include a book on Augustine's *De doctrina Christiana* (Fribourg 1996) and an edited volume *Double Standards in the Ancient and Medieval World* (Goettingen 2000).

Roger Rees, Lecturer in Classics at Edinburgh University, has written articles on Roman poetry and prose. His first book, *Layers of Loyalty in Latin Panegyric 289-307* (Oxford) was published in 2002.

Michael Roberts, Robert Rich Professor of Latin at Wesleyan University, Middletown, Connecticut, has published extensively on the poetry and poetics of late antiquity.

Danuta Shanzer, Professor of Classics and Vice-Chair, University of Illinois, is editor of *Illinois Classical Studies* and *Early Medieval Europe*. She specialises in the Latin literature of late antiquity and the early Middle Ages. Her publications include work on Augustine, Ausonius, Claudian, Licentius, Proba, Prudentius, and others beyond the fourth-century pale.

Catherine Ware is a graduate of University College Cork with a Masters degree from Brown University. She is currently researching Claudian for her doctorate at Trinity College Dublin.

Charles Witke is Professor of Greek and Latin Emeritus at the University of Michigan, Ann Arbor, and Fellow of the American Academy in Rome. His publications on classical and medieval Latin literature include *Numen Litterarum; the Old and the New in Latin Poetry from Constantine to Gregory the Great* (Leiden and Cologne 1971).

Timeline

Imperial dates, publication dates and other relevant events are given below as a guide. Usurpers appear in quotation marks.

Date	Politics	Literature
284-305	Tetrarchy with Diocletian and Maximian Augusti, and Constantius and Galerius Caesars	
287-96	'Carausius' and 'Allectus'	
289		*Pan. Lat.* X(2)
291		*Pan. Lat.* XI(3)
297		*Pan. Lat.* VIII(4)
298	Victory over Persians	*Pan. Lat.* IX(5)
303	'Great' Persecution	
306-37	Constantine emperor	
306-12	'Maxentius'	
306-10	'Maximian'	
307-24	Licinius emperor	
307		*Pan. Lat.* VII(6)
311		Lactantius *Divinae Institutiones*
312	Battle of the Milvian Bridge	
313	Edict of Milan	*Pan. Lat.* XII(9)
314/5		Lactantius *De mortibus persecutorum*
321		*Pan. Lat.* IV(10)
325	Council of Nicaea	
326	Foundation of Constantinople	
329-30		Juvencus *Evangeliorum libri*
337-61	Constantius II	
337-50	Constans	
337-40	Constantine II	
350		*fl.* Avienus, Aelius Donatus
353-70		Proba *cento*
361-3	Julian	
362		*Pan. Lat.* III(11)
363-4	Jovian	
364-75	Valentinian	
364-78	Valens	
367-83	Gratian	
369		Symmachus *Or.* 1, 3
370		Symmachus *Or.* 2

Timeline

374(?)		Ausonius *cento nuptialis*
374-97		Ambrose, Bishop of Milan
375-92	Valentinian II	
377(?)		Ambrose *De virginibus*
378	Battle of Adrianople	Ambrose *De excessu fratris*
378-80		Ambrose *De fide*
378-95	Theodosius	
379		Ausonius *Grat. actio*
381	Council of Constantinople	
384-6		Augustine, Professor in Milan
383-8	'Magnus Maximus'	
383-408	Arcadius	
384	Altar of Victory removed	
387-9		Ambrose *Exaemeron*
388(?)		Ambrose *De officiis*
389		*Pan. Lat.* II(12)
390	Theodosius excommunicated	
390-406(?)		*fl.* Prudentius
391-2		Augustine *De utilitate credendi*
392-423	Honorius	
394	Battle of Frigidus	
395		Claudian *Prob. et Olyb.*
396		Claudian *III Cons.*
397(?)		Augustine *Conf.*
398		Claudian *IV Cons.*
398(?)		*Historia Augusta*
400-10(?)		Servius *Ad Aen.*

Abbreviations

Full details for note references by author and date are given in the bibliography. The abbreviations *Ecl.*, *Geo.* and *Aen.* are used for Vergil's works. Otherwise, standard abbreviations (as listed on pp. xxix-liv of the *Oxford Classical Dictionary*, 3rd edition) are used for ancient authors and works. Journal abbreviations, when used, follow *L'année philologique*. The following abbreviations for modern works are also used.

ANRW = *Aufstieg und Niedergang der römischen Welt* (1972-)
CCSL = *Corpus Christianorum series Latina* (1977-)
CIL = *Corpus Inscriptionum Latinarum* (1863-)
CSEL = *Corpus Scriptorum Ecclesiasticorum Latinorum* (1866-)
EV = *Enciclopedia Vergiliana* (1984-91)
Harvard Edition = E.K. Rand et al., *Servianorum in Vergilii carmina commentariorum editionis Harvardianae volumen II* (1948); A.F. Stocker and H.T. Travis, *Servianorum in Vergilii carmina commentariorum editionis Harvardiane volumen III* (1965)
ILS = *Inscriptiones Latinae Selectae*, ed. H. Dessau, 3 vols (1892-1916)
LSJ = Liddell and Scott, *Greek-English Lexicon*, 9th edition, rev. H. Stuart-Jones; suppl. by E.A. Barber et al. (1968)
MGH = *Monumenta Germaniae Historica*, 15 vols (1877-1919)
OCD^3 = *Oxford Classical Dictionary*, 3rd edition, ed. S. Hornblower and A. Spawforth (1996)
OLD = *Oxford Latin Dictionary*, ed. P.G.W. Glare (1982)
PLRE = *Prosopography of the Later Roman Empire*, vol. 1, ed. A.H.M. Jones, J.R. Martindale and J. Morris (1971); vols 2 and 3, ed. J.R. Martindale (1980-92)
RAC = *Reallexikon für Antike und Christentum* (Stuttgart 1941-)
RE = *Paulys Realencyclopädie der classischen Altertumswissenschaft* (1894-)
RIC = *Roman Imperial Coinage* (1923-)
ThLL = *Thesaurus Linguae Latinae* (900-)

Introduction

Roger Rees

Dead Poet's Society

In the late 280s and early 290s, the inhabitants of Britain and the northernmost reaches of Gaul had good reason to feel nervous. They were under the aegis of Carausius, who in 286 or 287 had abandoned his position as the Roman commander of the Channel fleet, detailed to clear the water of pirates, and proclaimed himself emperor. Carausius' claims had not been recognised by the joint emperors Diocletian and Maximian, who were in fact preparing a new fleet to confront him. But those of Carausius' subjects lucky enough to have two or three coins to rub together will have noticed his unprecedented creativity and energy in self-promotion.[1]

A silver coin depicting Carausius, and assumed to date to the period immediately following his assumption of office, bears the legend EXPECTATE VENI ('Come, o expected one!');[2] this clearly recalls Aeneas' question to the ghost of Hector during the fall of Troy (*Aen.* 2.283) and the opening words of Anchises to Aeneas when his son visits the Underworld (6.687).[3] This coin issue was considered unique in its verbal reference to Vergil until 1998, when Guy de la Bédoyère proposed ingenious but very convincing expansions for the enigmatic abbreviations RSR and INPCDA, both of which appeared on Carausian issues and had mystified numismatists. Using Vergil as his key, Bédoyère suggested that these were abbreviations for *redeunt Saturnia regna* ('the Saturnian kingdoms return') and *iam nova progenies caelo demittitur alto* ('now a new offspring is sent from lofty heaven'), both taken from the opening lines of *Eclogue* 4.[4] With the resonant associations of familial and national duty in the epic phrase, and of a golden age restored in the pastoral abbreviations, Carausius sought to legitimise and consolidate his claims to power through Vergilian idiom. For Carausius, a Menapian by birth who grew to usurp power, the poet is the authorising voice of Roman imperial identity.

But if these Vergilian intertexts could give articulate expression to the ambitions and ideology of Carausius, they were to be strangled. He was murdered in 293, and his successor Allectus was finally crushed in 296 by the emperor Constantius. One feature of Constantius' celebration of the reconquest of Britain was the issuing of the Arras medallion. A magnificent piece in gold, it shows a victorious Constantius on horseback as he

1

enters London. The legend reads REDDITOR LUCIS AETERNAE ('Restorer of the eternal light'); not Vergilian, but perhaps inspired by Horace's grandly panegyrical *Ode* 4.5 to Augustus, *lucem redde tuae, dux bone, patriae* ('Great general, restore the light to your country', line 5). Whether or not the Arras medallion was a direct riposte to the Vergilianised claims of Carausius, the exchange reveals that in challenging for and defending power, usurper and emperor alike were fighting for a culture, positioning themselves at the centre of that culture and expressing their claims through an idiom which gave it voice. The poets Vergil and Horace were dead – long dead – but by now Vergil in particular was more than a poet. He had become a cultural icon and political touchstone to be invoked by any who wanted to vaunt their claims to *Romanitas*.

The fourth century

Constantius' victory over the separatist British empire ushered in the fourth century, a period of profound change in the Roman empire.[5] Constantius himself was part of Diocletian's Tetrarchy, a college of four emperors which in many respects steadied Roman affairs after turbulent decades in the mid third century.[6] With two Augusti and two subordinate Caesars, in theory this hierarchical form of collegiate government could face challenges on several fronts without compromising unity. The Tetrarchy's notable achievements included decisive victory over Persia, reforms in economic, fiscal and legal administration, and fabulous provincial palaces, such as those of Split, Trier and Thessaloniki. Its most notorious act was the 'great' persecution of Christians. The Tetrarchy appears to have been meant as a system of non-dynastic succession, but rivalrous discontent in the new century's first decade precipitated the end of the constitutional experiment.

The man to emerge from the collapse of the Tetrarchy was Constantius' son Constantine.[7] Collegiate government would feature regularly in the fourth century, but Constantine eliminated other pretenders to power. Proclaimed emperor on his father's death in 306, Constantine spent the first six years of his reign in the north-western corner of the empire. Meanwhile, the usurper Maxentius held Rome. The two clashed at the Battle of the Milvian Bridge near Rome on 26 October 312. The battle was brief and decisive. Maxentius was drowned in the river, his troops crushed. Constantine was left the unchallenged emperor of the West. Twelve years later he became sole emperor of the united empire after the defeat of Licinius.

Constantine died in 337, to be succeeded in a fretful alliance by his sons Constantine II, Constans and Constantius II. In the fifty years since Diocletian's accession to the throne in 284, despite some significant consti-

Introduction

tutional fractures, the Roman world had experienced a prolonged period of managed change and consolidation. Two features of Constantine's long reign merit particular notice. The first was his patronage of the church.[8] Within ten years of Tetrarchic persecution, the church enjoyed a remarkable change in fortunes; in 313 the 'Edict of Toleration' was published by Constantine and Licinius, decriminalising Christianity.[9] But Christianity was more than legalised. With Constantine as patron, it was enriched, dignified and given prestige; magnificent churches were built, such as the Lateran Basilica in Rome or the Church of the Nativity in Bethlehem; the vast riches endowed to the church from soon after 312 are recorded in the book of the Pontiffs;[10] and clergy were privileged with exemption from curial obligations. However, there were still severe troubles to come for the church, of different kinds.

In the 320s, Arius, a priest from Alexandria, provoked a christological debate which divided the church for many decades. With his authority as emperor and patron of the church, Constantine tried unsuccessfully to reconcile Arius and his followers to the orthodox church at the council of Nicaea in 325. Arius was excommunicated, later to be readmitted to the fold, but the lines of division were clear and deep-seated; in the decades to follow, the Arian/Orthodox faultline regularly informed church and wider politics alike. The attempt of emperor Theodosius in 382 to enforce uniformity through legislation did not rid the world of Arians; but the episode does reveal how highly the emperor valued the possibility of church unity.

A further check to the church's prosperity was the brief reign of Julian (361-3). Although a nephew to Constantine, this 'apostate' attempted to reverse the headway the church had made; a famous example was his decision in 362 to bar Christians from teaching in schools.[11] But Julian died within two years of taking office, and his successors embraced the church with considerable enthusiasm and generosity. Pagan resistance, such as that mounted in 384 by the aristocrat Symmachus in a public debate about the traditional Altar of Victory in Rome, was spirited but doomed. Under the House of Valentinian (Valentinian I, his brother Valens and sons Gratian and Valentinian II) and, in particular, the House of Theodosius (Theodosius I and his sons Honorius and Arcadius), the church gained in strength. Gratian refused the quintessentially pagan position of *pontifex maximus*, the first emperor to do so; in 391 Theodosius outlawed pagan sacrifice and entry to pagan temples.[12] It had not always been smooth, but the fourth century had witnessed a radical change in the fortunes of the church in Roman society, from persecution to privilege.

One immediate effect of this was the new prominence granted to Christians in Roman society. In the fourth century, clerics began to enjoy a platform denied them before. Some even had the ear of the emperor. If in his prolific writings in the first decades of the fourth century Eusebius the

Romane memento

Bishop of Caesarea exaggerated his closeness to Constantine, the claim must at least have been plausible.[13] Athanasius, Bishop of Alexandria from 328, was certainly an influential figure in imperial affairs over several decades. In 390 Ambrose, Bishop of Milan, was able to refuse Theodosius communion until the emperor did public penance for a civil massacre he had countenanced.[14] Careers such as that of the politician Symmachus or the court poet Claudian clearly indicate that pagans could still enjoy prominent status, but the congruence between Christian and imperial discourse was beginning to be pronounced.

The second fundamental redirection of Roman culture under Constantine was his attitude towards the ancient capital.[15] If Rome had seen little of her Tetrarchic emperors, the city would see even less of Constantine.[16] After his defeat of Maxentius in 312 he visited Rome on two further occasions only, and on 11 May 330 the city of Constantinople was consecrated in his name on the site of Byzantium on the Bosphorus. The city had its own forum, senate and imperial palace; it was the new seat of empire, the new Rome.[17] The Eternal City was not forgotten – Rome remained the traditional heartland of the empire, the 'mistress of nations' – but her influence was more ideological than political. Spending on imperial building projects at Rome was minimal. Instead, the emperors spent much more time in newly embellished 'provincial' capitals such as Trier, Antioch, Milan and Nicomedia.[18] In 410 Rome was to be sacked by the Visigoths.

The move to provincial capitals was, no doubt in part, a strategic response to the variety of civil and foreign challenges which threatened Roman government in the fourth century. Only three royal houses consolidated power in the 300s, most frequently in power-sharing colleges of two or more emperors, and altogether many fewer men claimed the throne in the fourth century than had done in the unstable middle decades of the previous century; nonetheless, the record of civil war, usurpation and feuds among reigning families reveals the tense and precarious nature of imperial authority from Diocletian to Honorius.[19] This was further exacerbated by intensification of pressure on the frontiers.[20] The Tetrarchy had secured a resounding victory over the Persians in 298, but tension continued to simmer, and Constantine was planning a new campaign when he died in 337. Hostilities were renewed under Constantius II and Julian, and resulted in a disastrous Roman campaign, in the course of which the emperor Julian died. In the ensuing peace treaty the decades of Persian resentment were calmed by significant Roman concessions.

Furthermore, Gothic threats from the Danube area occupied the attention of many fourth-century emperors, from Constantine on. These culminated in 378 at the Battle of Adrianople, in which the emperor Valens was killed. In only fifteen years, Rome had suffered two very damaging reverses. The effect was for the emperor Theodosius to pursue a more compromising policy, which saw barbarian leaders with confederate status intimately involved in serious affairs of state. The various strains exerted on the vast geography of the empire are crystallised in 395, when Theodosius died. The empire was split east/west between his sons Arcadius and Honorius, never to be reunited.

Latin literature

The fourth century was, then, a time of great political, social, religious and administrative change. It also witnessed a revival in the fortunes of Latin literature.[21] Little in the way of enduring secular Latin literature had been written since the early second century; the fraught third century was particularly unmemorable.[22] But in the so-called 'renaissance' of the fourth century, Latin letters were to flourish. Modern readers occasionally remark upon the irony that in the case of the lofty genres of Latin historiography and hexameter poetry, the last great classical exponents, Ammianus Marcellinus and Claudian respectively, were not native Latin speakers.[23] Their decision to enter the world of Latin letters must have been peculiarly self-conscious. They were both writing in the final decade of the fourth century, but Alan Cameron makes the important point that a revival in the fortunes of Latin had taken hold outside of Italy many decades before. He cites the example of the Schools of Gaul, the orators they trained, and Ausonius, their most distinguished alumnus.[24] If we add Paulinus of Nola, also from Gaul, then Juvencus and Prudentius from Spain, Arnobius, Lactantius, Nemesianus and Augustine from Africa, possibly Aelius Donatus too, and Firmicus Maternus from Sicily, we can identify a distinctively provincial profile emerging amongst prominent Latin writers in the fourth century. The revival in Latin literature did not originate in Rome and varied in intensity, time and momentum across the empire.

A similar variety can be seen in the types of literature that the revival inspired. Historiography and Claudian's poetry have been mentioned, as has the oratory from Gaul. To augment the traditional genres of didactic, pastoral, panegyrical and occasional poetry, biography, philosophy, epistolography and epideictic prose, new categories began to materialise; biblical epic, Christian *centos*, autobiography, Christian exegesis, polemic and homily, church history. Clearly, the new genres were essentially forged amid the fundamentally changing status of the Church; but the vitality of works of non-Christians such as Avienus, Symmachus and Claudian make it clear that the revival was inspired by other factors too. With Roman political geography, religion and social determination being renegotiated and contested, Latin literature, both secular and Christian, was a vigorous and strident aspect of cultural transition. In the chapters which follow, arranged in roughly chronological order, many of the cultural preoccupations which characterise the age are canvassed. The reader is invited to consider if the truism is upheld that times of upheaval and watershed are graced by new energies and ambition in artistic achievement.

The common lens through which the literary and cultural landscape of the fourth century is here viewed is the work of Vergil.[25] A consistent interest in Vergil lay at the heart of the Latin renaissance. Of course, Vergil was not rediscovered in the fourth century; a foundational classic within Latin literary education since the early principate, his oeuvre did consistent service as the primer through which Roman schoolchildren learned their letters, grammar and rhetoric well into late antiquity.[26] Here Vergil was preserved and revered, together with Cicero, Terence and Sallust.[27] Beyond the lecture-room, at various levels Vergil permeated the public realm and informed Roman cultural consciousness; from the high literature of the aristocratic elite and the exquisitely and luxuriously illustrated manuscripts of Vergil they commissioned;[28] to provincial graffiti, papyri, mosaics and wall-paintings, and to the civic stage of late Roman Carthage.[29] Thus the fourth century did not see a revival in interest in Vergil so much as a new energy and variety in the way Vergil was read, understood and inscribed. Carausius' coinage is a fine example; his confident and novel engagement with Vergil indicates very close acquaintance with the poet on the part of usurper and alike those expected to use the coins. His intertexts and abbreviations confirm the pride in their knowledge of Vergil that aristocrats were ready to parade, and as coin legends with manifest political ambitions, they indicate the variety of uses to which Vergil could be put. Not only was Vergil widely known, and well-known too, but he enjoyed canonical status as a defining characteristic of Roman culture. His appeal as a bedrock of *Romanitas* was no doubt keener for the other changes in the essence of Roman culture that the fourth century encompassed. Against the fourth century's shifting landscapes sketched above, Vergil could provide a much needed sense of continuity with the past.

The continuities explored in this volume are essentially intertextual and exegetical in nature. Intertextuality, a prominent sub-category of ancient reception, has received much recent scholarly attention, both in theoretical and, more frequently in applied form. Vergil's chosen genres – pastoral, didactic and epic poetry – all feature in fourth-century Latin, and the *Eclogues*, *Georgics* and *Aeneid* clearly serve as the respective paradigms, the *modello-codice* ('code-model') in Conte's terminology.[30] This was particularly the case in pastoral and didactic works; unconventional aspects of works like Juvencus' biblical epic, Claudian's small-scale

Introduction

historical *Gothic War* and Prudentius' allegorical *Psychomachia* mark these texts out as 'epic successors' to Vergil in rather different ways to earlier epicists such as Lucan, Statius, Valerius Flaccus and Silius Italicus.[31]

In Roger Green's analysis of the fortunes of Latin pastoral from the late third to the early fifth century, it becomes clear that intertextual engagement with Vergil functions most prominently at the level of generic *imitatio*. Servius described Vergil's *Eclogues* as imitations of Theocritus, but in appropriating the Alexandrian form for the Latin language, Vergil had transformed pastoral's frames of reference.[32] Pastoral was still set in the countryside, but the genre's thought-world had metamorphosed. Beginning with late antiquity's use of marked identifiers of the pastoral genre, Green highlights the profoundly Vergilian style and format; but in addition to these code-examples, he demonstrates too how the genre had again transformed to embrace contemporary preoccupations. Christian reactions to pastoral and pastoral reactions to Christianity reveal the genre's flexibility and fertility; the substratum of Vergilian aesthetic is modulated to late antique sensibilities.

Generic *imitatio* is more complicated in the discussions of fourth-century didactic. Juvencus published his Latin gospels in hexameter verse in 329/30, that is, during the ascendancy of the church under Constantine. Juvencus, the subject of Michael Roberts' study, is comfortably categorised as the first Christian epic poet; but his biblical paraphrase, divided like Vergil's *Georgics* into four books, contains narrative and doctrine, inviting identification as epic and didactic respectively. Roberts highlights how Vergil's presence in the *Evangeliorum Libri* demands both literary and religious interpretation. The translation of pronounced Vergilian form and idiom into explicitly Christian discourse was a radical and self-conscious watershed in Latin letters; its reverberations were to be deep-seated and enduring. The continuities implicit in formal *imitatio* are seen to heighten appreciation of differences, a literary dynamic which Roberts argues, might enjoin re-evaluation of Vergil and the Evangelists alike.

Roy Gibson highlights a similar challenge in his discussion of the apparently pagan *descriptio orbis terrarum* by Avienus. Written in the mid-fourth century, the *descriptio* is another paraphrastic text, a Latin version of the *Periegesis* of Dionysius, a Greek Alexandrian from the reign of Hadrian. The poem is nominally a work of geographical description, but Gibson reveals how in this work of literary and cultural translation, evocation of Vergilian didactic (and epic) arrogates for Avienus' poem some surprising and controversial textures. Avienus' accommodation of and resistance to Vergilian influence is a revealing aspect of an unusual complex of compositional factors underlying this neglected text.

In my own contribution, I identify an assertive political agenda in the use of Vergil made by panegyrical orators of the late third and fourth centuries. In discussion of the narrative accounts in speeches from 313 and 321 of the Battle of the Milvian Bridge, I argue that without the complicating effects of paraphrastic ambition or generic determinism, the orators' appropriation of Vergil is essentially as model-example, that is, available for precise imitation.[33] The speeches' extensive engagement with the poet marks a significant departure from the theory and practice of late republican and early imperial oratory, including Pliny's *Panegyricus*, the exemplarity of which for late antique orators has long been heralded. I argue that this confident new aesthetic reveals the orators' drive to advertise their complete acculturation to *Romanitas*.

Vergil's status as an irrefutable indicator of good taste is used in the *Historia Augusta* to characterise some of its subjects. From this opening observation about the cultural assumptions made in this enigmatic collection of imperial biographies, Daniel den Hengst moves to consider what light is shed on the notorious issues of the text's composition by its evocation of Vergil. Quotation is the normal practice here; the distribution of references across the biographies illuminates the questions of authorship and reliability; and their religious dimension prompts speculation about the relationship between the biographies and Augustine's *Confessions*.

A peculiar practice mentioned in the *Historia Augusta* and attested elsewhere was consultation of the *sortes Vergilianae*. A verse or verses from Vergil would be selected at random and interpreted to illuminate the reader's own circumstances. (Parallel practice involved Homer or the Bible.) The *sortes Vergilianae* were predicated on the vatic qualities and omniscience of the poet; at the same time, as den Hengst stresses, in recontextualising verses, this form of consultation negated any authorial intentionality and risked trivialising the text.[34] As a literary parallel to the *sortes*, Karla Pollmann cites the form of the *cento*. A centonist reassembles fragments from a canonical text (the 'hypotext') to create a new work ('hypertext'). Ausonius was the first to articulate a theory of the *cento*, in the introduction to his *cento nuptialis*, where he claims, in self-deprecation, that the new work 'devalues' the hypotext. The *cento* already had considerable ancestry and both of Pollmann's fourth-century subjects, Ausonius and Proba, adhere to the conventions of a deconstructed, cellular collage of quotations. But both too it seems were innovative, Proba (writing between 353 and 370) for her Christian purpose and Ausonius (c. 374) for his theorising and scurrilous pornographic content. The polarised tones and subjects of their *centos* reveal at the same time the flexibility of the genre and the wide appeal of Vergil's 'hypotext'. Whatever their different ambitions, Ausonius and Proba confirm the universally high value of the currency of Vergilian discourse.

If Ausonius' *cento* is the most outrageous Latin poem of the fourth

Introduction

century, his *Mosella* is the most famous. A survey of the different functions and tones of Vergilian allusion across the work of this most prolific author – at times, learned, clever, witty, scandalous, pathetic, religious, parodic, political, and always, it seems, peculiarly self-conscious – prefaces Gerard O'Daly's analysis of this hexameter poem about the river Mosel. The variety and sophistication of Ausonius' engagement with Vergil, especially his *Georgics* and *Aeneid*, are seen to characterise the *Mosella* as representative of his *oeuvre* as a whole; in this case, the Mosel region of north-east Gaul is transformed by Vergilian allusion into the true heir of *Romanitas*; Ausonius himself as narrator is aligned with Aeneas. O'Daly's formulation challenges the inclination of recent scholarship towards a unitary interpretation of the poem.

A markedly different agenda dominates the polymetric collection of Prudentius, known as the *Peristephanon*, written in the closing decade of the century. A native of Spain, Prudentius wrote the *Peristephanon*, consisting of fourteen poems, to promote the cult of Christian martyrs. The subject of the eleventh poem, addressed to Bishop Valerian of Calahorra, is St Hippolytus, martyred by dismemberment at Ostia by Roman authorities probably in the third century, and buried in the catacomb of the Via Tiburtina in Rome itself. Charles Witke demonstrates how the chronological and topographical sequencing of Prudentius' account of the martyrdom of St Hippolytus accentuates contemporary appreciation of the nature of civic identity by retrojecting onto Vergil's *Aeneid* a new Christian order. Figures of Vergilian language and thought give powerful voice to a new unVergilian world. The retrojected *interpretatio*, whereby the redeployment of Vergilian diction in the hypertext henceforward inspires and even compels a new reading of the hypotext, is perhaps the most proactive (and controversial[35]) hermeneutic in the range of intertextuality and allusion. The strain of Prudentius' work which Witke argues functions as a corrective to Vergil does not preclude a broad reverence for the Vergilian original.

If a certain tension between evocation of Vergil as an authority and revision of his texts' message underlay retrojected *interpretationes*, especially those of Christian authors such as Juvencus, Proba and Prudentius, the attraction of the accommodation of Vergilian discourse within a changing religious landscape offered a different challenge to the poet Claudian, operating in the Christian court of Theodosius and, according to modern consensus, a pagan. Catherine Ware considers Claudian's panegyrics to the emperor Honorius on the occasions of his third and fourth consulships (396 and 398). Both works, in hexameter verse, consider in detail the Battle of Frigidus, fought in 394 between Honorius' father Theodosius and the pagan pretender Eugenius. Theodosius' emphatic victory was hailed by some as a Christian success; but not by Claudian. Ware shows how

Claudian turned to Vergil to resolve any apparent contradiction. Vergilian ethics and characterisation provided Claudian with a template for his representation of the protagonists at Frigidus in a way designed to appease Christian and pagan alike. Vergilian allusion works to construct imperial legitimacy and literary status. Both Honorius and Claudian have much to gain.

The pagan literary legacy was a prominent concern to exercise the Church fathers of late antiquity, two of whom are discussed in this volume. Neither Ambrose, Bishop of Milan, nor Augustine, Bishop of Hippo (in present-day Algeria), shared the forthright and consistent misgivings of Jerome, who boasted he had not read a page of Cicero or Vergil for fifteen years, effectively demonising the great works of ancient Rome.[36] Instead, in their engagement with Vergil, Ambrose and Augustine are seen to accentuate (though not to simplify) the continuities between the pagan past and their Christian present. Ivor Davidson discusses how for Ambrose in his very public capacities of debating theologian and moral preacher, the text of Vergil was a vital and versatile medium for wider appreciation of personal obligations in a catholic society. Davidson selects four areas of Ambrose's ministry in which Vergil provided recognisable templates and points of reference. Ambrose clearly appreciated the reassuring effect Vergilian aesthetics promoted; but that at the same time they had to be subordinated to the demands and ambitions of the Christian state.

Vergil's cultural authority was also to be exploited by Augustine, who in Richard Lim's contribution is seen to be assured in his distinction between the sacred and the secular. Lim focuses on the writings of Augustine in the five-year period from 386. In his early thirties by this stage, Augustine had already turned his back on the Manichaean doctrine which had attracted him as a youth and still enjoyed great appeal in North Africa as an alternative to Christianity. In 387 Augustine was baptised into catholic Christianity. He had been educated according to the traditions of the pagan grammarian, and in his search for an appropriate and compelling means to refute the claims of Manichaeism, he turned to scholarly exegesis of Vergil as a model of sound practice for those reading sacred literature.

Today the best known literary exegete whose methodology seems representative of the practice Augustine would bring to the world of biblical analysis is Servius. Servius' commentary was probably written in the first decade of the fifth century; it is the fullest surviving work of the many of its kind written in antiquity. In late antiquity in particular, when as we have seen, some of the cultural assumptions of the early principate simply no longer persisted, the privileged status Vergil enjoyed as faultless and omniscient necessitated learned and assertive exegesis of his works by his

Introduction

commentators. In the final essay, Charles Murgia highlights the contrasting ambitions and limitations evident in the Vergilian commentaries of the late fourth and early fifth centuries. The effects of this hermeneutic culture impacted upon commentaries and their authors alike; tensions emerge between the claims and approaches of Servius (with his various sources), and those of Tiberius Claudius Donatus (*fl.* late fourth/early fifth centuries). Not for the first time in the volume, a mixture of inherited tradition and an impulse to innovate is seen to animate and complicate the reception of Vergil.

Given the range of texts that are discussed below and the ideological positions they defend, it is not surprising that the dynamics of reception are used variously and to different ends. In the Janus-like culture of the fourth century – at the same time looking forward and looking back – Vergil was available to be digested, explained, rejected or redeployed.[37] Vergil could variously be secular, sacred, political, ethical, providential and authorising. That this was appreciated at the time is established by the marked self-consciousness of much of the fourth century engagement with his work. Vergil was available for appropriation, and politicians, Christians, intellectuals and poets all recognised this potential. When even Jerome's non-engagement with Vergil, mentioned above, is explicitly proclaimed, the ideological charge of Vergilian reception is manifest. As Lim and Murgia illustrate below, the search for 'truth' could be conducted in more than one way, but Vergil provided a reliable discourse in the matrix of possibilities.

Vergil

The broad range of perspectives and approaches to Vergil adopted in the fourth century was complemented by a resurgence of interest in him as an historical figure. This even extended to material form. In the forum in Aquileia, a statue was erected in the fourth century with its dedication 'to Publius Valerius Maro, the father of Vergil'.[38] Scholarly debate about the inaccuracies of the inscription's nomenclature should not lose sight of the fact that the dedicant/s clearly believed – in fact insisted – they had it right.[39] This monumental celebration of association with the family of Vergil in the heart of Aquileia's civic showcase would be seen as an emphatic claim to a distinguished cultural pedigree.

The fourth century was a key period in the history of the biography of Vergil. Interest in the biography of Vergil influenced contemporary literary criticism, best witnessed in the *Life of Vergil* by Aelius Donatus.[40] Donatus was a grammarian practising in Rome in the mid-fourth century, and had among his pupils Servius and Jerome.[41] The *Life* survives with an accompanying letter (to L. Munatius, perhaps a former pupil, or Donatus' literary patron) in which Donatus claims to have studied almost all work on Vergil in preparation for his own; that he has exercised a rigorous selectivity in his ambition to keep the work arresting; and that he has chosen to follow his source material *verbatim*, with his own observations added.[42] Donatus' *Life* is therefore thought to have relied very heavily on that of Suetonius, Vergil's only serious biographer before the fourth century. What rendered Suetonius' *Life* unsuitable for the needs of Donatus' readership is not clear: certainly the biographer enjoyed considerable popularity in the fourth century.[43] Perhaps Suetonius' *Life* lacked the brevity Donatus valued so highly. The fact that Donatus' *Life* was itself influential on later *Lives* such as that by Servius suggests that it replaced Suetonius' as the archetype. If Donatus lacked independent sources and his biography was accordingly an unoriginal if thorough synthesis, it should be acknowledged it fulfilled a perceived need. The *Life* may reveal little of value to modern readers about Vergil, but it has much to say about the cultural preoccupations of the fourth century.

For all of Donatus' insistence on brevity, the *Life* is characterised by a keen interest in incidental and unsubstantiated detail. For example, three of the 46 chapters are given over to miracles associated with the poet's birth. Publius Vergilius Maro is said to have been born near Mantua on 15 October 70 BC, of parents of meagre means (his bricklayer father bought some woodland and kept bees) (§§1-2). When pregnant, Vergil's (unnamed) mother dreamt that she gave birth to a laurel branch which immediately took on the appearance of a mature tree, heavy with different fruits and blossom (§3). She gave birth to Vergil the following day in a roadside ditch in the countryside; the quiet baby's calm expression inspired confident expectation of a rather prosperous fate (*prosperioris geniturae*) (§4). Then to mark his birth according to local custom, a poplar branch was planted; it flourished and matured so quickly that it became known and dedicated in ritual as the 'tree of Vergil' (§5). In rehearsing these miraculous events in all their detail, Donatus reveals his willingness to perpetuate a romanticised, spiritualised and teleological attitude to Vergil. At once Donatus' Vergil is the pre-ordained child of *Eclogue* 4; the *Georgics*' literal man of the soil; and the supernatural branch, like the *Aeneid*'s golden bough, a totem.

The reverential tone of the *Life*'s symbolic opening chapters is offset by more mundane observations thereafter. Donatus tells of the poet's move to Rome, his physique and health, his dietary and sexual habits, his ultimate financial security and preference for country retreats over his house on Rome's Esquiline; the death of his parents and brothers, his own interest in medicine and mathematics, his solitary experience as a barrister (§§6-16). Such biographical niceties carry little conviction nowadays; often

Introduction

traced to inferences from his texts and anecdotes of no reliability, they have the air of legendary accretions.

Without questioning the authenticity of several works now conventionally thought not to be Vergilian, Donatus discusses the poems approximately in order of publication, and allocates most space to the *Georgics* and *Aeneid* (§§17-34). The majority of poems now relegated to the *Appendix Vergiliana* are merely named in a catalogue; three are not even mentioned.[44] However, without endorsing their quality or otherwise accounting for his selection, Donatus provides the context for and quotes an epigram against a gladiator-trainer called Ballista who had turned to crime, and offers a résumé of the plot of the *Culex* ('Gnat') complete with quotation of its sentimental closing lines (§§17-18). In the economy of Donatus' chapters on Vergil's bibliography, these are curious choices for expansion; perhaps the biographer is indulging his own tastes; making conspicuous display of his own erudition; or meeting what he sees to be a genuine pedagogical *desideratum*. In the context of the *Life* the selections accentuate the moral character of the discourse; because in tender childhood Vergil wrote sharply against the violent criminal Ballista, and then as a young man, gave touching voice to his sensitivity for rural simplicity and duty, his life and poetry are granted teleological inevitability and ethical coherence.

Donatus' brief comment on the *Eclogues* assumes considerable acquaintance with the poems. Nothing is said of the models, content or even number of poems. Simply, Vergil's purpose is said to have been 'to glorify' (*celebraret*) Pollio, Varus and Gallus because they ensured his indemnity from land confiscations after the battle of Philippi (§19). Similarly baldly, Donatus says that Vergil wrote the *Georgics* 'in honour of Maecenas' who had saved him from a violent disagreement with a veteran soldier about landholdings (§20). Vergil read the *Georgics* to Augustus after his return from Actium, with Maecenas taking up the recital when Vergil's voice failed him (§§27-8). Perhaps appreciation of the collections' literary pedigree and originality could safely be taken for granted, and their political inspiration and context was all that needed to be explained.[45] Vergil is said to have dictated many verses for the *Georgics* early each morning and then spent the day revising and reducing them to but a few, likening this process himself to the contemporary belief that a bear would fashion her cubs by licking them into shape (§22). The image keeps in tension Vergil's political interests and the more romantic aspect of an earthier side.

The *Aeneid* is said to have a varied and complex plot, to match Homer's two epics, to share in Greek and Roman terms and customs and, most especially, to cover the origins of Rome and Augustus (§21) Its incomplete state is explained by Vergil's method of composition; it was originally written in prose and then organised into twelve books (§23). To maintain his momentum in the subsequent translation into verse form, Vergil left some lines incomplete (*inperfecta*) and supported some others, as it were, with very slight lines; these, he joked were props to hold the work up until solid columns arrived (§24). Vergil died at Brindisium on 21 September 19 BC, before he had completely revised the poem (§35), but polish had been applied in some areas. Inspiration for completing two particular lines (6.164-5) is said to have come to Vergil when reciting the poem, a practice he seems to have favoured in order to seek the opinions of others (§§33-4). Vergil could recite well (§29). Augustus pestered Vergil for an advance brief about the poem and at last Vergil recited for him books 2, 4 and 6, but Octavia fainted on hearing (*Aen.* 6.884) about Marcellus, her deceased son (§§31-2). These anecdotal glimpses figure a man of great reputation, influence and popularity (Donatus quotes too Propertius' acclamation of the *Aeneid*, 2.34.65), but also of personal sensitivity, charm and humility. What can be identified with confidence is an overwhelming determination to relate biography to bibliography; the life which begins in a calm rural setting and ends in the company of Augustus before Vergil could be done with poetry and dedicate himself to philosophy as he had planned (§35), follows the contours of Vergil's literary output so closely that poet and poetry are perfectly aligned.[46] This schema accommodates Vergil's frustrated perfectionism and his epic's unfinished state; his integrity is preserved, even enhanced by the legend of his deathbed wish to burn the *Aeneid* (§39).[47]

The *Life* is conservative and uneven; it is unreliable as biography and flawed as an aid to literary criticism. Donatus' individual details about Vergil are not presented in an overtly judgmental tone; but the process of selection he claims in his covering letter seems to have been underpinned more by a moralising instinct than what might be termed an attempt at an objective enquiry. The *Life*'s lack of clear differentiation between biography and bibliography will strike most modern readers as naïve; yet Donatus' insistence on hermeneutic interplay between the poet and his poetry contributes significantly to the *Life*'s quasi-hagiographical tone. The *Life* illustrates the desire in the fourth century to preserve the tradition of Vergil and at the same time to see his poetry as symbolic. To redeploy the words of the *Life*, this symbol could be *refertae variis pomis et floribus* ('laden with various fruit and flowers', §3). The *Life* acknowledges different responses to Vergil from his own era, some critical (§43-6). Detractors of Vergil are of course, implicitly yet thoroughly condemned by the tone and detail of Donatus' biographical project – yet the idyllic image of the supernatural tree of indeterminate significance both treats Vergil the man with fateful awe and also arrogates a range of interpretative responses to his work. It is the ambition of this collection to discuss some such reactions from the biographer's own century.

Introduction

Notes

1. Casey (1994).
2. BM 1900-11-5-10; *RIC* 5 ii p. 510.
3. Shiel (1972-3).
4. Bédoyère (1998); *Ecl.* 4.6-7.
5. The fullest treatment is Jones (1964). See also Averil Cameron (1993).
6. Williams (1985).
7. Barnes (1981).
8. Frend (1984).
9. Preserved in Lactantius *De mortibus persecutorum* 48 and Eusebius *HE* 10.5.2-14.
10. Davis (1989).
11. Ammianus Marcellinus 25.4.
12. Theodosian Code 16, 10, 10; Curran (2000) 215-17.
13. Barnes (1981) 265-6.
14. McLynn (1995) 315-30.
15. Nicholson (1999) discusses the theme in the contemporary author Lactantius.
16. Barnes (1982) 71-80; Curran (2000) 43-50.
17. Sarris (2002).
18. Millar (1977, 1992^2), 44-53.
19. The House of Constantine was conspicuously explosive; usurpers included Maxentius, Magnentius, Silvanus, Procopius, Magnus Maximus and Eugenius; civil wars included those between Constantine and Maxentius, Constantine and Licinius, Julian and Constantius II.
20. Blockley (1992) 5-39.
21. Alan Cameron (1984).
22. Diehle (1994) 363, Von Albrecht (1997) vol. 2, 1281ff. Christian Latin was relatively thriving, but the Church as yet enjoyed no franchise.
23. Ammianus came from the Greek East and Claudian from Egypt.
24. (1984) 54-5. See the Timeline, pp. x-xi above.
25. See Glover (1901), Binns (ed.) (1974), Herzog (ed.) 1989.
26. Kaster (1988) 45; Horsfall (1995) 249-52, 298.
27. Haarhoff (1920) 56, 69-70.
28. The so-called 'Vatican Vergil' dates to the late fourth century. See Wright (1993).
29. See e.g. Horsfall (1995) 251-5; August. *Serm.* 241.5.5.
30. Conte (1986) 31; and Hinds (1998) 41ff.
31. Hardie (1993); and Barnes in Horsfall (1995) 257-92. For a survey of late Latin epic see Pollmann (2001).
32. Servius *proem Ad Buc. Intentio poetae haec est, ut imitetur Theocritum Syracusanum* ('the intention of the poet is this, to imitate the Syracusan Theocritus'); Du Quesnay (1979).
33. Conte (1986) 31; Hinds (1998) 41ff.
34. See also den Hengst's discussion of Augustine's condemnation of biblical *rhapsodomanteia*, below.
35. Fowler (2000) 130.
36. *Ep.* 22.30. Note Markus' characterisation of Jerome as 'a wayward and idiosyncratic scholar' (1974) 6.

37. Elsner (2000a) 175-7.
38. Sotinel (2000) 27-8.
39. The ancient lives of Vergil variously identify his father as Vergilius (Servius and Probus) and Maro (Focas); and his stepbrother as Valerius Proculus (Donatus 37).
40. See Upson (1943); Horsfall (1995) 3-25 with bibliography. Aelius Donatus is to be distinguished from Tiberius Claudius Donatus.
41. Kaster (1988) 275-8.
42. Text in OCT *Appendix Vergiliana. Vitae Vergilianae Antiquae* (1954).
43. e.g. *SHA Prob.* 2.7 and Ausonius' *Caesares* 1.3-5.
44. *Copa, Moretum* and *Elegiae in Maecenatem*.
45. Cf. Murgia below on the ambitions of Vergil's commentators.
46. Theodorakopoulos (1997); cf. Servius' identification of Vergil as Tityrus (*Ad Buc.* 1) and *Corydon* (*ad Buc.* 2).
47. Suetonius is not considered Donatus' source for 37-8; Horsfall (1995) 3, 22.

1

Refinement and Reappraisal in Vergilian Pastoral

Roger Green

'Take two or three shepherds. Add Greek-sounding names and place them in a shady spot in the sunny Mediterranean countryside with appropriate plants, animals and deities. They need plenty of leisure to converse and make music with each other. Give them a soft and simple life, with only occasional things, other than rivalry in love, to disturb the happiness of their little community. Serving suggestion: vary names, formats and themes between your eclogues.' This is the basic recipe, in formal terms, for Latin pastoral[1] – and Latin pastoral is to a noteworthy extent Vergilian pastoral. Pastoral is a strange congeries of conventions, as has been remarked,[2] and yet it became a popular and distinctive part of the European literary tradition, steadily increasing its referential and thematic scope through the centuries, without any erasure of its origins, and strongly influencing vernacular literatures. It is understandable that the same scholar (Jenkyns is comparing with it epic, lyric and satire) can say that pastoral 'does not belong to the nature of things'[3] – especially when it is recognised, as it must be, that pastoral poetry is not poetry about the country in general but poetry about the sentiments of fictive shepherds – but from this apparently humble and restricting template something surprisingly durable emerged.

This was, then, the creation of Vergil himself, drawing on material in the Greek poet Theocritus among others. The subsequent history of the pastoral genre shows it to be not only permeated by his language and motifs but also, and no less importantly, engaged in an exploration and occupation of the imaginative space outlined by him. His dominance is not due to the fact that his followers were writers of pastiche;[4] indeed, when there is pastiche in the strict sense a particular purpose may be suspected. Themes recur, certainly, and sometimes the repertoire may seem small: but scholars do not complain of yet another Funeral Games in epic, nor that a lyric poet keeps mentioning the weather; and if epic writers compete in longing for multiple mouths to express a large subject,[5] why should shepherds not competitively boast of owning a thousand animals? Nor is it right to dismiss antique Latin pastoral as consisting of 'Vergil and one or two imitators'.[6] This chapter, going up to the beginning of the fifth century, will mention at least six.

A new approach is needed: one that posits not a petering out after Vergil, to be followed by an outburst of activity in the Renaissance inspired by some misguided notions – especially the idea based on the schematism of Servius[7] that tone and style are humble, and the idea, certainly post-Vergilian,[8] that antique pastorals are set in Arcadia – but rather one that leaves room for tracing how poets of various eras worked with the possibilities of relating Vergilian form and subject-matter to new conditions. This paper will contribute by presenting first the eclogues of Nemesianus, written not long before the beginning of the fourth century, which are apparently very traditional, and then some fascinating Christian experiments in the rapidly changing cultural atmosphere of the fourth and early fifth. We will see not only the continuing appeal of the genre but also its fertility and flexibility in an educated environment in which Vergil was regularly regarded as the 'greatest' or the 'noblest' poet.

Nemesianus

The poet Nemesianus is regarded by many as one of the humbler occupants of the mansions of the Minor Latin Poets,[9] but in late antiquity he was more famous. At least, he is given high praise in the *Historia Augusta*, in which it is said of Numerianus, a son of the emperor Carus, that 'in verse composition he is said to have been such that he surpassed all the poets of his time. For ... he competed with Olympius Nemesianus, who wrote *Cynegetica*, *Halieutica* and *Nautica* and emerged as one distinguished by all the colours of poetry' (*Carus* 11.2).[10] Nemesianus probably never wrote the epic or panegyric on the sons of Carus and their conquests that he promised in *Cynegetica* lines 63-75, but we may add to the above list of works by this aspiring Vergil – an African Vergil, to judge from various indications[11] – a small set of pastorals, confused until 1854 with the pastorals of Calpurnius because of a false attribution in most of his manuscripts.[12]

These are very much in the Vergilian tradition, and are composed with elegance, insight and economy.[13] In a very literal, and programmatically significant, sense, Nemesianus begins where Vergil left off, for the first two words recall the end of Vergil's last *Eclogue* (*haec sat erit, divae, vestrum cecinisse poetam, dum sedet et gracili fiscellam texit hibisco, Pierides*, 'This will be enough, Muses, for your poet to have sung while he sits and weaves a basket from the slender mallow', 10.70-2). Nemesianus begins with these words from Thymoetas:[14]

1. Refinement and Reappraisal in Vergilian Pastoral

> dum fiscella tibi fluviali, Tityre, iunco
> texitur et raucis immunia rura cicadis,
> incipe, si quod habes gracili sub harundine carmen
> compositum. nam te calamos inflare labello
> Pan docuit versuque bonus tibi favit Apollo.
> incipe, dum salices haedi, dum gramina vaccae
> detondent, viridique greges permittere campo
> dum ros et primi suadet clementia solis. (*Ecl.* 1.1-8)

While you are weaving a basket with river rushes, Tityrus, and while the countryside is free from the rasping cicadas, begin, if you have a song composed for your slender reed-pipe. For it was Pan who taught you to blow into the reeds and good Apollo who blessed you with verse. Begin, while the kids graze on the willows and the cows on the grass, and while the dew and the gentleness of the morning sun urge you to send the flocks into the verdant plain.

Other Vergilian features are immediately apparent: the name of Tityrus in the first line; the river and the grassy meadows; the flora and fauna, including Vergil's cicadas (*Ecl.* 2. 13); Pan and Apollo, the most important deities; the time of day. The assumption, integral to pastoral, that shepherds sing songs whenever they meet is found here too, conveyed in the polite insistence of repeated *incipe*.[15] Tityrus successfully excuses himself from song, as one too old and now immune from sexual passion (love is a major theme of pastoral); and so Thymoetas, the rising star, modestly obliges, and sings a song that he has previously carved on a tree.[16] This is a lament for the deceased Meliboeus, who was not only an admirer of Thymoetas (17-18) but a respected benefactor of the rural community, notably in settling legal disputes (49-55). It has been well observed that the tone here is not that of imperial panegyric or an encomium like Vergil's lament for Daphnis;[17] whoever he was, Meliboeus was human, and had suffered the *communis causa* ('the common lot of mankind': 1.48).[18] But the literary lineage of the name is obvious: there are predecessors in Vergil *Eclogue* 7, where a Meliboeus is a judge (or at least gives a verdict), and in Calpurnius 1 and 4.

Tityrus ends by complimenting Thymoetas:

> nam sic dulce sonas, ut te placatus Apollo
> provehat et felix dominam perducat in urbem.
> iamque hic in silvis praesens tibi Fama benignum
> stravit iter, rumpens livoris nubila pinnis. (83-6)

For you sound so sweetly, that a favourable Apollo carries you forward to the city and auspiciously leads you into the queen of cities. And already here in

the woods Fame is present and has paved your way, scattering with her
wings the clouds of envy.

Evidently Thymoetas (who could stand for the poet) is already making a
reputation for himself, and following in the footsteps of the Tityrus of
Vergil's first *Eclogue*, who actually returned from the city but was later
seen as a kind of poetic (and catless) Dick Whittington, or a Scottish 'lad
o'pairts', who went to the Smoke and made good. He might even be
identifiable with the poet Calpurnius, if it is true that the two poets could
have known each other in real life.[19]

The second *Eclogue* of Nemesianus presents the songs of two shepherd-
boys, Idas and Alcon, distraught by the absence of their beloved Donace,
who had been raped by them and strictly confined by her parents when
they detected signs of pregnancy. The first word (*formosam*, 'beautiful')
echoes the second *Eclogue* of Vergil, where *formosum* is the first word, and
the first line echoes also the first line of Calpurnius' second *Eclogue*,
intactam Crocalen puer Astacus et puer Idas (... *dilexere diu*), 'the boy
Astacus and the boy Idas (loved for a long time) the virgin Crocale'. The
form of the eclogue, with its two matching songs of exactly equal length (in
this case 33 lines), is that of Vergil's fifth; this is now used to develop an
interesting contrast between the two singers. Idas is a wimp, a self-
confessed shrinking violet (*pallidior buxo violaeque simillimus erro*, 'I
wander paler than boxwood and very like a violet': 2.41);[20] Alcon, by
contrast, has a well-massaged ego, claiming that he is superior to Idas both
in his choice of presents (a caged bird is certainly unusual) and in beauty
(lines 60, 78). At the end, after enthusiastically describing his beautiful
face (in seven lines, whereas Vergil had used less than two), Alcon echoes
Tityrus' tribute to Thymoetas in the first *Eclogue*, saying that he will make
a name for himself in the city. Modesty is not his strong point, and so in
terms of the pastoral ethic he is the less attractive personality, rather like
Thyrsis in Vergil's seventh *Eclogue*, who loses the contest to Corydon (at
least on the usual interpretation of line 69[21]) on what scholars see as both
moral and poetical grounds.[22] (In terms of poetics, Idas is made to quote
Vergil to the point of pastiche, while Alcon shows a leaning to Calpurnius).
Here in Nemesianus we seem to have the interesting notion of a character
breaking ranks, as it were, and aspiring to follow the poet's own journey,
or poetic trajectory, to the city as presented in the first *Eclogue*. The closing
lines bring him down to earth; both are, after all, *pueri*, and they have been
singing throughout the daylong heat of north Africa, just like the agitated
Corydon in Vergil's second *Eclogue*.

Eclogue 3 proclaims its ancestry in two ways. Its second line, *torrentem
patula vitabant ilice solem* ('they were avoiding the blazing sun under a
broad holm-oak'), is identical to the second line of Calpurnius' fifth *Eclogue*

1. Refinement and Reappraisal in Vergilian Pastoral

(actually a mini-*Georgic* in which the pastoral character Micon gives instruction on the care of young farm animals), but the key to the poem is to be seen in the allusion in lines 61 and 62 to the Silenus of Vergil's sixth *Eclogue, inflatum hesterno venas, ut semper, Iaccho* ('puffed up with yesterday's wine throughout his whole body, as always', 6.15). Nemesianus goes behind Vergil's picture of Silenus (and, one might add, behind Vergil's second *Georgic*, which is on viticulture) to tell the story, through the character Pan, of how the satyrs discovered wine under the guidance of the young Bacchus. The content of Pan's song has nothing to do with Vergil's sixth, and although there may be hints of Vergil's fourth *Eclogue* in the baby Bacchus and the simultaneous growth of the vine it is a strikingly original variation, perhaps inspired by the Bacchic scenes popular on contemporary sarcophagi.[23] Mock-didactic and mock-hymnic, the tale is told with great comic brio; in the merry chaos at the end of this first ever Bacchanal the god even gives a winebowl to a lynx.[24] The closure of the poem wryly highlights the task of milking.

Another form of the traditional eclogue, the amoebaean, is adopted in his fourth *Eclogue*. In short songs of five lines each – Vergil had favoured two and four in *Eclogues* 3 and 7, Calpurnius four and five in *Eclogues* 2 and 4 – Lycidas and Mopsus vocalise their disappointment with their absent lovers. As in Vergil's eighth, there is a refrain at the end of each short song: *cantet amat quod quisque: levant et carmina curas* ('let everyone sing of what he loves: songs too relieve love's pangs'). Each of the five pairs of songs develops a commonplace theme from earlier pastoral and other love poetry. The refrain does not mutate in any way at the end, as it does in Vergil's eighth, and in this poem, unless the mention of the beloved at the end of each man's final stanza is intended as a closing feature, there is no ending at all. This is also the only eclogue of the four that does not end with the coming of evening, a Vergilian motif that, as we have seen, Nemesianus likes to exploit. The poem, and with it the whole set, peters out, and the possibility must be considered that we have lost two stanzas, and its true ending. It is worth asking, too, whether the extant set of four poems corresponds to Nemesianus' intentions. Just as Calpurnius wrote seven *Eclogues*, with 1, 4 and 7 distinguished by an unusual theme and treatment, so Nemesianus was perhaps minded to add a fifth, thus sandwiching the poems on familiar themes between poems of greater originality, and making the flamboyant third a centrepiece. A final eclogue might have dealt with the poet's own role – or did he reach the city, whether literally or metaphorically, sooner than he expected, and, more impatient than Vergil (who is sometimes surmised to be disillusioned with pastoral),[25] simply drop his Pan-pipes and pruning-hook?

Fourth-century developments

The next individual poem to be examined is some hundred years away; the work of a dedicated Christian, it will be very different in context and content. The religious revolution, though strong in the late third century and certainly powerful in Africa, seems to have left the poetry of Nemesianus untouched. The significance of the word *paganus* in 4.62 is not that Amyntas, that son of a witch, is a 'pagan' (still less an especially bad one!) but simply that he is a rustic like the others: the poet drops his guard for a moment, for the epithet is otiose.[26] A case might be made for seeing parody of Christian thought in one or two places, but this would be speculative and tenuous. The triumph of Christianity through the intervention of Constantine – which Nemesianus could well have lived to see, though we know nothing of his life after the *Cynegetica* – created a radically new situation, and one which the Christians were not slow to exploit. Constantine himself, in his *Oration to the Saints*, a sermon delivered to a Christian audience between 317 and 324,[27] appealed to Vergil's fourth *Eclogue* to show that Vergil had foretold the birth of Christ, though it seems that most Christian interpreters did not go so far; it was generally thought, especially in the Latin speaking West, that Vergil was citing a Sibylline oracle.[28] Another sign of Christian interest in Vergil is the work of the Spanish priest Juvencus (*c.* 329/30).[29] Juvencus does not avoid pastoral intertexts, but they are not conspicuous. In the *cento* of Proba some thirty years later, citations of the *Eclogues* are proportionately fewer than those of the *Aeneid*.[30] The explanation may be the obvious one that the subject-matter of the pastorals is more esoteric and its wording less amenable to borrowing; but it is to be noted that Proba, like Juvencus, holds back from using pastoral material even in contexts that invite it. A rather different approach was taken later – perhaps in the late fourth century, when Proba's work finds renewed interest,[31] by the Christian centonist Pomponius, who has his Tityrus and Meliboeus sing beside a river.[32]

Paulinus of Nola makes considerable use of Vergil's *Eclogues*,[33] more so than his contemporaries Prudentius and Claudian, and does so long after he has bidden farewell to the Muses; and so too does Ausonius, though seldom in his *Mosella*. To take one of several possible examples, there is an exquisite use of pastoral convention in a letter to his beloved Paulinus (*Ep.* 21.62-72).[34] Lamenting his pupil's sudden and unexplained absence, he prays that the person responsible may be deprived of the use of his own voice, and of the converse that is part and parcel of pastoral, and the pleasures of the pastoral world. These pleasures include those of song (*querella*[35]), the kindly attentions of the animal world,[36] and the sympathetic echo which is described as 'hidden in the

1. Refinement and Reappraisal in Vergilian Pastoral

groves of shepherds'.[37] This rich recreation of pastoral is a metaphor for the communication that Ausonius so misses, and for the poetic exchanges of time past.

Another great scholar of the time, perhaps no less aware of pastoral charms, takes a very different line. Jerome, explaining the significance of the pigs' food eaten by the Prodigal Son in the parable, fulminates that 'now we see priests leaving aside the gospels and the prophets and reading comedies, singing the erotic words of bucolic verse, clasping their Vergil and wilfully and willingly doing what schoolboys are obliged to do'.[38] For Jerome pastoral was out of bounds to the Christian because it was the poetry of love, and also because classical poetry was *in idolorum laudes composita*, 'written for the praise of idols'.[39] The attractiveness of the poetry only makes the damage more insidious. Elsewhere he inveighs against misinterpreting Vergil's fourth *Eclogue* and making it speak of Christ.[40] These views are not untypical of articulate Christians: we may add Gregory of Nazianzen's disapproval of the 'personal pleasure' enjoyed by the shepherds of the pastoral ideal.[41]

Christian experimentation in pastoral

There are various lesser-known writers who devise interesting approaches within the space between total acceptance and total rejection defined by Ausonius and Jerome. Only one can here be presented in detail: Endelechius, whose single poem, entitled by the two extant manuscripts *De mortibus boum* ('on the deaths of oxen'),[42] may well refer to the plague of *c.* 386 attested by Ambrose.[43] Lines 21-4 make it likely that its setting is Gaul, perhaps eastern Gaul, though Aquitaine would fit his connection with Paulinus better.[44] In form this poem is strikingly different from conventional pastoral – not least in its use of a Horatian lyric metre[45] rather than the otherwise normal hexameter – but it cannot be understood without a knowledge of pastoral convention and was written for people of considerable learning.

Lack of space prevents the presentation of the whole text or a complete translation, but what follows will suffice to demonstrate its remarkable inventiveness. The text is that of Riese and Korzeniewski.[46] The names of the three characters are Aegon, Bucolus and Tityrus, of which Aegon and Tityrus are Vergilian, that of the victim Bucolus ('cowherd', 'shepherd') presumably made up.

A. Quidnam solivagus, Bucole, tristia
   demissis graviter luminibus gemis?
   cur manant lacrimis largifluis genae?
      Fac, ut norit amans tui!   4

B. Aegon, quaeso, sinas alta silentia
   aegris me penitus condere sensibus.
   nam vulnus reserat, qui mala publicat;
      claudit, qui tacitum premit.   8
A. contra est quam loqueris, recta nec autumas.
   nam divisa minus sarcina fit gravis.
   et quicquid tegitur, saevius incoquit.
      prodest sermo doloribus.   12
B. scis, Aegon, gregibus quam fuerim potens,
   ut totis pecudes fluminibus vagae
   complerent etiam concava vallium,
      campos et iuga montium;   16
   nunc lapsae penitus spes et opes meae,
   et longus peperit quae labor omnibus
   vitae temporibus, perdita biduo.
      cursus tam citus est malis!   20
A. haec iam dira lues serpere dicitur.
   pridem Pannonios, Illlyrios quoque
   et Belgas graviter stravit et impio
      cursu nos quoque nunc petit.   24
   sed tu, qui solitus nosse salubribus
   sucis perniciem pellere noxiam,
   cur non anticipans quae metuenda sunt
      admosti medicas manus?   28
B. tanti nulla metus praevia signa sunt,
   sed quod corripit, id morbus et opprimit;
   nec languere sinit nec patitur moras.
      sic mors ante luem venit.   32
   ....
A. quidnam, quaeso, quid est, quod vario modo
   fatum triste necis transilit alteros
   affligitque alios? en tibi Tityrus
      salvo laetus agit grege!   100
B. ipsum contueor. dic age, Tityre:
   quis te subripuit cladibus his deus,
   ut pestis pecudum, quae populata sit
      vicinos, tibi nulla sit?   104
T. signum, quod perhibent esse crucis dei,
   magnis qui colitur solus in urbibus,
   Christus, perpetui gloria nominis,
      cuius filius unicus.   108
   hoc signum mediis frontibus additum
   cunctarum pecudum certa salus fuit.
   sic vero deus hoc nomine praepotens
      salvator vocitatus est.   112
   fugit continuo saeva lues greges,
   morbis nil licuit. si tamen hunc deum

1. Refinement and Reappraisal in Vergilian Pastoral

	exorare velis, credere sufficit:	
	votum sola fides iuvat.	116
	non ullis madida est ara cruoribus	
	nec morbus pecudum caede repellitur,	
	sed simplex animi purificatio	
	optatis fruitur bonis.	120
B.	haec si certa probas, Tityre, nil moror,	
	quin veris famuler religionibus.	
	errorem veterem defugiam libens,	
	nam fallax et inanis est.	124
T.	atqui iam properat mens mea visere	
	summi templa dei. quin age, Bucole,	
	non longam pariter congredimur viam	
	Christi et nomina noscimus?[47]	128
A.	et me consiliis iungite prosperis.	
	nam cur addubitem, quin homini quoque	
	signum prosit idem perpete saeculo,	
	quo vis morbida vincitur?	132

A. 'Why, Bucolus, do you wander alone and groan sadly with sorrowfully downcast eyes? Why are your cheeks running with copiously flowing tears? Let your loving friend know!' (4)

B. 'Aegon, I beg you to allow me to maintain deep silence within my distressed mind. For a man who divulges grief opens up a wound, but one who keeps it within himself, closes it.' (8)

A. 'It is the opposite of what you say, and you do not speak correctly. For a burden shared becomes less heavy, and whatever is covered festers more cruelly. Conversation helps grief.' (12)

B. 'You know, Aegon, how rich I was in flocks, so that my flocks wandering over whole rivers filled even the hollows of the valleys, the plains, and the mountain ridges: now my hopes and my livelihood have completely crashed, and whatever my long labours in all periods of my life have produced has been lost in a couple of days. So quick is the course of disaster!' (20)

A. 'This terrible plague is already said to be spreading. For a long time it has devastated Pannonia, Illyria too, and northern Gaul, and now is attacking us in its inexorable course. But you have become expert in knowing how to drive away harmful disease with healing drugs – why did you not anticipate this fearful disaster and apply your medical skill?' (28)

B. 'For such a horror there are no advance signs, but what the disease takes hold of it also overwhelms; nor does it allow respite or brook delay. So death comes before the plague (32) ....

A. 'Why is it, I wonder, that the sad fate of death passes over some and afflicts others, inconsistently? Look, there is Tityrus, happy and leading a healthy flock!' (100)

B. 'I see him. Tell me, Tityrus, what god has rescued you from this disaster, so that you don't have the plague which has ravaged your neighbours?' (104)

T. 'The sign which they say is that of the cross of the god who is worshipped alone in great cities, Christ, the glory of the eternal godhead, whose only-begotten son he is. This sign, applied to the centre of their foreheads, was the sure salvation of all my animals. So the god who is powerful with this true name has been called the saviour. The cruel plague fled immediately from my flock: disease had no power. But if you wish to prevail upon this god, it is enough to believe; faith on its own helps prayer. There is no altar wet with blood, nor is the disease of the livestock driven away by slaughter, but simple purification of the mind secures enjoyment of the good things that you desire.' (120)

B. 'If you can vouch for these things as true, Tityrus, I do not hesitate to subject myself to the true rites. I will gladly flee ancient error, for it is deceitful and empty.' (124)

T. 'And yet my soul is eager to visit the temple of this greatest god. Come, Bucolus, why don't we join together for our long journey, and acknowledge the power of Christ?' (128)

A. 'Include me too in your happy plans. For why should I doubt that the sign which conquers the power of disease also benefits a man for eternity?' (132)

This description of a plague and its ravages is new in pastoral; though occasionally in danger, the animals are unaffected by disease.[48] The theme of the poem actually looks back to the *Georgics*, especially the passage where Vergil describes a severe outbreak in Noricum (3.440-566). From this Endelechius borrows certain words and phrases – *serpere* (469, in his line 21), *ilia* (507, in line 51), *medicas ... manus* (455, in line 28); he adapts *immemor herbae* (498) in line 65 and recasts a simile (470-1) in lines 85-8.[49] Yet this poem owes much to the pastoral tradition. The names are a pointer to this, but more important, and indeed crucial to the structure of the poem, are verbal reminiscences that occur at three particular moments.

The poem begins with Aegon asking Bucolus what is wrong; we may compare the beginning of Calpurnius' third *Eclogue*, where Meliboeus asks *quid tacitus, Corydon?* ('why are you silent, Corydon?'), and the similar beginning of the second of the Einsiedeln *Eclogues*,[50] where Glyceranus asks *quid tacitus, Mystes?* These take a hint from the beginning of Vergil's

1. Refinement and Reappraisal in Vergilian Pastoral

ninth *Eclogue*, and in all these cases the sorrowful shepherd is prevailed upon to speak. Bucolus is told that a problem shared is a problem solved; exposing one's distress is better than hiding it – which is why the shepherds in Nemesianus' fourth *Eclogue* (in particular 4.12, *nudantur vulnera*) ventilate their frustration in song. The second pivotal moment is found at the beginning of Bucolus' sad story, as he bemoans the wealth he has lost: *scis, Aegon, gregibus quam fuerim potens* ('You know, Aegon, how rich I was in flocks', 13). Here he is using a theme which goes back to Theocritus (11.34); after Vergil had adapted it for the raving Corydon (2.21) it became a regular, one might almost say obligatory, motif,[51] to be found in Calpurnius (2.68-9), Nemesianus (2.34-5), the Carolingian court poet Modoin (5.47),[52] Sannazaro (*Eclogue* 2.30-2: oysters!), and Sir Philip Sidney. Its use now in a context of dejection makes for a telling contrast: deluded the other characters may be, but their wealth is a cause for confidence, if not happiness, whereas the flocks of Bucolus are all lost.

The third of these moments brings the poem to its climax. After the long sad story of Bucolus, punctuated by Aegon's well-meaning but lame interventions in lines 21-8 and 53-6, they see Tityrus, his flock evidently unscathed, and ask him what god rescued him from the pestilence that ravaged their other neighbours. Just so in Vergil's first *Eclogue*, where Meliboeus, dispossessed and demoralised, and trying to fathom why Tityrus is so happy, asked *sed tamen iste deus qui sit da, Tityre, nobis* ('But tell us, Tityrus, who this god of yours is', 18). The influence of Vergil may go further. Both characters begin their explanations with a single word – in Vergil 27 it is *libertas* ('freedom') and in Endelechius *signum* ('the sign') – and both answers show a certain incoherence, perhaps a suggestion of euphoria. Then the Christian Tityrus tells us that this sign, branded onto his sheep's foreheads, is that of the cross of Christ, the deity worshipped alone in cities: he has triumphed in the cities but not yet in the countryside. Bucolus is convinced. The nearest church, we learn, is some way away, but they all decide to go there (flocks and all). This journey recalls the journey to Rome that was forced on Tityrus by the danger of land confiscation, or rather the journey to Rome which (with the embellishment of biographical tradition) was the making of Tityrus/Vergil;[53] and it inverts the sad journey of Vergil's ninth *Eclogue*. Tityrus does not gloat, though he is allowed to preach and instruct the new believer before they reach the city, the place of salvation. Though the city – it hardly matters which city – remains on the periphery in formal terms, it is the place of salvation, and its dominant deity is now at the centre of the world. The country in this poem is no longer idealised; we hear but little of its music (*crepitacula*, 'cowbells' – and in unison! – in lines 35-6), and there is no description of its aesthetic appeal, no mention of leisure or song, no hint of pagan deities. Love is banished, but the sympathy between shepherds already inherent in the genre is easily transmuted into Christian *agape*. There are strong bonds of love (*pietas* in line 80) in the animal world too, a note already strong in republican times; the picture of the steer 'mourning for the death of his brother' in *Georgics* 3.518, a line recast by Endelechius in line 47, is one of many that show the influence of Lucretius' picture of a sorrowing cow in 2.355-66.[54]

This is a remarkable poem. Pastoral takes in preaching. Bucolus has no doubt that the whole of 'ancient error' is vain (123-4); he is told that all he needs is 'faith alone' (116: *sola fides*). It is not to be regarded as an allegory: we naturally think of a Christian pastor and his flock, but if that idea were relevant there would be no point in the unbelieving Bucolus having a flock, and it would be inappropriate for members of his flock to be portrayed as capable of loving conduct. Admittedly they suffer 'the sad fate of death' (99), which might suggest the unregenerate; but some of the animals die within two days (19), which may be a hint of the death of Christ. The thought that humans may be saved in the same way, and that the sign of the cross may be somehow beneficial to them – both physically (for Ambrose seems to imply a plague that destroyed oxen and humans alike) and spiritually – only enters in the last stanza; the poem's main concern is the efficacy of the sign of the cross in branding animals. That this reflects actual practice is clear from John Chrysostom and other sources.[55] It is a rural tale, and one of greater moment than the stories that Paulinus used in his later poems to show the power of faith and God's care for the animal world.[56] The recent ravages of foot and mouth disease in Britain have made clear the magnitude of the effects, both emotional and material, of such a disaster on the rural community, and the sympathetic interest aroused within society as a whole; Endelechius recalls a similar disaster, presenting it within a Vergilian frame to increase its resonance with the educated élite.

The last poem to be discussed in this paper is a poem of perhaps twenty years later, generally known (insofar as it is known) under the misleading and unhelpful title of *Epigramma Paulini*.[57] About a hundred lines long, it is not an epigram in the familiar sense; and the Paulinus to whom it is attributed cannot be confidently identified.[58] Two Christians – their names, Salmon and Thesbon, are not taken from the pastoral store, but because they are porte-paroles and have Grecising endings are not far from the world of Aegons and Corydons – meet after an absence of some time and discuss the present situation of their faith (rather as academics meeting at a conference will usually begin a conversation by asking how their specialism is faring at the University of Poppleton, or wherever). The setting is a 'temple' of the Christian God, a detail that tells us something about the implied readership, for the use of this word, rather than the word *ecclesia*, the normal term for 'church', exemplifies a linguistic concession to educated tastes of a common type.[59] Rural detail is sparse, although they

1. Refinement and Reappraisal in Vergilian Pastoral

are certainly in the country. Thesbon, having given his visitor the opportunity of going straight to church to pray (for he is a *peccator*, 'sinner') directs him to a seat

> cui fratrum ad requiem frondosae vitis in antro
> herbida caespitibus sunt structa sedilia vivis. (6-7)

'by whom' [he refers to himself] 'for the repose of the brothers grassy seats have been created from the living turf in a cave entwined with a leafy vine'.

The pastoral underpinning of the scene is obvious: the leafy vine is paralleled in Vergil *Eclogue* 2.70, and the cave in pastoral (as opposed to epic) is always welcoming. It is combined interestingly with a reference to *Aeneid* 1, *vivoque sedilia saxo* ('seats from the living rock', 167), that recalls Aeneas' landfall on a remote African beach. Here they discuss the damage done to the countryside by its new invaders; verbally at least the words *agris opibusque hominum terraeque colonis ... barbarus incumbit* ('the barbarian has fallen upon the fields, upon the wealth of men and upon the tillers of the soil'), allude to the first *Eclogue* of Vergil, especially his emphatically placed word *barbarus* (71). Nonetheless there is now a greater enemy, *interior pestis bellumque profundum* ('inner pestilence and a deep conflict'), and here the poem becomes more ambivalent about the countryside, for one of the complaints is the selfishness and complacency of the owners of villas. Repairs to house and garden (including vines evidently unpruned for some time) are more important than the cultivation and restoration of the mind (26-9), and the tone becomes both self-culpatory and satirical. The second half of the poem (after a brief intervention by Thesbon) begins with a furious tirade on the morals of women; the problem is that they read about Dido and Corinna, and the odes of Horace and the mimes of Marullus, instead of Solomon and Paul. Salmon tries to put a brighter side – either sex may attain the crowns of martyrdom – but the conversation must end as the time of day warns them to rise (the same word as in Vergil *Eclogue* 10.75) and proceed to worship. This final touch (anticipated by *ante diem, Thesbon, tenebris nox umida condet*, 'Thesbon, damp night will cover the daylight with its darkness before ...', 55) confirms the impression that the poem is designed as a pastoral.

Many traditional pastoral features are lacking in the *Epigramma Paulini*, as in Endelechius; but here we must also note the treatment of the relationship between country and city. In Vergil there is a marked opposition between them: the city from which Tityrus gained his freedom is also the city where it was decided that land must be lost; and there is no affection for the city in *Eclogues* 8 and 9. In Calpurnius the city acquires a positive charge:[60] his Corydon goes so far as to deplore the country garb which prevents him from seeing his new master. For Nemesianus, as we have seen, the city is the goal of the ambitious poet. Endelechius uses as his backdrop the unconverted countryside, but the city is the locus of salvation. In pseudo-Paulinus, too, we are in the countryside, but there is no city. Social and historical factors have no doubt played a part here: the cities or towns may no longer, after the destructive barbarian invasions, be seen as viable, and in any case the territory in question is one dotted with large villas, like so much of the Western empire. As always in pastoral,[61] there is a strong sense of community – the widely spread but sympathetically united Christian community, which in spite of its denunciations has a feeling of responsibility to society as a whole – but here it is in no way defined by contrast with the city. The traditional polarity is elided. The enemy is from without, the literal *barbarus*; but, more importantly, it is also within, in the morally recalcitrant human mind, as will be said increasingly in later centuries as pastoral poets lay claim to wider perspectives. Just as epic has developed, by the early fifth century, into the *Psychomachia* enacted within the 'cave' of the human mind, so pastoral, though still recognisably in its sylvan grotto, has acquired the possibility of being a landscape of the soul.

Notes

1. This (home-made) recipe is similar to that found in Greg. Naz. *Orat.* 2.9 (*SC* 247 [Paris, 1978] 102), derived presumably from Greek sources.
2. Jenkyns (1998) 180.
3. Ibid.
4. Jenkyns (1998) 179, (1992) 153.
5. See Hinds (1998) 41-7; Conte (1986) esp. 31; and the Introduction above.
6. Jenkyns (1992) 153.
7. See Thilo (1887) 1-2; Paterson (1988) 20-42.
8. Jenkyns (1989), summarised in Jenkyns (1998) 157-69.
9. See Duff and Duff (1968); Volpilhac (1975) (critical text with French translation); Williams (1986) (critically established text with commentary).
10. *versu autem talis fuisse praedicatur ut omnes poetas sui temporis vicerit. nam...cum Olympio Nemesiano contendit, qui Halieutica, Cynegetica at Nautica scripsit quique in omnibus coloribus illustratus emicuit.* So Hohl (1927): *coloribus* is a conjecture. See Chapter 11 below for the *Historia Augusta*.
11. Volpilhac (1975) 8-10; Smolak (1989) 309.
12. See Haupt (1854) and (1875); Williams (1986) 3-8.
13. These features are well brought out in Schetter (1975) and Walter (1988).
14. Some manuscripts give *Timetas* here, a name difficult to justify. It is likely that the various readings are corruptions of the name *Thymoetas*, which although not a traditional pastoral name, fits the pastoral context better. See Schetter (1975) 9-11.
15. Cf. Verg. *Ecl.* 5.10 and 12.
16. Compare for this motif Verg. *Ecl.* 5. 13-14. In Calpurnius 1.20-32 one

1. Refinement and Reappraisal in Vergilian Pastoral

shepherd draws the other's attention to a divine prophecy cut into the trunk of a beech tree, which, being tall, he can read (and does: lines 33-88).

17. See Verdière (1974); Volpilhac (1975).
18. Himmelmann-Wildschütz (1972).
19. In his challenging article about the date of Calpurnius (1978, 109) Champlin made the suggestion that if the poems of Calpurnius are dated to the third decade of the third century, as he argues they should be, then Tityrus could actually be Calpurnius, and the two poets could have met in the 260s or 270s. There has since been much discussion of Calpurnius' date, detailed, complex and variously instructive, but the question remains tantalisingly open.
20. Korzeniewski (1976) appropriately cites Ov. *Met.* 4.134-5, 11.417-18 ad loc.
21. This line, pronounced by Meliboeus (nowhere stated to be the umpire) could be translated 'I remember contending in vain that Thyrsis had been defeated' rather than in the usual way as 'I remember that Thyrsis contended in vain'. Perhaps Vergil foresaw both, a puzzle for the perceptive.
22. See Coleman (1977) 226-7; Clausen (1994) 210-12 and the literature quoted there.
23. See Verdière (1966) 181; Smolak (1989) 310-11.
24. We are not told what happens when a lynx drinks, but for artistic depictions of other animals with Bacchus see Korzeniewski (1976) ad loc.
25. Coleman (1977) 32, 35, 296-7.
26. On the meaning of this word see Schmid (1953) 160-5; *ThLL* X 1.78-84, esp. 81. Cf. Chapter 12 below.
27. Printed in Heikel (1902) 181-7. For discusssion, see Barnes (1981) 73-6.
28. Courcelle (1957) 294-319, esp. 311-13; but his arguments do not refute Schelkle (1939) 16-21, esp. 20.
29. See Chapter 3 below.
30. See Chapter 5 below.
31. Green (1995) 560-3.
32. See Schenkl (1888).
33. See Hartel and Kamptner (1999).
34. This reference follows the numbering in Green (1991) and (1999).
35. Cf. Nemesianus 1.48, 2.15, 4.13.
36. Cf. Verg. *Ecl.* 1.58, 5.24-8, 10.16.
37. For the echo as a feature of pastoral, see Rosenmeyer (1969) 148-50.
38. Jerome *Ep.* 21.13.9: *at nunc etiam sacerdotes dei omissis evangeliis et prophetis videmus comoedias legere, amatoria bucolicorum versuum verba cantare, tenere Vergilium et id, quod in pueris necessitatis est, crimen in se facere voluntatis.*
39. Ibid.
40. Jerome *Ep.* 53.7.
41. See n. 1.
42. The version in Bücheler and Riese (1894) no. 893 derives from a manuscript, now lost, copied by Pithou; it is closely related to the manuscript of the sixteenth century described by Cock (1971) 156-60. This is used by Korzeniewski (1976).
43. Ambrose *Expositio evangelii secundum Lucam* 10.10 (*CCSL* 14, 348), where a plague that affected 'oxen and humans alike, and other livestock' is cited as one sign of the approaching end of the world . See Schmid (1953) 122-3 and (1962) 52.
44. For details see Schmid (1953) 120-2; *PLRE* 2 975.
45. The metre is usually now known as the Second Asclepiad; see Nisbet and Hubbard (1970), xxxviii-ix.

46. Korzeniewski (1976) translates it into German, and also mentions a Polish adaptation (6).

47. For *agnoscimus* in the manuscript, which does not scan; such an error would be untypical.

48. e.g. Verg. *Ecl.* 3.100 (a lovesick bull), and 7.9.

49. Schmid (1953) 125-8. Weyman (1926) 103-10 finds similarities of expression to a wider range of authors, of a less significant kind.

50. See Duff and Duff (1968) 319-35.

51. And one with some basis in fact: cf. La Roy Ladurie (1980) 103-4, observing that shepherds tended to get carried away by the wealth to be derived from wool.

52. Green (1980) 18; Korzeniewski (1976) 90.

53. Cf. Introduction above.

54. Lucretius 2.355-66 with Bailey ad loc.

55. John Chrysostom *Contra Judaeos et Gentiles* 9 (*PG* 48. 826). Schmid (1953) 135; Korzeniewski (1976) on lines 105ff.

56. Schmid (1953) 116-20, (1954).

57. Text in Schenkl (1888), 499-510.

58. See Green (1984) 75-8.

59. Green (1971), 95; Mohrmann (1958), 62 and 157.

60. Fear (1994).

61. Cf. Coleman (1969) 103: 'The Pastoral Concept is ... a longing ... for an ideal community set in an ideal landscape.'

2

Praising in Prose: Vergil in the Panegyrics

Roger Rees

In his dramatised debate about oratory, Tacitus casts Marcus Aper as the defender of an elaborate, sparkling style of speech. Contemporary taste in oratory, he argues, is for something 'more beautiful and ornate' (*pulchrior et ornatior*) than had been popular in the time of Cicero. The contemporary orator, he argues, strives for poetic decor, drawing not on the ancient works of Accius or Pacuvius, but Horace, Vergil and Lucan (*Dial.* 20.5-6). Cicero had certainly urged caution in using poeticism in oratory; the occasional poetic word, such as an archaism, could bring dignity to a speech (*De or.* 3.153), but unless it was for the purposes of ornamentation (*ornandi causa*), the poetic register should not, he insisted, be imported into oratory (*De or.* 3.39).[1] Quintilian, Professor of Rhetoric under Vespasian, took a similar line to Cicero. Recommending moderation, he observed that orators could quote poetry not just to show learning, but for pleasure (*iucunditas*); the sentiments of the poetry could even be used in evidence to support the case (*Inst.* 1.8.10-12). Poetry could give an orator inspiration, elevation in diction, versatility in moods, and decor in characterisation (10.1.27). In general, however, poetry and oratory should preserve their distinctions; each had its own conventions and decor (10.2.21). So, in celebrating the poetic decor to be found in contemporary speeches, Aper was promoting a controversial aesthetic in classical oratory.[2]

The question of the suitability of poetic ornament in oratory is raised within the broader context of the Attic/Asiatic polarity which informs much literary theorising in the late republic and early empire, and to which Tacitus' *Dialogus* makes an important contribution. Modern engagement with the controversy is hampered by our lack of any complete speeches from the death of Cicero until the *Panegyricus* of Pliny the Younger.[3] In several of his letters, Pliny discusses literary style in general;[4] and twice he touches on the suitability of poeticism in prose in particular.[5] However, perhaps not even the most confirmed Atticists would have objected to distinctively poetic elements in epideictic ('showpiece') oratory, of which panegyric was classified as a subsection. Epideictic oratory was the third branch in ancient rhetorical taxonomy, after forensic and deliberative.[6] Where forensic oratory sought to further legal claims and deliberative to advance philosophical understanding, epideictic had a more ornamental, less proactive function – to impress, to please, to enrapture.[7] Panegyrics were delivered in praise of individuals, cities, gods and so on.[8] Originally, praise had been in verse, such as was the case in Pindar's victory odes. Isocrates' *Evagoras*, published in 365 BC, marked a crucial watershed, as he proudly advertised; he claimed it to be the first prose panegyric.[9] Prose and verse panegyrics were to thrive in Roman literary culture.[10] Inevitably, the two traditions, prose and verse, had much in common.[11] Perhaps because of origins in archaic poetry, or because of the elevated form of expression which the grand occasions for delivery demanded, epideictic oratory had more in common with poetry than did the two main branches of oratory.[12]

Just as Cicero had been, separately, an orator and a poet, so too Pliny composed his own poetry.[13] However, there is no suggestion that his *Panegyricus*, which was in fact his *Gratiarum actio* ('thanksgiving') to Trajan for the consulship of AD 100, should or could have been in verse. Such a speech had been a senatorial convention, so it seems, as early as the reign of Augustus.[14] In two letters Pliny discusses his *Panegyricus* (3.13 and 18); in the latter he speaks of its *laetioris stili* ('more exuberant style'). This characterisation is not explained in any detail, but could account for, among other things, vocabulary with poetic resonances. The classification of vocabulary as 'poetic' or 'prosaic' is awkward, especially in this instance if, by the time of Pliny's inclusion in his *Panegyricus* of a word first attested in poetry, it had already featured in prose authors such as Livy, Velleius and Pliny the Elder.[15] However, it is clear that Pliny deployed far more 'poetic' diction in the *Panegyricus* than in the *Epistles*.[16] In doing so, Pliny could indulge his poetic instincts within a work of prose to give it suitable elevation and ornamentation.[17] But it should be noted that the many examples of poetic ornamentation are isolated words (or sometimes two), drawn, it appears, from a range of poetry and authors. By this means Pliny creates a generally Augustan and post-Augustan poetic texture without privileging any particular genre or poet.[18] For despite its poetic character, the *Panegyricus* does not name, quote *in extenso* or paraphrase poets.[19]

Imperial Latin panegyrics continued to be delivered, but none are preserved from the next 189 years.[20] Twelve complete and three fragmentary prose panegyrics survive from the late third and fourth centuries. All were delivered in Gaul or by a Gallic orator. Eleven belong to the collection known as the *Panegyrici Latini*, which seems to have been put together in the late fourth century.[21] Ausonius' speech of thanksgiving to Gratian for the consulship of 379 is his only surviving prose work;[22] and Symmachus'

2. Praising in Prose: Vergil in the Panegyrics

fragmentary panegyrics were addressed to Valentinian and Gratian.[23] We should exercise some caution when generalising about late antique panegyric – in many respects, the fifteen surviving works are unlikely to be representative of the original output.[24] However, across the variety of occasions and circumstances the speeches commemorate, the sociology of panegyric seems reasonably consistent. Celebrating imperial accessions, victories, anniversaries, marriages, birthdays, consular appointments and so on, panegyrics articulated a commitment. The Gallic orators, most obviously those of Trier where the majority of surviving works were delivered, acted as spokesmen for their city in underlining their commitment to the imperial centre.

In the third and fourth centuries, this commitment was of supreme political importance to the people of Gaul. From 260 to 269, a 'Gallic empire' had been proclaimed by Postumus. This had been recognised in Gaul, Spain and Britain. The 'Emperor' Postumus was followed in quick succession by Marius, Victorinus and Tetricus until the separatist regime was finally ended in 274 by Aurelian.[25] A decade or so later, a people known as the Bagaudae so ravaged Gaul that the emperor Diocletian appointed an imperial colleague (Maximian) to crush them.[26] In the late 280s and 290s, the so-called 'British empire' of Carausius and Allectus extended to northern Gaul.[27] In the fourth century further challenges to imperial authority were mounted in Gaul; Magnentius usurped power for three years, having killed the emperor Constans in 350; in 355 Silvanus reigned there very briefly, and from 383 when he defeated the emperor Gratian, Magnus Maximus held power in Gaul for five years, basing himself at Trier. Usurpations occurred elsewhere too in this period, but Gaul's record of loyalty to the central Roman empire was notably weak.

Against this backdrop of wavering loyalty, it is inviting to see the body of surviving panegyrics as a welcome protestation of political allegiance. Indeed, the hypothesis that the *Panegyrici Latini* were put together (perhaps by Pacatus, the author of the speech of 389) as an expression of Gallic loyalty to the empire is now quite orthodox.[28] This allegiance finds form not only in the specific lauding of the imperial honorand but also, more generally, in the orator's participation in the communion of Roman culture. An orator in 313 and later Pacatus may have voiced doubts about their own Latinity, no doubt disingenuously;[29] in reality, panegyrics were at pains to enact a cultural togetherness which (in detail and discourse) defined what it was to be Roman.[30]

It is no surprise, therefore, that the most prominent model for these fifteen speeches was Cicero.[31] Not only was his corpus a cornerstone of education, but he had been an important pioneer of panegyrical oratory in Latin.[32] He was the model for the panegyrics of late antiquity in various ways; from the structure of the speeches (often based on the honorand's virtues), to the strategies used to generate praise (such as comparisons with historical figures), to lexical echoes.³³ For an orator in 297 Cicero and Fronto were the two ornaments of Roman eloquence (*Panegyrici Latini* [=*Pan. Lat.*] VIII(4)14.2); in 313 another anonymous panegyrist refers to Cicero simply as the 'greatest orator' (*Pan. Lat.* XII(9)19.5); speaking to the emperor Theodosius, Pacatus imagines the ghosts of Cicero and other orators before him (*Pan. Lat.* II(12)1.5). These orators were very conscious of their inheritance.

Together with the fundamental influence of Cicero on third- and fourth-century panegyric, Pliny seems to have contributed significantly to the genre's evolution. Although historically and geographically anomalous, his colossal *Panegyricus* heads the *Panegyrici Latini*; if, as seems most probable, the collection was put together in the late fourth century, the *Panegyricus* appears to have effected a monumentalising and exemplary role as a direct model for imperial prose panegyric.³⁴ Given this pedigree, it is not surprising to encounter poetic decor in these speeches. However, one feature which distinguishes these late antique works from their exemplars Cicero and Pliny is their close engagement with poetry. On several occasions the orators refer in very vague terms to poets. In 289 an orator speaks approvingly of some particular promises made by 'Greek poets' (*Pan. Lat.* X(2)11.3); addressing Julian in 362, the consul Claudius Mamertinus begins an assertion 'poets say' (*Pan. Lat.* III(11)28.5); 'as the poets say', says Nazarius when comparing Constantine with the mythical Lynceus; in 389 Pacatus commends the regular poetic and pictorial image of winged victory (*Pan. Lat.* II(12)39.1). This tendency to appeal to the authority of a literary canon no doubt had an ornamental function, considered appropriate to the occasion; at the same time it would confirm the cultural pedigree of orator and audience alike. Poetry enjoyed status as an avowedly authorising discourse within oratory.³⁵

This reverence towards poets, however, was not without its problems for the orators. One constant throughout antiquity was the allegation of insincerity levelled at panegyric. In response, panegyrics tend to labour to assert the transparency and authenticity of their claims. With their deliberate evocation of poets as a cultural authority, orators of late antiquity seem to have been particularly sensitive to the possible identification of a more fictional atmosphere in their work. It seems that in order to counter this possibility, on occasion they asserted the truth of their own claims by highlighting the extravagance of poets'. As a result, the 'licence of poets' became a topos of panegyrical oratory. In 289 an orator speaks of the 'stories from the licence of poets' and then later compares the circumstances of Jupiter's infancy (as told in poetry) with the real hardships experienced by the infant Maximian (*Pan. Lat.* X(2)1.3, 2.5); addressing Valentinian eighty years later, Symmachus similarly denounces the

2. Praising in Prose: Vergil in the Panegyrics

licence of poets as 'fictions of poetry' (*Or.* 1.4). The following year, the same orator decided not to mention many of Valentinian's achievements 'in case a high style breaks out into poetic exaggeration of great affairs' (*ne in poeticos flatus rerum ingentium cothurnus erumpat, Or.* 2.26).[36] Thus we see that the engagement of third- and fourth-century panegyric with poetry was generally very self-conscious; at times it was confident and assertive, at others it was far more qualified. Either way, it is clear that poetry provided the orators with widely recognised reference points, designed to embellish but not to undermine their rhetoric.

While poetry in general was invoked as a means of validating the various claims of prose panegyric, certain poets were quoted and paraphrased in detail in the speeches.[37] This new licence to meld genres and literary registers produced energetic, flamboyant rhetoric. With the exception of Ennius, whose popularity had waned dramatically over the previous 300 years, citations in panegyric were from authors who were the mainstays of education in Latin literature.[38] Identified as the 'first founder of Roman poetry' (*Pan. Lat.* XI(3)16.3) and the 'greatest poet' (*Pan. Lat.* IX(5)7.3), Ennius' attraction seems to have been his great antiquity.[39] Otherwise, the panegyrics are marked by recollections of Augustan poets; echoes of Ovid and Horace can be detected, but pre-eminent was Vergil.[40] For an orator in 291 Vergil was simply 'the Roman poet';[41] he was the 'great poet' for a speaker in 313;[42] Ausonius too felt no need to identify him by name when speaking of his wonderful account of Numidian riding.[43] In his address to Gratian in 368/9, the *Eclogues* inspired Symmachus. The orator defends his intention to use a poetic style of oratory and identifies his source before indulging in what are even for this genre, sentences of highly embroidered praise:

> If I could now range higher in poetic style, like the bard I would pen in your name a whole excursus of Vergil about the new era. I would say that Justice has returned from heaven and that teeming nature now promises rich produce without prompting. Now I would say that of their own accord the ripe crops turn golden in the unfenced fields, the grapes grow heavy on the vine, dewy honey sweats from oak-leaves. Who would deny belief in this under your reign, when your character has already given much and expectation promises still more? (*Or.* 3.9)

The fourth *Eclogue* was much contested in late antiquity.[44] Although his addressee was a Christian, the pagan Symmachus' panegyrical deployment of some of the poem's most memorable details arrogates a reading firmly rooted in the imperial cult.[45] The Golden Age is Gratian's reign. The opening clause reveals the orator's awareness of the controversies he might be initiating when invoking Vergil (although they perhaps more concern the aesthetic integrity of oratory than politics); nevertheless, he continues in confident Vergilian vein. It seems that for Symmachus at least, the motif of a Golden Age could not find convincing, resonant expression without Vergilian figures of thought and language. What these examples reveal is the confidence a late antique orator could feel that direct references to Vergil would be welcomed and appreciated by the audience.

Another example of direct citation appears in the speech addressed to the joint emperors Maximian and Diocletian in 291. A brief quotation from the *Eclogues* introduces the theme of imperial omnipresence.

> I now make bold to announce about each of you what the Roman poet sang about your Jupiter, that 'everything is full of Jupiter', I suppose figuring that although Jupiter holds the highest point of heaven sitting above the clouds and winds in everlasting light, nevertheless his godhead and mind are infused throughout the whole world: wherever you are, even if you withdraw into one palace, your divinity is everywhere, all lands and seas are full of you. (*Pan. Lat.* XI(3)14.2-3)

The argument is ponderous, but its style and premise are revealing.[46] The signalled quotation (*Ecl.* 3.60) is followed by adaptations of other lines from the *Aeneid*.[47] The high poetic style of the passage befits the grandness of the orator's claims and the ceremonial of the occasion. More specifically, the orator's engagement with Vergil confirms the poet's standing as the supreme cultural authority. This appeal to Vergil thus has the twofold effect of elevating the stylistic register of the speech and validating the orator's extravagant assertion.

However, such intense and direct invocations of Vergil are unusual in surviving panegyric. All but one of the extant speeches accommodate Vergilian references by one means or another.[48] The manner, frequency and effects of these references vary across the corpus. Whereas direct quotation is relatively rare, the simplest and most common means of engagement is by short intertext.[49] In the same speech of 291, for example, on several occasions the orator embellishes his panegyric with two word phrases: *annis volventibus* ('as the years roll by', *Pan. Lat.* XI(3)2.3), *nemora pacavit* ('he pacified the groves', 3.6), and *arces Monoeci* ('the heights of Monaco', 4.2) from the *Aeneid*, and *gens effrena* ('unrestrained people', 17.1) the *Georgics*.[50] Intertexts such as these provide what Walker has recently termed 'noble ornament for the ritual praise of emperors'.[51] Through poetic ornamentation an orator also appealed to the high-cultural pretensions of the (Gallic) aristocratic elite. Literary aesthetics had a determined social function.

Together with the cultural cohesion which isolated Vergilian references

2. Praising in Prose: Vergil in the Panegyrics

could embody, the poet was also invoked to pointed political effect. Addressing Constantine and Maximian in 307, an anonymous orator broached the delicate matter of Maximian's unconstitutional return to power after his abdication two years earlier. The orator turned to Jupiter and Vergil, bedrocks of Roman culture, for his justification of the current regime.

> For what, Maximian, do you think Jupiter himself replied to you when you magnanimously said 'Take back, Jupiter, [the authority] you lent me'? For sure, he replied as follows: 'I did not grant it to you on loan, but for ever; I will not take it back but I will keep it safe'. Therefore, as soon as you curbed the state as it fell headlong and took up the unsteady rudder, hope of salvation dawned on everyone. Winds dropped, clouds dispersed, waves drew back. (*Pan. Lat.* VII(6)12.6-7)

As a convention of epic narrative, dialogue between immortal and human confers privileged status on the latter. Maximian is thus cast as Jupiter's favourite. Furthermore, his role as the saviour of the troubled ship of state recalls Aeneas taking control of the rudder after the helmsman Palinurus fell overboard (*Aen.* 5.854-71).[52] The felicitous weather conditions which followed his return to the helm likewise recall the end of the *Aeneid*'s opening storm scene, the calm which greeted Aeneas on the Tiber, and the West Wind's subservient repose as Jupiter begins his response to Juno in book 10.[53] Later the orator includes in his description of Maximian's imperial duties his responsibility 'to impose laws when peace is to be concluded' (*componendis pacibus leges imponere*, 14.1) recalling Aeneas' duty as dictated by Anchises 'to impose custom on peace' (*pacique imponere morem*, *Aen.* 6.852). These marked associations between epic hero and emperor enrich the speech's texture and insinuate Maximian's imperial legitimacy.[54]

Sustained engagement with his works is best exemplified in two Constantinian speeches which took as their main subject the emperor's victory over Maxentius at the Battle of the Milvian Bridge in 312. The anonymous *Pan. Lat.* XII(9) was addressed to Constantine in 313 in Trier; the Gallic professor Nazarius delivered his panegyric IV(10) in Rome in 321, in Constantine's absence. Between them, the speeches provide the most detailed account of Constantine's campaign against Maxentius, which was launched from Gaul. Military success was a regular subject-matter of imperial panegyrics, but the pronounced Vergilian flavour of these two speeches might have been inspired by the similarities between Constantine's campaign against Maxentius and many of the details of the narrative and historical circumstances of Vergil's poems.[55] Both Octavian and Constantine had been victorious in civil war; both Aeneas and Constantine fought their decisive battles in the environs of Rome, both near the river Tiber. The orators exploit these similarities to give their speeches highly elaborate styles and depth of association.

The earlier orator is the more explicit of the two. Referring to Vergil as the 'great poet', he quotes from the *Georgics* the famous line about curved sickles being melted down into hardened swords (1.508).[56] The orator's inspiration for this is Constantine's treatment of the prisoners he took at the siege of Aquileia. There, it is claimed, Constantine had the enemy's swords melted down into fetters for them, lest they do themselves further mischief (11.2-4). The Vergilian quotation leads to a comparison between the poet's time and the present; 'that very sad era' contrasts with the current emperor's blessed reign (12.4). The orator's sheer laboriousness dilutes the force of his argument, yet by making Vergil his reference point but inverting the conceit, he contrives to deny the realities of the recent civil war.[57]

In the narrative of the final confrontation with Maxentius, both orators evoke Vergil in their attitude towards the Tiber. In 313 an intertext recalls how Aeneas foresaw the river rolling weapons and bodies headlong (17.3).[58] The river is then addressed, 'Sacred Tiber, onetime adviser of your guest Aeneas', in both its high style and content recalling the scene early in *Aeneid* 8.[59] The Tiber is said to moderate its nature according to circumstances, as it did to the Trojans' advantage in the *Aeneid* (18.2).[60] Using their alternative names the Albula and the Alba, the orator contrives a link between the Tiber and Elbe rivers, again recalling Vergil's interest in the Roman river's name (21.5).[61] Both orators personify the river when it is said to act against Maxentius (XII(9)17.2, IV(10)30.1-4). Nazarius speaks of the river banks covered with endless heaps of dead, of the Tiber itself filled with piles of corpses, and its bloodied waves inflicting on Maxentius no noble death but one worthy of his cowardice and brutality.[62] Such grand figurations of a river begin with Homer's Simois and Xanthus – an epic conceit – but more immediately the speeches resonate with Vergil. The Tiber's beneficent agency generates an epic context for the battle of the Milvian Bridge and equates the significance of that clash with that between the Trojans and Italians in the *Aeneid*.

The panegyrics indulge in other identifiably Vergilian tropes of this kind. Maxentius is said to have been 'exercised by terrible dreams and driven by night-time Avengers' (*somniis terribilibus agitatus et nocturnis pulsus Ultricibus*, XII(9)16.5), a typically epic style motivation recalling the *Aeneid*'s furious Tisiphone and Allecto.[63] 'Fear revealed the degenerate's mind, as it is said' (*degeneris, ut dictum est, animos timor arguebat*, XII(9)14.2), echoing Dido to Anna.[64] In a Vergilian flourish, the war-god Mars is *dubius* ('wavering', IV(10)7.1);[65] his name is associated with the noise of battle, *strepitus Martii* ('the din of Mars', 30.4).[66] The implications

2. Praising in Prose: Vergil in the Panegyrics

of these Vergilian personifications and characterisations of the Tiber, Ultrices and Mars are probably more literary than religious. Constantine's patronage of the church would render unlikely an orator's fulsome promotion of ancient pagan beliefs. However, even when the speeches take a more explicitly theological turn, Vergil remains the fundamental cultural reference. Both orators speak in vaguely monotheistic terms, but use carefully adapted Vergilian language.[67] In 313 the orator uses cautiously syncretistic terms in addressing the 'supreme creator of things' (*summe rerum sator*, 26.1);[68] in characterising a divine mind, spread through the whole world and mixed in all the elements, the orator draws directly from Anchises' revelations to Aeneas in the Underworld.[69] To similar effect, Nazarius' monotheistic description 'that majesty which distinguishes right and wrong' (*illa maiestas fandi ac nefandi discriminatrix*, 7.4) recalls Ilioneus' 'gods who are mindful of right and wrong' (*deos memores fandi atque nefandi*, *Aen.* 1.543). This engagement with Vergil does not represent a Christian appropriation of, nor a slavish adherence to the poet, but deployment of him as a consistent and reliable cultural norm in the hesitant and delicate negotiation from a pagan past to a new religious dispensation.[70] Any necessarily tentative religious posturing is authorised by reference to the bard.

In terms of characterisation of individuals, inevitably Constantine himself is the principle beneficiary from the orators' Vergilian approach. Like Aeneas, Constantine is of notable piety (XII(9)4.4, 11.2, IV(10)7.4).[71] Like Vergil's hardy farmer, Constantine does not reject life's difficult roads (IV(10)33.5); likewise he can withstand the harsh winter weather (36.5).[72] In battle Constantine is said to have been 'like a rushing river which is followed by trees torn from their roots and rocks wrenched from their deep holds' (*torrenti similis amni quem abruptae radicitus silvae et convulsa funditus saxa sequerentur*, XII(9)9.5).[73] Selflessly he went 'into the midst of the enemy's arms' (*in media hostium tela*, 9.4).[74] In Nazarius' speech, Constantine's 'fiery soldiery' (*fulmineus miles*, 7.4) recalls Aeneas' ally Mnestheus (*Aen.* 9.812). The 'great mass of war' (*tantam belli molem*, 18.2) at which Constantine did not flinch resonates with Aeneas' own ktistic mission (*Aen.* 1.33). 'Invisible outcomes' (*caecos eventus*) exercised Constantine (19.3) as they had Aeneas (*Aen.* 6.157-8). Vergil resounds in Nazarius' account of a night battle at Verona, earlier in Constantine's campaign (26.1-2) – the 'thick shadows', 'fractured voices of trumpets', 'heavy groans of the fallen';[75] the consolation his victims might have in identifying their killer.[76] When Nazarius turns to the battle at the Tiber, he 'shudders when about to speak' (*dicturus horresco*, 29.5) as Aeneas did when remembering Laocoon's death (*Aen.* 2.204); Nazarius' shudder was at the recollection of the possibility of Constantine's death in action, for, like Aeneas, he was first into battle (*invadis primus*, 'you make first attack').[77] Within this framework of epic warfare and heroism, Constantine is cast as an epic, quintessentially Roman leader. Because in character and actions Constantine chimes so sonorously with Vergil's Aeneas, his rise to power is presented as the welcome fulfilment of fate's decree.[78]

This method of characterisation diverges from the practice recommended by rhetorical treatises, where the traditional canon of virtues provides the ethical blueprint.[79] The orators are demonstrating their literary flair and sensitivity to the pulse of Roman politics. That is not to say, however, that virtues and vices have no part in these speeches; personal ethics had been central to Vergil's epic design and were to provide a grand model for Nazarius when recounting Constantine's triumphal procession through Rome.

> duci sane omnibus videbantur subacta vitiorum agmina quae Urbem graviter obsederant: Scelus domitum, victa Perfidia, diffidens sibi Audacia et Importunitas catenata. Furor vinctus et cruenta Crudelitas inani terrore frendebant; Superbia atque Arrogantia debellatae, Luxuries coercita et Libido constricta nexu ferreo tenebantur.

> Certainly everybody thought that the train of vices which had blockaded the City grievously had been conquered: Crime was tamed, Treachery conquered, Impudence which cannot trust itself, and Insolence in chains. Fettered Fury and bloody Cruelty gnashed their teeth without causing fright; Haughtiness and Arrogance were subdued, Luxury held back and Lust held tight in iron bonds. (31.3)

In style and detail the description's debt to Vergil is profound. In the *Aeneid*'s first great prophecy scene, Jupiter describes the predestined triumph over impious Fury, chained and snorting (1.294-6). Vergil's was the original literary personification of Fury, and Nazarius' version builds on his trope in lavish fashion. Not all of Nazarius' catalogue of personified vices have Vergilian predecessors, but the very form of a catalogue of qualities was a distinctively Vergilian figure of thought.[80] Perhaps most arresting here is the personification of subdued Haughtiness, clearly recalling Anchises' advice to Aeneas 'to spare the defeated and subdue the haughty' (*parcere subiectis et debellare superbos*, 6.853). This intensely metaphorical account of the effects of Constantine's victory at the Milvian Bridge is a mosaic of Vergilian intertexts and figures. In one compressed passage, Nazarius presents moralising character sketches of Constantine and Maxentius, and he legitimises the outcome of the battle of the Milvian Bridge by phrasing its triumphal celebration with deliberate reference to Vergil's well-known teleological lines from *Aeneid* 1 and 6. The effect of this is not simply that Constantine is *like* Vergil's Aeneas or Augustus; rather, that he *is* himself the fulfilment of the ancient prophecy of Rome's

2. Praising in Prose: Vergil in the Panegyrics

imperial mission. Aeneas' *telos*, as told to Venus by Jupiter in *Aeneid* 1 and to the hero himself by Anchises in *Aeneid* 6, is fulfilled by Constantine. Nazarius' argument situates the emperor at the centre of Roman culture; this culture has effectively been inscribed and enshrined by Vergil but is lived by the emperor, the orator and the audience.

Nazarius' rich description of Constantine's triumph is not typical of surviving fourth-century panegyric, no doubt even less of the thousands of lost speeches from that time. However, it does indicate the new potential of epideictic oratory. The observation that late antique panegyric ignored the strictures of its models Cicero and Pliny to glitter with Vergilian intertexts and allusions of course confirms the central position Vergil held in Roman literature. At the same time, it signals an important stage in the evolution of the aesthetics of Roman oratory; now speeches could reach out without apology to embrace the icons of Rome's poetic inheritance. In the late third and fourth centuries Cicero and Vergil were the two core school texts; but in the elevated discourse of aristocratic culture they could also be bedfellows in a way denied them by earlier prescriptions and practice.

Furthermore, the prominent position accorded to Vergil in late antique panegyric is suggestive of the way the poet was read, at least by the orators themselves but perhaps also by their wider audience. Manifold invocation of Vergil in speeches designed to praise emperors would be inappropriate if the *Eclogues*, *Georgics* and *Aeneid* were considered subversive or even qualified in their own politics, particularly in respect of Augustus. Certainly in the fourth century Tiberius Claudius Donatus and Servius interpreted the *Aeneid* as an epic in praise of Augustus.[81] The panegyrical orators did not grant Augustus any privileged status as a cultural or political icon, preferring, it appears, some of the heroes of the republican era.[82] If, as seems likely, orators too read the *Aeneid* as effective panegyric, it was that ideological and cultural status which recommended the poem to them rather than the achievements of its honorand.

However, as we have seen, the orators' evocation of the canonical cultural icons Cicero and Vergil was not without political effect. A fundamental ambition of the genre's literary texture was to authenticate the orators' own claims to *Romanitas*. What the introduction of Vergilian resonances into provincial epideictic rhetoric of the time represents is as potent and authentic a display of *Romanitas* as bathhouses or the toga. To speak Latin was not enough, even in the fashion of Cicero or Pliny. To assert an irresistible claim to *Romanitas* the orators subscribed to national, imperial poetics; above all, this meant Vergil. Orators would weave into their work sophisticated and allusive Vergilian references to create depth of association and a sense of cultural belonging. Repeated and reworked, the poet's verses represented a meta-narrative about cultural identity. Vergil was an established and proven symbol of a shared culture.

The *Aeneid* in particular was a powerful cultural signifier for any orator keen to indicate his political loyalty and common *Romanitas*. Vergil's Anchises had crystallised what it was to be Roman, emphasising in this definition the ethics of war (*Aen.* 6.851-3); for the panegyrical orators of the fourth century, claims to *Romanitas* were just as likely to be founded on a generalised celebration of the poet as a key Roman imperial icon as on any intricacies of national self-definition and determination through ethics. For them at least, to be Roman was to be Vergilian.[83]

Notes

1. Hagendahl (1947) 121-2; Walker (2000) 71-83.
2. Leeman (1963) 311-14; Walker (2000) 103-9.
3. For a recent discussion, see Webb (1997).
4. e.g. *Ep.* 1.20, 2.5, 3.13, 3.18, 5.20, 7.9, 9.26.
5. *Ep.* 2.5.5 *poetice*; 9.26.8 *alia condicio oratorum, alia poetarum*, 'orators and poets differ'; see also 7.9.8.
6. Arist. *Rhet.* 1.iii.1-3.
7. Note Quint. *Inst.* 3.4.15-16 on the dangers of oversimplification in classification.
8. See the various treatises by Menander Rhetor.
9. Russell (1998) 23-4; Morton Braund (1998) 53-4.
10. Early prose panegyric in Latin, e.g. Cic. *Marcell.*, Sen. *Clem.*, Plin. *Pan.*; verse panegyric, e.g. *laus Messallae, laus Pisonis*, Stat. *Silv.* 4.1, and then in late antiquity, esp. Claudian.
11. Russell (1998) 48.
12. Walker (2000) 114-18, 307-8; Russell (1998) 21-9; Børtnes (2000) 183.
13. Herschowitz (1995).
14. Plin. *Pan.* 90.3; on Verginius Rufus *Ep.* 2.1, *Ep.* 6.27.1; Ov. *Pont.* 4.4.35-42; Durry (1938) 3-5; Ausonius' only surviving prose work is his *Grat. act.* to Gratian for the consulship of 379. Verse panegyric was thriving in Rome too – see above n. 10.
15. Durry (1938) 55-6.
16. e.g. *exuberet* (29.3), *inevitabile* (42.4) and *interfuso* (16.5) appear first in poetry before being adopted in post-Augustan prose; others, such as *caesaries* (4.7), *freta* (81.4) and *tellus* (31.6) were still confined almost exclusively to the poetic register in Pliny's day; Gamberini (1983) 458-60, 517-24. For poetic constructions in the *Panegyricus*, Durry (1938) 57.
17. Durry (1938) 59, 'L'élément poétique est dans le *Panégyrique* essentiel.'
18. Durry (1938) 56; Gamberini (1983) 458-60, 517-24.
19. Hagendahl (1947) 122. For Pliny's engagement with Cicero and Tacitus see Suster (1890), Mesk (1911), Durry (1938) 60-6, Bruère (1954). Durry (1938) 57 identifies five Vergilian phrases in the speech; not all are convincing and none are striking. Cf. Vergil in Pliny's letters, e.g. 1.2, 5.8, 6.20, 6.33, 7.20, 8.2, 9.13. Terzaghi (1949) 126-7 identifies traces of *Aen.* 8.367ff. underlying *Pan.* 15.4, and notes this very sophisticated method of exalting Trajan. If the intertext is accepted (cf. Fedeli [1989] 416), it is inconspicuous and uncharacteristic.
20. As with books 1-9 of his letters, Pliny saw to the publication of his

2. Praising in Prose: Vergil in the Panegyrics

Panegyricus himself (*Ep.* 3.13 and 18). Lost panegyrics include Fronto's speech to Antoninus; Nixon and Rodgers (1994) 3.

21. Text, translation and commentary by Nixon and Rodgers (1994).
22. Edited with commentary by Green (1991).
23. Edited with commentary by Pabst (1989).
24. Russell (1998) 17; Rees (2002) 19-23.
25. Drinkwater (1987).
26. Lassandro (2000) 105-44 surveys the evidence for the Bagaudae.
27. See Introduction above.
28. Pichon (1906).
29. *Pan. Lat.* XII(9)1.2; II(12)1.3-5.
30. Woolf (1998) 12-13.
31. Galletier (1949) xxxiii-iv; Nixon and Rodgers (1994) 2-3, 14-19.
32. Morton Braund (1998) 68-75.
33. On strategies see Maguinness (1932), (1933); for some intertexts from Cicero, see Klotz (1911) and Nixon and Rodgers (1994).
34. Pichon (1906), Galletier (1949) xxxiii-iv, Klotz (1911) and Nixon and Rodgers (1994) 18 mention specific verbal echoes of Plin. *Pan.* in the later speeches. Cf. Vereeke (1975) 151-3. The *Panegyricus* is placed first in the collection although the order of the speeches generally is not chronological; see the timeline above for the dates of delivery.
35. For similarities between prose and verse in late antiquity, see Roberts (1989) 63; writing in the late third century, Menander Rhetor (*Basilikos logos* 369, 374) briefly mentions the suitability of Homeric features at certain points in a panegyric.
36. See also *Pan. Lat.* II(12)4.4, 17.2, 44.5; Aus. *Grat. act.* 1.5; Symm. *Or.* 3.9.
37. Of these two methods of citation, paraphrasing was by far the more common: Hagendahl (1947) 119-24; Russell (1998) 39.
38. Skutsch (1985) 9-10.
39. Klotz (1911) 538-9.
40. Klotz (1911); Nixon and Rodgers (1994) 16-17; Russell (1998) 44-5. The generally Augustan character of this intertextuality contrasts with the panegyrists' preference for republican figures in establishing historical comparisons for their addressees: Nixon (1990).
41. *poeta Romanus* (*Pan. Lat.* XI(3)14.2).
42. *magnus poeta* (*Pan. Lat.* XII(9)12.3).
43. *mirabamur poetam*, 'we used to wonder at the poet' (*Grat. act.* 65) recalling *Aen.* 4.41.
44. Courcelle (1957); Monteleone (1975); Benko (1980). See Green above.
45. *Ecl.* 4.6, 28-30.
46. A similar but more succinct version appears in Aus. *Grat. act.* 5.
47. *Aen.* 1.225, 6.726-7.
48. The exception appears to be *Pan. Lat.* V(8).
49. Hagendahl (1947).
50. *Aen.* 1.234, 6.803, 6.830; *Geo.* 3.382. The brevity of such phrases might indicate less marked redeployment of Vergil than general and thorough acquaintance with his idiom.
51. Walker (2000) 308. Schenkl (1881) 129-30, Klotz (1911), and Nixon and Rodgers (1994) ad locc. identify other intertexts.
52. *praecipitantem* 'falling headlong', cf. 860; *gubernacula* 'rudder', cf. 859; *fluitantia* 'unsteady', cf. 867.

53. *Aen.* 1.143, 7.27, 10.103.
54. See Introduction above.
55. On Tiberius Claudius Donatus' ignorance of much Augustan history, Starr (1992) 159-68. 'Victory' panegyrics include *Pan. Lat.* VIII(5) and II(12). Cf. Roberts below, pp. 47-8, and Ware below, pp. 157-8, on the narrative character of epic.
56. *Pan. Lat.* XII(9)12.3.
57. Galletier (1952) 119; Nixon and Rodgers (1994) 313.
58. *Aen.* 8.538-40; *ripae ulterioris* at 17.2 and *Aen.* 6.314; Lubbe (1955) 96.
59. *Aen.* 8.31-78, 188, 364.
60. e.g. *Aen.* 8.86-9, 548-9, 9.124-5. On this passage, see Roberts (2001) 551.
61. *Aen.* 8.332.
62. e.g. *Aen.* 6.87, 10.592-3, 11.393-4, 12.35-6.
63. e.g. *Aen.* 6.555-70, 7.324-31, 12.846; Lubbe (1955) 95.
64. *Aen.* 4.13; Lubbe (1955) 88.
65. *Geo.* 2.283. For 7.1 cf. also *Aen.* 10.159-60.
66. Cf. *Geo.* 4.71.
67. Liebeschuetz (1990) 369-70.
68. Cf. e.g. *Aen.* 1.254.
69. *Aen.* 6.724-7.
70. Cf. Christian exegesis of Vergil discussed by Roberts, Witke, Pollmann, Lim and Davidson below.
71. Cf. e.g. *Aen.* 1.545.
72. *Geo.* 1.122, 1. 211.
73. Cf. e.g. *Aen.* 2.305-7, 2.496-9, 10.362-3.
74. Cf. e.g. *Aen.* 2.353, 408, 10.237; *Ecl.* 10.44-5.
75. *spissis tenebris, Aen.* 2.360, 621; *tubarum fractae voces, Aen.* 2.313, 3.556, 5.139, 8.526, 9.503, 11.192; *cadentum graves gemitus, Geo.* 3.506, *Aen.* 2.288, 10.674.
76. *Aen.* 10.829-30, 11.686-9.
77. *Aen.* 10.310 *primus invasit,* 'he made first attack'.
78. This method of characterisation extends to Constantine's son; Nazarius calls Constantine Caesar ('the greatest increase in the public good' (*incrementum maximum boni publici,* 37.5) recalling the boy of *Ecl.* 4 (49).
79. Morton Braund (1998) 57-8.
80. e.g. *Aen.* 6.273-81.
81. Starr (1992) 169-74; Williams (1967).
82. Nixon (1990).
83. With thanks to audiences at Edinburgh and Manchester.

3

Vergil and the Gospels: The *Evangeliorum libri IV* of Juvencus

Michael Roberts

The *Evangeliorum libri IV* (hereafter *Ev*.) of the Spanish priest C. Vettius Aquilinus Juvencus recounts in four books of dactylic hexameters the story of the Gospels, following primarily Matthew, but supplemented by John and, especially for Christ's birth and early life, Luke. Jerome registers the poem in his *Chronicon* under the year 329/30, a date broadly confirmed by the praise of Constantinian peace with which the poem ends. Juvencus' work is the first substantial Latin poem in classical metre on Christian subject matter.[1] It inaugurates a tradition of biblical epic that was to continue throughout late antiquity.

The date of Juvencus' work is significant. After the Edict of Milan and the emperor's increasing patronage of Christianity, the poet could count on attracting cultivated readers for whom a recasting of the biblical narrative in the culturally prestigious idiom of Latin (primarily Vergilian) epic would have a special appeal.[2] Lactantius, Juvencus' older contemporary and tutor to the emperor's son Crispus, had laid the groundwork for such an undertaking. In his *Divinae Institutiones* he called for the best stylistic practices of classical eloquence to be put to the service of the Christian message (*Inst.* 1.1.10). By recasting the Bible in the idiom of Vergilian epic, Juvencus followed Lactantius' programme for a new Christian literature, accommodated to the taste of the cultivated reading classes.[3] Such readers, deterred by the low stylistic level of the Old Latin versions of the Bible (cf. *Inst.* 5.1.15), could be expected to respond favourably to such a project of cultural translation. At the same time, Lactantius' practice of frequently citing or alluding to classical poets and his high valuation of pre-Christian poetry as preserving, if in disguised form, intimations of the Christian truth (e.g. *Inst.* 1.11.30 and 34) will have helped legitimate from a Christian perspective such an act of translation.[4]

Juvencus' poem is framed by a 27-line preface and an 11-line epilogue that reflect on his poetic undertaking. Juvencus clearly understands his poem as epic. He compares it with the songs of Homer and Vergil. But while they sang of the deeds of great men of the past, thereby preserving the memory of those figures and gaining near-eternal fame as poets for themselves, Juvencus will sing of the actions of Christ and in so doing win the reward of eternal salvation (*pr.* 6-24). He understands the epic as a poem of praise, hymning the deeds (*sublimia facta*, 6; *gesta*, 19) of a hero or heroes. But whereas classical epic celebrates worldly glory, Juvencus' subject is the 'living/life-bringing actions of Christ' (*Christi vitalia gesta*, 19): that is, not just the actions of his life, but the actions that bring salvation to humankind ('life-bringing' in a specifically Christian sense). The formulation already implies a challenge to classical epic. Though epic is essentially a narrative genre, in its Christian exponents it is capable of taking on a further spiritual dimension that transcends the historical sequence of events.

Juvencus' preface concludes with a prayer for inspiration, not to the Muse but to the Holy Spirit. The poet asks that his mind be washed by the waters of the Jordan 'in order to speak worthily of Christ' (*ut Christo digna loquamur*, 27). The language is significant. Vergil had included among the inhabitants of the Elysian Fields 'holy poets who had spoken worthily of Apollo' (*pii vates et Phoebo digna locuti, Aen.* 6.662).[5] In the new context Juvencus speaks of himself as a 'holy poet', in that he sings a poem in praise of Jesus. He, too, hopes for posthumous reward, but in the form of Christian salvation, not Elysium. The Vergilian language lends intertextual density to the concluding words of Juvencus' preface. As often, it is difficult to know how to evaluate the play of similarity and difference in such an intertextual exchange. Is Juvencus correcting Vergil – the truth is that only Christian poets can expect such posthumous reward – or does the language imply a Lactantian reading, that the classical poet already contains disguised presentiments of the Christian truth? Vergil's words then would receive an allegorical, prophetic reading, reaching their fulfilment only with the figure of the Christian poet. Conversely Juvencus' anticipation of Christian salvation potentially takes on the colours of the happy abodes of Vergil's underworld.

The programmatic language from the *Aeneid* at the beginning of the poem corresponds to a clear echo of the ending of the *Georgics* in the epilogue. In this case the similarities in language are not close (only *haec ... canebam*, *Geo.* 4.559; *haec mihi ... tribuit*, *Ev.* 4.806, in both cases at the beginning of a line and sentence). In content, though, the parallels are marked: Vergil sets his poem in the context of the warlike achievements of Augustus and the civilising mission they make possible (*Caesar dum magnus ad altum / fulminat Euphraten bello victorque volentis / per populos dat iura*, 'while great Caesar wields his lightning in war by the deep Euphrates and victorious brings laws to a welcoming people', *Geo.* 4.560-2); Juvencus emphasises the peace promoted by Constantine, which

3. *Vergil and the Gospels: The* Evangeliorum libri IV *of Juvencus*

he associates with the peace of Christ and which provides the conditions for his poetic project (*haec mihi pax Christi tribuit, pax haec mihi saecli, / quam fovet indulgens terrae regnator apertae / Constantinus*, 'the peace of Christ granted me this, the peace of the world, which Constantine, merciful ruler of the earth's wide expanse, promotes', *Ev.* 4.806-8). Vergil declares that by his achievements Augustus 'is winning his way to heaven' (*viamque adfectat Olympo, Geo.* 4.562). Constantine, on the other hand, rejects the title of divinity (*sacri sibi nominis horret / inponi pondus*, 'he dreads the weight of a sacred title being forced upon him', 4.809-10), but his exemplary conduct as Christian ruler will win him eternal life (*aeternam capiat divina in saecula vitam*, 'may he receive eternal life for centuries divine', 4.811).[6] The reader has already been alerted in the epilogue to the relevance of the *Georgics* as comparandum. In book 1 of that poem Vergil characterises his subject as 'the glory of the divine countryside' (*divini gloria ruris*, 1.168); in the *Ev.* the 'glory of the divine law' (*divinae gloria legis*, 4.804) receives the 'earthly ornaments of language' (*ornamenta ... terrestria linguae*, 4.805).[7] Although every example of intertextuality contains elements of similarity and difference, the evocation of the last lines of the *Georgics* highlights in particular the contrasts between the two situations, between war and peace, Olympus and eternal life. Juvencus' Vergilian echo here is an example of contrast imitation (a term initially coined by Thraede for Christian Latin poetry, but subsequently adopted by Vergilian scholars to Vergil's relationship with Lucretius):[8] the Christian ruler who promotes peace – the peace of Christ – and who will enjoy eternal life is polemically opposed to the warlike would-be god of the *Georgics*.[9]

In his preface Juvencus represents his poem as a Christian epic of praise, a narrative of the redemptive acts of Christ, for which Vergil's *Aeneid* provides the pre-eminent classical counterpart. His epilogue adds a new dimension of Vergil-reception. Implicitly the poem can also be read as a Christian *Georgics*. Its division into four books recalls not only the four Gospels but also the four books of Vergil's didactic poem (though the books are of epic length). With its emphasis on Christ's teaching and the soteriological dimensions of the narrative, Juvencus' poem does contain a large didactic element, although as a narrative of *gesta* it remains generically a form of epic.[10]

Already the discussion of the preface and epilogue to Juvencus' poem has revealed some of the issues in the Juvencan (and, more broadly, Christian poetic) reception of Vergil. As Herzog insists, every example of intertextuality potentially involves a hermeneutic process, a process definable in terms of metaphor and exegesis.[11] The play of similarity and difference in such textual exchange is analogous to the workings of metaphor.[12] But at the same time Juvencus' re-use of Vergilian phraseology in a Christian context is inherently exegetical, constituting an *interpretatio Christiana* of epic, but also potentially, as in the case of the implicit identification of heaven and Elysium, an *interpretatio epica* of the Bible.[13] Because of the strong confessional opposition between pagan and Christian authors, the play of similarity and difference with a classical text can often take on the polemical connotations of contrast imitation. At the same time, the hermeneutic availability of the Vergilian text for such appropriation opens the classical author to the interpretative practices of biblical exegesis, as in the case of the *pii vates* of Vergil's underworld.[14] The potential for such semantic complexity lends much Christian Latin poetry a special appeal. Prudentius at the end of the fourth century marks a first high-point of such Christian poetics, but already in Juvencus the distinctive possibilities of Christian-classical intertextuality are evident.[15]

This is not to say, of course, that all use of Vergilian language in Juvencus invites such interpretative complexity. In some cases there is little or no conceptual or contextual similarity between two passages, beyond a basic coincidence of language. Herzog speaks of neutralisation in such passages, citing as an example *Aeneid* 3.102 (*veterum volvens monimenta virorum*, 'pondering the memorials of men of old', of Anchises mentally reviewing the traditions of Troy) and *Ev.* 4.707 (*veterum monumenta virum patuere*, 'the monuments of men of old lay open', of the splitting open of tombs at the Resurrection).[16] In this example contextual links between the two passages are elusive. Although one could imagine a reading that detected such connections, in Herzog's classification Vergilian language here becomes a neutral component of Juvencan diction, contributing to the *Ev.* as Vergilian epic, but without a more specific, context-based relevance to the earlier poem.[17]

The presence of Virgil in Juvencus is substantial. At its lowest level intertextuality can take the form of coincidences of lexicon and metrical *sedes*. Borrell Vidal has studied *Ev.* book 1 closely and concluded that in that book over 92% of the vocabulary is Vergilian and that all lines in the book but two contain words that occur in the same place in the line in both authors.[18] The next stage in lexical distinctiveness involves certain (frequently periphrastic) turns of phrase, so common or unmarked as to be constituents of a standard poetic *koine*; for instance, *figit vestigia* (*Ev.* 3.115, *Aen.* 6.159) or *sumere poenas* (*Ev.* 4.630, *Aen.* 2.576).[19] Beyond these, periphrases for basic human activities and experiences – birth, sleep, death, or burial – an element of epic code, recur in Juvencus and are often of Vergilian inspiration, amounting to small-scale genre scenes. To take one example, Lazarus' limbs, according to his sister Martha, 'lie at rest in the earth' (*membra solo conposta quiescunt*, *Ev.* 4.377). The language recalls the Vergilian Antenor, founder of Padua, who 'now lies at rest in composed peace' (*nunc placida compostus pace quiescit*, *Aen.* 1.249). As

3. Vergil and the Gospels: The Evangeliorum libri IV of Juvencus

always, the presence of difference in similarity opens the way for interpretation: Lazarus, unlike Antenor, will come back to life. But Vergil is here primarily a code model; such periphrases are expected in epic.[20] A more complicated example concerns Jesus' healing of the son of a *regius iuvenis* (John 4:46-54). As the father is returning home, the news comes to him that 'sudden health/salvation (*subitam salutem*) had brought his boy back from the threshold of death to the shores of light' (*in luminis oras*), *Ev.* 2.342-3. The phrase 'shores of light' is Vergilian, frequent in Lucretius, and ultimately derived from Ennius.[21] In one sense Juvencus' *in luminis oras / ... remeasse* echoes an epic periphrasis for birth. But it is birth with a difference. Healing is represented as a kind of *rebirth* (*remeasse*), analogous to the rebirth experienced by the believer in baptism. Every act of healing is a drama of salvation in miniature; the word *salus* encapsulates this double meaning. In this context the Vergilian locution *in luminis oras* takes on further connotations. Light imagery is widespread in Christian literature in general, and in Juvencus in particular, to express the opposition between salvation and damnation: so, at the Resurrection, Jesus came back 'from the darkness of death to the light of life' (*e mortis ... tenebris ad lumina vitae*, 4.734). In its new context the word *lumen* takes on distinctively Christian connotations. Here is an example of Juvencus combining the resources of epic idiom and Christian allegory to forge a new poetics of the miracle episode.[22]

In addition to such small-scale genre scenes epic reshaping is also evident in more extended descriptive passages. For example, biblical banquets and feasts frequently take on the colours of or make allusion to the rhetorical *convivium luxuriosum*. In the epic tradition Dido's banquet in book 1 of the *Aeneid* is the epitome of dining luxury.[23] So Vergilian language from this scene is detectable in the parable of the marriage feast (Matthew 22:1-4) and in the dinner given by Herod that led to the execution of John the Baptist (Matthew 14:6-11), where the *luxuria* of the banquet communicates the pride (*superbia*) of the banqueters.[24] In the case of the marriage feast at Cana, the location of Jesus' first miracle (John 2:1-11), Juvencus has the servants of the house, on Jesus' orders, 'wreathe the waters, filling the stone jars to their brims' (*undasque coronant, / completis labiis lapidum*, 2.142-3). The phrase *undasque coronant* plays on the Vergilian 'wreathe the wine' (*vina coronant*), used of Dido's banquet and of the feast of the Trojans after their arrival on the shore of Italy.[25] Readers of Juvencus will recognise that the verb *coronant* is regularly applied to wine. Of course, the apparent anomaly of applying it to water will soon be explained, when the water changes to wine: Juvencus' choice of language anticipates the miraculous outcome of the story. At the same time, the participial phrase (*completis labiis lapidum*) makes clear that Juvencus understands the Vergilian expression in a metaphorical sense, of 'filling to the brim.' This is one of the two possible meanings cited by Servius. (His other alternative is that wreathes literally garland the drinking bowls.) Juvencus goes on to speak of the water foaming to the lips of the jar as it transforms itself into wine (*spuma per oras / ... volutat*, 2.143-4). In the Christian poet's account the ring of foaming liquid can be read as an explanatory gloss on *coronant*.

A fourth biblical feast also betrays the influence of Vergil's Dido. At the Feeding of the Five Thousand, Jesus bids the assembled crowd 'recline and stretch out on the grassy couches' (*tum mox discumbere plebem / gramineisque toris iussit conponere membra*, 3.83-4); later he 'loaded the tables with rich fare' (*dapibus mensas oneravit opimis*, 3.87). Compare Vergil's account of Dido's palace servants who 'load the tables with fare' (*dapibus mensas onerent*, 1.706) and of the Tyrian guests who are 'bidden to recline on embroidered couches' (*toris iussi discumbere pictis*, 1.708). A coincidence with the language of the Bible (*cum iussisset turbam discumbere supra faenum*, Matthew 14:19) will have promoted the perception of similarity between the two passages.[26] From the perspective of the biblical text *supra faenum*, 'on the grass', is paraphrased (and Romanised) by *gramineis toris*. From the perspective of the *Aeneid* the richly embroidered (*pictis*) coverlets of Dido's banquet-hall give way to open-air couches of grass. The use of the epithet 'grassy' (*gramineus*) assimilates the Feeding of the Five Thousand to another, similar meal in the *Aeneid*, the outdoor feast celebrated by Evander in the company of Aeneas on the site of the future Rome, where the king 'disposes his guests on seats of grass' (*gramineoque viros locat ipse sedili*, 8.176). In this way the idealised simplicity of Evandrian proto-Rome qualifies the potentially suspect luxury of Dido's court.

Such passages rely on the reader's familiarity with the conventions of Vergilian banquet descriptions. Dido's court epitomises regal luxury. The specific character of Dido is generally not relevant to the biblical context. In other cases, however, the parallels are closer to Vergilian figures. But typically comparisons are localised and depend on coincidences of situation. Aeneas, for instance, leaves a relatively faint trace in the text of the *Ev*.[27] Language used of the Roman hero is rarely used of Jesus. A striking exception, in the story of the Gadarene swine, depends on a close situational parallel between the two texts: in both cases the hero is greeted with strong emotions by a second person whom he is approaching. In the *Aeneid* Anchises in the underworld 'saw Aeneas walking toward him over the grass' (*tendentem adversum per gramina vidit / Aenean*, 6.684-5) and greeted him with joy; in the *Ev.* the possessed man 'saw Christ coming toward him over the shore' (*pergentem Christum per litora vidit*, 2.53) and hailed him as the true son of God. The meeting of Aeneas and Anchises in the underworld is one of the most resonant moments in book 6 of the

3. Vergil and the Gospels: The Evangeliorum libri IV of Juvencus

Aeneid. The passage in the *Ev.* re-enacts that scene not in the accents of paternal affection for a long-lost son, but in the terrified voice of the devils who possess the demoniac. They worship Jesus as 'truest offspring of the ever-reigning Lord' (*regnantis semper Domini certissima proles*, 2.55), language which recalls the Sibyl to Aeneas earlier in book 6: 'son of Anchises, truest offspring of the gods' (*Anchisa generate, deum certissima proles*, 6.322). Juvencus' choice of language here implies Christian polemic against pagan views of divinity.[28]

A second case of assimilation of Jesus to a figure from the *Aeneid*, in this case Iulus, also depends on a situational parallel, a prophetic meteorological phenomenon. Matthew's Gospel (2:9) refers to a star which the wise men saw in the East going ahead of them. In Juvencus this becomes:

> ecce iteris medio stellam praecurrere cernunt
> sulcantem flammis auras, quae culmine summo
> restitit ...

Behold, directly in their path they see a star run before them, furrowing the air with flames, a star which came to rest over the top of a building ... (1.243-5)

Juvencus' account is much more circumstantial than the biblical text. It owes much of its detail to the comet that appeared over Troy in *Aeneid* 2 (692-8) to confirm the omen of the tongues of flame seen over the head of Iulus. That comet too ran through the sky trailing fire (*stella facem ducens ... cucurrit*, 694), appeared over the roofs of a building (*summa super labentem culmina tecti*, 695), was perceived by observers (*cernimus*, 696), and likened to a furrow (*longo limite sulcus*, 697). The flames of the star settling over 'the rooftop' (*culmine summo*) of Jesus' dwelling presumably also recall the tongues of flame visible on 'the top of the head' (*summo de vertice*, 682) of Iulus. Christian Latin poetry often derives specific detail in this way from reminiscences of classical texts. In the present instance the reader will perceive the parallels between Iulus and Jesus, both children of special destiny, parallels that will prompt comparison between Christian salvation history and the future allotted to Rome and the Julian line.

In a third case paternal affection for a dearly loved son provides the point of contact between biblical text and Vergil. In the Transfiguration God acknowledges his son: 'This is my beloved son in whom I am well pleased' (*his est filius meus dilectus, in quo mihi bene complacuit*, Matthew 17:5). Juvencus' version, 'this is my only son, my greatest delight' (*unicus hic meus est natus, mea summa voluntas*, 3.333) calls upon Evander's farewell to his son, Pallas, in book 8 of the *Aeneid*: 'Dear boy, my late, sole joy' (*care puer, mea sera et sola voluptas*, 8.581). *unicus* in Juvencus presumably reflects the influence of the Vergilian *sola*; *mea summa voluntas* must mean 'the object of my greatest affection', though at least one scholar has proposed emending the difficult *voluntas* to the Vergilian *voluptas*.[29] The effect of the Vergilian language is to intensify the emotional force of the passage.[30] The relation between God the Father and his son takes on the colours of human paternal devotion. In this case the parallels are all the closer because both sons are destined soon to die.

Pallas again comes to mind near the end of the *Ev.*, when the risen Christ bids the women at the tomb carry to the disciples his instructions that they should meet him in Galilee: 'quickly convey these instructions to our brothers' (*ista / fratribus en nostris propere mandata referte*, 4.772-3). In the *Aeneid* Evander gives instructions to the Trojans who have returned his son's body to him, in which he seeks revenge for Pallas' death: 'go and forget not to convey these instructions to your king' (*vadite et haec memores regi mandata referte*, 11.176). *mandata referte* is exactly the kind of periphrastic verbal phrase that could easily become a standard component of poetic idiom, the equivalent of a faded metaphor. But the marked contextual parallels – both instructions are delivered after a recent death of a hero – prompt the kind of comparisons characteristic of intertextual play.[31] While Pallas' death inspires in Evander the very human desire for revenge, in Jesus' case his victory over death in the Resurrection is the crucial event of salvation history. He can deliver in his own person his instructions to the women at the tomb, instructions that will set in motion, in his subsequent meeting with the disciples, the Christian mission in the world.

It is easy to see how recollections of Pallas, Iulus, and, on a particularly charged occasion, Aeneas contribute to Juvencus' account of the *gesta Christi*. A fourth figure, Sinon, comes as more of a surprise. Yet as Jesus appears before the Sanhedrin the mistreatment he suffers twice echoes Sinon's situation when first captured by the Trojans: in the *Ev.* Jesus' tormentors 'all strive to mock him in speech' (*verbisque omnes inludere certant*, 4.568) and he is finally led away 'with his hands tied behind his back' (*post terga revinctum*, 4.588); in the *Aeneid* Sinon too has 'his hands tied behind his back' (*post terga revinctum*, 2.57) and his captors encircle him and 'strive to mock their captive' (*certantque inludere capto*, 2.64). Both figures have surrendered themselves voluntarily to the abuse of their enemies. Again the parallel is primarily situational. The comparison has the capacity to enhance our appreciation of the coolness and daring of Sinon. But primarily the Greek captive is the antitype of Christ. His self-sacrifice is illusory, he will not die nor be the saviour of the Trojans. By comparison Jesus is truthful in answering his examiners and goes to his death. But that death will bring salvation, not destruction. He enacts the role that Sinon falsely attributed to himself, of a human sacrifice dying

3. Vergil and the Gospels: The Evangeliorum libri IV of Juvencus

not, as in Sinon's fiction, to bring favourable winds for the voyage back home, but to bring redemption to the human race. Earlier in the *Ev.* Jesus foresees his death: 'soon the day will come (*iamque dies aderit*) when the bridegroom will be snatched away' (2.368-9). The language corresponds to Sinon's, announcing that the day of his supposed sacrifice had come (*iamque dies infanda aderat*, 2.132). Sinon in this reading becomes a kind of false prophet, the mirror image of Christ (though acting on a human scale). But he is a diabolical version whose motives are duplicitous and self-representation deceitful.

Vergilian language in the *Ev.* can evoke familiar episodes as well as characters. To take a prime example, Aeneas' descent to the underworld in *Aeneid* 6 figures in a variety of biblical contexts. For instance, in the Transfiguration story 'a bright cloud overshadowed' Jesus and his disciples (*nubs lucida inumbravit eos*, Matthew 17:5). Juvencus paraphrases this text as 'a brilliant cloud from heaven surrounded their eyes and cloaked the mountain in light' (*caelo praefulgida nubes / circumiecta oculis vestibat lumine montem*, 3.330-1). The first five words remain close to the content of the original, though with a participle (*circumiecta*) replacing the finite verb (*inumbravit*). The second half of 331 then completes the sense with the anticipated finite verb in a metaphor derived from Vergil's account of the groves of the blessed. There the air is more expansive and 'cloaks the fields in warmly glowing light' (*lumine vestit / purpureo*, 6.640-1). The heavenly aura that surrounds Jesus in the Transfiguration appropriately calls up the heaven-like fields of the blessed in the *Aeneid*. Both passages describe sacred topography (the Juvencan *montem* reinforces the sense of location). In this case it is difficult to speak of spiritualisation since the *Aeneid* passage already has a strong sacral content. As with the previous passage discussed, the reader can see the Christian usage as contrasting with and correcting Vergil's pagan view of the underworld or as pointing to a telling point of agreement between the two poets. Ultimately the two approaches are not necessarily mutually exclusive.

Commentators have noted a number of other passages with verbal similarities to the descent to the underworld in *Aeneid* 6.[32] In two cases such correspondences contribute to the visual imagination of a biblical scene. In John's Gospel Lazarus' tomb is described as 'a cave with a stone placed on top' (*erat autem spelunca et lapis superpositus illi*, John 11:38). For Juvencus this becomes 'a tomb in a hollowed cliff' (*sepulchrum / rupe sub excisa*, 4.372-3). The descriptive detail comes from Vergil's account of the Sibyl's cave, 'a huge cliff of Euboean rock hollowed into a cave' (*excisum Euboicae latus ingens rupis in antrum*, 6.42). Caves might serve literally as tombs, as they did in the case of Lazarus; but in classical and Christian texts the underworld itself can be imagined metaphorically as a cave.[33]

Aeneas himself begins his descent from 'a deep cave' (*spelunca alta*, 6.237). Though Vergil is careful to distinguish this from the Sibyl's prophetic grotto (cf. Servius ad 6.237), Juvencus' application of language used of the Sibyl's cave to a place of burial blurs the distinction. Lazarus' *spelunca / sepulchrum* in its likeness to the Cumean grotto takes on numinous, but not ominous, connotations. The language perhaps anticipates Lazarus' resurrection. Like Aeneas he too will pass, or apparently pass, from the realm of the dead back to that of the living. In both cases the cave is a liminal location, permitting movement between life and death; both Vergil and Juvencus describe sacred landscapes.

Lazarus' tomb-cave anticipates the *antrum* (4.724) in which Jesus is buried. In the latter case it is not the topography of the monument but the rock by which its mouth is closed that attracts Vergilian language. Juvencus refers twice to this feature. When the chief priests and Pharisees set guards on the tomb, concerned that Jesus' disciples will steal his body, 'they roll huge weights of rock' (*saxique ingentia pondera volvunt*, 4.741) before the tomb entrance. The detail is not present in the biblical text here (Matthew 27:66), though earlier we learn that Joseph of Arimathaea closed the chamber with a rock (Matthew 27:60). Juvencus apparently here reinterprets that procedure as a security measure. The language recalls Vergil's account of punishments in the underworld, where some of the criminals are sentenced to 'roll a huge rock' (*saxum ingens volvunt alii*, 6.616), the punishment traditionally attributed to Sisyphus. Although the specific actions in the two cases are identical, the larger contexts of each action show few situational parallels, though both actors in their different ways defy divinity. Perhaps the most obvious point of comparison is that neither action achieves its purpose. The sinners in Vergil's underworld are condemned to repeat perpetually the same tasks; the Pharisees' and chief priests' attempt to thwart Christ's resurrections is destined to failure. The Vergilian associations convey the idea that the efforts to secure the tomb are a fruitless expenditure of labour and a sinful act that has implicit in it its own punishment. By comparison a second Vergilian phrase describes the stone at the mouth of the tomb set there by Joseph of Arimathaea. In this case the connotations are morally neutral: 'a huge boulder of rock shuts off the entrance' (*limen concludunt immensa volumina petrae*, 4.725). The word *volumina* here means 'an object rolled' – Matthew has 'he rolled up a large rock' (*advolvit saxum magnum*, Matthew 27:60). In the *Aeneid* the same phrase refers to the boxing gloves of the legendary fighter Eryx, 'immense strapping of thongs' (*vinclorum immensa volumina*, 5.408). The gloves are *volumina* because they are made of straps that the fighter wraps (*volvo*) round his hands. In this case the contextual relevance is slight. Yet the words are something more than simply a convenient, semantically neutralised turn of phrase. Eryx's boxing gloves metonymi-

3. Vergil and the Gospels: The Evangeliorum libri IV of Juvencus

cally embody the physical strength and pugilistic valour of a past generation of heroes, qualities that the present combatants cannot match. In Juvencus' account Jesus' tomb too takes on a special monumentality and superhuman status. (It is significant that unlike Matthew's Gospel, Juvencus does not speak of Joseph rolling the stone into place. No personal agent is mentioned.) The passage is all the more distinctive because of the unusual sense of *volumina*. Normally used of animals (a snake) or objects that are pliant or readily twisted and turned, the application to a rock (*volumina petrae*) will first strike the reader as paradoxical. The sense is clear, but the unusual language suggests a certain literary virtuosity on Juvencus' part.

All the examples of intertextuality cited so far from the main body of the poem derive from the *Aeneid*. Juvencus' poem, as the narrative of *gesta Christi*, has most in common with that poem of Vergil. But the *Ev.* also contains a strong didactic element. Juvencus retains in his account much of Jesus' teaching. Such passages, because of their frequent use of pastoral and agricultural metaphors, accommodate readily turns of phrase from the *Eclogues* and the *Georgics*. The cultivation of the individual soul, conversion and the winning of souls to salvation, and the missionary activity of the disciples all lend themselves to such figurative language. Juvencus, as the author of the first substantial Christian Latin poem, plays a foundational role in initiating this georgics and bucolics of the soul. Such pastoral and agricultural language was to become commonplace in the poetry of subsequent centuries. The evocation of the *Georgics* in the epilogue foregrounds such a reading of the *Ev.* as a work of Christian spiritual husbandry.

Much of the figurative language in Jesus' teachings finds Virgilianising equivalents in Juvencus, for threshing, the ripening of crops, the growth of weeds, ploughing and viticulture.[34] One passage in particular, combining pastoral and agricultural language, takes on almost programmatic significance through its evocation of the beginning of the *Georgics*. In Matthew's Gospel (9:36) Jesus takes pity on the crowd that follows him: they are 'like sheep without a shepherd' (*sicut oves non habentes pastorem*). He goes on to speak in a second metaphor of the multitude of souls among whom the mission must be preached: 'the harvest is abundant, but the harvesters few' (*messis quidem multa, operarii autem pauci*). Juvencus paraphrases the passage as follows:

> ingemit ut ruris dominus, cui pascua laeta
> innumerae tondent pecudes rectoris egentes.
> tunc ad discipulos depromit talia dicta:
> 'quam laetae segetes ruris per terga patescunt!
> sed rarus messor frugis superatur acervo.'

He grieved like the master of an estate whose rich pastures countless flocks graze without a leader. Then he pronounced to his disciples the following words: 'How richly the crops extend over the surface of the land. But the reapers are few and unequal to the abundance of the harvest.' (2.423-7)

Lines 423 (*cui*) to 424 in Juvencus' version echo Vergil, *Georgics* 1.14-15. There the rural divinity Aristaeus is hailed as 'denizen of groves, for whom three hundred snow-white steers crop the rich thickets of Cea' (*cultor nemorum, cui pinguia Ceae / ter centum nivei tondent dumeta iuvenci*). Although there are only two exact verbal parallels, *cui* and *tondent*, the Juvencan language is clearly calqued on Vergil: *pascua laeta* corresponds to *pinguia Ceae / ... dumeta*, and *innumerae ... pecudes* to *ter centum ... iuvenci*. The biblical *non habentes pastorem* plays a less prominent role in the poetic version, corresponding to the participial phrase *rectoris egentes*. Juvencus' emphasis on the richness of pasturage and the size of the flock anticipates the following metaphor, but it also serves to elaborate the metaphorical characterisation of Jesus as a rich estate-owner of a kind familiar in the late antique world. The rich crops (*laetae segetes*) of the second metaphor will then call up the first line of the *Georgics*, where Vergil announces as one of his subjects 'what makes the crops abundant' (*quid faciat laetas segetes*, 1.1). In Juvencus the Christian mission takes on the colours of the idealised pasturage and plenty of the beginning of the *Georgics*. In Vergil that bounty is associated with the munificence of the pagan gods; his poem aspires to that happy agricultural abundance. For the Christian poet Jesus replaces the representative pagan divinity Aristaeus. Implicit in these lines is a vision of the Christian world corresponding to an ideally productive country estate, a vision that is inspired by and derives imaginative power from the evocations of Vergil. Here once again contrast and assimilation are in uncertain relationship: Vergil as a pagan antitype to Christianity and Vergil as a proto-Christian.

Within the scope of this paper it has been possible only to survey and give a few examples of the presence of Vergil in the *Ev.* By its very nature the project of recasting the Gospels in Vergilian hexameters raises questions of form and genre. The biblical text, despite its large narrative content, includes much preaching and Christian protreptic. If I am right, Juvencus turns to the Vergilian corpus to explore the generic implications of his Gospel poem. His framing allusions to the *Aeneid* and *Georgics* point to a work that combines elements of epic narrative with instruction and exhortation in the manner of didactic. Juvencus' own poem exemplifies this combination; the simultaneous presence of narrative and didaxis/exegesis was to remain a defining feature of the sub-genre of biblical epic throughout late antiquity.

The *Ev.* could expect an enthusiastic readership among cultivated

3. Vergil and the Gospels: The Evangeliorum libri IV of Juvencus

Romans for whom its Vergilian idiom would only enhance the appeal of Juvencus' version of the biblical text. Vergilian language frequently reinforces the edifying content of the original by intensifying the moral or emotional force of the narrative. Specific, often visual or topographical, detail derived from Vergil or other classical poets counteracts the general tendency in the *Ev.* to eliminate or generalise distinctive features of the biblical setting and frequently brings into relief the moral or spiritual content of a text.[35] But Juvencus' adoption of a Vergilian idiom was not unproblematic for the Christian reader. Use of Vergilian language necessarily prompted comparisons between the contexts of the source and target texts. From one perspective this process could be viewed positively as a spiritualisation of Vergil's poetry by bringing it into line with the message of Christianity. But equally, as in the case of the application of language used of the Evander-Pallas relationship to that between God the Father and the Son, it could be read as secularising and humanising the biblical text.[36] Such reservations seem to resonate in Jerome's otherwise positive appreciation of Juvencus: 'he did not fear (*nec pertimuit*) to submit the majesty of the Gospel to the laws of metre' (*Ep.* 70.5). Ultimately, though, Juvencus' achievement was to be foundational for the development of Christian Latin poetry in late antiquity and for the creation of a Vergilianising Christian poetic idiom. Despite his reservations about the boldness of Juvencus' undertaking it was Jerome who gave the stamp of approval to the *Ev.* by including its poet in his catalogue of Christian writers, the *De viris illustribus* (84).

Notes

1. The *Laudes Domini* (148 hexameters) is a little earlier, while Lactantius' *De ave phoenice*, though capable of a Christian interpretation, does not require such a reading. The poetry of Commodian, probably of the third century, does not follow classical metrics. I cite Juvencus in the edition of Huemer (1891).
2. Cf. Introduction above.
3. Van der Nat (1977) 215-25; Roberts (1985a) 67-70.
4. For Lactantius' attitude to classical poetry see Goulon (1978), especially 147-52; for the importance of Lactantian practices of citation and allusion for Christian Latin poetry Herzog (1975) 167-211.
5. It is relevant that Juvencus uses the phrase *carminis auctor*, found in Tibullus (2.4.13) and the *Culex* (12) of Apollo as source of poetic inspiration, of the Holy Spirit.
6. For a discussion of this passage, though without taking into account the *Georgics* intertext, see Fontaine (1984) 111-13. The parallel with the *Georgics* is noted in Huemer's edition.
7. I owe this parallel to Herzog (1989) 334.
8. Thraede (1962) 1039-41. Both Thraede and Herzog (1975) 195 and 201 are concerned to define the category narrowly. For its application to the relationship between Lucretius and Vergil see Buchheit (1972) 77 and Hardie (1986) 233.

9. Of course, the historical Constantine was no less warlike in his early career than Augustus. Juvencus' image of Constantine is an ideological, panegyrical construct.

10. Röttger (1996) 129-30 compares the poem to didactic and suggests the division into four books may owe something to the *Georgics*, but without discussing the presence of the *Georgics* in the epilogue.

11. Herzog (1975) 202 (cf. 194-5).

12. So Conte (1986), especially 52-6.

13. Thraede (1962) 1035: 'The question of the *interpretatio Christiana* of ancient epic must be completed by that of the *interpretatio epica* of the biblical tradition.'

14. On the poetry of Vergil as an 'open work' in late antiquity, available for formal and semantic reconfiguration see McGill (2001) v-xiv. Cf. Lim below on Augustine and biblical and classical exegesis.

15. Cf. Witke below.

16. Herzog (1975) 197.

17. The distinction has something in common with the distinction Conte (1986) 31 makes between exemplary model and model as code (so McGill [2001] 39-52). Such neutralised locutions, though reproducing single *loci* from Vergil, contribute meaning primarily at the level of epic/Virgilian code.

18. Borrell Vidal (1991) 20-2. For compilations of Vergilian parallels see also Hatfield (1890) and Widmann (1906).

19. This category might also include epic formulas for introducing and concluding speeches of the form *et (ac) talia fatur, olli respondit, talia dicentem, talibus attoniti* and the like.

20. For other examples in Juvencus see 2.33 (*Aen.* 4.555, sleep), 2.342 (*Aen.* 7.660, birth), 2.384 (*Aen.* 2.14, passage of time), 4.368 (*Aen.* 2.62, death). See Roberts (1985a) 151-3.

21. 109 and 135 Skutsch.

22. Juvencus uses the phrase *in luminis oras* also of literal births (1.106 and 3.486). The phrase *lumina vitae* is also Vergilian (*Aen.* 6.828 and 7.771 – the latter of the reborn Hippolytus). For light imagery in Juvencus see Röttger (1996).

23. This tradition continued throughout late antiquity; see Roberts (1995) 94-100.

24. Compare 3.743 and 753 (parable) and 3.52-3 (Herod's banquet) with *Aen.* 1.637-8.

25. *Aen.* 1.724 and 7.147.

26. I quote the *Vetus Latina* from the edition of Jülicher (1963-76).

27. It is perhaps relevant that both Tertullian (*Nat.* 2.9.12-14) and Lactantius (*Inst.* 5.10.2-9) question Aeneas' piety on the grounds respectively that he abandoned Troy and committed human sacrifice.

28. See Servius ad loc.

29. Petschenig (1891) 139-40. In at least one other passage (1.418) the manuscripts of Juvencus show confusion between *voluntas* and *voluptas* (Röttger [1996] 59-62).

30. On the enhanced emotional force of Juvencus' biblical epic see Herzog (1975) 145-50. He sees this as an aspect of epic reception, mirroring the psychological sensitivity of Vergilian epic. As with scenic detail, so too psychological detail often finds expression in the language of classical epic.

31. Fowler (1997) 19-20 = (2000) 121-3 speaks of 'markedness' and 'sense' as criteria for accepting a correspondence between two texts. In the present case I would say the contextual parallels between source and target text prompt compari-

3. Vergil and the Gospels: The Evangeliorum libri IV of Juvencus

son and hence produce meaning, even though the phrase itself is not particularly distinctive (i.e. marked). Because of late antique readers' intimate familiarity with the works of Vergil there is a less heavy burden of proof when arguing for a correspondence with a Vergilian text than with the works of other authors.

32. See, for instance, 1.759 (*Aen.* 6.288), 2.161 (6.258), 2.211 (6.626), 2.346 (6.408), 2.652 (6.696 – but also 2.321), 2.702 (6.430), 3.592 (6.486), 4.574 (6.255).

33. *ThLL* 2:192.17-22.

34. Threshing: *purgabitur area frugum* (1.343) and *terit area fruges* (*Geo.* 1.298); ripening of crops: *laeta ... fruge salutis* (2.505 – no equivalent in the biblical text) and *laetis ... frugibus herbae* (*Geo.* 1.69); weeds: *lolium infelix* (3.7) and *infelix lolium* (*Ecl.* 5.37); ploughing: *iugera laeta / infindent ... sulcis* (4.170-1, of literal ploughing) and *telluri infindere sulcos* (*Ecl.* 4.33); viticulture: *vitis ... semiputata iacet* (3.693-4) and *semiputata ... vitis* (*Ecl.* 2.70), *falce premens* (3.695) and *falce premes* (*Geo.* 1.157).

35. Herzog (1975) 124-54 is the classic discussion of emotional intensification in the *Ev.*, the contribution of visual detail to such intensification, and its relation to Christian edification.

36. Compare Jerome's criticism of Proba for applying *Aen.* 1.664 to the relation between Father and Son (*Ep.* 53.7).

4

Vergil, Homer and Empire: The *Descriptio orbis terrae* of Avienus

Roy Gibson

Rufius Festus Avien(i)us was the most prolific producer of didactic poetry in late antiquity.[1] From Volsinii in Etruria, Avienus held two proconsulships (Achaia and Africa) in the middle of the fourth century,[2] and authored three substantial didactic works: *Descriptio orbis terrae*, a geographical and ethnographical work (1,393 hexameters); *Ora maritima*, a description of the Atlantic, Mediterranean and Black Sea coasts (713 surviving iambics); and *Phaenomena*, an astronomical poem (1,878 hexameters).[3] Avienus' vigorous poems are little read today. One reason for this is that the first and the last of these didactic works are translations of surviving Greek poems, respectively the *Periegesis* of Dionysius and the *Phaenomena* of Aratus. However, it is the precisely the status of the *Descriptio* as a paraphrastic text which is of interest in the context of a collection on the reception of Vergil in the fourth century. For Avienus' poem, although a relatively close paraphrase of its Greek source, contains Vergilian allusions and consistently seeks to downplay the Homeric themes of the original. To understand the significance of the role played by Vergil in this transformation is the task of this chapter.[4] In particular, I shall argue that the presence of Vergil creates problems for Avienus and his readers in a work where the vision of empire is contracted to the north and west, where Italy is neither the geographical nor the emotional centre of the work, and where the city of Rome is all but erased from the text.

Avienus' source: the *Periegesis* of Dionysius

Two acrostics concealed within the *Periegesis* (112-34, 513-32) appear to identify the author as Dionysius, native of Alexandria in the time of Hadrian.[5] The work commences with an overview of the three main continental divisions (Libya, Europe and Asia) and seas interior and exterior (1-173); follows with a detailed geographical and ethnographical review of Libya (174-269), Europe (270-449), the islands (450-619) and

4. Vergil, Homer and Empire: The Descriptio orbis terrae of Avienus

Asia (620-1166); and closes with a poetic farewell to the subject (1167-86). The poem has recently been summarised as a work 'describing in pseudo-epic style the known world chiefly after Eratosthenes, taking little account of subsequent discoveries'.[6] To accuse the author of bypassing discoveries made since the third century BC is to miss the point of his poem. Dionysius refers to no scholarly sources, involves himself in no disputes, and makes no pretence of scientific rigour. He is careful also to distance himself from the more mundane tradition of the *periplus* (description of coastlines). Numerous references are made to travel in ships (e.g. 154-5, 473ff., 580, 719ff.), but numerical indications of distance are excluded and in general suitable landing places are not described. Rather, he declares his reliance, in explicitly Hesiodic fashion, on the Muses alone (707-17).[7] This 'reliance' has far reaching consequences; as Jacob (1990) 42 remarks, Dionysius does not so much describe a place as reproduce the image found of it in earlier poets. As a result Dionysius' geographical description of the world is also a 'guide' to Greek literary culture. How Avienus deals with this we shall see below.

Avienus' translation of Dionysius

Although over 200 lines longer than its source, Avienus' text follows the structure of the Greek text closely. Like the *Periegesis*, it starts with an overview of oceans and continents (11-256), follows with a systematic review of Libya (257-393), Europe (394-604), the Islands (605-816), and Asia (817-1384), and concludes with a short epilogue (1385-93). Avienus is also faithful to the character of his source in his exclusion of numerical distances and the description of suitable stopping places. For Roman readers this would serve not only to distinguish the text from the *periplus* tradition, but also from the distinctively imperial genre of *itineraria* (descriptions of routes and distances by road).[8]

Avienus' decision to translate this particular 200-year-old Greek poem is less surprising than it initially appears. Dionysius' work attracted – or went on to attract – a considerable body of Greek scholarly commentary, and elicited another Latin translation from Priscian in the sixth century.[9] Furthermore, Avienus' younger contemporary Ammianus Marcellinus – despite the availability of more up-to-date works – appears to have used it as a source for his digressive description of the Black Sea area (*Res gestae* 22.8.1-48).[10] Like Ammianus' use of Dionysius, Avienus' decision to translate the *Periegesis* may be accounted for satisfactorily enough by the appeal to the author – and perhaps to some of the audience – of a familiar literary work. But it is worth asking whether there also might be some cultural significance in Avienus' choice of text. The *Descriptio* is not simply a 'school' exercise, but apparently part of a programme to offer a complete description of the ancient universe: land (*Descriptio*), shores (*Ora maritima*) and sky (*Phaenomena*). We have no firm evidence for the exact date of publication of the first poem in this programme, but it was certainly written some decades after Constantine's legalisation of, and subsequent programme of official support for, Christianity.[11] In both the *Descriptio* and the following two poems there is no reference to Christianity (not necessarily significant in itself at this date). But some notably pagan features suggest that Avienus' silence in this matter does not imply neutrality.[12] In this context, Avienus' decision to translate a product of Hadrianic Alexandria may appear part of a programme to offer a non- or pre-Christian view of the world. The *Descriptio*, in this one respect, can be compared to a near-contemporary anonymous text of the fourth century entitled *Expositio totius mundi et gentium* (hereafter *ETM*).[13] A description of the known world, with special emphasis on the systematic coverage of the provinces of the Roman empire, this text 'emphasises Hellenism (by reference to the ancient authors and deities) and it studiously ignores Christianity, even to the extent of omitting all mention of Jerusalem'.[14] The *Descriptio* is similarly devoid of reference to Christianity and is Hellenic and pagan in its emphasis. What role Vergil – although fundamental to the education of both pagan and Christian – might play in the perpetuation of a pagan character for the earth in Avienus' poem is a question worth bearing in mind.

Vergil in the *Descriptio*

Avienus never openly acknowledges that his poem is a translation of Dionysius' poem (contrast his naming of Aratus at *Phaen*. 172-3). However, the references in the opening ten lines of the poem to *Pierides*, Helicon and Phoebus combined with the appeal to the native Italian Muses, the *Camenae*, implicitly acknowledge that this is a Latin translation of a Greek original. Nevertheless, the influence of the *Camenae*, in the first instance at least, is confined to the transforming effects of the Latin language itself, as the text of the poem is not dense with allusions to earlier Latin poets. But this was hardly to be expected in the translation of a text from another language. However, such allusions as Avienus chooses to include are of more than ordinary significance precisely because the *Descriptio* is a translation. Allusions are not part of the fabric of translated texts to the same extent or even in the same way as of other texts: the use of an allusion in a translation represents a highly-conscious importation of another author into a context where – in the first instance – he or she does not belong.

Avienus weaves into the fabric of his text the ideas or phrases of a number of earlier poets, including those of Lucretius (*Descript*. 257-62; cf.

4. Vergil, Homer and Empire: The Descriptio orbis terrae of Avienus

Lucr. 1.921ff.), Ovid (*Descript.* 183; cf. Ov. *Met.* 7.785), Seneca (*Descript.* 7; cf. Sen. *Oed.* 269) and Lucan (*Descript.* 303f.; cf. Lucan 9.439; and *Descript.* 942; cf. Lucan 2.585). But the author to whom Avienus refers most often is Vergil, particularly to his *Georgics* and *Aeneid*. The reasons for the prominence of Vergil in this regard I discuss below. First, I offer a few straightforward examples of Avienus' exploitation of the Augustan poet.[15]

Avienus has a habit of preferring Vergil's report of a particular tribe or area over that found in his Greek source. For example, Avienus' Seres, like Vergil's, card silk from trees rather than producing garments from the flowers of the field.[16] And the thronged but wind-swept Scythia of Dionysius is transformed by Avienus into a barren quarter modelled on Vergil's Scythia.[17] Avienus also adds colour to his text by importing Vergilian phrases, as in his account of the 'blood and milk' diet of the Massagetae, or his description of the latter as 'men of hardy of stock'.[18] One may see here a simple taste for the deployment of Vergilian phrases in fresh contexts; or, more ambitiously, an attempt to stamp Vergil on a Greek text – and on the outermost reaches of the earth.

More extensive allusions by Avienus to the Augustan poet may also be discovered in the *Descriptio*. At the end of the review of the islands of the globe, Dionysius concludes with one of didactic and technical writing's most characteristic conventions, namely the indication of the infinity of subject matter (which defies proper coverage).[19] Avienus expands the final line of Dionysius' epilogue ('Of all these islands, it is not easy for me to speak the name', 619) into a full-blown figure (*Descript.* 811-16):

> harum quis ualeat *numerosa* ut *nomina* fari?
> si uelit hoc ullus, *uelit* idem *scire quot* alto
> curuentur *fluctus* pelago, quot sidera caelo
> elucent flammas, quot robora proferat Ida,
> quantus *harenarum numerus* uerratur ab *Euro*.

Who would have the strength to reveal the numerous names of these islands? Were anyone willing, he would likewise be fain to know how many billows curve on the deep sea, how many stars in the sky shine forth their light, how many oaks Ida puts forth, the number of grains of sand swept by the East wind.

This clearly draws on the similar 'uncountable number' passage which Vergil uses to bring his review of vines and grapes to a close (*Geo.* 2.103ff.):

> sed neque quam multae species nec *nomina* quae sint
> est *numerus*, neque enim *numero* comprendere refert;
> quem qui *scire uelit*, Libyci *uelit* aequoris *idem*
> dicere quam multae Zephyro turbentur *harenae*

> aut, ubi nauigiis uiolentior incidit *Eurus*,
> nosse *quot* Ionii ueniant ad litora *fluctus*.

But for the many kinds, or the names they bear, there is no numbering – nor, indeed is the numbering worth the pains. He who would have knowledge of this would likewise be fain to learn how many grains of sand on the Libyan plain are stirred by the West wind, or when the East wind falls in unwonted fury on the ships, would know how many billows of the Ionian sea roll shoreward.

Here Avienus has transformed some of Vergil's details, amalgamated others, and added fresh examples (i.e. the stars, Ida). An important transition in the text is thus marked, significantly, with lines original to the Latin poem, whose strongly Vergilian character is clear. Again, Vergil is stamped on a Greek text, and – by extension – on the map of the world. The importance of Vergil for Avienus' project is confirmed in other, more symbolic, ways too. Upon reaching Italy during the initial review of seas and coasts, the Greek original comments: 'the sons of the Italians inhabit the land, the Ausonians offspring of Zeus, always lords far and wide' (*Perieg.* 77-8). These Homeric-style lines are expanded by the Latin poet into (*Descript.* 114ff.):

> ... indomito tellus iacet Itala regno.
> Ausonis hic regio est; pubi genus ab Ioue summo.
> qua se flabra trucis boreae per inhospita terrae
> eructant caelo, populis caput Aeneadarum

[Here] lies the land of Italy, its kingdom unconquerable. This region is Ausonian, the population descended from highest Jupiter. Where the blasts of the fierce north hurl themselves from the sky across shelterless regions, [that is the northern] summit for the peoples of the *Aeneadae*.

The Latin poet generally follows his Greek counterpart in referring to Italians as *Ausonidae* (*vel sim.*). Here this name is supplemented with the term *Aeneadae*, which – hardly an indication of the true lineage of the peoples on the Italian peninsula – acts as a precise signal of the Vergilian cultural heritage of the Italian peoples. The deliberateness of this signal is confirmed by the allusion in 115 *pubi genus ab Ioue summo* to Aeneas' proud declaration before the Sibyl at *Aeneid* 6.123 *et mi genus ab Ioue summo* ('I too am descended from highest Jupiter').[20] Avienus pointedly substitutes *pubi* for Vergilian Aenes' *mi*; the Italian peoples are truly *Aeneadae*.

4. Vergil, Homer and Empire: The Descriptio orbis terrae *of Avienus*

Vergil as model

Examples of Avienus' use of, and reference to Vergil may be multiplied.[21] The appeal of Vergil to the fourth-century poet, at least in terms of similar subject matter, is not hard to account for. Included within the text's review of the three continents are features associated with the 'ethnographical' tradition, such as an interest in the physical geography of an area, and its climate, produce and inhabitants. As Thomas (1982) has shown, this ethnographical tradition is used prominently by Vergil both in the *Aeneid* and particularly in the *Georgics*. The best known passages in the former poem include Evander's review of the various inhabitants of Rome and Numanus Remulus' boast of the hardiness of Italy's sons (*Aen.* 8.314-36; 9.598-620), while the *Georgics* contains such memorable 'ethnographic' passages as the *laudes Italiae* (2.136-76), the excursus on the extreme climates of Libya and Scythia (3.339-83), and the description of the old man of Tarentum (4.116-48). A number of these passages share obvious similarities with the subject matter of Avienus' text, which covers the harsh climates and barbarous peoples of north and south, and includes within its review the geography and peoples of Italy.

But why does Avienus allude to Vergil more than to other poets? The relative prominence given to Vergil in this respect is hardly to be explained by the lack of other suitable material for Avienus to exploit. The geographical and ethnographical excursuses contained in (e.g.) Lucan's epic poem were presumably available to the fourth-century poet, but he appears to choose not to exploit them so frequently as Vergil's. One explanation is that Vergil is for Avienus both *modello-esemplare* and *modello-codice*.[22] That this is the case is perhaps suggested by the prologue to Avienus' poem.[23] The poem begins with a series of four clauses introduced by *qua* – no equivalent is found in Dionysius – which indicate in some detail the subject matter of the poem (*Descript.* 1-5). These appear to align the poem with the opening lines of the *Georgics*, where the content of that poem is also summarised in four clauses introduced by the pronoun (*Geo.* 1.1-5).[24] No doubt the use of pronouns in this fashion was a common device by Avienus' time, but the specifically Vergilian reference contained within them is confirmed in the verses immediately following by Avienus' use of the scene of Apollo's invasion of the Sibyl to express his own poetic inspiration (*Descript.* 6-7 *deus, en deus intrat Apollo / pectora*, 'The god, look, the god Apollo enters my breast').[25] Just as the Vergilian Apollo spoke through the Sibyl, so he will also speak through Avienus. To put it in modern terms, Avienus is signalling that Vergil offers a canonical text for his ethnographic poem.

Roy Gibson

Avienus' Vergil versus Dionysius' Homer

The presence of Vergil in Avienus' prologue is significant in ways other than that indicated above. The corresponding opening lines in Avienus' source contain a number of allusions to texts of programmatic significance for the Greek poem (*Perieg.* 1-4):

> Starting my song of the earth and the vast sea,
> The rivers, the cities and the countless tribes of men,
> I shall recall deep-flowing Ocean. For in it
> All land is encircled like an immense island.

Avienus' prologue, as we have seen, is rather more expansive. Mention of Ocean (the first subject) is delayed until line 9 of the *Descriptio*, and Dionysius' opening two lines are expanded into four. However, what is of interest here is not what has been added, but what has been omitted. Dionysius' four lines of prologue are packed with adaptations and allusions: particularly clear are the expansion of the opening sentence of Apollonius' *Argonautica* (1.1-2 'Taking my start from you, Phoebos, I shall recall the glorious deeds of men of long ago'), and the use of Homeric phrases (e.g. 'vast sea', 'countless tribes') in the build-up to the adaptation in line four of *Odyssey* 10.195 (Circe's island) 'an island encircled by immense ocean'.[26] Of these allusions no trace remains in the Latin translation. Of course, Avienus may not have recognised these allusions (how likely this is in the case of a translator of Hellenistic epic poetry I leave to the reader to decide). Or he may simply have wished to compose a completely new prologue for his translation. But the omission of the references to the two Greek epic poets and the substitution of allusions to Vergil may find a new significance in the context of Avienus' practice – observed below – of downplaying and eliminating Homeric references from his text, or over-writing Homeric characters and episodes with their Vergilian counterparts.

Geographical knowledge is routinely contextualised within a mythological framework in ancient geographical and 'travel' literature, whether in relatively sophisticated compositions such as the second-century *Periegesis* of Greece by Pausanias, or in more mundane works, such as *periploi,* the third-century *Antonine Itinerary*, or the *ETM*.[27] Although neither an itinerary nor a *periplus*, myths are likewise a part of the fabric of Dionysius' *Periegesis*; references to these tales at the appropriate landmarks in his review – as in the case of Herodotus and the authors of other *periegeseis* and *periploi* – aid the cultural Hellenisation of the earth. But the same myths are part of the cultural heritage and education of Latin-speakers (cf. the presence of Greek myth in the *ETM*), and Avienus

4. Vergil, Homer and Empire: The Descriptio orbis terrae of Avienus

reproduces and even occasionally extends those found in his source.[28] Indeed so attuned is Avienus to the story of the Argo – one of the cycle of stories most closely associated with the Hellenisation of the globe – that he even adds a reference to her voyage 'missing' from the text of the original.[29]

However, Avienus' attitude appears to be rather different when the Greek original includes references to Homeric characters and episodes. For example, at the beginning of his review of the islands, Dionysius implores the aid of the Muse after the manner of the opening of the *Odyssey* (*Perieg.* 447-8). Avienus replaces this once more with an appeal to the native Italian *Camenae* (*Descript.* 608-9) – a preface to a series of transformations loaded with cultural tension. The Greek original moves on in an easterly direction from Cadiz, and soon reaches the islands of Aeolus (*Perieg.* 461-4):

> After [Corsica] there are in the sea the circular [floating?] islands of Aeolus,
> Aeolus son of Hippotas, a king hospitable to strangers,
> Aeolus who has received gifts wonderful amongst mortals as his share
> – Sovereignty over the winds, both raging and at rest.

Here reference to the Aeolus episode in book 10 of the *Odyssey* is underlined with an adaptation of the opening lines of that book ('We came to the Aeolian island; here lived Aeolus, son of Hippotas; the deathless gods counted him their friend'). But what are the isles of Aeolus doing in the middle of the Hadrianic Mediterranean? However, as we saw earlier, the character of Dionysius' poem makes it clear that he is not providing a traveller's chart, but rather a map of Greek literary culture.[30] Against this background, Avienus' Latin version makes interesting reading (*Descript.* 625-9):

> has dudum tenuit *rex Aeolus*: Aeolus illic
> hospita iactatis indulsit litora nautis,
> Aeolus *imperio* summi Iouis arbiter alto
> *impositus* pelago est, effundere *carcere* uentos
> et sedare salum.

Long has king Aeolus held these [islands]: there Aeolus bestowed his hospitable shores on storm-tossed sailors, Aeolus – through the dominion of highest Jupiter – is installed as overseer of the deep sea, to send forth the winds from their prison or restrain the swell.

Debts to the Aeolus episode in the *Aeneid* are readily detectable (1.52ff., 60ff.):

> hic uasto *rex Aeolus* antro
> luctantis uentos tempestatesque sonoras
> *imperio* premit ac uinclis et *carcere* frenat ...
> ... pater omnipotens ...
> ... montis insuper altos
> *imposuit*

> Here king Aeolus in a vast cavern keeps under his dominion the brawling winds and howling storms, chained and bridled in their prison. ... the all-powerful Father ... installed massive mountains over them

Avienus, notwithstanding the oblique reference to Odysseus (626), has 'overwritten' the Homeric episode with its Vergilian counterpart and apparently transformed a map of Greek culture into a Latin one.

This transformation of a Homericising original forms part of a wider pattern of the omission or significant alteration of Iliadic or Odyssean characters or episodes in Avienus.[31] As we saw above, references to Homer (and Apollonius) in the prologue are replaced with language which aligns the text with significant passages in the *Georgics* and the *Aeneid*. We shall see in more detail below how explicit mention of Odysseus is omitted from Avienus' reference to the area inhabited by the Lotus-eaters, and replaced by allusion to Vergil. But other examples may be found. For instance, during the survey of Italy, Dionysius refers to the famous rock of the Sirens near Naples (*Perieg.* 360). Avienus simply omits the Homeric landmark, and adds in a reference to what the viewer can see with their own eyes (*Descript.* 498-500). The process of eliminating or downplaying Homer occurs outside Italy too. For example, Dionysius identifies the island of Leuce in the Black Sea as one of the 'isles of the blessed', home to Achilles and other heroes – a gift from Zeus in recognition of their valour (*Perieg.* 541-8). Avienus extends the description of the isle, transforming Dionysius' home for war heroes into a residence for the just (*Descript.* 723-9). Most significantly, from our point of view, Achilles is removed from the scene altogether.

A similar process of erasure can be seen in the Latin poet's treatment of Dionysius's passage on Troy. Dionysius accords the Homeric city an encomium similar, in terms of structure, to that which had been given earlier in the text to Rome (*Perieg.* 351-6). The city is described in five hexameters – the first four beginning with its name – which list with pedagogical earnestness the site of the town, its claim to fame, and builders and destroyers (*Perieg.* 815-19). Avienus, however, renders this passage simply as (*Descript.* 985-6):

> quae iacet immensae late sub rupibus Idae,
> infortunatam pertingens caespite Troiam.

4. Vergil, Homer and Empire: The Descriptio orbis terrae *of Avienus*

[Phrygia Minor] lies under the crags of boundless Ida, reaching with its turf as far as unfortunate Troy

The glorious rise and fall of Troy is reduced by the Latin poet to a single epithet. The Homeric city is all but erased from the Latin text, and its history is, by implication, irrelevant or uninteresting to Latin readers.[32] Furthermore, Homer is clearly being singled out for special treatment, for, as we saw above, Avienus is happy to include characters and episodes associated with other mythic cycles, including those connected with the voyages of the Argo. This reduction of the presence of Homer is matched by the elevation of the presence of Vergil (whose own scenes are used on occasion by Avienus to overwrite the Homeric originals).

This striking feature of Avienus' translation is thrown into even greater relief by comparison with the practice of the author of the *ETM*. This Latin treatise follows the normal practice of geographical works in setting topographical lore within a mythological framework – both Greek (Apollo and Diana at Naxos, 63) and Roman (Romulus at Rome, 55). Indeed the anonymous author of this treatise makes explicit in his text what is implicit in the text of others (including Dionysius and Avienus), by actually naming the authors of those myths which he is 'inscribing' upon the map of the world. Thus Homer is mentioned by name in connection with Mount Olympus and its gods (52), Vergil in connection with Carthage and Dido (61), and both authors together in connection with Phrygia (42). By contrast, as we have seen, Avienus seeks to downplay Homer – often to the benefit of Vergil. Not only is Vergil *modello-codice* for the fourth-century poet, but apparently also a Latin cultural icon to be elevated at the expense of his Greek 'rival'.

Vergil and the Romanisation of the *Orbis*

Vergil's role in the Latin transformation of the original text is complemented by an increased emphasis in Avienus on Roman perspectives of the *orbis*, particularly where empire is concerned. Here too Vergil has a role to play. For example, in his review of North Africa, Dionysius alludes to the pre-Roman story of the bull-hide used to measure the territory of Carthage (*Perieg.* 197). Avienus, however, offers an explicitly Roman and imperial perspective on the city ('readily inclined to cruel war', *Descript.* 290), in tandem with an introduction to the city ('After [the Massylii] there rise the renowned walls of Tyrian Carthage', *Descript.* 287-8) which echoes Vergil ('You will now see the great walls and the rising citadel of the new city of Carthage', *Aen.* 1.365-6). However, the most obvious attempt to introduce imperial perspectives follows not long after, on that part of the North African coast associated with the Lotus-eaters. The Greek original offers a cocktail of Homer and a genocide recently inflicted on the author's North African neighbours (*Perieg.* 205-10):

> Beyond the territory [of Neapolis] dwell the Lotus-eaters, friendly to strangers. There once in his wandering came wily Odysseus. In that region you might behold the deserted homes of the Nasamones, an annihilated race: they did not respect Zeus and the spear of Ausonia destroyed them.

The Lotus-eaters, considered an 'historical' people already in Herodotus (4.177), are here identified through a reference to the Homeric visit of Odysseus. Yet immediately following is a reference to an event of AD 85-6, namely the revolt of the Nasamones against their tax collectors during the reign of Domitian. Dionysius' description of the Nasamones as 'not respecters of Zeus' (Διὸς οὐκ ἀλέγοντας) hardly suggests criticism of the Romans.[33] Nevertheless, Dionysius' vision of Roman imperialism in general is indifferent or grim; as Jacob notes, Roman power in Dionysius is generally identified with brute force, and not with imperial wars of conquest or the protection of the provinces against exterior incursions.[34] Somewhat different in effect is the expansion of this passage offered by Avienus (*Descript.* 302-12):

> ... hanc rursum gens late prisca uirorum
> Lotophagi includunt; durosque Nasamonas inde
> accipe, quis quondam populorum examina multa
> uersauere solum, multo sonuere per agros
> balatu pecudes: nunc lati iugera campi
> et grege nuda iacent, et sunt cultoribus orba.
> Ausonis haec duro uastauit dextera bello;
> Ausonis inuicti gens roboris una per orbem
> arma tulit: pubem Latiam ferus horruit Hister,
> Romanas aquilas Rhodanus tremit, Italidum ui
> maesta paludiuagos Germania fleuit alumnos.

> An ancient race of men, the Lotus-eaters, surrounds [Neapolis] to the rear. Next consider the hardy Nasamones: their many multitudes once dug the earth, their livestock sounded many a bleat through the fields. Now their expanses of plain lie devoid of flocks and deprived of farmers. These Ausonian might laid waste in unbending war; the Ausonian race – its strength invincible – alone has waged war throughout the earth: the wild Danube trembled before the people of Latium; the Rhone quakes before Rome's standards; Italian force made gloomy Germany weep for her fen-wandering sons.

At first sight the proconsul of Africa appears to have a produced a piece more critical than its Greek source of the effects of imperial might: the

4. Vergil, Homer and Empire: The Descriptio orbis terrae of Avienus

'deserted homes' of Dionysius are developed into a vast plain emptied of its cultivators and their flocks. By the end of the passage, however, it is clear that Avienus is using the scene as an occasion for the celebration of the might of Roman arms and the extent of imperial power. The Latin poet has found an opportunity to supply something missing in Dionysius. The latter's silence on the actual extent of the Roman empire is notable. Indeed, Dionysius has nothing to say on the organisation of the empire, its different provinces, or the relations of emperor and subjects.[35] It is precisely this sense of the extent of empire, and Roman domination of it, which is restored in Avienus' text. Furthermore, it is to Vergil that Avienus turns when he wishes to express his vision of empire; the list of rivers and places which fear, or have experienced Roman might is reminiscent of the final lines of the catalogue of peoples who have yielded to Caesar on the shield of Aeneas (*Aen.* 8.726-8):

> ... Euphrates ibat iam mollior undis,
> extremique hominum Morini, Rhenusque bicornis,
> indomitique Dahae, et pontem indignatus Araxes.

The Euphrates was now moving with chastened current, and here were the Morini from the ends of the earth, the two-horned Rhine, the undefeated Dahae and the river Araxes chafing at his bridge.

Where Dionysius makes a reference to Homer ('There once in his wandering came wily Odysseus', 207), the Roman poet removes the reference – and once again substitutes Vergil. The emphasis on the reality of the extent of empire, missing in the Greek text, is apparently matched by the literary 'imperialism' which replaces Homer with Vergil.

Yet, to the modern reader, the pitfalls of offering an explicitly Roman and imperial perspective on the *orbis* through this Vergilian passage may be all too obvious. Where, for the Augustan poet, the Euphrates, the Rhine, Gaulish and Scythian tribes and an Armenian river mark the limits of empire, in the later poet the empire is identified by reference to the Danube, the Rhone and Germany. Here we may contrast Claudian who, in his *Panegyric for the Consuls Probinus and Olybrius*, has Dea Roma offer a rather different vision (*Prob. et Olyb.* 160-3):

> ... so may Scythian Araxes be our vassal
> And Rhine's either bank; so may the Mede be overthrown
> And the towers that Semiramis built yield to our standards,
> While amazed Ganges flows between Roman cities.

Both Claudian and Avienus are drawing on the same Vergilian passage. But where Claudian offers a vision of empire expanded in an easterly direction beyond its Vergilian limits, Avienus contracts the Vergilian model effectively to the western and northern sections of the empire. This un-Vergilian confinement of imperial perspectives returns during Avienus' review of the East. After a long excursus on the warlike habits of the Parthians, the Greek original adds a celebration of their defeat by Roman imperial might – presumably Trajan:[36] 'but nevertheless, for all that they were irresistible in battle, the spear of the Ausonian king tamed them' (*Perieg.* 1051-2). No equivalent reference or celebration is to be found in Avienus' text (*Descript.* 1247-8).[37] The empire – somewhat ironically in a fourth-century Latin translation of a Greek text – has effectively shrunk to the West.

Vergil and the 'decentering' of Italy in Avienus

Vergil proves to be a two-edged weapon for the later poet. On the one hand the Augustan author is a poetic resource for the 'Romanisation' of the text. But on the other, as we saw in the final example above, the presence of Vergil in the text may also serve to highlight the un-Vergilian features of Avienus' poem. This latter process can be seen most clearly in the Italian sections of each text. For Vergil, Italy's capital is 'Rome ... of all things the fairest' (*Geo.* 2.534), and the peninsula, whether in the *Georgics* or the *Aeneid*, is the geographical and emotional centre of his work. One could hardly expect a native of second-century Alexandria to award Italy a similar position in a description of the inhabited earth. Yet he does place the city of Rome at the centre of his description of Europe. What is surprising is that the fourth-century Roman, by comparison, all but erases Rome from his text. Dionysius writes (*Perieg.* 351-6):

> Through the middle [of the land inhabited by the Latins]
> The Tiber rolling sends its clear current into the sea,
> Fair-flowing Tiber, much more kingly than other rivers,
> Tiber who bisects lovely Rome,
> Honoured Rome, great home of my lords,
> Mother of all cities, opulent foundation.

In Avienus this is rendered baldly as (*Descript.* 494-5):

> per quos flauentis Tybris pater explicat undas,
> Romanosque lares lapsu praelambit alumno.

Through the midst [of the Latini] Father Tiber stretches out his tawny waves, and Roman dwellings he laps first with his native flow.

The Latin poet, an inhabitant of Rome,[38] has stripped his text of the

4. Vergil, Homer and Empire: The Descriptio orbis terrae of Avienus

elaborate encomium found in Dionysius' text (and replaced it with a domestic reference to Roman *lares*). This omission materially contributes to the decentering of Italy in the Latin text. The Greek poem as a whole may betray little sense of the actual extent or the workings of the Roman empire, as we saw above, yet here Dionysius looks to Rome as 'home of my lords, mother of all cities'. Avienus' lack of emphasis or focus on Rome is all the more surprising, found as it is at a time when the 'idea' of Rome was beginning to develop and grow as the political importance of the city itself declined.[39] In the near-contemporary *ETM*, for example, the city is hailed as 'enjoying supremacy' (54), the chief good of Italy, 'a city most great, most eminent and royal' (55), and the home of the Senate (55) – if not of the emperor, who is resident in Antioch (23, 32).

This 'failure' to sustain a centralising focus on Rome and Italy, noticeable precisely because of Avienus' use of Vergil elsewhere, is given further prominence by a number of passages in which Avienus retains Dionysius' attribution to lands outside Italy of features which Vergil had confined to the Roman homeland. For example, the wonderful climate and fertility of Egypt are described in a passage which, if anything, elaborates on the Greek version (*Descript.* 359ff.; cf. *Perieg.* 239ff.) – and in terms which, for a Roman reader, may recall the Vergilian *laudes Italiae*, particularly the miraculous spring, super-fertility and excellent ports of the Italian peninsula.[40] Despite the evident attempt above to stamp the Roman empire on the Greek text, Avienus is happy elsewhere to contribute to the dislodging of Italy from its place at the heart of the Vergilian world.

Conclusion

In Avienus' transformation of the *Periegesis* of Dionysius we have seen Vergil play various roles: Vergil the *modello-codice*, symbol of the institution of Latin didactic and ethnographic poetry; Vergil the Roman cultural icon, rival and supplanter of Dionysius' Homer; and Vergil as poetic well-spring for the conceptualisation of empire. But Vergil's role also raises questions. A text which replaces Homer with Vergil, which uses the Augustan poet to stamp Roman values and the Roman empire on the map of the world, yet lacks a centre in Italy, may appear to be something of a paradox. Avienus, admittedly, has attempted neither to structure nor to exploit this paradox. But what are readers to make of it? Of course, the lack of a centre in Italy is in good part a product of the poem's source: the Greek original has no reason to locate its geographical or emotional centre there. Yet Avienus, as we have seen, was prepared to make changes to his source (and inflate it by 200 hexameters) – but not in the case of Italy. More strikingly, he declines to follow Dionysius in making Rome the centre of Europe. Was the pagan Avienus alienated from the contemporary Christianisation of the city? Or is his neglect of Rome a symptom of that city's decline in importance, a dim reflection of the emergence of Constantinople and provincial capitals such as Trier and Antioch? Yet if the poem lacks a centre in Rome and Italy, Avienus does claim a special Vergilian heritage for the people of Italy, and on occasion describes the rest of the world in Vergilian terms or attributes to it qualities reserved in the Augustan poet for the peninsula. Perhaps Vergil's Italy has become a 'landscape of the mind' – a phrase easier to use than explicate – a literary landscape fit for export to the *orbis* (as more obviously in Ausonius' *Mosella*).[41]

Notes

1. For the controversy over the spelling of his name, see most recently Cameron (1995).
2. On the provenance and career of Avienus, see Matthews (1967).
3. Lost are the iambic *Vergilii fabulae* attested by Servius (*Ad Aen.* 10.272).
4. Translations from Avienus and Dionysius are my own. Others are taken or adapted from H.R. Fairclough (*Georgics*), D. West (*Aeneid*), W. Shewring (*Odyssey*), R. Hunter (Apollonius), and M. Platnauer (Claudian).
5. The acrostics, discovered by Leue (1884), are perhaps allusions to the famous acrostics in Nicander and Aratus; see Reeve (1996-7). On Dionysius, see most recently Khan (2002).
6. OCD^3 s.v. Dionysius 'Periegetes'.
7. Cf. Hesiod *Op.* 678ff. For the relationship of the poem to the Greek geographical tradition, see Jacob (1990) 18-28, also 39-44.
8. For a brief overview of the *periplus* tradition and Roman *itineraria*, both pagan and Christian, see Elsner (2000b) 184-6.
9. Gualandri (1982), which I have not seen, apparently argues on the basis of Avienus' translation that scholia on Dionysius were in circulation already in the fourth century. For the surviving scholia, prose paraphrases, commentary of Eustathius, and verse translation by Priscian, see Bernhardy (1828). On the reception of the poem, see further Jacob (1990) 13-14.
10. See Drijvers (1998). For Latin translations of Greek texts in the fourth century, both pagan and Christian, see Cameron (1977) 13-15.
11. See Matthews (1967) 487-90; and Introduction above.
12. E.g. the reference, in language which recalls Vergil (*Aen.* 4.53), to the poet's autopsy of the god at Delphi at *Descript.* 603ff. (there is no equivalent in Dionysius). Zehnacker (1989) 326-9 argues that Avienus' attempt at a third Latin translation of the *Phaenomena* of Aratus is primarily pagan in inspiration; certainly the prologue to that poem is strongly Stoic (Zehnacker, op. cit., 325-6). Apparent evidence of Avienus' pagan sympathies may also be found in the epitaph which the poet composed for himself (*CIL* 6.537 = *ILS* 2944), where the Etruscan goddess Nortia is addressed (see Matthews [1967] 490-1). More radically, Marcotte (2000) sees in *Descript.* 1077-93 a sympathetic allusion to Julian's *Misopogon* (which, if correct, would have important consequences for the dating of the poem).
13. The text is dated by Rougé (1966) 19 to 359.
14. Elsner (2000b) 188. Contrast the 'Christian' empire which emerges from the slightly earlier *Itinerarium Burdigalense* (the subject of Elsner's paper).
15. The text of the *Descriptio* used is that of P. van de Woestijne (1961).

4. Vergil, Homer and Empire: The Descriptio orbis terrae *of Avienus*

16. *Descript.* 936; cf. Verg. *Geo.* 2.120-1; cf. *Perieg.* 753ff.
17. *Perieg.* 758ff.; cf. *Descript.* 937-40 and *Geo.* 3.352-5.
18. *Descript.* 921-2: cf. Verg. *Geo.* 3.463; *Descript.* 918 *durum ab stirpe genus*: cf. *Aen.* 9.603
19. For the convention, see Gibson (2003) on Ov. *Ars* 3.149-52.
20. *Aen.* 1.380.
21. Cf. e.g. *Descript.* 141 and *Aen.* 8.691; *Descript.* 494 and *Aen.* 8.540; *Descript.* 752 and *Geo.* 4.521; *Descript.* 801ff. and *Aen.* 1.416ff.; *Descript.* 948 and *Geo.* 2.540; *Descript.* 1003 and *Aen.* 1.492.
22. See Introduction above.
23. On the prologue, see Santini (1992).
24. The same Vergilian passage lies behind *Phaen.* 67-70. Also prominent in the *Descriptio* prologue is a reference to the opening of the *De rerum natura*: both texts employ the phrase 'every kind of living thing' (*genus omne animantum*); cf. *Descript.* 4 and Lucr. 1.4.
25. *Aen.* 6.46 *deus ecce deus*.
26. For the extensive influence of Apollonius Rhodius on Dionysius, see further Jacob (1990) 47-50.
27. See Elsner (2000b) 186; for Christian equivalents in the *Itinerarium Burdigalense*, see op. cit., 189-90.
28. E.g. Io (*Perieg.* 140-1 = *Descript.* 198ff.); Memnon (*Perieg.* 249-50 = *Descript.* 368-9); the Heliades (*Perieg.* 290ff. = *Descript.* 425ff.); Cadmus and Harmony (*Perieg.* 390ff. = *Descript.* 540ff.); Boreas and Orithyia (*Perieg.* 425 = *Descript.* 585); Diomedes (*Perieg.* 483ff. = *Descript.* 648ff.); Sinope (*Perieg.* 775ff. = *Descript.* 953ff.); Heracles and Cerberus (*Perieg.* 788ff. = *Descript.* 960fff.); Pegasus and Bellerophon (*Perieg.* 869ff. = *Descript.* 1032ff.).
29. Compare *Descript.* 249-56 with *Perieg.* 167-9. For other references to the cycle of myths associated with the voyages of the Argo, cf. e.g. the isles of Apsyrtus (*Perieg.* 487ff. = *Descript.* 655ff.); the Hellespont (*Perieg.* 516ff. = *Descript.* 689ff.); Hylas and the nymphs (*Perieg.* 807ff. = *Descript.* 977ff.); Medea and the Medes (*Perieg.* 1020ff. = *Descript.* 1216ff.)
30. See further Jacob (1990) 44-51.
31. Compare the first-century Latin geographical work of Pomponius Mela, where Batty (2000) 72-5 detects active and passive resistance to Homer in the search for 'a new [geographical] model for the world of the West'.
32. Avienus does also cut down the original's extended praises of Rome (see below). But note that he matches the length of Dionysius' praises of his native Alexandria (*Perieg.* 254-9; cf. *Descript.* 374-80), while omitting reference to the Homeric Eidothea, daughter of Proteus (*Od.* 4.364ff.), whose tomb lay on Pharos. On one occasion Homer is not erased, but – rather ambivalently – 'restored' to the text: compare the description of Ithaca at *Perieg.* 494-5 with *Descript.* 662-5, noting the application of the dubious *tyrannus* to Odysseus (who is absent from the Greek text).
33. The massacre even of the non-combatants elicited from Domitian the famous remark to the senate 'I have forbidden the Nasamones to exist' (Dio 67.4.6). People in this part of the world had a habit of disappearing off the face of the earth: the Nasamones occupied the land of the Psyllians who had been obliterated by the south wind (Herodotus 4.173).
34. Jacob (1990) 64-5.
35. See Jacob (1990) 62, also (1991) 46-7.
36. See Jacob (1991) 47.

37. It is possible, but not certain, that we see here the effect of contemporary concerns with the military situation in the East. See Introduction above.
38. According to the epitaph he composed for himself: see n.12 above.
39. See Introduction above.
40. *Geo.* 2.149ff., 161ff.
41. I would like to thank the following for help and advice: Catherine Conybeare, Roger Green, Yumna Khan, Andrew Morrison, Roger Rees, and Michael Reeve.

5

Sex and Salvation in the Vergilian *Cento* of the Fourth Century

Karla Pollmann

I. Theory

'Every book is a quotation; and every house is a quotation out of all forests and mines and stone quarries; and every man is a quotation from all his ancestors.'[1] This pre-postmodern claim of a universal intertextuality has gained strong prominence in post-war theoretical discussions concerning the nature of literature. In a less sharply focussed way, such a perception of language or literature can already be observed much earlier. Lucretius in the *De rerum natura* (written before 55 BC) compares the versatility and endless possibility of recombining atoms to create things to the same ability of letters to be combined into different words (1.197-9, 823-7, 912-4; 2.688-9, 1013-22).[2] In an analogous way, this is exactly what happens when a poet writes a *cento*[3] by rearranging an original hypotext into a new, equally meaningful but different hypertext. This method can best be called hypertextuality.[4]

The writing of *centos* goes back to the Alexandrian period,[5] though the first extant *centos* date to the first[6] and second centuries AD.[7] This literary technique remained popular till at least the nineteenth century.[8] In a *cento*, a writer uses fragments from texts of canonical authors (Gennette's hypotext) taken out of their original context to create a new work (Genette's hypertext), which one could indeed call literary 'patchwork' (κέντρων[9]) or an assembly (*collage*) of quotations.[10] It is in the truest sense 'littérature au second degré' (Genette). It is important that the authors whose texts were used for a *cento* should be canonical and well known in order to assure the recognition of the technique by the readers. In practice this meant especially, though not solely, Homer and Vergil.[11]

In a different context,[12] I have shown two possible roots for the technique of the *cento*. First, the method of Alexandrian grammarians of making a difficult text more plausible by changing its word-order, which was justified by the rhetorical figure of *anastrophe*, that is, the inversion of the natural word-order. The context of this method is *exegetical*. Second, the Aristophanic mockery of the syntactical monotony of Euripidean verse, which is exposed in *Frogs* 1238ff. by quoting half-lines from Euripidean prologues that can always be completed by the mock ending 'He has lost his flask', thus creating a new, ridiculous meaning. The challenge is to maintain the syntactical and metrical coherence of the lines. The context of this method is *parodical*.

In a *cento*, the author's ambition would be to recombine parts of verses from one[13] author's works in order to create a new, unexpected sense, while at the same time moving (almost) exclusively within the metrical and lexical material of this author.[14] A computer program run over the new text would not be able to detect that it was not, in fact, the authentic work of the original author. However, in antiquity the verse *cento* was normally not intended as forgery. In order to make the *cento* more practicable, minor alterations of the original hypotext were allowed, as, for example, changing a noun in the singular into the plural, or a verb in the indicative into the subjunctive etc.[15] The crucial difference from the original is the semantic change of the material. This is possible on the micro-level of individual words or phrases that are sometimes employed in the new context in a meaning different from that of their original context; and this is necessary on the *cento*'s macro-level, as the whole of the new text conveys a completely different message.

The possibilities of how to apply the technique of a *cento* range on the semantic level from sheer parody and caricature to serious interpretation with the intention of revealing a hitherto hidden and thus ultimately true meaning of the text. In the former case the noble style of the hypotext is applied to a vulgar subject in the hypertext, implying the parodical *transformation* of the hypotext; in the latter the noble style of the hypotext is applied to a noble subject in the hypertext, implying the serious *transposition* of the hypotext.[16] It is noteworthy that the pagan tradition from Alexandrian times up to late antiquity stayed more or less on the *parodical* track, whereas the Christian tradition, with Proba as its first Latin representative,[17] pursued the *serious* intention of revealing the hidden Christian message contained in the pagan canonical poets.[18]

Though *centos* had been written well before Ausonius,[19] he was the first to write what could be called a 'theory of the *cento*' in the preface to his *cento nuptialis*.[20] I quote some extracts that are crucial for our context:[21]

> Those who first trifled with this form of compilation (*concinnatio*)[22] call it a 'cento'. It is a task for the memory (*memoria*)[23] only, which has to gather up scattered tags and fit these mingled scraps together into a whole, and so is more likely to provoke your laughter (*ridere*) than your praise. ... For it is vexing to have Vergil's majestic verse degraded (*dehonestasse*) with such a

5. Sex and Salvation in the Vergilian Cento of the Fourth Century

comic theme (*ioculari ... materia*). ... So take a little work, continuous, though made of disjointed tags; one, though of various scraps; absurd, though of grave content; mine, though the elements are another's. ... A *cento* is a poem compactly built out of a variety of passages and different meanings, in such a way that either two half-lines are joined together to form one, or one line and the following half with another half. For to place two whole lines side by side is weak (*ineptum*), and three in succession is mere trifling. But the lines are divided at any of the caesurae which heroic verse admits. ... This my little work, the *cento*, is handled ... so as to harmonise different meanings (*sensus diversi ut congruant*), to make pieces arbitrarily connected seem naturally related, to let foreign elements show no chink of light between, to prevent the far-fetched from proclaiming the force which united them, the closely packed from bulging unduly, the loosely knit from gaping.

In this passage, Ausonius emphasises the importance of the formal success of the poem, which is as relevant as the unity of its new content. The convincing combination of formerly heterogeneous parts into a seamless whole has, moreover, the function of giving the impression that the 'new' poem is an original creation of the centonist.[24] Ausonius' characterisation of the *cento* is dominated by paradoxes: the dignity of the Vergilian poetry versus the comic theme of his own *cento*; the erudition of Valentinian I[25] versus the playfulness (*ludus*[26]) of his *cento*; the continuity of the *cento* versus the disjunction and disparity of its elements; the seriousness of the hypotext versus the ludicrousness of the hypertext; the tension between the different ownerships of hypotext and hypertext. Defining the genre of the *cento* as essentially paradoxical corresponds to its particular nature as a text that in itself exposes the paradoxicality of texts or literature in general as potentially or necessarily fluid entities capable of conveying various meanings (*parole*) as long as the author and the reader (who is also the second author who transforms the hypotext into a *cento*) operate within the same *langue*.[27]

In the prose passages framing the *cento*, and in the digression (*parecbasis*) before the detailed description of sexual intercourse, there are several features bearing upon the meaning of the *cento*: (a) the apologetic tone of the author; (b) the repeated references Ausonius makes to his *cento* as a (*nullius pretii*) *opusculum*, which is apparently carelessly composed; (c) the description of the *cento* as jocular entertainment.

Concerning (a), Ausonius' poem may first have been composed around 374,[28] and so, presumably, after Proba. Yet, although Vergilian *centos* had been written before Ausonius,[29] the need for apology may be explained by the fact that here for the first time Vergil was used in an extensively obscene way. Ausonius may have felt he had to give some warning, which at the same time served to incite the readers' curiosity. Moreover, he combined this with the remark that the emperor Valentinian I himself indulged in such *nugae*, and that he was really writing at his command. His apology thus turns into confirmation that his literary activity had the backing of the emperor and was thus above reproach.[30]

On (b), his repeated emphasis on the formal carelessness of his *cento* could be understood as a modesty topos, though possibly there existed technically more successful specimens of this genre.[31] It seems more likely, however, that this statement of 'unpolishedness' is to be understood as hinting at the nature of the literary genre: the theme of the *cento nuptialis* is completely different from the high and serious topics of epic and tragedy. At the same time, however, the author's thorough knowledge of Vergil and his ingenuity are highlighted, both facilitating the speed with which a cento could be created.[32] In this, Ausonius follows a tradition as it can be observed in Catullus 1.1 'my pretty new booklet' (*lepidum novum libellum*). However, the playfulness of Catullus' work nevertheless claimed to be 'polished' (1.2 *expolitum*), in opposition to Ausonius, who in his letter to Paulus (from which his theory of the cento was quoted above) emphasised the roughness of his work, *nec labor excudit nec cura limavit, sine ingenii acumine et morae maturitate* ('[the cento which] no hard work has shaped nor care polished, without spark of wit and the ripeness which deliberation gives').[33] Ausonius uses this kind of terminology several times in his oeuvre.[34] That the statement cannot simply be taken at face value is clear from its aim of giving the appearance of authenticity, unity and originality. The hypertext should no longer bear any traces of the original content or context of the hypotext. This ideal of Ausonius' aesthetics of production does not necessarily contradict the fact that the readers have to be able to recognise the poet's model in order to appreciate the cento properly. Moreover, as we shall see below, the contrasting comparison of the old and the new contexts of the reassembled phrases adds a crucial dimension to an enhanced understanding of the cento's content and message.

Concerning (c), the characterisation of the cento as something one could rather laugh at than praise is clearly not meant with regard to the semantic surface of the hypertext. Its content as such is not funny at all, with its elements of solemn marriage ritual and, at its end, 'one of the most detailed descriptions of sexual intercourse in Latin literature, and also one of the most violent'.[35] The humour comes in only when the readers recognise that the poetic material used is entirely taken from Vergil (see also on (b) above). This mechanism had already been described by Seneca the Elder with regard to Ovid's technique of Vergilian allusion: 'Something he (i.e. Ovid) had done with many other lines of Vergil, with no thought of plagiarism, but meaning that his piece of open borrowing should be noticed (*agnosci*)' (*Suas.* 3.7). Though such a cento expresses a certain irreverence towards the poet, this does not necessarily mean that the hypotext as such is not respected. On the contrary, it is the implicit acknowledgement of the

5. Sex and Salvation in the Vergilian Cento of the Fourth Century

familiarity of the reader with Vergil's works and their canonicity that guarantee that the *cento* will work and be recognised for what it is. In a similar way parody in general only works if the text to which it refers is taken entirely seriously.

As already hinted at under (b), it is noteworthy that the theoretical statements made in the preface to the *cento nuptialis* are not always followed by the poet (or indeed by other poets, including Proba[36]) in practice. First and foremost, Ausonius himself frequently uses whole lines, even two consecutive ones (25-6, 75-6, 97-8), though he describes this as *ineptum*. Secondly, not only caesurae are used as cut-off points for the addition of another phrase. Thirdly, though the smoothness of the *cento* in syntax and content should be as successful as possible, it only achieves its full effect if the reader nevertheless recognises the underlying original context. All in all, Ausonius' theory of a *cento* does not present rigid guidelines, but is rather to be understood as an ideal programme.

II. Sex: Ausonius' *cento nuptialis*

Ausonius was not the first to use Vergil's poetry for vulgar effect in a *cento*. This was previously undertaken by Petronius in his *Satyricon* 132.11. In that context the hero Encolpius blames his penis for not having performed in the required way when he was last together with his lover. Petronius describes the reaction of the scolded penis in Vergilian verse combined in a *cento*:

> illa solo fixos oculos aversa tenebat, (= *Aen.* 6.469)
> nec magis incepto vultum sermone movetur (= *Aen.* 6.470)
> quam lentae salices | lassove papavera collo. (= modified *Ecl.* 3.83 *lenta salix* ~ 5.16 *lenta salix quantum* + *Aen.* 9.436)

> That one turned aside and gazed fixedly at the ground,
> nor is moved by the beginning of the speech any more
> than drooping willows or poppies on their tired necks.[37]

The first two lines are taken directly from two successive lines in Vergil (which according to Ausonius is inept[38]), where he describes Dido's refusal to speak to Aeneas in the Underworld: *illa*, referring in the original to Dido, denotes in the new context Encolpius' penis (*ea* or *illa pars corporis*, cf. *Sat.* 129.1 and 132.12).[39] The crude 'identification' is almost macabre, but at the same time has a comic effect, as one imagines the shyly cast-down eyelids of the thus anthropomorphised penis in the first line.[40] In the next line the anthropomorphic aspect continues, especially in *vultum*, but with *movetur* the physiological state of the penis as such is

83

expressed, making use of the double meaning of *movere* as metaphorical (of emotional movement, as in the Vergilian original) and literal (the lack of physical movement, i.e. erection of the penis, in Petronius). This is reinforced by the comparison in the third line, where the reader is invited to refer the figurative level of the comparison again to the physiological behaviour and appearance of the flaccid penis: it hangs down like the drooping branches of willows, and its red glans is tilted like red poppy blossoms on their tired necks.[41] This interpretation is supported by the fact that Petronius does not continue after *Aeneid* 6.470 with 471 *quam si dura silex aut stet Marpesia cautes* ('as if it stood like hard flint or a Marpesian crag'). Apart from the fact that he might have considered that as too awkward (anticipating Ausonius' verdict to avoid line clusters),[42] stiffness or hardness is the last thing Petronius wants to evoke in this context.

In contrast with the original context, where Dido's lack of reaction to the entreating Aeneas is a sign of her bitter and unyielding resentment,[43] in the case of the penis its lack of response is a sign of its exhaustion. On each occasion the subject in question does not behave as the other side (Aeneas, Encolpius) expects. Similarly, the *lentae salices* ('drooping willows') were in the original (where the singular is used) inferior to the pale olive tree, as was, in Menalcas' judgment, Amyntas' song inferior to that of Mopsus. In Petronius there is no verdict of inferiority connected with the comparison but solely that of physical incapability. Therefore, equally incongruent is *Eclogue* 3.83, where the *lenta salix* is as dear to cattle as Amyntas is to Menalcas. Here the epithet *lenta* is an adornment (*epitheton ornans*) without much semantic content, whereas in Petronius its significance is vital. The discrepancies become even stronger in the second half of this line, where the romanticised image of the dying Euryalus, compared in Vergil to a flower (in the tradition of Catullus 11.21-4 and *Iliad* 8.306-7),[44] clashes harshly with the crudeness of the new context's meaning. At the same time, the bitter-sweet pathos of the Vergilian original confers to the new context an emotional depth which, in an analogous way, Encolpius may well have felt facing his predicament of sexual impotency and its negative consequences for him. On the one hand, the context of the original has to be neutralised to make the new meaning possible. At the same time, however, the old context has to stay in the readers' awareness in order to achieve its telling effect by way of contrasting transformation.[45]

In the following, I wish to demonstrate with a few select examples how Ausonius in his *cento nuptialis*[46] employs in principle the same techniques, which are an intentional application of a stylistic fault criticised by the grammarians, viz. an awkward combination (*iunctura*) of words that involuntarily creates a vulgar sense and is therefore an ill-sounding expression (*cacemphaton*).[47] Martianus Capella (*De nupt.* 5.518) advises that a *cacemphaton* which is caused by the 'intrusion or alteration of

5. Sex and Salvation in the Vergilian Cento of the Fourth Century

words' (*vel interpositione vel commutatione verborum*) should be avoided and quotes as an example *Aeneid* 2.413 *atque ereptae virginis ira* ('the anger of the *ereptae* maiden') because *ereptae* can not only mean 'rescued' but also 'raped'.[48]

After the epistolary introduction in prose and a metrical preface to the *cento nuptialis*, there follow six roughly symmetrical sections: II. The Marriage Feast (*Cena nuptialis*), III. The Bridal Portrait (*Descriptio egredientis sponsae*), IV. Portrait of the Groom (*Descriptio egredientis sponsi*), V. The Wedding Gifts (*Oblatio munerum*), VI. Epithalamion (*Epithalamium utrique*), and VII. The Entry into the Bedchamber (*Ingressus in cubiculum*). Then a prose apology (*Parecbasis*) separates this from the final VIII. 'Bumping of the Uglies' (*Imminutio*),[49] which is again followed by a prose apology. This structures the sequence of action in a subtle way, while also evoking the satirical tradition of the prosi-metrical form.[50] Ausonius' *cento* tells the 'story of a wedding' (*fabula de nuptiis*).[51] However, not the whole wedding is described, as, for instance, the actual ceremony of uniting bride and groom as husband and wife and the signing of the wedding contract are missing. After that, a meal would normally take place at the house of the bride. Then first the bridegroom, then the bride would leave the house to go in procession to the house of the bridegroom where the marriage would be consummated.[52] Sometimes the whole ceremony could take place in a country estate. We have to assume an arrangement like that in this *cento*, as the procession is not mentioned. Other details are documented elsewhere, like the offering of gifts to the couple (lines 57-66),[53] the throwing of nuts (73),[54] and the emphasis on the good looks of bride and groom.[55] The term *epithalamium*, literally a 'song given at the bridal chamber', did not emerge from the marriage cult, but was created in Hellenistic times as a technical term for the literary genre of songs sung at the bridal chamber. Later the term's meaning widened to 'wedding song' in general, which could be sung at various stages during the wedding.[56] Ausonius follows a combination of the two meanings, as the *Epithalamium* is obviously sung before the bridal chamber, but with the bride and groom still outside and not already inside as would usually have been the case. Another problem is that elements one would normally expect to be addressed in the epithalamium with its intention to praise the bridal couple (with the topoi of the luckiness of the day, the hope for offspring, etc.),[57] are dealt with separately in the *cento*, especially the description of bride and groom (lines 33-56). Therefore we have a partial overlapping of the genre: the *cento* as a whole contains elements of an epithalamium, and the *Epithalamium* (VI) itself is part of the *cento* (lines 70-8).[58] The mirroring of the *cento* as a whole in the *Epithalamium* is also visible from the statement that the young men and women 'sing playfully in unpolished verse' (line 69 *versibus incomptis ludunt*) echoing in a

85

self-referential way Ausonius' characterisation of the weakness of his *cento* (quoted above).

The difference between the first six parts and the final much cruder *Imminutio* can be described in Genette's terms as transposition versus transformation.[59] In the first six parts it is easier to transpose the original context into a new one, often without harsh contrast. This can, for instance, be seen in the *Epithalamium* for bride and bridegroom (lines 67-79). First the bride is addressed (lines 70-2) in phrases originally applied to Nysa in the context of her happy but ill-assorted marriage to Mopsus (70a ~ *Ecl.* 8.32), to Juno (addressed by Jupiter, 70b ~ *Aen.* 10.607), to Venus (addressed by her son Aeneas, who does not yet know her identity, 71a ~ *Aen.* 1.330), to the blonde nymph Lycorias (71b ~ *Geo.* 4.340), and to the nymph Cyrene (72 ~ *Geo.* 4.380, a particularly clever transposition, as in the original it is Cyrene [= *mater*] who urges her son Aristaeus with the words *cape ... Bacchi* to pour a libation of wine to Oceanus, whereas in the *cento* it is not the *mater* who utters the rest of line 72). Then the bridegroom is addressed (73-6); the original addressees were Mopsus (73a ~ *Ecl.* 8.30), an enchantress (73b ~ *Ecl.* 8.64), Aeneas (74a ~ *Aen.* 8.500), and Mopsus (74b ~ *Ecl.* 8.29). While the bride is associated with nymphs and the divine sphere, the bridegroom belongs to a bucolic-heroic context. In a way, this continues in 75-6, taken from *Aeneid* 1.74-5, where Juno promises Aeolus (the bridegroom in Ausonius) her most beautiful nymph Deiopea (the bride in Ausonius). The following two lines have a more tragic undertone: 77a is taken from *Aeneid* 9.446, where the fallen warrior pair Nisus and Euryalus are promised immortality through Vergil's poetry; 77b from *Aeneid* 4.382, Dido's evocation of the divine powers in a curse when Aeneas announces to her that he wants to leave her; 78a from *Aeneid* 3.493, spoken by Aeneas to Andromache and Helenus at Buthrotum as a farewell, adding that their toils are now over. This and the allusion to the Parcae (78b-79 ~ *Ecl.* 4.46-7[60]) give the epithalamium an almost ominous ending.

In contrast, in the *Imminutio*, the break with the original context has to be much stronger (Genette's transformation), and therefore the effects are more intensive, verging on the grotesque. This technique is facilitated by the fact that certain phrases were already considered in antiquity to be ambiguous, potentially obscene or metaphorical. This becomes clear from scattered comments by the grammarians.[61] For instance, Diomedes (*Ars* 2, Keil 1, p. 451.7) comments on *Aeneid* 6.406 (~ *cento* 105b) *ramum qui veste latebat*, ('the bough which lay hidden in the Sibyl's clothing') that this is a *cacemphaton*, caused by a 'mistake in word-arrangement' (*vitio compositionis*).[62] Servius points out concerning *Aeneid* 1.159 (~ *cento* 110a) that the area described is purely fictitious (*topothesia est, id est fictus secundum poeticam licentiam locus*, 'an imaginary landscape, that is a place made up

5. Sex and Salvation in the Vergilian Cento of the Fourth Century

according to poetic licence'). Such a comment almost justifies Ausonius' transformation of this line for the area of the female genitals. Similarly, Servius remarks on *Aeneid* 2.19, that the *caverna* described there and at 2.53 (~ *cento* 119) is also to be understood metaphorically, which in Ausonius' case again means the female genitals. Servius' learned comment on *Aeneid* 11.817 (~ *cento* 121b) that *mucro* ('sharp point') could denote the point (*acumen*) of any weapon makes it easy for Ausonius to transfer it to the penis. Macrobius *Saturnalia* 6.6.17 quotes among other references *Aeneid* 11.804 (~ *cento* 118) as a praiseworthy example of Vergil's ability to give words or phrases a 'new meaning' (*excogitatio novorum intellectuum*), which Ausonius certainly matched by applying the line to the penetration of the virginal bride. Ti. Donatus' comment on *Aeneid* 2.52 (~ *cento* 126b) that *recusso* means *omnia illa percussa ictu validissimo* ('everything was thoroughly shaken by the strongest blow') also illustrates the point well when transferred to sexual intercourse.

But there are also instances, where the centonist breaks with the commentary tradition in addition to ignoring the original meaning of a phrase.[63] Servius on *Eclogue* 10.27 (~ *cento* 106) offers an allegorical interpretation for *minium* ('red pigment') as *aether* and therefore as the god Pan, whereas Ausonius takes it in its material appearance and applies it to the red glans of the groom. Ti. Donatus comments on *Aeneid* 4.690-691a (~ *cento* 122-123a) that Dido's final convulsions before her death express her remorse. In the context of the *cento* these lines describe the resistance of the bride while being penetrated. Macrobius *Saturnalia* 4.5.2ff. explains that *Aeneid* 6.122 (~ *cento* 126a) expresses *pathos* and *misericordia*, which is completely lost in the *cento*, where the phrase refers to the coital movements of the groom.[64]

III. Salvation: Proba's *cento*

Unlike Ausonius, Proba's Christian *cento*[65] serves a serious exegetical purpose, similar in fact to that intended by the *sortes Vergilianae* from at least the third century onwards.[66] She wrote it presumably between 353 and 370[67] and can thus be seen as inaugurating the tradition of the Christian *cento*. Before Proba, *centos* were associated by Christians with heretics and condemned as intending to convey dogmatic lies in a manipulative way.[68] Her poem comprises 694 Vergilian hexameters,[69] and is thus substantially longer than Ausonius' *cento nuptialis* of 131 hexameters. Her *cento*, providing a brief survey of the history of salvation, can only be fully appreciated if one has knowledge of the Vergilian text, the biblical text, and the commentary tradition linked with both.[70] The *cento* has two aims:[71] first it conserves Vergil's verse and language for the Christian reader by using them to paraphrase the Bible (and we may remember that Christianity at her time had not produced much poetry of its own), and secondly it provides an exegesis of Vergil's *Aeneid* acceptable to a Christian reader.[72] The exegetical figure used here for literary interpretation is *typology*, i.e. the exploitation of scenes, figures or phrases of the hypotext to illuminate corresponding parts of the hypertext.[73] Truly innovative is the idea that Proba (in contrast to many other Christian authors) accepted that Vergil in all his works proclaims *Christian* truth and that she therefore understood her *cento* as a kind of Vergilian exegesis, as stated in the programmatic verse 23: 'That Vergil sang of Christ's sacred duties let me tell' (*Vergilium cecinisse loquar pia munera Christi*).[74] This leads to the self-confident position that Proba on the one hand refuted pagan poetry, including her own previous poetry (which dealt with the traditional pagan themes of panegyric and war), and on the other felt able to use Vergil to convey the Christian message of truth. This, in turn, makes her *cento* superior to pagan poetry: it is a *sacrum ... carmen* ('sacred song', 9), not *ludus* ('game', 'trifle') as Ausonius' *cento* (see above), and it intends to reveal *arcana ... cuncta* ('all mysteries', 12) and the *altae res* ('profound affairs', 50-1) of the history of salvation.[75] This justifies her pride in assuming the title *vatis* ('prophetess and poetess') in line 12.[76]

Scholarship, apart from criticising Proba's poem as absurd and unoriginal,[77] has accused her *cento* of being not properly structured, with episodes following one after another at random.[78] This is not correct. A close analysis shows that both the selection and the sequence of the episodes follow theological principles to give a brief survey of the crucial points in the history of salvation. The Old Testament section ranges from the creation of the world up to the flood with the sole survival of Noah and his family, with God's purpose 'to have the fundamental stock from which a new stem's roots could be revived' (*ut genus unde novae stirpis revocetur haberet*, 316), echoing the traditional view of Noah's survival as a second creation and a new order, 'after that flood, the Almighty summoned the patriarchs and gave them laws: they lived the age under great laws' (*diluvio ex illo patribus dat iura vocatis / omnipotens: magnis agitant sub legibus aevum*, 317-18). *Cento* 316 is taken from *Georgics* 4.282, where it refers to the death of the beehive. *Cento* 317 is partly based on *Georgics* 4.154 (after the passing of the Golden Age, in the Age of Jupiter laws are necessary). The original contexts of both these adapted phrases help to mark the change to another era in the *cento*, that is the age of the patriarchs; it lasts from the second flood till the birth of Christ and can therefore in a theologically stringent way be encapsulated in a *praeteritio* (319-22). The birth of Christ initiates a prophesied new era ('future kingdoms', *regnisque futuris*, 414; 'not unaware of the prophets and knowing the age to come', *haut vatum ignarus venturique inscius aevi*, 447) as he will rule the earth and save humanity ('help', *auxilium*, 340; 'who would

5. Sex and Salvation in the Vergilian Cento of the Fourth Century

fill the world with his strength', *qui viribus occupet orbem*, 345; 'sent for dominion', *missus in imperium*, 348; 'rule the peoples by your power', *tu regere imperio populos*, 409;[79] 'concern for salvation', *cura salutis*, 418; 'the main path to salvation', *via prima salutis*, 472; 'triumphs', *triumphi*, 666). This second era supersedes the first and the poetic task is therefore greater ('I begin a greater work', *maius opus moveo*, 334).[80] It is not surprising that Proba uses verses from *Eclogue* 4 to illustrate the birth of the Saviour, as this eclogue had been interpreted as a prophecy of Christ's birth by Christians from Lactantius onwards.[81] But there are also other instances where she offers a theological interpretation of Vergil. For instance, Jesus as a Christian Aeneas is also a saviour who transcends the past and by his suffering transforms the future, thus representing a truly epic hero.[82] This characterisation consolidates the christocentric unity of the *cento*.[83]

Furthermore, there are typological correspondences within the poem between events from the Old and New Testament, like the Serpent's successful temptation of Eve, which is undone by the Serpent's unsuccessful temptation of Christ.[84] This is an unusual constellation, because from Romans 5:12 onwards Christ had been seen as the anti-type to Adam, whereas here Eve and Christ form a typological pair. This serves to strengthen Eve's position and to see her as a representative of humanity in general and not as a negative counterpart to Adam.[85] Another motif linking the Old and New Testament part of the poem is the reversal of the role of the Jews according to Proba: the persecuted Hebrews of the Old Testament (317-32) become the persecutors of Christ in the New Testament (600-24).[86]

In striking contrast to Ausonius' profuse apology for his *cento*, Proba is concerned with emphasising the soteriological framework of her *cento* which has a strongly didactic aim: in view of Jesus' mighty deeds for humanity and his power, and in the face of a final judgment, it is important that people keep their faith and lead a good life. This protreptic aim places this *cento* between an epic (with narrative action and a hero) and a didactic poem (with personal address to the reader and exemplary illustrative episodes), a fairly common transgeneric combination in late antiquity.[87]

In order to illustrate Proba's centonic technique more clearly a passage may be analysed in which she paraphrases the event of Jesus walking on water, both in relation to her biblical model and to an analogous paraphrase of the same passage in Juvencus. As is commonly acknowledged, Juvencus aims at following the biblical text as closely as possible; the changes he makes are very 'discreet'.[88] He follows the version of Matthew 14:22-33 with details missing in Mark 6:45-54 and John 6:16-21.

Proba makes some remarkable alterations. First, she adds a complete section (531-44) without a biblical equivalent, which can best be described as amplification with the aim of universalising the biblical message. She puts the sea-journey of the disciples in the context of the general human achievement of catching fish from a boat, and later of travelling over water. The latter, especially, risks exposure to the elements, and sailors often have to fear for their lives. This general setting, which echoes pagan ideas about the dangers of technological progress,[89] serves to assimilate the biblical narrative to pagan ideas and to make the biblical message more easily palatable and convincing for both educated unconverted pagans and converted educated ex-pagans. After this, Proba turns in a rather abrupt way to the specific event of the disciples on a boat caught by a storm (545-61; 545, *ecce*, marking the transition from the general to the specific). Whereas in Juvencus it is quite straightforward to determine the exact biblical model, this is not the case in Proba. This is not simply due to her being restricted by Vergilian verse, but by the fact that she purposefully reshapes the biblical episode.

Jesus' approach towards the disciples' boat is richly embellished (547-9), emulating Juvencus' amplification (*Ev.* 3.102-4). In *cento* 550-1 the disciples recognise Jesus at once and salute him. This blatantly contradicts Matthew 14:26 and Mark 6:49-50, where they mistake Jesus for a ghost and are frightened. In John 6:19 and Juvencus *Ev.* 3.104-6 the disciples are also frightened at the sight of Jesus. Notably, Proba omits the scene between Christ and Peter who wants to walk on water as well, though this scene is related in Matthew 14:28-31 and Juvencus 3.110-23,[90] but is also missing in Mark 6:48ff. and John 6:18ff. The instantaneous and unquestioning acknowledgement by the disciples of Christ as king is corroborated by his description as a powerful giant: 546, *cui summa potestas* ('who has greatest power' ~ *Aen.* 10.100 of Jupiter); as soon as Christ touches the water the storm subsides (552-5)[91] without him even wetting his 'giant loins' (556, *latera ardua* ~ *Aen.* 3.665 of Polyphemus); he is immediately acknowledged as the *rector* of the boat (558 ~ *Aen.* 5.176 of Gyas, having thrown Menoetes overboard), an element that is missing in the biblical pericopes. Finally, the boat groans under the great weight of Christ (559 ~ *Aen.* 6.413 about Aeneas climbing into Charon's boat, with him being heavier than the shadows[92]), which is in ancient thought generally a sign of divinity; 560-1 suggests that no rowing is necessary anymore now Christ is on board, again a pagan idea of a god's ship moving without physical effort. Instead of the merciful and educational attitude of Christ in the biblical model, Proba focuses in her depiction of the scene on Christ's power and the spontaneous response of his disciples, thereby describing the act of faith as joyful worship instead of the existential doubt and angst of the disciples, especially of Peter, in the biblical narrative.[93]

5. Sex and Salvation in the Vergilian Cento *of the Fourth Century*

IV. Conclusion

According to Genette, the relationship between a hypotext and its hypertext is always that the latter *comments* on the former.[94] As we have seen, this is certainly true for the *cento* as well. Several differences between Ausonius and Proba are illuminating: Ausonius takes the grammarians' tradition of finding *cacemphata* in an author to its extreme, while at the same time claiming that he speaks the truth, because these things really happen in a wedding night, *aliter haec sacra non constant* ('the rites are exactly as I have described'), and by mentioning Vergil and others as his predecessors, even regarding obscenity. However, Ausonius confesses in the *Parecbasis* that (by manipulation) he makes Vergil *impudentem* 'shameless', which means that he, as the 'second' poet, *devalues* his model (*dehonestasse*). The need for ample apology is therefore understandable. In contrast, Proba, while also insisting that she tells the truth, does not do so by claiming to manipulate the poet's works (as it were, against the grain of their intended content), but by revealing the true and hidden message of the hypotext. Thus, she *revalues* or enhances the status of her hypotext. She does not have to apologise to lovers of Vergil as Ausonius has to, but rather to lovers of Christ. Hence she offers a lengthy renunciation of pagan sources of inspiration and of her own previous (pagan-style) poetry (*cento* 1-55).[95] As her *cento* has a missionary aim, and intends to promulgate the history of salvation, Proba can well describe herself as part of this history and thus, as part, also, of the content of the poem.[96] This contrasts sharply with Ausonius, who in his own original way follows, at the very end of his *cento*, the path of Catullus 16.5-6 ('For the pious poet ought to be chaste himself, though his poems need not be so'), emphasising the strict separation of the life-style of the poet from the content of his poetry.[97]

For later Christian poets, Proba's technique of abbreviating and amplifying her biblical model became clearly influential. On a formal level she (even more than Juvencus) encouraged the further development of a Christian poetic language based on classical models, first and foremost Vergil, but also others.[98] The intentionally anti-classical (because anti-pagan) poetical enterprise of Commodian remained the exception. On the level of content she helped to establish a genre of epic-like poetry with non-martial content.[99]

In both Ausonius' and Proba's *centos*, part of the ambition, and of the play, is the enigmatisation of Vergil's phrases.[100] The necessary and intended way of speaking in an obscure way urges the reader to try to make sense of the verses with the frame of reference in mind (wedding celebration or biblical text). The collage of verses always requires a hermeneutical frame within which it may be understood.[101] In particular, as our analysis of a single passage in Proba has illustrated, more consideration should be given to Proba's theological intentions that go beyond literary artistry. Despite the Vergilian strait-jacket, her considerable modifications of the biblical text aim at making her own theological statement with a protreptic perspective oriented towards her fellow human beings, urging them to remain steadfast in the Christian faith.

Surprisingly (or maybe not, after the preceding argument), if one judges the quality of a *cento* in terms of the degree of transformation of a given phrase in its new context, then Ausonius' sexualisation of Vergil in his *Imminutio* and Proba's Christianisation in her *cento* are closely related from a technical point of view. The extent of the success of this technique can be seen in particular clarity when one looks at *Aeneid* 7.66, *pedibus per mutua nexis* ('feet mutually entwined', of a swarm of bees clinging together), which is one of only two Vergilian phrases[102] used in both Proba's *cento* and Ausonius' *Imminutio*. Whereas in Proba (618) it describes the fixing of Jesus' feet when he is mounted on the cross, in Ausonius (107) it refers to the intertwining of the couple's limbs during sexual intercourse. If deconstructionism aims at the elimination of the author from the work, and seeks to dismantle the signifier in order to reconstitute what is always already inscribed in a phrase, this would be a prime example to put this theory to the test.

Notes

1. Emerson (1876) 42.
2. Pollmann (1996) 115-17.
3. In all cases known to me words or phrases are recombined. But Ptolemy Philadelphos went a step further and even recombined syllables to mock this method, cf. Pollmann (1997) 87-8.
4. Genette (1982) 11-15. It is not clear to me why Genette does not discuss the *cento* in his book, though it would illustrate his point in an extreme fashion. His categories and criteria of narratological analysis will prove useful for the following discussion.
5. Döpp and Geerlings (1998); Kunzmann and Hoch (1994) 148.
6. In Petronius *Satyricon*, see Herzog (1975) 13 and Section II of this chapter.
7. Ermini (1909) 41-55, among them especially the 'tragedy' *Medea* by Hosidius Geta consisting of Vergilian hexameters.
8. Slavitt (1998) 43-75 has rendered the *cento nuptialis* by Ausonius in a Shakespearean *cento*, thus extending the history of the genre into the twentieth century. For examples from late antiquity and the Renaissance see Herzog (1975) 13, 17-18; for the Middle Ages up to the twentieth century, see Kunzmann and Hoch (1994) 152-6.
9. For the etymology of '*cento*', see Kunzmann and Hoch (1994) 148. The term *cento* is not found in the sense of 'poem composed of odd fragments' before Ausonius, but Tertullian speaks of *Homerocentones* in *Praescr. haer.* 39.5; it may have been current long before that.
10. This became again popular in the eighteenth century, where parts of various newspaper headlines were assembled to produce amusement or criticism

5. Sex and Salvation in the Vergilian Cento of the Fourth Century

of society. In the twentieth century similar effects were achieved by photographic montages, often as a means of political agitation; cf. Riha (1971) especially 7-46.

11. For the superior status of Homer and Vergil as almost universal poets cf., e.g., Sen. *Consol. ad Polyb.* 8.2; Quint. *Inst.* 1.8.9; Aus. *Epigr.* 137.1; Macrob. *Sat.* 1.24.5; August. *De civ. D.* 1.3; Orosius *Hist.* 1.18.

12. Pollmann (1997) 87-90.

13. Whereas it is common to combine phrases from several works of one author, it is less frequent to combine bits taken from various authors into a new unit, but cf. Lucian *Symp.* 17 (a certain Histaeus when drunk had quoted a ridiculous poem consisting of verses from Hesiod, Anacreon, and Pindar). A third of the Byzantine *cento Christus patiens* consists of verses from Euripides; to a much smaller degree verses are taken from Aeschylos and Lycophron, see Pollmann (1997) 92 with n. 16.

14. The literary *cento* had its 'haptic' equivalent in various forms of ancient and Chinese puzzles (the tangram), see Evelyn White (1919) vol. 1, 394-6.

15. For examples in Proba cf. Schenkl (1888) 556-9 and his *apparatus fontium* under the text 569-609; for Ausonius see Green (1991) 519, 522-4.

16. Genette (1982) 30-7.

17. In the Greek world, the *Homerocentones* by Eudocia and others follow, according to Zonaras *Ann.* 13.23, the tradition of a bishop Patricius.

18. Kunzmann and Hoch (1994) 149, summarising earlier scholarship.

19. Herzog and Schmidt (1989) § 554.

20. Ermini (1909) 31-6. The text of the *cento nuptialis* is quoted from Green (1991) 132-9.

21. Translation with slight modifications taken from Evelyn White (1919).

22. For *concinnatio* as a crucial term in Ausonius' poetics in general see Sánchez Salor (1991) passim, esp. 133-4.

23. The mnemotechnic artistry links the *cento* to the rhetorical training at schools, cf. Herzog (1975) 5; Herzog and Schmidt (1989) 296; Kirsch (1989) 67-8.

24. Herzog (1975) 4-6.

25. Sivan (1993) 106-11; Green (1991) 520.

26. Cf. Green (1991) 132.3; 139.19

27. Kirsch (1989) 120-2.

28. Green (1991) 518; Herzog and Schmidt (1989) 296 suggest AD 368/9.

29. See pp. 83-4 for Petronius.

30. His emphasis on composing this *cento* by imperial command is repeated in the poetic preface (line 10, *non iniussa cano*). For Proba's completely different strategy of framing her *cento* see Section III of this chapter.

31. Herzog (1975) 10; Laelius Capilupus, *centones ex Virgilio* (Rome 1555).

32. Slavitt (1998) 75 about the *Imminutio*: 'a dirty mind is a great comfort, and ... if the devil can cite scripture to his purpose, at least he can take credit for having read some.'

33. Green (1991) 132.2-3. In a similar way, Statius *Silv.* 1 *praef.* emphasised the improvised state and speedy composition of his *Silvae*.

34. Sánchez Salor (1991) 114-21.

35. Green (1991) 519.

36. Herzog (1975) 39.

37. The translation is taken from Connors (1998) 32, who analyses this passage 30-3.

38. See Section I of this chapter.

39. *illa* can also be interpreted as elliptic for *mentula*, see *ThLL* s.v. *mentula* 782.52-4.

40. This is of course made plausible by the preceding personification of the penis in *Sat.* 132.9-10. For the personification of the penis, see Adams (1981) 205.

41. The glans or the whole penis are often described as red, see Ausonius below and Adams (1981) 204.

42. See Section I of this chapter.

43. Macrobius *Sat.* 5.2.14 speaks of *infesta* ('hostile') *Dido*. In *Sat.* 4.1.1 he lists the passage under those describing *pathos* (unfortunately the text is incomplete).

44. Connors (1998) 32.

45. Term after Gennette; see Section I of this chapter, and Chapter 3.

46. Evelyn White does not translate the *Imminutio*, hence Slavitt (1998) 67.

47. Adams (1981) 201, 203-4; Lausberg (1998) §964.

48. Ausonius does not use this line in his *Imminutio*. Servius does not criticise the line in the way of Martianus.

49. The translations of the subtitles are taken from Slavitt (1998). The noun *imminutio* ('diminution', 'violation') is used only here in the meaning of 'defloration', see *ThLL* s.v. *imminutio* 463.11; for the verb *imminuere* in this sense cf. Green (1991) 518.

50. Gruber (1981) 215-19, who emphasises that in a *prosimetrum* an author wishes to show his erudition and expects his or her readers to be sufficiently educated to recognise this.

51. Green (1991) 139.20.

52. Treggiari (1991) 161-70.

53. Terence *Phorm.* 39-40; Livy 42.12.4.

54. Cat. 61.121; Verg. *Ecl.* 8.30 (used in line 73), for which cf. Coleman (1977) 234; Festus 183 (p. 178 Lindsay).

55. Generally considered to be of importance, cf. Treggiari (1991) 101, 260.

56. Contiades-Tsitsoni (1990) 31-2.

57. Typical elements of an epithalamium were the praise of the happiness and the beauty of the couple; wishes for a happy consummation of the marriage, for offspring and marital harmony; cf. Keydell (1962) 938 who emphasises the purely literary character of Ausonius' epithalamium.

58. This differentiation is not made by Green (1991) 518.

59. Genette (1982) 33ff.; 237ff.

60. The Parcae announce the Golden Age which will be inaugurated by a second Achilles, cf. Coleman (1977) 150-2; in Cat. 64.321-2 the Parcae sing at the wedding of Thetis and Peleus, hinting at the violent deeds and death of Achilles.

61. The following examples serve as an illustration of the general approach to canonical authors possible in late antiquity. Owing to relative scarceness, some of the material included is slightly later than Ausonius.

62. Adams (1981) 201 with n. 1. This is again equivalent to the technique of a *cento*; see Section I of this chapter.

63. Herzog (1975) 7; cf. Chapter 3 above.

64. See Petronius in Section II of this chapter.

65. Schenkl's edition (1887), reprinted with English translation by Clark and Hatch (1981), is still standard.

66. For the *sortes*, which also fractured Vergil's text, see Chapter 11 below; Ermini (1909) 37.

67. Shanzer (1986b), (1994); Green (1997).

68. Cf. Tert. *Praescr. haer.* 39 passim.

5. Sex and Salvation in the Vergilian Cento of the Fourth Century

69. The 55 lines of introduction to the *cento* are mainly non-Vergilian. Some manuscripts also transmit a prefatory poem, not by Proba, of fifteen non-Vergilian hexameters, beginning *Romulidum ductor*; Green (1997) 548-9.

70. Herzog (1975) 36. For a discussion of *cento* 38-42 and 108-9 in this light see Pollmann (2002) 226-30.

71. See especially Herzog (1975) 16-46; Kirsch (1989) 120-3; Jensen (1991a) 47-8; 55; Margoni-Kögler (2001) 143, 151.

72. Cf Roberts above. It is not clear why Green (1997) 556 denies that Proba reinterprets Vergil whereas 558 he says so himself.

73. In a literary way, this is partly the case in Ausonius' *cento*, see Section II of this chapter; cf. Margoni-Kögler (2001) 141-2. Augustine *De ordine* 1.5.12 and 7.24 (AD 386) allows a Christian to write philosophical poetry that is wholly allegorised, so that, e.g., the story of the lovers Pyramus and Thisbe would appear as a rarefied allegory of the love of the wise man for wisdom.

74. Buchheit (1988) 166; 172; 175-6; Jensen (1991b) 87.

75. Kartschoke (1975) 60-3 with parallels in other Christian writers. Proba shares this ambivalent attitude towards pagan culture and literature with many of her Christian contemporaries, cf. the survey in Kirsch (1989) 140-50. Nodes (1993) 13-16 rightly emphasises the theological ambitions of Proba, who does not intend just to offer literary play for an educated audience.

76. For *vatis* as nominative see Green (1997) 553 n. 28.

77. Cf. e.g. recently Smolak (1999) 12-13. This eventually goes back to Jerome's hostile assessment in *Ep.* 53.7. In reality, however, Proba's *cento* was very popular, as is already visible from the numerous manuscripts and editions, Ermini (1909) 63-70; cf. Isidorus *De vir. ill.* 18.22; *Etym.* 1.39.26. Even Boccaccio dedicates a chapter to Proba in his *De claris mulieribus*.

78. Even Kirsch (1989) 127. Herzog (1975) 14ff. emphasises the unity of the *cento*, but is wrong in stating (19) that Proba does not have any theological aims (which he concedes (41) for parts of the poem).

79. Clearly a Christian adaptation of the Roman missionary self-awareness as a force civilising humanity, as expressed in the famous lines *Aen.* 6.851-3, with the quotation here taken from 851.

80. See Clark and Hatch (1981) 191 n. 33.

81. *Div. inst.* 7.24 quoting *Ecl.* 4.21-45. See especially *cento* 34 *iam nova progenies* ~ *Ecl.* 4.7 and the cluster at *cento* 377-9 which takes up phrases from *Ecl.* 4.18-20; 23; 28; cf. in general Clark and Hatch (1981) 171-81. Benko (1980) 670ff. does not mention Proba at all.

82. Kastner and Millin (1981) 39-42.

83. Margoni-Kögler (2001) 149.

84. Clark and Hatch (1981) 161-9; Margoni-Kögler (2001) 151.

85. Jensen (1991a) 51-6; Leisch-Kiesl (1992) 150-7; Margoni-Kögler (2001) 149; cf. Clark and Hatch (1981) 151-9.

86. Poinsotte (1986) 101, 111.

87. See Roberts above; Kirsch (1989) 123-5; Genette (1982) 15 emphasises the partly transgeneric character of hypertextuality in general.

88. Cf. Roberts above.

89. e.g. Horace *Ode* 1.3; see Nisbet and Hubbard (1970) 43-4.

90. Cf. Röttger (1996) 108-9.

91. This is not explicitly stated in the biblical models. In Matthew 8:26-7 this is said in a different context.

92. Christ is modelled throughout the *cento* after Aeneas.

93. In Matthew 14:33 the disciples recognise Jesus eventually as the son of God; cf. Mark 6:54.
94. Genette (1982) 14-15.
95. Herzog (1975) XLIX-LI.
96. Herzog (1975) 46-51.
97. Quoted for a similar purpose by Plin. *Ep.* 4.14.5, Ov. *Tr.* 2.354, and Martial 1.4.8. Ausonius quotes Juvenal *Sat.* 2.3.
98. Kirsch (1989) 139. Ermini (1909) 109-41 offers a list of phrases in Proba's *cento* which appear also in Juvencus and in later Christian poets.
99. Kirsch (1989) 137.
100. Therefore the criticism in Kirsch (1989) 133 that Proba's *cento* is not clear enough, is not quite appropriate. The character of riddle and allusion are an essential part of a *cento*, cf. Kartschoke (1975) 35.
101. Kirsch (1989) 122-3.
102. The other is *Geo.* 1.142 *alta petens* ('seeking the bottom' of a river while fishing), which in Proba (534) denotes the same thing, and in Ausonius (105) is used for the groom seeking to penetrate. These two instances do not provide sufficient evidence to regard Ausonius' *Imminutio* as a literary 'answer' to Proba's *cento*.

6

Doing What Comes Naturally? Vergil and Ambrose

Ivor Davidson

Ambrose, bishop of Milan from 374 to 397, is justly famous as the churchman who spearheaded the political success of Nicene Christianity in the late fourth-century West. The product of a privileged background, Ambrose became a bishop after a career in the imperial civil service, in which he attained the post of governor of Aemilia-Liguria. Though hampered at first by a lack of theological preparation and constrained over a longer period by an assortment of powerful opponents, Ambrose exercised a remarkable ministry that had deep and lasting effects, both in northern Italy and much further afield. His achievements were far harder won than has often been supposed, but by a combination of political skill, intellectual ability, and spiritual determination he was able to package his conception of the Catholic faith in a way that proved powerfully relevant to his social world.[1]

Approaching Vergil's legacy: Ambrose and classical Rome

Like every Roman of his class, as a schoolboy Ambrose had been thoroughly grounded in the great *quadriga* of Vergil, Cicero, Terence and Sallust. He never appears to have struggled much with the legacy of this literature, or with that of the other classical authors he had read, who included Ovid, Horace, Lucretius, the Elder Pliny and Tacitus. Nowhere does he record the kind of psychological tensions made famous by Jerome in his account of his dream in *Epistle* 22, or by Augustine in his rueful depiction of his boyhood love for the *Aeneid* in the *Confessions*.[2] Of course, the narrative of Jerome's dream is itself a stylised affair, in which the conflict between renunciation of the classics and devotion to their literary culture is presented in carefully wrought prose, and Jerome later concedes that pagan books may in fact be profitably exploited if they are first sanitised of dangerous elements.[3] Again, while Augustine's writings after

391 may reflect a general absence of classical quotations, Augustine can also famously appeal to the notion of *spoliatio* to justify the usefulness of retaining elements of classical learning.⁴ For Ambrose, though, not even these kinds of gambits are very pertinent. He takes some standard Christian swipes at the corruptions of pagan thought and the frivolities of traditional rhetoric, contrasting their empty follies with the satisfying nourishment of God's Word.⁵ His references to 'philosophy' are overwhelmingly negative,⁶ and even where secular thinkers are acknowledged to have seen elements of truth they are usually said to have plagiarised them from the Hebrew Bible.⁷ But never does Ambrose express a wish to dislodge the influence of classical texts from his memory.

His approach, rather, is to show that he is at ease with the cultural legacies of the *saeculum* while he contends that the Christian message more than fulfils the ends to which classical wisdom aspired. He can show sufficient knowledge of pagan learning to make the sophisticates among his hearers and readers take notice, but never so much as to compromise his overriding contention that his message is a matter of scriptural *simplicitas*, not secular *ars*. In his most famous treatise, *De officiis*, he models his work openly on Cicero's textbook of the same name, and takes over the structure, themes, language, and father-to-son style of Cicero's text. But he goes out of his way to contend that an ethical system built upon biblical principles is far more profound than anything 'the philosophers' (Cicero and his sources, chiefly Panaetius) can offer. Roman Stoic morality contains much that Ambrose still admires, and the ideals of public conduct presented by Cicero continue to inform his understanding of the etiquette of leadership, but he seeks to show that the standards of the world are far surpassed by the Christian servant, who is summoned to a nobler task than that of the secular statesman.⁸

No classical author left such an impression on Ambrose as Vergil. His extant works reveal several hundred clear evocations of Vergil's poetry and many other probable echoes of his diction. Allusions can be found in all the main parts of his literary corpus – in his exegetical works, his moral-ascetical treatises, his dogmatic writings, his sermons, hymns and letters. Not every text contains Vergilian language, but every genre does, from every period of his creative output. Yet Ambrose nowhere mentions Vergil by name, and only three times quotes him explicitly.⁹ Ambrose never tries to do with Vergil quite what he does with Cicero: that is to say, he never attempts to utilise any continuous stretch of Vergil's poetry as the basis of a written work. But what this means is that, even more obviously than is the case with his *De officiis*, his subordination of his classical source to the plot-line of a scripturally-focused narrative is unambiguous.

In many instances, Ambrose's allusions to Vergil can hardly be deliber-

6. Doing What Comes Naturally? Vergil and Ambrose

ate at all: he has simply absorbed the poet's phraseology so deeply from boyhood that it has become a natural element in his own vocabulary. Even where he is aware of what he is doing, the echoes belong in a strategy that resists formal imitation in favour of insouciant reminiscence. No matter how extensive the allusions can be – and, as we shall see, Ambrose often produces entire mosaics of diverse Vergilian phrases within a few lines or paragraphs – he cannot be accused of simply producing crude pastiche, even where the evocation is calculated. As Ambrose sees it, the lingering charm of poetic language and imagery is a natural thing for the educated Christian mind; but it deserves to be handled with a light touch – as something that is part of an assured elegance rather than a studied effort to conjure up images that might distract from the supremacy of biblical themes.[10]

Vergil was special nevertheless. His poetry symbolised, however loosely, a nostalgic vision of *Romanitas* with which everything in Ambrose's make-up encouraged him to identify. Ambrose had grown up surrounded by the physical emblems of Rome's historical glory (and doubtless pictorial representations of Vergilian scenes). He had pursued a secular career in which he had been a prominent representative of Rome's authority. As bishop, he was part of an emerging class of new imperial power-brokers, whose duties reflected the patronal dynamics traditionally associated with civil political leadership. A strong patriotism and pride in the glory of the Roman order are widely present in his thinking. He may famously insist that episcopal authority is, in the end, superior to the *potestas* of even the emperor himself, but he made sure to exert all the leverage that a Christianised imperial system could afford, berating those who implicitly jeopardised the church's advantages by 'insolently abusing the powers that be' (*Off.* 1.208) and eliding the crime of political treason with that of attacking the church (*Off.* 1.144).[11] The kingdom of God could not be directly equated with the empire, but the church's place at the heart of society was key to the endurance of the Roman peace. The Roman world was a realm of civilisation surrounded by the shadow-worlds of the pagan (or heretical) barbarians, and those who sought to undermine the advance of the Catholic faith were not only perfidious in religious terms: they were also traitors to Rome.[12]

Vergil's poetry never had been about a crude ideologising of empire (despite the uses to which it had been put), but it clearly bespoke a cherishing of Rome's status that resonated deep in Ambrose's spirit. Since the time of Constantine himself, and his apologist Lactantius, it had been possible to read in the author of the Fourth *Eclogue* a prophecy of the coming of the virgin-born Christ-child, and to fuse the ideals of triumphant Christian imperialism with poetic anticipations of a new age of peace: now, definitively, 'the final age of Cumae's prophecy' (*Ecl.* 4.4) had indeed arrived.[13] Ambrose does not try to copy Juvencus in synthesising Vergil directly with the gospels, or follow the Christian *centones* in elaborating a pastiche of Vergilian citations in celebration of the gifts of Christ, but he must have been well aware of the extent to which Vergil's poetry had been absorbed into a new metanarrative: the story that the Roman world had come to its true fullness in the official ascendancy of the gospel.[14] The political instability of Ambrose's society was in reality considerable, but the rhetoric lost none of its potency because of it: Rome's vulnerability could variously be attributed to an as-yet-incomplete security for the true faith, or to the pressures that were concomitant with fidelity to righteousness in the last times.

Ambrose's reception of Vergil has been the subject of a number of studies, ranging from brief articles to at least one doctoral dissertation.[15] In the space of a brief treatment, it is possible only to glance at a few of the most striking debts, in the attempt to assess what they imply about his approach to his classical inheritance. In what ways is Ambrose's natural affinity for Vergil manifested, and what does such evidence reveal about Vergil's place in Ambrose's overall Christian style? I shall take examples from four areas, which together reflect a number of the major aspects of Ambrose's work as bishop: the defining of truth against heresy; the exposition of biblical narratives; the promotion of asceticism; and the task of delivering funeral or memorial speeches for prominent individuals. Here we glimpse Ambrose the theological instructor, Ambrose the exegetical preacher, Ambrose the moralist, and Ambrose the public rhetor. In each of these categories, his utilisation of Vergilian language and imagery hints at his cultural *modus operandi*. His style is at one and the same time 'urbane' in a conventional sense, in its unmistakable evocation of Vergilian diction and characterisation, and powerfully 'different', in its sponsorship of ideals that speak ultimately of a very un-Vergilian world.

Truth and falsehood

A key element in Ambrose's rhetoric is the building up of what has aptly been described as a 'siege mentality', whereby the church is seen as a community of the righteous surrounded by vicious satanic forces, constantly scheming to engineer its downfall.[16] The supreme manifestation of this hostile alliance, not surprisingly, is Arianism (a term that, for Ambrose, described a more or less homogeneous evil: modern usage is much more qualified).[17] In his *De fide* 1-2, dated variously to 378 or 380, Ambrose responds to the young emperor Gratian's request for an exposition of his theological position by setting out his first serious manifesto against Arian beliefs. He depicts all forms of Arianism as equally bad, and presents the disaster of Rome's defeat at the battle of Adrianople in the summer of 378

6. Doing What Comes Naturally? Vergil and Ambrose

and the ensuing Gothic devastation of the Danubian provinces as divine judgements on Arian strongholds.

The general standard of Ambrose's grasp of contemporary doctrinal debates as evidenced by this work is poor; but what is of interest is his use of Vergilian imagery in the debunking of theological errors. Heresy is 'like some hydra of the fables', which 'has grown from its own wounds, and as often as it is beheaded it gives forth new shoots; but, doomed to the fire, it will perish in flames'. Further, it is 'like some dread, monstrous Scylla, divided into many shapes of unbelief'; with part of its body it appears to be Christian, but, for those who are caught as they are tossed to and fro in the waves of its 'unholy strait', amid 'the wreckage of their faith' (cf. I Timothy 1:19), it turns out to be 'girt with beastly monsters', and quick to rend its victims with 'the cruel fang of its foul teaching' (*Fid.* 1.46). Both of the key images come from Vergil: *Aeneid* 6.576 ('the huge, black-throated, fifty-headed Hydra'); *Aeneid* 7.658 ('the Hydra and its snakes, the hundred snakes encircling it'); and *Eclogue* 6.74-5 ('Why should I speak of Nisus' Scylla, who (so runs the rumour), with white groin girt with barking monsters ...'). The Scylla's cavern contains 'hidden lairs', where 'the rocks of unbelief echo to the howling of her black dogs' (*Fid.* 1.47). Her dread depths recall *Aeneid* 3.424 ('But Scylla lurks in the dark recesses of her cave') and 3.431-2 ('... the hideous Scylla, deep in her cavern, and the rocks echoing with the howling of dogs as blue as the sea'). Like prudent pilots, true believers must 'set the sails of their faith' (cf. *Aen.* 3.268) so as to pass by such perils in safety, and follow the 'coasts' of the Scriptures, like Aeneas passing round the coast of Sicily (*Aen.* 3.692-715).

When *De fide* 1-2 was delivered to Gratian, the emperor showed the work to Palladius of Ratiaria, the ablest of the clergy of Illyricum. The Illyrican church was Arian-dominated, and Ambrose had already annoyed Palladius and his colleagues by his interference in an episcopal election at Sirmium around 377/8 to ensure the consecration of a pro-Nicene candidate. Palladius, keen to get even, set out to refute Ambrose's anti-Arian logic in a short but forthright exposé (preserved in his *Apology*, 81-7). Appalled at Ambrose's accusations about homoian theology, and angered by what he saw as the upstart bishop's shoddy understanding of the issues, he launched a blistering attack on Ambrose's reasoning. In particular, Palladius objects to Ambrose's attempts to equate his opponents' doctrinal positions with images of pagan mythology: 'Desist from your monstrous comparisons, with which you have fitted out your long-winded address to show off your knowledge of literature; abandon the prodigies, the highly polished but vain recitation of which has caused the shipwreck of your faith, and recover at last an understanding of the truth from which a treacherous and unholy heresy has lured you ...' (Pallad. *Apol.* 87). The rebuke is revealing: Palladius sees Ambrose's evocation of classical images as a piece of intellectual showmanship, designed to impress his readers and so, implicitly, to divert attention from the weakness of his theological arguments. He urges him instead to pay attention to 'the divine Scriptures, which you have neglected' (ibid.). Palladius elects to pick up metaphors implicit in his opponent's own allusions: Ambrose's faith is said to have been shipwrecked, and it is *he* who has been 'lured' from the truth by the errors of false doctrine.

The dynamics behind Palladius' charges deserve to be assessed with care, but it is interesting that a capable critic should choose to draw attention to Ambrose's classical allusions in particular as ground for reprimand, singling out his use of Vergilian mythology as an empty display of learning. Probably Palladius had a point: Ambrose may well have been appealing to an anticipated taste for the baroque, and mythological imagery in particular, at the imperial court. Ambrose certainly caught the edge of the rebuke. At the end of 380, he published a sequel to his previous text, in a treatise which makes up the second part of *De fide* (books 3-5), and at the start he sought to respond to Palladius' attack on his literary references. He accuses Palladius of focusing on his language for want of substantive things to say about his faith, and defends his own use of such images as a practice that has the highest of precedents: 'not only phrases but complete verses of poetry have been woven into the divine Scriptures' (*Fid.* 3.3). As an example, he quotes the apostle Paul's citation of Aratus/Cleanthes in Acts 17:28. He then goes on to argue that such creatures as the Giants, the Titans and the Sirens can all be identified in the Old Testament (*Fid.* 3.4).[18]

At this point, he wanders somewhat off his theme, and proceeds to warn against the enticements of worldly pleasures and indulgence in general rather than the dangers of heresy in particular (*Fid.* 3.4-6). What is striking, however, is his effort to justify his mythological illustrations as scriptural. He does not say that pagan thought stole the Giants and others from the Bible; he simply pretends that the preaching of the Hebrew prophets 'did not avoid' these images (*Fid.* 3.4). Ambrose refuses to be diverted from his penchant for poetic allusion by the allegation that such a habit is at odds with a biblical faith. By implication, classical, and in this case Vergilian, language, judiciously applied, is no more alien to Christian discourse than the citation of Scripture itself, so long as it is deployed in the furtherance of Scripture's own truth. This logic would remain basic: 'Gentile [pagan] writers' may not have been able to 'imbibe the truth of the Spirit', but when they discerned such realities as the fact that (as Anchises has it) 'in the beginning the Spirit nourished all things from within, the sky and the earth, the level waters, the shining globe of the moon and the Titan's star' (*Aeneid* 6.724-6), they recorded something worthy of recollection (*Spir.* 2.36). In any event, heresy in the Christian faith deserves to be

6. Doing What Comes Naturally? Vergil and Ambrose

denounced in whatever terms best serve to expose its horrors, and if a Vergilian image might facilitate the depiction of its dangers, Ambrose has no problem with that. Thus the heretic is one who prowls like a wolf besieging Christ's sheep (*Luc.* 7.49), like Turnus in the dead of night, growling at the gaps in the Trojans' walls (*Aen.* 9.59-61).

Preaching and teaching

This basic confidence about the legitimacy but subordinate status of Vergilian evocation suffuses Ambrose's moralising expositions of biblical stories. Abraham, like Corydon, the great shepherd whose ewe-lambs range the Sicilian hills (*Ecl.* 2.20), is 'rich in flocks' (*Abr.* 1.68). He it is who sets out faithfully, Aeneas-like, in pursuit of his own and his people's destiny, checking sexual passion (though not his own) and facing great dangers in obedience to a divine summons.[19] The behaviour of Jacob, who, to avoid further problems, allowed his daughter Dinah to be given in marriage to Shechem the Hivite (*Off.* 1.121), despite the fact that Shechem had raped her (Genesis 34), recalls Dido, screening her sin with the name of marriage.[20] The harmony of the seven-stringed lyre of Orpheus (*Aen.* 6.646) is turned into the music of the 'sevenfold Spirit' (cf. Isaiah 11:2-3) in the baptised soul;[21] the seven Maccabees martyred in front of their mother (II Maccabees 7) also created a harmony 'sweeter than every strain of the lyre'.[22] The mother of the Maccabees shows remarkable fortitude in her grief, forbearing to 'close their eyes or wash their wounds', knowing that her children will be all the more glorious if they are seen as bloodied warriors, bearing the 'trophies' of their conquest in the fight of faith (*Iac.* 2.56): her behaviour is very different from that of the mother of Euryalus, standing on the ramparts in defiance of the Rutulians in mourning for her son, who lies bereft of his due maternal death-rites in a strange land, his body food for the dogs and birds of Latium – but the words recall hers.[23]

The rich man, selfishly hoarding his wealth and ignoring the needs of the poor, is so opulent in material things that he has a horse that 'champs gold between its teeth' (*Nab.* 56), like one of the champion steeds of Father Latinus.[24] The Philistine giant, Goliath (I Kings 17), is a figure of 'vast bulk' (*Off.* 1.177), like Polyphemus, heaving his great frame among his flocks.[25] Samson, after the Spirit of God had departed from him (Judges 16:19-21), is 'changed from the man who returned clothed in the spoils' of his enemies (*Spir.* 2, prol. 13): he is like the dead and humiliated Hector, 'changed from the man who had cast Trojan fire on the Greeks' ships or returned clothed in the spoils of Achilles'.[26] And so it goes on: such echoes, whether in letter-perfect form or, as more often, with inflectional variations and scant concern to replicate metrical prosody, are to be found again and again throughout Ambrose's recitations of biblical stories.

By far the most extensive evocation of Vergil in all of Ambrose's *corpus* is to found in his *Exaemeron*, an exegetical treatment of the six days of creation. The work was composed originally out of nine sermons, delivered over six consecutive days one Holy Week in the latter half of the 380s, and edited into a series of six books. Ambrose draws heavily on an existing *Exaemeron* by Basil of Caesarea, and there are a few further possible debts to Philo, Origen and Platonist authors. Among the most remarkable features of the work, though, is its reference to Vergil. In a standard edition, *Exaemeron* presents an average of around three Vergilian echoes per page, which, all told, amounts to considerably more than a quarter of the total number of borrowings from Vergil to be found in all of Ambrose's extant works.[27] When Ambrose is celebrating the beauty and usefulness of creation, he has no greater treasury of language than Vergil's depictions of nature. Whether he is describing the earth, the sea, or the sky, the activity of birds, insects, or animals, his characterisations are pervaded by a strong poetic strain that reaches automatically for Vergilian formulae.

In *Exaemeron* 5.66-72, Ambrose pictures the republic of the bees, with its harmonious community life and shared labours. His opening words, 'And now I shall explain' (5.66) directly echo Vergil's opening to his account of the bees at *Georgics* 4.149-50, and what follows in 5.66-72 is strongly reminiscent not just of the whole famous passage in *Georgics* 4.149-227 but of much else in Vergil besides.[28] The bees (5.67) 'alone ... hold their progeny in common', 'all inhabit one dwelling', and are 'contained by the dwelling of a single homeland'.[29] 'They all toil in common'; they bear their young in a way that Ambrose especially approves, 'without any intercourse between them', instead 'gathering their children in their mouths from leaves and herbs'.[30] 'They themselves appoint their king' (5.68); and 'no peoples, neither the Persians ... nor the Indians, nor the peoples of Sarmatia, show as much reverence and respect for their king as the bees do for theirs.'[31] The bees proceed (5.69) through the 'redolent' countryside, where there are 'gardens breathing with flowers', and 'hurrying through the grass, a stream': there, in 'the pleasantness of its banks', lies 'sport for the young ones in their energy'.[32] From the flowers and the sweet herbs 'they lay the first foundations' of their 'camp', which is what the 'honey-comb' amounts to.[33] The 'drone is driven from the common fold'.[34] Their combs are elaborate in 'trellis-form', brilliantly constructed by natural craftsmen with no architectural instruction, who know by instinct how to 'suspend the wax within the walls of their homes', to 'pack the honey', and to 'distend their plaited store-rooms with the nectar from the flowers'.[35] They vie with one another to complete their tasks: some stage a 'careful watch' on their camp, 'looking out for signs of rain and keeping an eye out for gathering clouds'; others gather their treasures, but do not try to 'live off what is plundered' from others.[36] Nevertheless, 'they have their stings, and pour poison in

6. Doing What Comes Naturally? Vergil and Ambrose

amidst the sweetness if provoked, and lay down their lives in this wound in the passion of revenge'.[37] 'They defend their king (5.71) with the utmost protection, and think it a splendid thing to perish on his behalf. So long as their king is safe they never think of changing their mind, but when he is lost they abandon their loyalty and plunder their honey ....'[38]

Even this string of allusions is by no means a complete catalogue of the Vergilian borrowings in these paragraphs (and several of the lines or phrases registered here are also to be found elsewhere in Ambrose), but it illustrates just how easily Ambrose resorts to Vergil when describing the natural world and extrapolating moral lessons from it. Two further brief examples from *Exaemeron* must suffice to extend the point. In *Exaemeron* 1.28, Ambrose is commenting upon 'the "unformed earth" of Genesis 1:2'. He reminds us that the earth 'even now is wont to shiver (*inhorrere*) with the wetness of a swamp, and not be submissive to the plough-share' when it has been inundated.[39] In its uncultivated state, the earth was bare of vegetation, without grass on 'the soft couches of the river-banks', not 'dense with groves', or 'joyous with crops', or 'shaded by mountain ridges ...: everything shivered in the darkness'.[40] At *Exaemeron* 3.23, on the gathering of the waters in Genesis 1:9, Ambrose speaks of the sea as an image of the church. People surge into it, and in turn it 'disgorges them as a tide from all its vestibules'. His words recall *Georgics* 4.262, on the 'ebbing waves of a disturbed sea dashing (*stridit*) on the shore'. The same line is then put to a different application: during the church's liturgy, 'there arises a noise (*stridit*) like the ebbing waves, when the whole congregation joins in the responses of the Psalms, the singing of men, women, virgins and children re-echoing with a great noise like waves dashing together and breaking'. The Vergilian depiction of the physical world can serve not just as a celebration of nature for its own sake, but also as a way of presenting the Christian community, united in praise of the God of nature.

Asceticism

Among the best-known notes of Ambrose's episcopate was his promotion of female asceticism. One of the ways in which he had set about making his mark in his early days as bishop was by staging public processions of teenage girls coming forward to profess vows of virginity and devote themselves to the spiritual life. Virginity was the theme of his first written work, his three books *De virginibus*, constructed in part out of sermonic material around 377. In this and in a further three or four texts besides (also mostly elaborated out of homiletic transcripts), Ambrose presents public consecration to Christ and the church as a matter of escaping the 'pollution' of the flesh and ascending to the utmost pinnacle of sexual virtue. Such devotion was thus symbolic of the otherness of a spiritual élite, and it had a powerful effect on a number of young women from upper-class North Italian families, who were encouraged to believe that the presence of a consecrated virgin in a household brought vicarious spiritual blessing to the rest of the family.[41]

Ambrose's success in encouraging such commitment brought certain risks. In the third book of *De virginibus* (3.16-17), he warns against excessive austerity, which can enervate the body prematurely. Instead of paying attention only to the duty of fasting, the virgin ought to devote herself to equally valuable interior virtues, such as prayer and the recitation of Psalms. There needs to be a moderation in which physical self-denial is not given an exclusive place. Ambrose proposes a prudent rotation of complementary virtues in order to maximise the spiritual 'yield' of the virgin body, and to prolong its usefulness into old age, so that it can serve as an example to younger women. The model here is the skilful cultivator, who puts his land to different uses over a period of years in order to make the most of its potential. 'He works his land by turns, or, if he does not want it to lie fallow, he alternates different seeds, so that the fields may have rest through a change of crops ...' (3.16). 'Not every land produces the same harvest. On one side vines rise on the hills, on another you can see the olives growing purple, elsewhere the scented roses ....' The farmer, 'with the same rough hands with which he steers the straining oxen in between the vine-rows, gently squeezes the udders of the sheep .... So you too, following the example of the good farmer, avoid cleaving your soil with perpetual fasts as though you were driving in the plough' (3.17). The imagery is straight from the *Georgics*;[42] there are also echoes of the Fourth *Eclogue* and of the *Aeneid*.

In his *Expositio evangelii secundum Lucam* (which is not a commentary in any modern sense, but a collage of redacted sermonic and written material on selected parts of Luke's text), Ambrose compares virginity to a lily (7.127-8). Commenting on Luke 12:27, 'Consider the lilies, how they grow', he notes that lilies require no annual cultivation, no 'treadmill of farmer's labour'.[43] Instead, they flourish even in drought conditions by virtue of their own sap, and yield their 'vigorous growth of leaves'.[44] In the 'enclosed garden' (*Cant.* 4:12) of purity, chastity, and piety they thrive. This is a space where there is the 'reverential silence' of the holy mysteries;[45] the context of Cybele-worship is translated into that of the Christian sacraments.

Virginity is Ambrose's sexual ideal, but he endorses a standard patristic schema in which the next best thing to virginity is consecrated widowhood, followed in turn by chastity within marriage. His *De viduis* was written to dissuade widowed women from entering upon second marriages and to urge devotion instead to a life of piety and good works. The faithful widow

6. Doing What Comes Naturally? Vergil and Ambrose

'labours night and day at her tasks' in order to 'preserve the bed of her deceased husband undefiled and to be able to support her dear children and minister to the poor' (*Vid.* 31). She resembles the dutiful woman whose task it is to support life by the work of her distaff in *Aeneid* 8.411-13, who, 'adding the night to the time for her labour, sets her slave-women going by lamp-light upon their long day's work, so that she can keep her husband's bed chaste and bring her young sons to manhood'. This time, the energies are expended specifically in honour of a dead husband, and an additional virtue is the Christian widow's ministry not only to her children but also to the poor. Vergil's touch about the 'undefiled' bed resonates nicely with Hebrews 13:4: 'Marriage is honourable in all, and the bed (*torus* rather than *cubile*) untainted.' In the end, however, Ambrose's widow has ascended to a stage beyond that of the Vergilian exemplar: her sexual fidelity is such that she does not just keep her marriage-bed chaste in commitment to a worthy husband; she now lives in purity without a husband at all.

Memorial speeches

When Ambrose became bishop, his brother Satyrus, also an imperial administrator, abandoned his career in order to devote his life to assisting with the running of the Milanese see. Satyrus undertook the supervision of the family estates in North Africa and (probably) Sicily, with a view to maximising their revenue in the interests of the Milanese church. On a return trip from Africa in the late summer of 378, Satyrus, who had always been of delicate constitution, fell ill and died. For all the intensity of his private grief, Ambrose used the opportunity to magnify his own public image. In his funeral homily, he presents Satyrus' virtues in the light of his value to Milan and its bishop. Episcopal grief is depicted in terms that evoke the lament of Evander for Pallas in *Aeneid* 11, particularly the celebrated words of Evander to his wife, who in dying previously had been spared the grief of losing her son: 'O my dear wife, most blessed of women, you were fortunate in your death, in not living to see this day. But I have outstayed my time ...' (158-9). Satyrus is said to have been fortunate to be spared the ravages from which Italy is suffering (*Exc. fr.* 1.30-3), at the hands of the Goths in the aftermath of Adrianople. 'Fortunate, then, was he in so opportune a death, because he has not been preserved for this sorrow' (1.33).

In a second sermon, delivered one week later, Ambrose put on a still more elaborate performance. Ciceronian consolation motifs are recast in the language of biblical faith in the resurrection of the body. The piece is much less personal than the funeral homily; instead, Ambrose offers an extensive dismissal of the beliefs of 'the poets' and 'the philosophers' (*Exc. fr.* 2.127-8) on death. The oration climaxes with a repudiation of the doctrine of the transmigration of souls, which is presented as consigning human beings to the fellowship of wild beasts rather than the heavenly company of angels (2.131). Ambrose scorns the errors of the philosophers who imagine that 'that soul which was accustomed to overcome anger by gentle and lowly purpose ... can now, inflamed by the raging impulse of a lion, impatient with anger and with unbridled rage, thirst for blood and seek for slaughter; or again, that that soul which as it were by royal counsel used to moderate the various storms of the people and calm them with the voice of reason can now endure to howl like a wolf in pathless, desert places; or that soul which, groaning under a heavy burden, used to low in sad complaint over the labours of the plough, now, changed into the form of a man, looks for horns on his smooth brow; or that another, which used once to be borne aloft on rapid wing to the heights of heaven, carried through the air by the oarage of wings, now thinks of flight that is no longer in its power, and mourns that it grows sluggish in the weight of a human body' (2.128).

The images come from *Aeneid* 7.15-20, on Circe: 'From her palace could be heard growls of anger from lions fretting at their chains and roaring late into the night, the raging of bristling boars and penned bears and howling from huge creatures in the shape of wolves. These had all been men, but with her irresistible herbs the savage goddess had given them the faces and hides of wild beasts.' Ambrose leaves out the boars and the bears, but, for good measure, he alludes also to *Eclogue* 6.48-51, on the daughters of Proteus, who 'with false lowing filled the fields, but yet not one pursued so base an intercourse with beasts, although she feared the plough's yoke on her neck and often would look for horns on her smooth brow'; and to *Aeneid* 6.14-19, on Daedalus' flight from the kingdom of Minos, 'floating off on swiftly driving wings' and then, at Cumae, returning to earth, dedicating to Phoebus Apollo 'the wings that had oared him through the sky' (which last words are a favourite Ambrosian trope). In the paragraph that follows (2.129), Ambrose recalls *Aeneid* 10.189-93, on Icarus/Cycnus, singing of the loss of his beloved Phaethon in his old age, 'with soft white plumage'.

In another highly-wrought set-piece, his commemoration address for Valentinian II in 392, Ambrose saluted the dead emperor (who had probably committed suicide) in terms which recall the lament of Anchises over C. Claudius Marcellus, the young son of Octavia and nephew of Augustus whose premature death in 23 BC had shattered dynastic plans. 'What a noise of mourning has come' from all the emperor's subjects, he laments (*Ob. Val.* 3 – considerably glossing the chequered history of Valentinian's career and his own relations with him), like 'the noise of the mourning of men' that is envisaged by Anchises as coming 'from the field of Mars to Mars' greatest city' in *Aeneid* 6.872-3. Anchises, in expression of his grief, says: 'Give lilies from full hands. Leave me to scatter red roses. These at

6. Doing What Comes Naturally? Vergil and Ambrose

least I can heap up for the spirit of my descendant and perform the rite, although it will achieve nothing.'[46] Ambrose says that he will not strew Valentinian's tomb with flowers: others may sprinkle it with basketfuls of lilies, but Christ is the Christians' 'lily'. The hands that may have scattered the classical emblems of remembrance are now to be 'lifted up to the holy places' (Ps. 133:2) in prayer for 'the descendant's spirit', which is commended to the God of Christian faith (*Ob. Val.* 56). Ambrose intermingles the Vergilian phraseology with biblical quotation, and fuses the poetic reminiscence with an image drawn from a Christian allegorical reading of Hebrew Scripture: Christ as lily.[47] The echoes of the classical past, however, are still clearly to be heard: the 'blessed pair' of Valentinian and Gratian will never be forgotten (*Ob. Val.* 78): like Nisus and Euryalus, 'fortune has favoured both'.[48]

Conclusion

What we glimpse in this rapid survey is that Vergil's poetry represents for Ambrose at one and the same time a highly congenial cultural companion and a force that must be kept in its place. It is there to be evoked spontaneously, but its world, in the end, is one that has gone: its complex divine machinery and superstitious rites have been replaced by a new faith, its moral structures transferred to a different foundation and a higher teleology. We must not be misled by the casualness of Ambrose's evocation into concluding that his use of Vergil is of only superficial or formal significance to his message, or that it is marked by a lack of creativity. Like many authors in late antiquity, Ambrose has suffered rather a lot at the hands of those who have treated his written legacy as, if not a spiritual treasury *tout court*, then little more than a literary puzzle – a kind of field within which to play 'hunt-the-quotation'. The place of Vergil in Ambrose's thinking needs to be gauged by subtler mechanisms that do justice to the bishop's own intellectual input to his material.

Of course Vergil gives great texture to Ambrose's style. He contributes much to the honing of the poetic talent that made Ambrose's own spiritual verse such a powerful medium in his church's liturgy (and such a great influence on subsequent hymnody in the West): so that, for example, he can sing to God the Creator as the one who 'clothes the day with fitting light' (*Hymn* 3[*Deus Creator Omnium*].2-3), like the sky which 'clothes the plains in glowing light' in *Aeneid* 6.640-1, or petition God as one of a company of believers 'bound by their vow' (*Hymn* 3.11), like Cloanthus invoking the help of the sea-gods and promising to offer sacrifice in fulfilment of his vow.[49] Of course it is a knowledge of Vergil's imagery that lends learned touches to Ambrose's prose works, too, enabling him to describe an incomplete treatise, say, as 'a repast left half-consumed' (*Paen.* 2.1), like the feast of the Harpies in *Aeneid* 3.244.

But Vergil imparts far more than an ornamental *color poeticus*. In so far as Ambrose operates at the interface of two worlds, Vergil provides a vital element in his intellectual capital. Ambrose is able to present his vision of a Christian future in terms that resonate suggestively with elements of the classical past; yet, by dramatically altering the contexts in which the classical verse appears and by ensuring its strict subordination to scriptural categories, he can contend that the arrival of this future involves a present acknowledgement that the past really *is* past. If it is natural to echo Vergil, it is natural also to insist that Vergil's realm has now become the kingdom of the one God and of his Christ. Thus deployed, Vergil belongs close to the heart of a vital fourth-century contribution to the 'totalising discourse' of catholic Christian imperialism.[50]

Notes

1. For modern characterisations, see McLynn (1994); Williams (1995); Moorhead (1999).

2. Jerome *Ep.* 22.30 (with Hagendahl (1958) 318-28); Augustine *Conf.* 1.13.20-3, 17.27-18.28.

3. Jerome *Ep.* 70.

4. Augustine *Conf.* 7.9.15; *Doctr. Chr.* 2.40.144-7.

5. For some examples, see Ellspermann (1949) 113-25.

6. See Madec (1974).

7. e.g. *Noe* 24; *Abr.* 1.82; 2.54; *Bon. mort.* 45, 51; *Exc. fr.* 1.42; *Expos. Ps.* 118.2.13; 18.4; *Ep.* 7 [37].28; *Off.* 1.31, 43-4, 79-80, 92, 94, 126, 132-5, 141, 180; 2.6, 48; 3.2, 80, 92.

8. See Davidson (2002), especially 1: 45-95.

9. *Abr.* 1.82 (*Ecl.* 1.45), citing him simply as *quidam poeta*, and noting that his wisdom is perhaps derived from the Scriptures; 2.4 (*Geo.* 4.208); *Expl. Ps.* 43.17 (*Geo.* 2.146-7).

10. Cf. Introduction above.

11. For some examples, see McLynn (1994) 298-309, 315-30.

12. See generally Meslin (1964).

13. For a survey of the tradition, see Benko (1980); see Green above, p. 22.

14. Cf. Roberts and Pollmann above.

15. e.g. Ihm (1890) 80-94; Weyman (1897); Diederich (1931); Consolo (1955); Alfonsi (1965); Charles (1968); Del Ton (1970); Opelt (1976); Nazzaro (1976 and 1988); Gioseffi (1998); Scarcia (1998). Several relevant citations are also recorded by Courcelle (1984) 1: passim.

16. So Meslin (1967) 51, cited by Brown (1988) 347-8.

17. Cf. Introduction above.

18. On the Sirens, cf. also *Expl. Ps.* 43.75, 80; *Ep. extra coll.* 11 [51].3; *Luc.* 4.2-3; and see Doignon (1983); Adkin (1998), especially 681-95: it is clear from Ambrose's words in *Fid.* 3.4 that he is also thinking of the Homeric narrative in *Od.* 12.39-54, 165-200. On the Titans, cf. also *Apol.* 33-4; *Off.* 1.177.

19. *Off.* 1.108.

6. Doing What Comes Naturally? Vergil and Ambrose

20. *Aen.* 4.172.
21. *Iac.* 2.39; cf. *Interp.* 4.36.
22. *Off.* 1.203.
23. *Aen.* 9.486-7.
24. *Aen.* 7.279.
25. *Aen.* 3.656-7.
26. *Aen.* 2.274-6.
27. Using the text edited by Schenkl (1896): so Diederich (1931) 6-32.
28. Cf. *Aen.* 6.756-9; 7.37-40; also Lucr. 2.62-6; 6.495-7, 738-9.
29. *Geo.* 4.153, 4.153-4, 4.155.
30. *Geo.* 4.184, 198, 200-1.
31. *Geo.* 4.201; 4.210-2, mentioning Egypt, Lydia, the Parthians, and 'Median Hydaspes', which is properly an Indian rather than a Median river, the Jhelum.
32. Cf. *Geo.* 4.169; *Aen.* 1.436; *Geo.* 4.109, 19, 23, 22.
33. *Geo.* 4.161.
34. *Geo.* 4.168; cf. *Aen.* 1.435.
35. *Geo.* 4.214, 159-64, 250; cf. also *Aen.* 1.432-3.
36. *Geo.* 4.158-67, *Aen.* 7.749; 9.613.
37. *Geo.* 4.236-8.
38. *Geo.* 4.212-8. For an overall discussion, see Nazzaro (1988); also Alfonsi (1965).
39. Cf. *Aen.* 3.195, of the sea's waves; *Geo.* 2.223.
40. *Aen.* 6.673; cf. also Stat. *Theb.* 4.819; *Aen.* 8.107-8; *Geo.* 1.1; *Aen.* 3.195.
41. See Brown (1988) 341-65, especially 356-7.
42. Cf. *Geo.* 2.356-7, on the time to 'work the soil by driving in the plough, and even steering your straining oxen in between the vine-rows'; 1.82, 'thus too, by change of crops, fields can be rested'; and 2.203, 'earth that is rich when you drive in the plough'; *Ecl.* 4.39 'every land will bear everything'; *Aen.* 3.642; cf. *Ecl.* 3.99, on Polyphemus 'squeezing the milk from the udders' of his sheep.
43. *Geo.* 2.401.
44. *Aen.* 12.413.
45. *Aen.* 3.112.
46. *Aen.* 6.883-6.
47. Cf. *Cant.* 2:1, etc.
48. *Aen.* 9.446. For a recent study of the rhetorical strategies employed in all of Ambrose's funeral *encomia*, see Biermann (1995).
49. *Aen.* 5.237.
50. On this theme more generally, see Cameron (1991).

7

Augustine, the Grammarians and the Cultural Authority of Vergil

Richard Lim

The portrait of Augustine as a young man shedding tears over the suicide of Dido vividly captures his deep personal engagement with the poetry of Vergil.[1] Evident through his many quotations and allusions to the works of the *summus poeta*, the lifelong relationship between the praise-singer of the Augustan empire and that of the *City of God* has rightly attracted much erudite scrutiny. Karl Hermann Schelkle's work provides a firm foundation for the analysis of Vergil's influence upon Augustine while that of Harald Hagendahl refines and corrects many of Schelkle's more daring conclusions.[2] More recently, the works of Brian Stock and Sabine MacCormack have further enriched our understanding of Augustine the reader of classical texts.[3] Notwithstanding the many differences in the scholarly assessment of Augustine's attitude towards classical literature, a consensus that his appreciation of Vergil changed markedly over the course of his career has emerged. According to Hagendahl, 'Augustine's use of Vergil rises and falls like a wave'.[4] It is not a question of tracing a linear progression or clear development of thought, however, for there existed 'fluctuations not only in the course of time, but also at the same time owing to special circumstances'.[5] A good starting point for approaching this question is the doubtless correct conclusion drawn by MacCormack: 'Augustine did not write about Vergil systematically or with the aim of providing a coherent interpretation of his poems .... If one inquires what specifically Vergil meant for Augustine, no single answer can be forthcoming. In addition, Augustine thought of Vergil over a very long time, in diverse contexts, and for different reasons.'[6]

My contribution contextualises Augustine's attitudes regarding Vergil and ancient poetry between his retirement to Cassiciacum near Milan in September 386 and his ordination to the priesthood in Hippo in 391; it will show why Augustine's engagement with Vergil cannot be examined in isolation or even as part of a dyad. Instead Augustine frequently articulated his relationship with the ancient literary tradition within a

7. Augustine, the Grammarians and the Cultural Authority of Vergil

triangular relationship. During the late 380s, the relevant triangle featured himself as a newly-rehabilitated catholic Christian, the Manichaean teachers with whom he used to associate, and Latin grammarians and Vergil's cultural authority.

The young Augustine was a self-reported seeker of truth. From his student days in Carthage to his retreat to Cassiciacum, he was seeking the means for wresting authentic meaning from authoritative texts, a common enterprise among late antique intellectuals. In addressing particular problems surrounding textual interpretation, Augustine was at once working out his rejection of the teachings of Manichaean *doctores* and establishing the principles for a Christian biblical exegesis that would prove robust enough to withstand anticipated Manichaean critiques. The cultural authority of Vergil and the classroom practice of the grammarians furnished Augustine with a familiar and expedient frame of reference; they also provided him with a compelling model of an interpretive community, in which teachers served as cultural intermediaries and choice interpreters of ancient authorities. Thus references to Vergil and ancient poetry in Augustine's early corpus are less preoccupied with the task of reconciling classical *paideia* with Christianity than with Augustine's desire to claim the authority of the poets in his controversy with the Manichaeans.

The influence that Vergil had on the formation of the young Augustine, especially in regards to his training in grammar and rhetoric, is well known.[7] According to his retrospective *Confessions*, Augustine, while still a rhetor-in-training, rendered one of the poet's lines (*irascentis et dolentis quod non possit Italia Teucrorum avertere regem*, 'angry and grieving because she could not keep the Trojan king out of Italy', *Aen.* 1.38), spoken by Juno, into prose:[8]

> A task was set which caused me deep psychological anxiety. The reward was praise but I feared shame and blows if I did badly. I was to recite the speech of Juno in her anger and grief that she 'could not keep the Trojan king out of Italy'. I had understood that Juno never said this. But we were compelled to follow in our wanderings the paths set by poetic fictions (*figmentorum poeticorum vestigia*), and to express in plain prose the sense which the poet had put into verse. The speaker who received highest praise was the one who had regard to the dignity of the imaginary characters, who most effectively expressed feelings of anger and sorrow, and who clothed these thoughts in appropriate language.

His comment here demonstrates a keen awareness of the openly competitive nature of the Roman rhetorical education to which he had been exposed as a young man. More importantly, it evinces a clear understanding of how an orator might at once gain honour and help to reinforce the cultural authority of ancient poets.

Augustine won this contest. Triumphant and confident in his own powers, the young rhetor embarked on a career that would take him to the pinnacle of literary success in the Latin west. In later years, Augustine would come to regard these early triumphs as hollow and of little worth:

> What could all this matter to me, true life, my God? What importance could it have for me that my recitation was acclaimed beyond many other readers of my age group? Was not the whole exercise mere smoke and wind? Was there no other subject on which my talent and tongue might be exercised? Your praises, Lord, your praises expressed through your scriptures would have upheld the tender vine of my heart, and it would not have been snatched away by empty trifles to become 'a shameful prey for the birds'. There is more than one way of offering sacrifice to the fallen angels.[9]

The younger Augustine was probably free of such retrospective doubts that plagued Augustine the priest. Instead he used his literary prowess as a primary vehicle for self-advancement. As the result of his victory at a public poetry contest in Carthage, Augustine won the friendship and patronage of Vindicianus,[10] *proconsularis Africae* in 379/382, who crowned the young man. Following this début, Augustine's mastery of poetry continued to help him unlock every door. In that same year, Augustine dedicated his first work, *De pulchro et apto*, a book on literary aesthetics, to Hierius, a Greek Syrian poet-laureate prominent in the elevated circles of the Symmachi in Rome.[11] Mastery of Vergil and the other poets promised to this young provincial, as to all aspiring Roman youths, an avenue for upward social mobility.[12] For Augustine, the journey would indeed also be a spatial one, taking him first from humble Thagaste to Carthage, thence to Rome and Milan, where in 383 he was appointed to one of the official chairs of rhetoric in the city.

Augustine's conversion to catholic Christianity and his baptism in 387 did little to diminish his high regard for the cultural relevance of Vergil. At Cassiciacum, he fashioned an intellectual environment in which the classical authors featured prominently. While Cicero, here embodying the ancient philosophical heritage, was manifestly the major presence, Vergil was another presiding spirit that shaped Augustine's conversations with cherished friends and pupils. The poet's works formed part of the fabric of their everyday life as selections from the corpus were recited on a regular basis. According to *De ordine*, a work composed in December 386, Augustine and his companions listened to a recitation of half a book of the *Aeneid* every evening prior to taking supper.[13]

At Cassiciacum, Augustine was working out with others the relative importance of philosophy and literature to a Christian life. His own interactions with Licentius, a younger man who played the role of a

7. Augustine, the Grammarians and the Cultural Authority of Vergil

discipulus, highlights this dialogue. A talented youth whose skills as a poet, together with the connections of a rich father, subsequently enabled him to enter high Roman society, Licentius was then so enamoured of the poetry of Vergil that he caused Augustine no small measure of alarm.[14] While he no doubt saw in Licentius intimations of his own youthful career, Augustine cautioned him against showing an excessive interest in poetry, suggesting that the study of philosophy would confer more wholesome benefits. Peter Brown has rightly warned against seeing this tension as evidence of Augustine's turn away from literature to philosophy, as he 'was not deserting an exhausted literary culture: rather, he was attempting to swim against an equally strong and self-confident current'.[15] Augustine's increasing emphasis on philosophy should be seen within the context of the ongoing competition between philosophers and sophists for prestige and legitimacy.[16]

Indeed Augustine himself felt no need to make an exclusive choice. When later he drew on his experiences at Cassiciacum to compose *De magistro* (389), quotations and echoes of Vergil would suffuse the work even though the subject matter of the treatise was clearly shaped by the philosophy of Plato, Plotinus and Porphyry.[17] Many of the exchanges seem to echo conversations between teacher and pupil within a grammarian's classroom. In book 1, he entered a discussion with his son Adeodatus regarding whether words are signs by citing Vergil's phrase *si nihil ex tanta superis placet urbe relinqui*, 'if the gods wish nothing to survive from so great a city' (*Aen.* 2.659) and discussing the eight words in turn:[18]

> Aug. Do we agree then that words are signs?
> Ad. We do.
> Aug. Well, can there be a sign unless it signifies something?
> Ad. No.
> Aug. How many words are there in this verse? *Si nihil ex tanta superis placet urbe relinqui.*
> Ad. Eight.
> Aug. Are there eight signs then?
> Ad. Yes.
> Aug. I believe you grasp the meaning of this verse.
> Ad. Well enough, I think.
> Aug. Tell me what the words mean, one by one.
> Ad. I certainly understand what *si* signifies, but I find no other word to explain it.
> Aug. Whatever it signifies, do you at least know where it occurs?
> Ad. It seems to me that *si* signifies doubt, and where, except in the mind, can doubt exist?
> Aug. I will accept that for the time being. Go on to the other words.

115

The question of whether words are signs that have a certain correspondence to an underlying reality featured centrally in Augustine's thinking at the time. To him, words, *uerba,* should be regarded as signs, *signa,* that point towards a higher reality, *res,* but only if the former could be appropriately understood. On the face of it, Augustine the Christian might be expected to conclude that the words of the poets convey nothing truthful. Indeed he frequently referred to works of poetry as *fabula* or *figmenta poetica*, however, he never completely rejected the possibility that Vergil's poetry might reveal truth. While the works of the poets feature outlandish and even immoral stories about the gods, the authors themselves were merely making use of received traditions that they themselves did not invent.[19] The ancient poems were not so much false as untrue. A poet such as Vergil transmitted traditions that were untrue – which he knew to be untrue – due to a desire to engage his audience. Such an exculpatory interpretation of an ancient author's role *vis-à-vis* the mythological tradition remained throughout Augustine's life. Even in a late work such as the *City of God*, he insisted that the ancient poets composed their poems about the gods without any explicit intention to create falsehoods.[20]

Not surprisingly, Augustine conceded a similar cultural role to contemporary grammarians. While these teachers required their students to read and memorise the poetry of Vergil and other poets while knowing that the fables in them were not true, they did so firmly believing in poetry's ability to confer benefits. The grammarians who taught fictitious tales about the gods were not harming the young so much as doing good by imparting a solid and useful literary training.[21] Augustine sought thereby to justify to himself and others the value of the *ars grammatica* for a Christian.[22] For him, when properly employed, it represented a form of *scientia* in which, according to Gerard Ellspermann, one 'collects all the fictions of the human tongue, teaches and enforces principles of interpretation concerning these fragments'.[23]

Augustine's views regarding the value of pagan poetry were not formed in a vacuum or in reference solely to the contents of the poems, nor was it always the much-trumpeted tension between classical *paideia* and Christianity that shaped his reflections. More pressing concerns weighed on the young Augustine's mind. During his student days in Carthage, Augustine became intimately involved with Manichaeans and this engagement lasted almost a decade.[24] When he retreated to Cassiciacum with his friends, he was still distancing himself intellectually from Manichaean ideas so that the greater part of his thinking during that time revolved around live disputes between Manichaeans and catholic Christians.[25]

In Roman North Africa, Manichaeism had presented itself as a rational alternative to catholic Christianity.[26] It was popular among the young men of Augustine's circle because it offered them a religious identity that

7. Augustine, the Grammarians and the Cultural Authority of Vergil

promised to be more rational and true. No longer would Christians have to attempt to use makeshift explanations to reconcile apparent contradictions in biblical passages in the Old and the New Testaments, a famously challenging task. Manichaeans were in the habit of accusing catholic Christians of corrupting the truth through accepting the Old Testament, which, as with many gnostic Christians, the former regarded as the work of a lesser god.[27] On their part, Manichaeans proposed a more apparently straightforward alternative. Acccording to Peter Brown, Augustine and his friends learned from the teachings of the Manichaean teachers that 'there was no need to 'water-down' so intimate an awareness, to obscure it with the clumsy scaffolding of Hebrew prophecies, that the Catholic Church had erected around the simple truth.'[28]

It was the Manichaean claim to afford a more direct path to the truth that first attracted and captivated Augustine.[29] After his conversion to catholic Christianity, he took notice of the fact that, while the Manichaean teachers made much of the contradictions and apparently irrational statements in the Christian scriptures, especially in the Old Testament, these *doctores* based their argument on the premise that catholic Christians must read sacred texts literally. Augustine now refused to grant this premise since catholic Christians should be entitled to read scriptures in a figurative or allegorical way whenever appropriate. The Manichaeans' insistence that catholic Christians read Genesis, for instance, literally appeared to Augustine as a calculated ploy, a kind of disingenuous reductionism designed to score points rather than discover the truth. The question of how Christians ought to read the stories in the Old Testament, especially Genesis, was nevertheless a real one that Augustine tried to address over his long career and to which he devoted at least five lengthy discussions.[30]

In their turn, Manichaean teachers were promoting Mani's teachings regarding the primordial elements of Light and Darkness, the accidental admixture of which led to the creation of the world, and the idea of salvation as the refining process for releasing the Light particles trapped in matter. In later years, Augustine regarded the Manichaean myths as just as incredible but very much less useful than the poems about the gods:[31]

> How superior are the fables of the masters of literature and poets (*grammaticorum et poetarum fabellae*) to these deceptive traps! For verses, poems, and 'the flight of Medea' are certainly more useful that the Five Elements which take on different colours, each in accordance with one of the Five Caverns of Darkness – things which have no reality whatever and kill anyone who believes they have. Verses and poetry I can transform into real nourishment. 'Medea flying through the air' I might recite, but would not assert to be fact

(*non adserebam*). Even if I heard someone reciting the passage, I would not believe it. Yet the other [Manichee] myth I did not believe (*non credebam*).

The topos of Medea's flight had so exercised Augustine that he wrote on it on at least three earlier occasions, as noted by James O'Donnell in his edition of the *Confessions*.[32] But the important points that Augustine raised here concern the connection between a specific belief and utility.

Rather than judge the value of a truth claim based strictly on its correspondence to *res*, Augustine proposed that its acceptability for Christians should instead be determined by the mental disposition of those who told the story, the willingness of others to believe in it, and the overall consequences of their belief. On the other hand, while the Manichaean teachers deliberately and knowingly misrepresented the truth, their audiences were not guilty of the same misdeed. In fact, Augustine's presentation of the teachings of the Manichaean *doctores* aimed to reinforce the distinction between the false teachers and those whom they misled: the *imperiti* who were impressionable and susceptible to the false claims paraded by the *doctores* as true.

His entanglements with Manichaeans greatly shaped Augustine's biblical hermeneutics.[33] This connection is made abundantly clear in the *De Genesi contra Manichaeos,* composed in 388 after Augustine had returned to Africa.[34] At the very beginning, Augustine explains how he came to write the treatise at the insistence of educated Christians who wished to have a formal refutation of the Manichaean arguments regarding Genesis aimed at those without training in the liberal arts.[35] Accordingly, Augustine employed the rather artless technique of rendering a verse-by-verse statement of Manichaean claims regarding Genesis followed by the correct Christian interpretations, often resorting to allegorical or spiritual readings.[36] He made the following contrast: [37]

> If the Manichees preferred to search out the secrets of these words, without finding fault and making accusations, but investigating with reverence, they would, of course, not be Manichees ... those who seek with pious diligence (*pia diligentia*) raise more questions on this discourse than those impious wretches (*impii*), but with this difference: the former seek in order to find; the latter work only at not finding what they seek. Hence, this whole discourse must first be discussed according to history (*secundum historiam*), then according to prophecy (*secundum prophetiam*). According to history, events are narrated; according to prophecy future things are foretold.

In addition, Augustine insisted that the practice of literal reading which Manichaean teachers attributed to catholic Christians would not pass muster in the grammarians' classrooms, given that the grammarians' exposition of poetry tended to be much more nuanced and multifaceted.

7. Augustine, the Grammarians and the Cultural Authority of Vergil

For instance, Servius' commentary on Vergil contains a large number of allegorical interpretations that are interspersed with appeals to history, etymology and other senses.[38]

Augustine drew upon his own background in the liberal arts, which he shared with his ideal intended audience, to make this an effective juxtaposition. Grammarians instructed the young that the work of an authority such as Vergil was capable of multiple levels of interpretation. With this insight, Augustine advanced an *a fortiori* argument that, given the greater value of scriptures over poetry, a multifaceted approach suited to the interpretation of poetry ought *even more* to be applied to the reading of inspired sacred texts. Secondly, he argued that the Manichaean teachers who insisted on a literal interpretation of scriptures did so with the intent to confuse and deceive the inexperienced, particularly those who did not have the benefit of a literary education. Indeed Augustine was here also implying that many of the Manichaean *doctores* were themselves autodidacts who lacked such an education.[39] Appealing to the common élite literary culture formed part of Augustine's effort to establish his own credentials and discredit those of Manichaean teachers.

His efforts to separate himself from his Manichaean past and to insulate others from the seductiveness of Manichaean arguments prompted Augustine to articulate his own theory of exegesis. Drawing upon his literary and philosophical readings, Augustine responded to the Manichaean claims regarding the literal reading of scriptures.[40] The first known discussion in which Augustine proposed a fourfold hermeneutical approach based on Greek literary theory – history, aetiology, analogy and allegory – appears in *De utilitate credendi*.[41] The work was dedicated in 391/392 to Honoratus, an old North African friend who had turned from the catholic Christianity of his youth to Manichaean teachings, having been attracted by their claim to demonstrate greater rationality.[42] Book 5 explains the four modes of interpretation: there is the reading according to *historia*, the more or less literal sense of what was written or done, and what did not happen but is nonetheless described in writings as if it has happened. Next comes *aetiologia*, the explanation of why something is either said or done. Then a reader may harmonise the scriptures through *analogia*, whereby the Old and New Testaments do not contradict (*non sibi aduersari*). Finally, *allegoria* attempts to construe a figurative meaning from something that has been written in such a way that it cannot be understood in a literal sense (*non ad litteram esse accipienda*). An awareness of these different ways of reading might help a reader avoid three common errors. As Augustine explained the matter in *De utilitate credendi*,[43] these occur when

(i) *id quod falsum est uerum putatur, cum aliud qui scripsit putauerit* ('that which is false is thought true, when the author thought otherwise').

(ii) *id quod falsum est uerum putatur, id tamen putatur, quod etiam ille qui scripsit putauit* ('that which is false is thought true, but the thought is also that of the author').

(iii) *ex alieno scripto intelligitur aliquid ueri, cum hoc ille qui scripsit non intellexerit* ('from another's writing some truth is understood when the author did not understand it').

While all three involved some misunderstanding or mismatch between what the author intended and what the reader understands, they do not incur equal risk or opprobrium for the misguided reader. Augustine went on to explain that the Christian church sees the first as a indeed a serious fault but also one that one could negate easily by realising and repudiating one's error. Nor does the church regard these errors in reading as equal:[44]

(i) *Graue omnino crimen, sed defensionem longam non requirit; satis est enim negare. ita nos intellegere, ut illi, cum inuehuntur, existimant* ('It is altogether a serious crime, but does not demand a lengthy defence; for it is enough to deny that we so understand as they who inveigh against us think').

(ii) *Non minus graue est, sed eadem uoce refellentur* ('It is no less serious, but they will be refuted by the same saying').

(iii) *Nullum crimen est* ('There is no crime').

According to Brian Stock, who recasts these points in terms of the reader's comprehension of the author's work, '… the reader errs (1) when the false is taken for the true, despite the author's perception of the opposite, (2) when both parties make the same mistake, and (3) when the reader sees what is wrong but the writer does not.'[45] Rather astutely, he further notices that these scenarios raise as a central issue the function of the interpretive community in the production of an authentic meaning of a given text. Neither author nor [the individual] reader appears to play a privileged role in this process, for 'if the true meaning of the text is not derived from the writer, it can potentially arise in the reader; but Augustine argues that it cannot reside uniquely there either because the text from which the reader derives meaning is probably not his or her own creation'.[46]

Here the grammarian/exegete comes to his aid once more as Augustine drew on his knowledge of their practice to advocate a respectful and truth-producing Christian exegesis. One superior aspect of the grammarians' approach to poetry that Augustine praised was their ability to draw on an established scholarly and authoritative apparatus rooted in a community of understanding. Indeed grammarians relied on the whole

7. Augustine, the Grammarians and the Cultural Authority of Vergil

trapping of learning – commentaries and learned ancient commentators – to create their own interpretations and, even more importantly, their own authority. A cornerstone of the primary Latin education dispensed by the grammarians, the *Aeneid* was seen in late antiquity as containing universally shared and still relevant linguistic norms and cultural truths.[47] But despite this cultural ubiquity, the contemporary understanding of the work was heavily mediated by the authoritative commentaries of individual writers on grammar who addressed their works to *magistri* and *discipuli* alike. Thus Augustine could take it for granted that his readers would agree that, just as no sane person would approach the *Aeneid* without resorting to these *auctores*, no Christian should expect to understand the gospels without consulting the learned commentaries of experienced exegetes. Addressing a Manichaean interlocutor, he asked:[48]

> Without being imbued with some poetic training, you would not venture to take up Terentianus Maurus without a teacher (*sine magistro*). Asper, Cornutus, Donatus, and countless others are required so that any poet can be understood whose verses are seen even to capture the applause of the theatre. But, against books which, however they may be, are reported by the acknowledgment of almost the entire human race to be holy and full of divine things, you let launch your attack without a guide, and you dare to pass sentence upon them without a teacher (*sine praeceptore*)!

Furthermore, their respectful attitude towards the *auctores* also served to distinguish the grammarians from the Manichaeans. The grammarians, Augustine proposed, validated the authority of Vergil and based their inquiry upon the premise that the poet could not be wrong whereas the Manichaeans challenged the authority of scriptures and were quick to point out their every deficiency, thereby disqualifying themselves as the ideal readers of such texts.[49]

> And this I must do in any other way, rather than by explaining their meanings and words. For, if we hated Vergil – rather, if we did not love him through the recommendations of our forebears before we had an understanding of him, never would we have been satisfied about these innumerable questions over which grammarians are generally agitated and disturbed; nor would we listen willingly to one who resolved these questions to the poet's credit, but would favour him who tried to show, through them, that he had erred and was off the track (*errasse ac delirasse*).

Thus the authoritative texts came to serve as the basis upon which later individuals competed to gain honour, doing so in such a way that the *auctores* were invariably built up as infallible. The prestige of a contemporary teacher was intimately connected to his ability to uphold or amplify the prestige of the classical author:[50]

> those men get the most applause through whose exposition the poet is found better, one who is believed (even by those who do not understand him) not only to have erred in no respect, but to have written nothing save what was praiseworthy. And so we rather become annoyed at the teacher (*magister*) who fails in some little question and has no answer to give than think that he is silent through Maro's fault. Now if, toward his own defence, he should wish to assert a defect in so great an author, it is not likely that his students will stay with him, even though their fees have been paid.

Augustine argued that the dialectial questionings of the Manichaeans, whose every manoeuvre sought to demonstrate the inadequacy or inconsistency of scriptural claims, undermined their search for truth. Rather than adopt such a critical, fruitless and ultimately dangerous approach, catholic Christians ought instead to treat the scriptures with the proper respect that grammarians paid to the ancient authorities such as Vergil. To advance his polemic:[51]

> How great a thing it would be to show similar good will to those through whom so old a tradition confirms that the Holy Spirit has spoken. But, of course, we brilliant young men and wondrous searchers-out of reason, not even having opened those books, without having looked for teachers, without directing the least accusation at our own dullness, and finally, not even conceding an average understanding to those men who for so long a time had wished books of this kind to be read and guarded and expounded throughout the entire world, we thought that no confidence should be placed in these men; and we were moved to this opinion by the words of those who were their enemies and foes and among whom we would be forced to cherish and believe under the false pretence of reason, untold thousands of fables.

What can the practice of late Roman grammarians tell us about Augustine's invocation of their craft? Keepers of the linguistic knowledge with which to access the ancient literary tradition, grammarians also laid claim to being themselves authorities in whom pupils should place their utmost confidence. They were culturally and institutionally enshrined as the intermediaries standing between authoritative writings and young pupils seeking to make those writings their own. But while the authority of the grammarians was inextricably tied to the authority of the texts of which they claimed to be privileged interpreters, they could and often did innovate.

In his study of the practice of late antique grammarians, Robert Kaster has convincingly shown that they were in reality neither passive recipients

7. Augustine, the Grammarians and the Cultural Authority of Vergil

nor mere conduits of the ancient literary tradition.[52] In Macrobius' *Saturnalia*, a text from the 430s, the figure of Servius is represented as a strong spokesman for the primacy of traditional authority. The author created an idealised portrait of the grammarian as someone who conserved the ancient tradition and who thereby acted as a guarantor for the continuation of a cultural legacy which, in the early fifth century, seemed fragile and vulnerable. The literary Servius was someone who stood watch over the *mos maiorum*; he was a *conservator* of *antiquitas* and an avowed foe of *novitas*.[53] This may not be too surprising as we have come to expect grammarians to be 'conservative'. Yet Kaster also shows that this Servius was in the main a literary cipher and did not correspond to the 'real' Servius, whose ideas and approach to *antiquitas* can be ascertained through reading his writings. In Servius' comments on Aelius Donatus' commentary on the *Aeneid*, one discerns a grammarian who forcefully and rather idiosyncratically fashioned special rules of grammar, which were then impressed upon his pupils as rules they themselves must follow.[54] Likewise, Peter Marshall commented on the magisterial tone that Servius adopted even as the latter was advancing tendentious readings or explanations of the poet's words.[55] Far from being a *conservator* of the *mos maiorum*, Servius regarded and presented himself as uniquely qualified to create a living literary Latin, 'as the maker of the *lingua aetatis suae* (voice of his own age) superior to the claims of *auctoritas* or *antiquitas*'.[56] The impetus for these innovations, Kaster has persuasively argued, derived from the grammarian's need to assert continually his own cultural authority and centrality within a broader social context in which his activities were regarded by others as preparatory.[57] The shared educational culture of the Roman élite and the grammarians' position at the lower rungs of literary culture served to circumscribe the latter's scope for clever or faddish innovations. Surrounded by other educated men who shared his expertise in literature, a grammarian was nevertheless the master of his own classroom insofar as he could persuade others that he was an authoritative and responsible exegete of ancient *auctores*. Thus, while the grammarian needed to be an entrepreneur and – to a lesser extent – an innovator, he could most expediently do so if he posed as a reliable guardian of the ancient tradition; however, this ironically also opened him to charges of uninspiring pedantry by members of the literary élite. A Christian exegete might not be caught in the same bind but Augustine understood well the limitations of all human exegetes for he would ultimately propose that neither the grammarian nor an ancient *poet* represented the ideal *magister*, a role that only Christ could play.[58]

Conclusion

In summing up Augustine's reaction to the pagan literary tradition, Gerard Ellspermann opines that 'in themselves the works of the poets fare badly. But compared to the errors of the heretics, they are viewed as less dangerous. On the other hand, compared to Sacred Scripture they are but nonsensical trifles.'[59] This comment summing up the common wisdom regarding Augustine's attitude towards poetry is essentially correct but fails to register important nuances. After he had become a priest and then a bishop, Augustine voiced heightened concerns about the influence of Vergil and the works of the pagan poets in writings such as *De civitate Dei* and *De doctrina Christiana*.[60] These concerns grew out of the constant demands of pastoral care, for Augustine had come to regard the classical literary tradition as one of the factors that were retarding the process of Christianisation. Poetry such as the *Aeneid* legitimised myths that buttressed traditional religious practices among the common people as well as solidified the 'pagan' cultural and religious outlook among the learned aristocratic élite.[61] Accordingly, Augustine began to treat his beloved Vergil as a cultural icon that had to be undermined.

But these reservations have yet to crystallise in the late 380s. Prior to his conversion, Augustine had been as much a Vergilian as a Manichaean. Unlike Jerome, who in his maturity claimed not to have read any Cicero and Vergil for some fifteen years, Augustine's deep connections to Vergil and other 'secular' Latin writers persisted from the time when an oration on the death of Dido won him his first prize. He returned to the *Aeneid* often in the years immediately following his conversion even as he attempted to fashion for himself a new identity as a catholic Christian. In assaying this task, he was less directly concerned with the value of pagan poetry for a Christian than with the need to counter widely accepted contentions made by Manichaean teachers. Augustine's appeals to classical literature at this juncture advanced a complex cultural claim. He recognised the universal appeal of a poet such as Vergil among educated men and sought to capitalise on this common culture in his fight against the Manichaean teachers and their doctrines. He also used the model of the relationship between the ancient poets, grammarians and their audiences to help develop the role of the Christian exegete, a figure who was coming into his own in the later fourth century. Some of his early works, such as *De utilitate credendi*, show how his views on Christian reading were shaped by the parallels he found between grammarian and scriptural exegete: both stand between an ancient, revered text and an (initially) unlearned audience. The manner in which he juxtaposed the two sets of texts, exegetes and exegeses demonstrates that Augustine's appreciation

7. Augustine, the Grammarians and the Cultural Authority of Vergil

of Vergil must yet be viewed against the backdrop of live controversies surrounding the interpretation of Christian scriptures.

Notes

1. See August. *De civ. D.* 1.17-18, 22, 26.
2. Schelkle (1939); Hagendahl (1967). Among the many other important works is Courcelle (1984).
3. Stock (1996) and MacCormack (1998). See also Eckmann (1988).
4. Hagendahl (1967) II, 445.
5. Ibid.
6. MacCormack (1998) 225-6.
7. See Hagendahl (1967) II, 384-463; and O'Donnell (1980).
8. Aug. *Conf.* 1.27 (trans. in text from Chadwick [1991] 19; Latin text from O'Donnell, [1992] I, 13). On this particular school exercise, see O'Donnell (1992) II, 91.
9. August. *Conf.* 1.27 (Chadwick 20). On the fallen angels as *daemones* and pagan gods, see O'Donnell (ed.), *Augustine* (1992) II, 92.
10. August. *Conf.* 4.3.5. See *PLRE* I, 967, s.v. (Helvius) Vindicianus 2, and 1074. This cultured man was a professional physician who had become a *comes archiatrorum* in 379 prior to taking up the proconsulship, at which point he was already a *senex*. On his interactions with Augustine, see Stock (1996) 51-2.
11. August. *Conf.* 4.14.21. See *PLRE I*, 431 s.v. Hierius 5: he mastered Latin in addition to Greek.
12. See Brown (1992) esp. 35-70, on the shared culture between the élite and the rhetors.
13. August. *De ordine* 1.8.26 (*CCSL* 29, 102) and *Contra academicos* 2.4.10 (*CCSL* 29, 23). For a sound assessment of the historicity of Augustine's representations of Cassiciacum, see McWilliam (1990).
14. For Augustine's comments regarding Licentius, see Mandouze (1982) 641-2, s.v. Licentius 1; and Romano (1961); Brown (1967) 118-19.
15. Brown (1967) 119.
16. See discussion in Stanton (1973), Hahn (1989), Lim (1995) 61-4, and Bowersock (2002).
17. See Madec (1975) and (1993).
18. August. *De magistro* 1.2 (*CSEL* 77, 6). Translation in text from Russell (1967) 12.
19. See MacCormack (1998) 53-4.
20. See, for example, August. *De civ. D.* 18.14 (*CSEL* 40:2, 285-6).
21. August. *De catechizandis rudibus* 6.10.20 (*CCSL* 46, 131). See now Chin (2002) 177-80.
22. See August. *Soliloq.* 2.11.19.
23. Ellspermann (1949) 188.
24. Among recent appraisals of Augustine's Manichaean background are: Van Oort (1997) and Coyle (2001).
25. On Manichaeans in the west, see, for example, Brown (1969); Decret (1970); Lieu (1985).
26. See Frend (1953) esp. 21; Lim (1992) 233-72 (revised and reprinted in Lim [1995] 70-108).
27. See August. *De utilitate credendi* 4 (*CSEL* 25, 6-7).

28. Brown (1967) 49.

29. August. *De utilitate credendi* 2 (*CSEL* 25, 4).

30. This corpus comprises *De Genesi contra Manichaeos* (388/389); *De Genesi ad litteram imperfectus liber* (393); *Conf.* books 1-2; *De Genesi ad litteram* (after 404 and before 420); and *De civ. D.* book 11. See Pelland (1972).

31. August. *Conf.* 3.11, Chadwick (1991) 42; O'Donnell (1992) I, 27.

32. O'Donnell (1992) II, 182: Aug. *Soliloq.* 2.15.29 (late 386) and *Ep.* 7.2.4 (to Nebridius, 389).

33. See, for example, Allgeier (1930); Ries (1961); Walter (1972); and Wenning (1990).

34. See August. *Retractationes* 1.10.1. See the recent edition by Weber (1998); and idem (2001).

35. August. *De Genesi contra Manichaeos* 1.1 (*CSEL* 91, 67).

36. Augustine adopted Origen's hermeneutical approach in places, see Teske (1992). On the underlying source, see Weber (1998) 24-9.

37. August. *De Genesi contra Manichaeos* 2.2. Translation in text from Teske (1991) 95; Latin text from Weber (1998) 120.

38. See, for example, Jones (1986) esp. 108-17.

39. Felix, one of the Manichaean *doctores* active in Roman North Africa (see August. *Retractationes* 2.34 [*CSEL* 36, 141]: *unus ... ex doctoribus eorum*) was famously described by Augustine as *ineruditus liberalibus litteris* ('uneducated in the liberal arts') in *Contra Felicem* 2.1 (*CSEL* 25, 828). See Mandouze (1982) 417-18, s.v. Felix 20.

40. On Augustine's exegetical methods, see La Bonnardière (1986).

41. See especially August. *De utilitate credendi* 5 (*CSEL* 25, 7-8). On the treatise, see Brown (1967) 43; Decret (1978), I, 72-8; and Bochet (2001) esp. 37-40. On the four modes of exegesis, see de Lubac (1959). More recently, see Stock (1996) 164-9.

42. On Augustine's long association with this individual, see Mandouze (1982) 564-5, s.v. Honoratus 4. On Honoratus as an *imperitus*, see Bochet (2001) 29-30.

43. August. *De utilitate credendi* 10 (*CSEL* 25, 13-15).

44. August. *De utilitate credendi* 11 (*CSEL* 25, 16).

45. Stock (1996) 170.

46. Ibid.

47. Cf. Murgia below.

48. August. *De utilitate credendi* 17 (*CSEL* 25, 21-2). Translation in text from Meagher (1947) 412-13.

49. August. *De utilitate credendi* 13 (*CSEL* 25, 18-9). Translation in text from Meagher (1947) 408-9.

50. Ibid.

51. Ibid.

52. Kaster (1988), 169-97; see also Marshall (1997).

53. See Kaster (1988) 169-97.

54. See Chapter 12 below.

55. Marshall (1997) esp. 3-4.

56. Kaster (1988) 195.

57. See the perceptive comments by Kaster on this issue and on how grammarians function within the broader élite society (1988) 201-30.

58. August. *De magistro* 46; and *Retractationes* 1.11.

59. Ellspermann (1949) 245.

60. See, for example, O'Daly (1999) 246-8, at 246: 'Vergil's *Aeneid* is the poetic

7. Augustine, the Grammarians and the Cultural Authority of Vergil

text most often cited by Augustine in the *City of God* .... Vergil is perceived by Augustine to be a repository and representative of the pagan Roman culture which he is combating.'

61. See Hedrick (2000) 85 on Vergil's role in Macrobius' *Saturnalia*: 'Vergil, then, is imagined as the head of the official state religion, and of the board of priests of which Flavian, Symmachus and Praetextatus were members.'

8

Recycled Words: Vergil, Prudentius and Saint Hippolytus

Charles Witke

Prudentius has received extensive study as a late antique poet.[1] His debts to such Roman poets as Ausonius,[2] Horace,[3] Seneca and Lucan,[4] and of course Vergil[5] have been as carefully explored as his presence in Rome and his composing the *Peristephanon* collection in order to foster the cult of the martyrs, especially in his native Spain. Prudentius thus confronts the physical fabric of Rome, Rome's centres of spiritual power and Christian devotion and mediates his reactions in awareness of Rome's literary monuments, the classical poets. What role does Vergil play in the formation of Prudentius' poetical reaction to the Rome of the martyrs?

A constant in the late antique Roman world was the presence of Vergil. The Augustan poet, particularly persisting in the *Aeneid*, functioned both as a literary monument (past which later Roman poets of epic had a hard time to move) and as the author of a text shaping, first in the collective encounters in the schools, and later in life as individuals appropriated the text, the cultural and especially civic awareness of its readers. Prudentius' assimilation of Vergil would seem to be typical of a highly educated person of affairs, working very likely at the court of Theodosius in Milan, even if he had provincial origins.[6] The number of citations and reminiscences in the standard works which cull these is impressive.[7] What is untypical is Prudentius' appropriation of the impact Vergil's poem made on the awareness of educated late fourth-century readers, impact comparable to that which the Augustan programme of building and decoration made on the physical fabric of Augustan and later Rome.[8] By the end of the fourth century, Vergil's works, particularly the *Aeneid*, had moved from offering a language of signs for articulating citizenship and its possible and potential duties and responsibilities in the Roman state, far-flung but centred on Rome itself, to constituting an environment where awareness of being a member or indeed citizen of that state could find a parallel Christian identity. Vergil as construed, corrected and indeed deconstructed by Prudentius could offer a framework of reference for the follower of Christ who

8. Recycled Words: Vergil, Prudentius and Saint Hippolytus

was also a Roman citizen, educated, civically aware, and often highly placed. Potential tensions were resolved in the grounding of Prudentius' fairly elite and very Roman literature in the fabric of faith.

In the Theodosian period, Latin Christians needed heroes too, not persons improving their minds with philosophy. Prudentius (to mention, among others, the subject of this inquiry) provides them in the *Peristephanon* with such heroes, and uses Vergil to set forth the heroic stature of many martyrs and the civic significance of their deeds.[9]

Prudentius studs his poems with references and quotations from Vergil. This has long been known and studied. Prudentius by doing this likewise uses the Vergilian texts (for this study, primarily the *Aeneid*) by putting colonising quotations and reminiscences from it into his sacred poems. Both texts are changed thereby. By doing this, Prudentius deepens a sense of the past being present to Christians. Prudentius 'translates' relics of Vergil, together with their contexts, into the Christian context of his poems, and reciprocal colonisation of Vergil's text by concomitant Christian reference results. Prudentius' work along these lines was not representative of literary activity at the end of the fourth century, the last quarter of which saw a growing rift between pagans and Christians. In resolving this tension, Prudentius forges a new path. In his recuperating from Vergil not only forms of words but also the insignia of civic worth and Roman identity, Prudentius as fervent Christian plays a significant role in the working out of these tensions between pagan religion, its cultural and literary vehicles, and the new literature, not least because post-pagan hardly meant Christian for any thoughtful producer or consumer of literature. Prudentius' innovations should be studied in some detail, to which we now turn.

As a poet of the later fourth century, Prudentius himself strives to be a poet addressing the whole Roman world, not just a segment or segments marked by a specially fervent life of devotion such as that lived by a Paulinus of Nola. Those who mirrored Ausonius in being indeed formally Christian yet bewildered by the faith's claim and its drive to sweep away from given individuals all remnants of pagan cult and individual compromise with it and with its secular society, and the elastic morals that went with it, were also among those whom Prudentius sought to address.

Peristephanon 11 on Hippolytus opens with Prudentius addressing Valerian, bishop of Calahorra, and closes in a similar way. At the outset, Prudentius tells Valerian it is difficult for him to comply with the bishop's request for the titles and names of the saints incised on their tombs.

> innumeros cineres sanctorum Romula in urbe
>   vidimus, o Christi Valeriane sacer.
> incisos tumulis titulos et singula quaeris
>   nomina: difficile est ut replicare queam.

>   tantos iustorum populos furor impius hausit,   5
>   cum coleret patrios Troia Roma deos.
>   plurima litterulis signata sepulcra loquuntur
>   martyris aut nomen aut epigramma aliquod,
>   sunt et muta tamen tacitas claudentia tumbas
>   marmora, quae solum significant numerum.   10
>   quanta virum iaceant congestis corpora acervis
>   nosse licet, quorum nomina nulla legas.
>   sexaginta illic defossas mole sub una
>   reliquias memini me didicisse hominum,
>   quorum solus habet conperta vocabula Christus,   15
>   utpote quos propriae iunxit amicitiae.
>   haec dum lustro oculis et sicubi forte latantes
>   rerum apices veterum per monumenta sequor,
>   invenio Hippolytum, qui quondam scisma Novati
>   presbyter attigerat nostra sequenda negans,   20
>   usque ad martyrii provectum insigne tulisse
>   lucida sanguinei praemia supplicii.

Countless are the graves of saints I have seen in the city of Romulus, Valerian, Christ's dedicated servant. You ask for the inscriptions cut on their tombs, and their individual names, but it is hard for me to be able to repeat them. Such great multitudes of the righteous did ungodly rage devour while Trojan Rome still worshipped the gods of her fathers. Many a grave is lettered and tells the martyr's name or bears some epitaph, but there are mute marbles too, which shut up the tombs in silence and only indicate the number; you may learn what masses of men's bodies lie gathered together in heaps, but read the name of none of them. I remember finding that the remains of sixty persons were buried there under one massive stone, whose names Christ alone knows since he has added them to the company of his friends. In surveying these memorials and hunting over them for any letters telling of the deeds of old that might escape the eye, I found that Hippolytus, who had at one time as a presbyter attached himself to the schism of Novatus, saying that our own way was not to be followed, had been advanced to the crown of martyrdom and won the shining reward for suffering bloodshed. (1-22, trans H.J. Thomson, Loeb)

As has been pointed out,[10] images of reading and of writing abound in the first nineteen lines of the text. In the first four lines alone we find incised names, titles, and (not noted hitherto) *replicare* in the sense of unrolling a *rotulus* or opening a codex.

The word *apices* (l.18, 'angles'), is used in the technical sense of the *ductus* or line strokes used by the *ordinator* and *marmorarius* of the inscription: a very emphatic direction of attention to the physical object itself.[11] The use of *invenio* ('I find'), in the sense of deciphering the name of Hippolytus functions similarly, and reveals how Prudentius is 'reading'

8. Recycled Words: Vergil, Prudentius and Saint Hippolytus

difference in varying sources or accounts, the multiple strands of, not a multiple personality, or a bogus martyr, but of a literary construct coming together from Prudentius' reading not only of the shrine's epigraphical evidence, but of his poetical predecessors, not least Vergil.

The poet emphasises the outward signs he is often unable to open up/*replicare*: again, one may say, relevant both to the inscriptions and to the literary tradition Prudentius inherits. Some tombs in this place are helped to speak by their *litterulae*, 'letterings', and name their dead or their *epigrammata*, whilst others are silent on identity but, like standardised commercial containers of the day give only a quantity, their occupants' *vocabula*, or 'namings', being known only to Christ. Prudentius ends this section by succeeding in 'finding' Hippolytus, that is, *invenio* both in the sense of reading his epigraphic name, and *inventio* as the rhetorical term for finding one's subject. This closely packed language about reading and writing provides, not coincidentally, the context for the first Vergilian contribution to the poem, surprisingly, one not cited hitherto by the great collectors of *Vergiliana* in Prudentius.[12] It is *furor impius* ('wicked madness', 5) If one recalls the opening of another poem on a hero who met conflict and achieved success (*Aen*. 1.291ff.), an interesting dialogue between Prudentius and Vergil is opened up. Prudentius asserts that when Trojan Rome was worshipping her fathers' gods *furor impius* swallowed up so many peoples from among the just (5-6). The Vergilian context comes with the words *furor impius* for anyone who has appropriated the famous Vergilian passage as the conclusion of a superbly wrought divine *allocutio*, the epic assertion of the god's plan for Rome, or who has assimilated it as a concatenation of the most powerful of Roman symbols (Venus, Aeneas, Lavinium, Alba Longa, the wolf, the twins, Mars, Caesar and all the rest); or who has seen it as all of the above, as any literate Roman of the fourth century would have done.

Note what Prudentius has done by using *furor impius* as he does. The peace promised by Jupiter Optimus Maximus in the first book of the *Aeneid* is now seen as no peace. Security and stability under law were not what the martyrs in these tombs experienced from the Roman state. *furor impius hausit*, 'engulfed and consumed' those who were *iusti*, 'righteous before Roman law and before God', and it did this in the setting of worship and cult of the ancestral gods. One might also note Prudentius' irony in using the adjective *Troia* with *Roma* (1.6): just whose gods are these Roman gods, and where do they come from ultimately?

For the contemporary Roman reader reading Prudentius' elegiac couplets here,[13] the most accessible of the metres he uses in the *Peristephanon*, *furor impius* calls into question, tension and ambiguity the validity and accuracy if not the disingenuousness of Vergil's Jupiter as seen from a fourth-century Christian perspective. And from a fourth-century non-

Christian or merely outwardly adhering Christian perspective it imputes to the Vergilian context an ambiguity which to say the least does not enhance it as a civic pronouncement of future benefits. There are of course modern critics of Vergil who would retroject this outlook back to the Augustan age itself. But for the readers of Prudentius, both Christians of whatever fervour and non-Christians alike (and one may confidently assume they read him too as a consummate metrical artist if nothing else), the words *furor impius* take on a new look whenever it will be encountered again in re-reading Vergil. Prudentius shows us that this is what it leads to, the destruction of countless *iusti*; this is what the cult of the ancestral religion civic religion, leads to: the poet of today standing amid tombs trying to read the names of the dead, mostly martyred co-religionists swallowed up by a state whose triumphant poet's words are deconstructed and assigned irrevocably a destabilised significance for all who have read Prudentius' *Peristephanon* 11.5-6, and the *Aeneid*: that is, many Christians on the one hand, and all educated citizens of the Roman world on the other.

At the outset of this poem, Prudentius writes for Valerian to read. He writes his own reading of the martyrs, his reading of Vergil, and his reading of Hippolytus as both martyr and literary construct.

After setting forth the background to Hippolytus, martyred it seems in the third century, his previous adherence to the Novatian schism, and his arrest by the Roman authorities, *vaesanus hostis*, 'the mad enemy' (1.25), he initiates Hippolytus' address to the crowd accompanying him by having it ask the prisoner *quaenam secta foret melior?* 'what religion it is better to follow?' (1.28)

> respondit: 'fugite, o miseri, execranda Novati
> scismata, catholicis reddite vos populis!'

> He replied, 'Flee, o wretches, the damnable schism of Novatus;
> return to the catholic people.'

Scholars have duly noted Vergil *Aeneid* 3.639.[14] In this passage Vergil revisits the famous episode in Homer's *Odyssey* where Odysseus accomplishes the blinding of the cannibalistic Cyclops and effects the escape of his crew. The narrator in Vergil is a member of the crew of Odysseus, Achaemenides, who was forgotten in the escape from Polyphemus' cave, and has been wandering (intertextually as it were) for three months in the wild. He enters the *Aeneid* and warns Anchises and the Trojans to flee from the imminent danger of Polyphemus who is emerging from his cave and leading his flock to the shore where the Trojan party has landed: *sed fugite, o miseri, fugite*, 'but flee, o wretches, flee'.[15] *miseri*, here, is proleptic;

8. Recycled Words: Vergil, Prudentius and Saint Hippolytus

if Aeneas and the Trojans stay, they will soon be 'wretched' when the Cyclops senses them. By inscribing this renowned Homeric episode in his epic, Vergil heightens his endeavour to be the Latin Homer. It is an intentionally memorable passage. Prudentius used it to initiate Hippolytus' discourse, his only speech in the poem (besides one line as his ordeal begins, 110). Hippolytus tells the crowd to flee the schism of Novatus and the educated reader will recall the dangerous context of Achaemenides' words, the imminent death threatened by the Cyclops, and will construe the schism as a lethal alienating danger. As Achaemenides was severed from his people, the crew of Odysseus, so followers of Novatus are schismatics, cut off from the catholics.[16] As Achaemenides was re-integrated into human society (albeit it Trojan not Greek) so the followers of Novatianism such as Hippolytus came back home. *fugite o miseri, fugite* in Prudentius also assigns a prophetic meaning to *miseri*, as well as a present one: schismatics are *miseri*, cut off from their true home, and will be *miseri* when devouring death, like a Cyclops, overtakes their souls. *furor impius hausit*; Trojan Rome drank the names of the martyrs along with their blood. Odysseus as Outis, 'Nobody', outsmarts Polyphemus the blood drinker, who now seeks new prey. The nameless have survived: both the Homeric hero and the anonymous martyrs among whom Hippolytus will rest.

Perhaps coincidentally, perhaps not, Hippolytus' encounter with Roman authority is at Ostia, a site on a shore like that of Achaemenides' encounter with Aeneas and his party. Prudentius is at pains to point out (1.39-48) that the *rector insanus* or 'mad magistrate'[17] has come from Rome to Ostia: *ostia Tiberina* (40); *Tyrreni ad litoris oram* (47); the epic names ring clearly. The magistrate has come to vex Christians (42). The Rome the persecutor has left is described in some detail; Vergil's poem begins with Aeneas coming to the Lavinian shore (where *Peristephanon* 11 begins) for the purpose of bringing his gods to Latium and establishing the walls of Rome. The itinerary of the Roman official in Prudentius has been in the opposite direction: from bloodshed within these same high walls, wherein he saw the Janiculum flowing with blood, blood-drenched *fora, rostra, Suburam* (45), to Ostia. This rehearsal of a good number of the canonical sites in Rome stresses the civic fabric of the city tinged with the blood of the persecuted *iusti* whose names and aggregate counts remain in Rome, *Romula in urbe* (1).[18] They have been persecuted because of the *una fides ... prisco quae condita templo est, / quam Paulus retinet, quamque cathedra Petri*, 'the one faith which was founded in the ancient sanctuary, which faith Paul and the chair of Peter hold' (31-2). The scene with Hippolytus moves from a Rome (re)founded by the Apostles to Portus, to Ostia, the shore of the Tyrrhenian sea where Aeneas made landfall to begin his own foundation.

The topographical trajectory of the Roman official from Rome to the shore is paralleled by the literary trajectory from Prudentius' poem back to Vergil's. It is as if (to be anachronistic) *Troia Roma, Furor impius*, and the *altae moenia Romae*, 'the tall walls of Rome', have been penetrated by a ticking time bomb which will go off when the reader of Prudentius revisits the terrain of the *Aeneid*. Vergil's high civic promise will be deconstructed into civic *furor*, which persecutes the new religion brought into Latium, and the cityscape will be irrevocably stained with civic blood: indeed, *fugite o miseri*.

In perhaps the most commented upon section of the poem, Prudentius presents an ecphrasis of a painted wall showing the event of Hippolytus' dismemberment in horrifying detail (123ff.) Some deny that a painting of such scope and nature would be found in a catacomb visited by Prudentius at the outset of the fifth century AD. However, it is now clear that it is well within the realm of the probable.[19] What is anomalous, however, is that the ecphrasis of the painting continues the narration in a direct way. The gathering of the bits and pieces and even blood of the martyred Hippolytus is described by the painting being described by the poet. Some have found the anomaly disconcerting: 'One is not sure where the description of the painting ends and the thread of the story is taken up again.'[20] And again: 'By erasing the boundary of the ambiguous painting, Prudentius forces his readers to experience the confusion and disorientation that are emblematic of his distracted saint.'[21] Awareness of Vergil can help understand this. While I agree that Prudentius does not signal the end of his ecphrasis in a formal way, nevertheless there is a line of demarcation. After the physical recollecting of the saint's body has been accomplished, in the same sentence that this is finished the place for posterity to recollect the saint's memory at his tomb is presented (147-52). Reference to Rome (152) shows that what began with 'an image painted above the tomb' (125) ends with the picture of the tomb being erected (151). After the tumulus is mentioned for the second time (151), Prudentius goes on to describe the catacomb, its means of access and its lighting, in detail which has fascinated archaeologists (if not literary critics of the poem) with its accuracy.

Early in his ecphrasis of the painting above the tomb Prudentius writes *cernere erat* (131, 'it was there to see'); together with *vidi, optime papa* (127, 'I saw, excellent Father', in reference to Bishop Valerian), this reinforces the visual basis and aspect of the narration. In *Aeneid* 6.595ff. the huge, intact body of a Titan is there to see, *cernere erat*; in *Peristephanon* 11, the body is dismembered. With this phrase, Prudentius signals his own excursus into ecphrasis and the underground landscape, but it is not a tour of the pagan Sibyl's underworld, with its gigantic body featured, nor of a shield animated with sufficient divine power to crush decisively the opponents of Rome's foundation at the Battle of Actium.[22] By

8. Recycled Words: Vergil, Prudentius and Saint Hippolytus

using *cernere erat*, the famous Vergilian introduction to two pregnant passages from the epic, Prudentius appropriates both their similarities and their differences, a torn-apart old man versus a sprawling Titan, a death witnessing to the power of faith versus a deadly battle establishing the power of Augustus Caesar. By retrojecting his tomb painting into Vergil's Underworld and the glowing gold of the shield's depiction of the battle to end all battles, Prudentius again seeks another dimension for the *Aeneid* to operate thenceforth within: the saint replaces in his underground reality the shadowy underworld purveyed by myth; the saint in his battle for his Christian Rome can be compared to Augustus Caesar's battle for his old version of Rome. All this *cernere erat*, 'is there to see' for the reader of the old and the new.

What we are dealing with hitherto in this use of words from Vergil is much more than verbal borrowing for metrical convenience, for local colour, for enhancement of the serious level of intent of Prudentius' text. Of course, where the metrical placement in both Vergil's line and that of Prudentius coincides, as with *cernere erat*, 'one could see', the dynamic parallelism is increased.[23] Rather than these effects, we are dealing with a programmatic effort on Prudentius' part to inform, to shape, to configure his text into a confrontation with the triumphalist epic of pre-Christian Rome, to enter into dialogue with it, and ultimately to correct it. The trajectory, it may be again asserted, is not only from Vergil to Prudentius, but from Prudentius back to Vergil, whose epic locales, often loaded with civic significance, here intersected by Prudentius' poetry, may never be the same.

The next section gives a detailed description of the catacomb, tomb and adjacent shrine, running to almost the end of the poem. We note that the tomb of Hippolytus in the catacomb of the Via Tiburtina is redolent with underworld colouring coming from Aeneas' descent to the underworld in book 6 of the *Aeneid*. In his description of the cult paid to Hippolytus, Prudentius presents the altar tomb with its silver coverings (185ff.) and tells how piety congregates people from morning to evening to venerate the saint, their faces wet with tears. In the *Aeneid*, after his encounter with his dead father in the Underworld, Aeneas hears from him a detailed description of Rome's future greatness, including the encompassing of various peoples into Rome's *imperium* (*Aen.* 6.760-87). Prudentius' description of the various peoples drawn to Hippolytus' shrine likewise follows the initial encounter with the saint's tomb (191ff.); Romans, people from the Alban towns, Piceni, Etruscans, Samnites, people from Capua, from Nola, all come to venerate Hippolytus (e.g. 199-210). The initial veneration of the shrine before the presentation of the ensuing gathering of these various peoples on the saint's *dies natalis* ('day of birth', 196; it is his day of death) concludes with the words *fletibus ora rigant* 'they wet their faces with tears' (194). This seems a realistic touch in such an emotional gathering, with the kissing of the silver shrine covering and the ritual offering in the old Roman way of perfumed unguents. However, *fletibus ora rigant* are also words encoded with more than descriptive force.

In *Aeneid* 6.699ff., we read in the initial encounter of Aeneas and father Anchises that Aeneas *sic memorans largo fletu simul ora rigabat* ('going over these things he likewise bedewed his face with many tears'). Prudentius has unpacked this line in polyvalent ways. First, placement: as in the *Aeneid* it comes as part of the opening of the encounter between worshipper and saint, before the recital of the origins of those who come to the tomb. Next, the context in the *Aeneid* is central. There, Aeneas has tried in vain to embrace his father's *tristis imago* ('sad form'); the gap between dead father and living son cannot be closed, *effugit imago* ('the form disappears', 701). There can be no physical closure. In Prudentius, the faithful have present their spiritual father in all his power, and imprint kisses on his shrine as they weep, not because they cannot bridge the gap between him and them, but because of joy at his accessibility. In the *Aeneid* the dead are but *imago*; in the church they are present, effective to help, and evoke not the tears of frustrated longing but the tears of joyful reunion.

In *Aeneid* 6, Anchises has foreshadowed for Aeneas a future Rome based on greatness of *imperium* achieved by military and political leaders of stature and power. In Prudentius' *Peristephanon* 11, Hippolytus calls forth to his tomb not only a wide variety of peoples from Italy but also the various social classes. This *fides* ('faith') has reconfigured Rome, her society and her leading poet as well. The tears of Aeneas flowed in the epic because of estrangement from the progenitor who prophesies. The tears of the Christian flow in Prudentius' poem because of communion with the saint who makes a social reality out of Rome's earlier promises. The collocation of the Vergilian reminiscence *fletibus ora rigant* in a position between the worshipper meeting the saint and the cataloguing of the people drawn together by the power released by the saint underscores the positioning of Vergil's *fletu simul ora rigabat* between the frustrated encounter with the father and the father's foretold programme for Roman greatness culminating in Augustus himself.

Aeneas' trip up the Tiber to Evander's Rome in *Aeneid* 8 results in a tour of the city site as it was before Aeneas.[24] The reader visits with Aeneas the site of the future altar of Hercules, the Aventine hill, and so forth. Part of the delight the reader experiences is the tension between the then of the text and the now of the time of Vergil and his audiences. Something of the same sort is going on with Prudentius' description of the structure that in the poem supplements (in time it has replaced) the cramped cave of the underground tomb shrine (213). The original catacomb site grows into an

8. Recycled Words: Vergil, Prudentius and Saint Hippolytus

ordered space above ground, a *templum*, a holy site, the description of which allows considerable accuracy in inferring its details from architectural parallels surviving in reality. 'A double row of columns supports gilden beams upon which the panelled ceiling lies.'[25] There is a high and wide middle area to this larger church, and lower and narrower side areas.[26] It has been compared in lay-out to the near-by basilica maior of San Lorenzo fuori le mura.[27] Prudentius in his text moves from the simple underground grave site to the *templum* nearby (*iuxta*, 215) as Vergil likewise moves from the narrated site of Evander's Rome to the architecturally achieved city known by his audiences, both contemporary and subsequent.

In much the same way Prudentius has inscribed the journey of Hippolytus into the journey of Aeneas, but in reverse direction. Vergil's hero makes landfall at Ostia, the mouth of the Tiber.[28] After hostility is stirred up against him he makes his way upstream to the site of Rome, meets Evander, and eventually returns to the encamped fleet and the battle with Turnus and the Italians and Etruscans. Prudentius shows Roman civic power coming from the city in the person of the Roman official, going to Ostia and slaying Hippolytus, whose body with its spiritual power is translated back to Rome to confront its civic power with that of Christ whose witness Hippolytus is. The Christian Roman reader of Prudentius would be provided in Hippolytus with a trajectory inverse to that of the Roman world's hero par excellence. The same terrain is traversed, but to different ends: radically different ends indeed. In death Hippolytus conquers; in life Aeneas is victor but at a great price, that of his inner self.[29] What happened to Aeneas at Ostia and environs prepared for Rome's founding. What happened to Hippolytus at Ostia refounds another kind of Rome. As a recent critic puts it, Prudentius is 'building a holy city with words'.[30] The *patronus* ('patron') is now the martyr; the *clientes* ('clients') his devoted worshippers. A new Christian community is precipitated out of the Vergilian language.

The final two lines of the penultimate section bear close study. The *domus*, the church together with its adjacent tomb shrine, is shown:

> maternum pandens gremium, quo condat alumnos
> ac foveat fetos adcumulata sinus.

> [The church] offers her maternal lap to receive
> her children and cherish her offspring. (229-30)

One may ask if *foveat* governs both *alumnos* and *fetos*, or whether *fetos* is an adjective going with *sinus*: 'the church is packed in regard to her *sinus* which are filled with her young'. If the former, *adcumulata sinus* refers

137

basically to being packed to the corners with people. If the latter, the idea is gained that the church brings forth her young as well as cherishes them. In either case, this is an apt conclusion to the main narration of the poem because it brings us back to the opening, with its presentation of *tanti populi, innumeros cineres* ('so many people, innumerable remains', 1-5), at the opening of the text. The *plurima sepulcra* ('plethora of tombs', 7) are now seen at the end of the poem to be seeds of life. The martyr Hippolytus, together with his countless buried companions, now find their analogues in the living worshippers brought forth by the church and welcomed into her maternal embrace. *Roma mater*, as *rûma* ('the nursing breast'), is now not the civic construct of Vergil but the ecclesiastical entity of Prudentius. Vergil's civic historical abstraction now has a face, not the face of a personification but of a living organism, the people of God.

We have noted earlier that Aeneas' visit to Evander in *Aeneid* 8 is the foil for Prudentius' description of the transformation of the narrow cave of Hippolytus' tomb into the spacious basilica filled to overflowing by a gathering of Romans of all ranks and origins.[31] Prudentius concludes this poem by animadverting to a scene in *Aeneid* 9 which presents what is happening while Aeneas is visiting Evander at the site of what will become Rome. Aeneas has ordered his fellow Trojans to keep to the camp by their ships and not to issue forth if provoked to combat (40ff.). The Italians under Turnus seek to draw them forth, to no avail. Turnus, enraged, prowls like a wolf about the Trojan encampment (59ff.). Just as the Trojans, led by Aeneas and safe in their encampment against the antihistorical forces represented by Turnus, will go on to found Rome, so the Christians, led by their bishop and safe in their community, will prevail. Valerian is exhorted to incorporate the feast of Hippolytus with that of the martyrs Cyprian, Chelidonius and Eulalia, subjects of preceding poems in the *Peristephanon*. By this means Christ will hear Valerian's prayers for the people, those sheep entrusted to his care as bishop. In that way the wolf will be kept from the fold: that is to say, the weak remnant under siege will be victorious, a new people founding a new community. And in that way Prudentius himself will be no longer a weak sheep, an invalid Christian, but will be incorporated into the flock after his tarrying in the grassy field. And in that way, when Valerian comes to the end of his shepherding, his episcopate, and has filled the folds with snow-white sheep, he will be *raptus*, 'taken up' to be a colleague of Hippolytus in heaven.

> sic te pro populo, cuius tibi credita uita est,
> orantem Christus audiat omnipotens;   240
> sic tibi de pleno lupus excludatur ouili
> agna nec ulla tuum capta gregem minuat;
> sic me gramineo remanentem denique campo

8. Recycled Words: Vergil, Prudentius and Saint Hippolytus

>   sedulus aegrotam pastor ouem referas;
> sic, cum lacteolis caulas conpleueris agnis,   245
>   raptus et ipse sacro sis comes Hippolyto.

So may all-powerful Christ heed your prayers for the people entrusted to your care, by this means may the wolf be kept far from the well-filled sheepfold, so may no lamb stolen away make smaller your flock; so may you my dutiful shepherd carry me back in my weakness as I tarry in the grassy plain, so when you shall have filled the pens with snowy sheep may you be taken up as a colleague of blessed Hippolytus. (239-46)

The counter-historical wolf, the Italian forces resisting Aeneas' hegemony and the founding of universal Roman rule, did not prevail. Neither will the Christian flock under its bishops throughout the Roman world, fall away. And so the poem concludes with this amalgamation of pastoral imagery into epic grandeur. The sheep of the world of the *Eclogues* rise to poetry of the highest serious intent. The cult of Hippolytus will expand from Rome to Spain; Valerian and Prudentius as well as the people of God will benefit from his intercession, and *pulcherrima Roma* ('fairest Rome', 231), again is universalised, not in the military and political sphere betokened by Aeneas and Turnus, but in the spiritual.[32]

We have seen how Vergil impinges upon Prudentius in a variety of ways: the preponderant role played by language in the structure of the Christian faith and practice; the function of pictures and their literary ecphrases; the borrowing of words, phrases and scenes from Vergil, and the retrojecting of their new meaning and context in Prudentius back into Vergil's texts. In a real sense an awareness of what it meant to be a Roman, a grasp of what the possibilities were for civic identity, and a conception of a world united as a Roman construct (ideally, at any rate), were recuperable from Vergil's *Aeneid*, as well as from his other poems and the works of other writers as well. Vergil's Rome and its extension through time provides for Christians in the fourth century and beyond a focus for a new kind of patriotism.[33] In using Vergil, not least in the *Peristephanon* and its eleventh poem on Hippolytus, Prudentius is not quarrying a disused or obsolescent cultural relic but as it were defusing powerful ordnance and turning it into Christian ammunition.

Notes

1. e.g. Roberts (1993); Palmer (1989); Malamud (1989).
2. Charlet (1980).
3. Opelt (1970); Witke (1968).
4. Sixt (1892).
5. Mahoney (1934); Schwan (1937).
6. Shanzer (1989) 461.

7. See Bergmann (1926); *Index Imitationum* 455-69; Mahoney (1934).
8. Zanker (1988).
9. Palmer (1989) 140, 205; Charlet (1980) 207.
10. Roberts (1993) 150ff.
11. Roberts (1993) 151.
12. Mahoney (1934); Bergman (1926); Palmer (1989).
13. Elegiac couplets are used by Prudentius elsewhere only in the brief *Perist.* 8, but are suitable for the personal reminiscence of religious tourism, like Ovid in the *Fasti*.
14. Bergmann (1926); Mahoney (1934).
15. The line is one of the unfinished ones.
16. Novatus was an anti-pope doctrinally orthodox but in schism since the election of Pope Cornelius because of the latter's accommodation with those who in persecution renounced their faith. The name is usually Novatianus in the west, Novatus in Greek writers such as Eusebius and Socrates. Prudentius uses Novatus *causa metri*. He likewise follows the epigram of Damasus who makes this Hippolytus the Novatian schismatic who reconciled before dying in Sardinia and who was translated to Rome.
17. A nice reversal of Jupiter Optimus Maximus as *regnator Olympi* etc. in *Aeneid* e.g. 2.779; 5.537; 7.558; 10.437, 621; 12.791.
18. Cf. Ov. *Fast.* 5.259-60.
19. Testini (1977).
20. Bertonière (1985) 42.
21. Cf. Malamud (1989) 111.
22. *Aen.* 8.676, *cernere erat*.
23. Palmer (1989) 104-7 presents rather different criteria for assessing reminiscences of earlier authors.
24. See also Prudentius *Contra Orationem Symmachi* 1.550, where the curia of Evander rushes to Christian faith, and the rich civic imagery there.
25. Bertonière (1985) 39.
26. Bertonière (1985) 40.
27. Schumacher (1960) 1-15.
28. *Aen.* 7.30ff.
29. e.g. *Aen.* 11.435ff.
30. Roberts (1993) 187. He also sees (160) in Prudentius' journey through the catacomb to Hippolytus an analogue to his journey from Spain to Rome and back to Spain. However, Prudentius' proximate trip may be from Milan to Rome.
31. *Perist.* 11.213, 199ff., 215ff.
32. Prudentius seems to have been successful in introducing the cult of Hippolytus into north-east Spain, in the region of Tarragona; see Palmer (1989) 257-8.
33. Cf. Palmer (1989) 123.

9

sunt etiam Musis sua ludicra: Vergil in Ausonius

Gerard O'Daly

For Ted Kenney

I

Decimus Magnus Ausonius of Bordeaux, grammarian and rhetorician, tutor at Trier to the young son of the emperor Valentinian I – the future emperor Gratian – and consul in 379, creates a poetic oeuvre that gives expression to the diversity of his career as teacher and courtier. His long life spans most of the fourth century, from the reign of Constantine to that of Theodosius. He is still corresponding with his pupil Paulinus of Nola in 393.[1] He is known above all as the author of a poem in hexameters of over 480 verses in praise of the river Mosel (*Mosella*), but his writings range widely, and include epitaphs on his family and poems commemorating professorial colleagues, didactic and technical poems, epigrams, letters in verse, a sequence of poems on the daily round, possibly intended as a mime, and a Vergilian *cento*.[2] Learned, playful wit is a common characteristic of his poetry, as is a high level of virtuosity. Neither quality is inconsistent with sincerity or seriousness: 'The Muses also have their own fun' (*sunt etiam Musis sua ludicra*, *Protrepticus ad Nepotem* 1). The influence of Vergil is paramount, but Ausonius also owes much to the Horace of the *Odes*, to Martial and Statius, and he is generally well-read in Greek and Latin literature: Plautus and Terence, Ovid, Lucan, Juvenal, and the later poets Juvencus and Nemesianus are among his favourites. His Christianity has left limited traces in his writings, only a few of which reveal or allude to his religious affiliation.

II

Ausonius recalls how a fellow-grammarian at Bordeaux, Crispus, emulated passages of Vergil and Horace, allegedly under the influence of wine

(*Professores* 21.6-8): this suggests improvisation in a drinking-party atmosphere. Ausonius' own poetic playfulness leads him to compose a Cupid in the Underworld, the *Cupido cruciatus*, in which the influence of Vergil is acknowledged explicitly (*Cup.* 1), and where the context of *Aeneid* 6, and its language and themes, make of Cupid a paratragic Aeneas, emerging at the end through the gate of ivory from a tormented journey (*Cup.* 101-3). The poem is an extended *ekphrasis* of a painting of Cupid crucified by his mythical female victims, which Ausonius had seen in a house in Trier: Dido is one of these victims, but Ausonius' brief presentation of her is, tantalisingly, Ovidian rather than Vergilian (*Cup.* 37-9, echoing Ov. *Met.* 14.80). The use of Vergilian language in this poem is at some distance from the systematic redeployment of Vergil in the *cento nuptialis*, but the element of witty re-casting is common to both, and is a challenge to the sophisticated man of letters, as Ausonius himself acknowledges in the prose epilogue to the *cento*, where Vergil's propriety makes the reproduction of his poetry in a context that is irreverent and bawdy all the more exquisite (*cento* pp. 153.15-154.22).[3]

Witty transposition of Vergilian poetry is also found in Ausonius' exhortation to his grandson, also named Ausonius, to work hard at his studies. The farmer's 'wicker utensil' (*virgea ... supellex*) of *Georgics* 1.165 becomes the schoolmaster's cane (*Protrepticus ad Nepotem* 29-30), and the master himself is described in language that Vergil uses of the Atlas mountain in *Aeneid* 4.249 (*Protr.* 21). The breaking of colts at *Georgics* 3.207-8 is recast as a metaphor for education (*Protr.* 75-6).[4] More seriously, the concluding words of an exhortation spoken by Aeneas to his son Ascanius, *et pater Aeneas et avunculus excitet Hector* ('may your father Aeneas and your uncle Hector stir you!', *Aen.* 12.440) influence Ausonius' words, also closing a part of his poem, *proconsul genitor, praefectus avunculus instant* ('[may you go where] your father the proconsul and your uncle the prefect advance', *Protr.* 44), in which there is similar emphasis on family continuity and emulation of antecedents. Vergil, of course, features in the syllabus proposed for Ausonius junior (*Protr.* 57), and is characterised in the phrasing of Juvenal (*altisonumque ... Maronem*, 'heaven-sounding Vergil', *Protr.* 57, from Juvenal 11.180-1), just as Homer has been earlier evoked in Juvenal's words (*conditor Iliados*, 'creator of the *Iliad*', *Protr.* 46, from Juvenal 11.180): similarly *orsa Menandri* ('Menander's words') at *Protr.* 46 borrows from Statius *Silvae* 2.1.114. In the rich cluster of associations generated by Ausonius, Vergil, like Homer and Menander, is seen from the perspective of later poets. Vergil is situated in a late Latin context. This happens also in a birthday poem for the same grandson, where Martial's poem on Vergil (12.67) is imitated and upstaged by Ausonius. Martial had referred to the Ides of May and August, sacred to Mercury and Diana, as well as to the Ides of October, Vergil's birthday, and added *Idus saepe colas*

9. sunt etiam Musis sua ludicra: *Vergil in Ausonius*

et has et illas / qui magni celebras Maronis Idus ('May you often celebrate the former and the latter Ides, you who celebrate the Ides of great Vergil', 12.67.4-5). Ausonius, exploiting the fact that his grandson's birthday falls on the Ides of September, after similar references to Diana, Mercury and Vergil, writes *idus saepe colas bis senis mensibus omnes, / Ausonii quicumque mei celebraveris idus* ('May you often celebrate all the Ides of the twelve months, you who celebrate the Ides of my Ausonius', *Genethliacos* 26-7). His proud compliment is daring, linking an allusion to the monthly worship, *bis senos ... dies* ('on twelve days'), of the divinised Octavian/Augustus in Vergil, *Eclogues* 1.43-5[5] to auspicious celebration of Ausonius junior's birthday. Here again, praise of Vergil is mediated through a later poet's praise – Martial – but the 'trumping' of Martial is achieved by means of a subtle allusion to a Vergilian poem.

Ausonius is sensitive to Vergilian pathos. The theme of premature death in the *Aeneid* is subtly alluded to in his eulogies of dead professorial colleagues. At *Professores* 6.36-7 the rhetor Alethius Minervius is celebrated in an allusion to Marcellus (*Aen.* 6.869-70): Ausonius' *ostentatus / raptusque simul* ('no sooner displayed than snatched away') echoes Vergil's *ostendent ... hunc tantum fata* ('the fates will only grant a glimpse of him'). The early death of the grammarian Acilius Glabrio (*praereptus*, 'prematurely snatched away', *Prof.* 24.12) is evoked in a line (*tam decus omne tuis quam mox dolor*, 'as much a glory to your people as you were soon to be their sorrow', *Prof.* 24.11) that alludes both to Daphnis (*tu decus omne tuis*, 'you are all glory to your own folk', *Ecl.* 5.34) and to Pallas (*o dolor atque decus magnum ... parenti*, 'o sorrow and great glory to your father', *Aen.* 10.507). Pallas' death informs Ausonius' poem on the death of his young wife Sabina (*et dolor atque decus, Parentalia* 9.24),[6] as it does the poem on Veria (*parva ingentis luctus solacia*, 'small comfort in great grief', *Parent.* 16.11), where *Aen.* 11.62-3 (*solacia luctus / exigua ingentis*, 'scant comfort in great grief') is recast. A young boy's death is lamented in an allusion to the killing of Euryalus in *Aeneid* 9 (*quam tener et primo, nove flos, decerperis aevo, / nondum purpureas cinctus ephebe genas!*, 'how tender and fresh a flower, you are plucked in your first youth, a boy whose rosy cheeks are not yet fringed', *Parent.* 23.15-16; *purpureus veluti cum flos succisus aratro / languescit moriens*, 'as when a crimson flower, cut down by the plough, droops in death', *Aen.* 9.435-6, itself famously using Catullus 11.22-4) together with *ora puer prima signans intonsa iuventa* ('a boy showing on his unshaven face the first traces of young manhood', *Aen.* 9.181), with a skilful use of *purpureus* to refer, not to the flower of the metaphor, but to the boy's cheeks, undarkened by any beard growth.

Vergilian pathos can extend to the living as well as the dead. In *Pater ad filium* 11-15 allusions to the *Eclogues* and *Aeneid*, contexts that evoke the pain of erotic loss (*Ecl.* 7.43) and longing (*Ecl.* 8.87), as well as punishing torture (*Aen.* 6.739), are blended in an image of familial loss: the theme is Ausonius' separation from his son Hesperius. Here the Vergilian allusions provide an appropriate emotional and psychological range for the expression of feeling, in a passage that also echoes phrases of Martial and Statius.[7] In *Pater ad filium*, erotically charged language is transposed to the father-son relationship. Elsewhere, Ausonius can transpose the erotic to the context of *amicitia*. A verse letter to his protégé Paulinus of Nola ends (*Ep.* 24.124) with a full-line citation of *Ecl.* 8.108 (*credimus, an qui amant ipsi sibi somnia fingunt?* 'Can I believe it? Or do lovers make up their dreams?'). The positioning mirrors the place of the line in Vergil's poem, where it is the penultimate line, followed only by the refrain. Anxiety, hope, and conciliation inform the Vergilian context: will Daphnis return to his lover? The emotions transfer to the context of Ausonius' letter, which is part of an exchange in which Ausonius is defending his use of the pagan poets against the strictures, reflecting his adoption of a monastic life, of Paulinus. Earlier in the correspondence Ausonius had added the relationship of Nisus and Euryalus, celebrated in *Aen.* 5 and 9, to the standard exempla of Pylades and Orestes, and others, to reinforce the theme of his *amicitia* with Paulinus (*Ep.* 23.20), an allusion that is gently provocative in the light of Paulinus' austere critique. Paulinus' verse letter (Poem 11) replying to Ausonius *Ep.* 24, implicitly suggests that *Eclogue* 1, rather than *Eclogue* 8, is a context in which their relationship should be read: its themes of separation, different life-styles, and friendship provide both the means of distinguishing and reconciling their differences.[8]

Ausonius was a Christian. His religion rarely encroaches on his poetry. But Vergil's virgin warrior Camilla becomes an emblem of the Christian virginity of his aunt Julia Cataphronia at *Parent.* 26.3-4, where *virginitatis amorem / ... coluit* ('she fostered the love of virginity') is closely modelled on *Aeneid* 11.583-4.[9] In the Christian prayer *Ephemeris* 3, allusions to all three works of Vergil achieve different effects. Sometimes the phrasing is verbal memory.[10] But Ausonius can also re-code a Vergilian phrase, as at *Ephemeris* 3.28, where *virtutes patrias* ('the father's powers/virtues') is an *interpretatio Christiana* of *Eclogue* 4.17, and the Vergilian context, referring to the divine son of a divine father, is crucial.[11] A Vergilian hero is recast in biblical form at *Ephemeris* 3.41, where Elijah borrows Latinus' chariot from *Aeneid* 12.162. Most striking of all is the use at *Ephemeris* 3.57 (*patiturque suos mens saucia manes*, 'the distressed mind suffers its own haunting') of the difficult Vergilian phrase *quisque suos patimur manis* ('each of us suffers his own haunting', *Aen.* 6.743) in a purgatorial sense that may reflect Vergil's meaning, even if Ausonius is referring to pre-death penance and repentance.[12]

Ausonius' interest in his dreams reveals him as a man of his time. In an

9. sunt etiam Musis sua ludicra: *Vergil in Ausonius*

incompletely transmitted poem (*Ephem.* 8), he dreams some characteristically Roman dreams – he is attacked by a wild beast in the arena, or wins a sword-fight there,[13] he is a prisoner dragged through the streets in a triumph – and the ideological context of his dreams is Vergilian. *Ephemeris* 8.22-6 alludes to the elm to which false dreams cling of *Aeneid* 6.282-4, and to the ivory and horn gates of sleep of *Aeneid* 6.893-6, combining them at *Ephemeris* 8.37 with the simplicity of Evander's hut (*Aen.* 8.366), with Ausonius' life-style thus evoked as a safeguard against evil dreams.[14] The poem ends with the dedication to dreams of a real elm-grove: the Vergilian underworld fantasy impinges wittily on Ausonius' world. He reads his elms in a Vergilian way.

Vergil is, for Ausonius, also the poet of political and imperial eulogy. Invited by the emperor Theodosius to do like the poets of the time of Augustus, and praise him,[15] Ausonius writes what is 'in spirit a *recusatio*'[16] but none the less conflates two Vergilian verses to magnify Theodosius' achievement:

Praefationes variae 3.21:
    tu ... pater Romane, memento
    ('you, father of Rome, remember')
Aeneid 6.851:
    tu ... Romane, memento
    ('you, Roman, remember')
Aeneid 9.449:
    ... imperiumque pater Romanus habebit
    ('the father of Rome will hold power')

This dual allusion combines the articulation of Rome's imperial mission in *Aeneid* 6 with the eulogy of Nisus and Euryalus, a part of the *Aeneid*, which, as we have already seen, is among Ausonius' favourite texts.[17]

The emperor Gratian, Ausonius' pupil, evidently dabbled in verse. Ausonius refers to a poem of his on Achilles and Penthesilea (*Precationes variae* 1.12-17), evoking Gratian's transition from warfare to poetry by alluding to Vergil's Sixth *Eclogue*, and referring wittily to Gratian's skills as an archer: *commutata meditatur harundine carmen* ('putting the reed to new use he composes a poem', *Prec. var.* 1.13); cf. *Ecl.* 6.8.[18] But Ausonius immediately qualifies his allusion to pastoral here by adding that Gratian's poem is *carmen non molle modis: bella horrida Martis / ... retractat* ('a poem not gentle in its measures: he deals again with the frightful wars of Mars', *Prec. var.* 1.14-15), thereby embracing at once Horace's famous judgement of the *Eclogues* as *molle atque facetum* ('gentle and whimsical', *Ser.* 1.10.44) and the *bella horrida bella* ('wars, frightful wars') of *Aen.* 6.86. In the *Gratiarum actio*, the speech that was the climax of Ausonius' consulship of 379, Gratian is eulogised by an allusion to the *omnia deo plena* ('everything is full of god') motif, echoing perhaps Vergil's *Iovis omnia plena* ('everything is full of Jupiter', *Ecl.* 3.60), and using a theme characteristic of late imperial panegyric (*Grat. act.* 5).[19] In *Gratiarum actio* 65 Vergil and Nemesianus are anonymously combined in an allusion to *Aeneid* 4.41: the *Numidae infreni* ('Numidians who use no reins') a wonder of epic poetry, become a reality when Gratian lets go of the reins to use his bow on horseback. The improbable becomes miraculously real, and the emperor fulfils a Vergilian reference.

III

Eulogy of the emperor is also a feature of Ausonius' masterpiece, the *Mosella*, the poem that, in addition, contains his most sophisticated allusions to Vergil. At *Mosella* 4 Vergilian echoes (several, most notably *Aen.* 6.325 ... *inops inhumataque turba est* ['all this crowd ... is helpless and unburied'] and 11.372 *inhumata infletaque turba* ['a crowd unburied and unlamented']) are found: referring to the battle of Bingen of AD 70, Ausonius writes *infletaeque iacent inopes super arva catervae* ('the hordes lie unlamented and helpless on the fields'). The first lines of the poem introduce several of its themes, and also some of its apparent contradictions. The opening *transieram* ... ('I had crossed ...', *Mos.* 1) recalls the informality of a Horatian *sermo* (*ibam ... via Sacra* ..., 'I was walking along the Sacred Way', *Ser.* 1.9.1), but we are almost immediately transported to military matters, with references to the walls of Bingen built by the emperor Julian in 359, and the battle of Bingen is itself hyperbolically compared with Cannae (*Mos.* 3), the first of several comparisons that magnify the importance of the Mosel region by linking it to events and places in Italy. In this context, references to the unburied dead who fell in battle are not out of place. We must read *Mos.* 4 as a historic present. The theme is none the less puzzling. The allusion to *Aeneid* 6 has been rightly seen to be crucial here. What we have is the first moment of a recreation of Ausonius' journey from the Nahe to the Mosel in terms of Aeneas' journey through the underworld. Ausonius as poet-narrator replicates the journey of Vergil's fictional hero. This Ausonius-Aeneas identification operates on a more limited scale at *Ordo urbium nobilium* 163, where Ausonius cites *Aeneid* 3.714 (*hic labor extremus*, 'this (was) my last task'). Aeneas is signalling the end of his long narrative in *Aeneid* 2-3; Ausonius the end of his poem. To return to the *Mosella*, if *Mosella* 5 (*unde iter*, 'From there my way') alludes to *Aeneid* 3.507 (*unde iter Italiam*, 'From there is the way to Italy'), we have another blending of the personae of the *Mosella* narrator and Aeneas-as-narrator. But whether this last reference is accepted or not, there is an undoubted epic colouring to the opening part of

146

9. sunt etiam Musis sua ludicra: *Vergil in Ausonius*

the *Mosella*, sustained in the following lines. *Mosella* 10, where Ausonius reaches Neumagen, at the confluence of Dhron and Mosel, *et tandem ... oris* ('and at last ... on the margin') echoes the arrival of Aeneas at Cumae, in *Aeneid* 6.2.[20] Arrival at the river itself is announced by an allusion to the Elysium of *Aeneid* 6: *purior hic campis aer Phoebusque sereno / lumine purpureum reserat iam sudus Olympum* ('the air is here clearer on the plains, and Phoebus, now cloudless, reveals bright heaven with calm light', *Mos.* 12-13) echoes *largior hic campos aether et lumine vestit / purpureo* ('here the sky is wider and clothes the plains with bright light', *Aen.* 6.640-1). Ovid's underworld also informs these lines: Orpheus' return from Hades is *per muta silentia trames / caligine ...* ('a path through the soundless silence in the dark', *Met.* 10.53-4), and these words are echoed in Ausonius' *nec iam consertis per mutua vincula ramis / ... caligine* ('no longer with branches intertwined, each linked to the other ... in the dark', *Mos.* 14-15).[21] And the scene is 'epicised' by the echo of *Aeneid* 11.187, describing funeral pyres, *conditur ... caligine caelum* ('the sky is hidden in the dark'), in *Mosella* 15 *quaeritur ... caligine caelum* ('the sky is sought in the dark'), as Ausonius-narrator emerges from the *viridi caligine* ('green dark') of the forests into the brightness of the river landscape. In *Mosella* 14-17 several passages in the *Aeneid* evoking dark foliage, crags and pathways have been identified as influences on Ausonius' language, though there are no close or sustained verbal echoes.[22]

Yet the *Mosella* is evidently not an epic, despite the emphatic positioning of its opening seventeen lines in an epic-related context. Why is Ausonius so deliberately post-Vergilian here, and why, given the allusions to the thematically closer *Georgics* and *Eclogues* which follow, does he insist on using the *Aeneid* so much in this part of the poem? The attempt to answer these questions will occupy much of the rest of this chapter.[23]

The description of the river begins in *Mosella* 20, and Ausonius' allusiveness shifts from the *Aeneid* to the *Eclogues* and, above all, the *Georgics*. The reference to *culmina villarum* ('the roofs of houses') in *Mosella* 20 recalls *Eclogues* 1.82,[24] and *culmina ... pendentibus edita ripis* ('roofs ... perched on the overhanging banks', *Mos.* 20) is the first of several allusions in the poem to the *laudes Italiae* of *Georgics* 2 (here 2.156 *tot congesta manu praeruptis oppida saxis*, 'so many towns built by human hand on sheer rocks').[25] Here syntactical parallelism and general thematic similarity suggest the allusion: that Ausonius has this Vergil passage in mind is shown by the influence of *Georgics* 2.157 (*fluminaque antiquos subterlabentia muros*, 'and rivers flowing beneath ancient walls') on *Mosella* 22 (*subterlabentis tacito rumore Mosellae*, 'the Mosel gliding beneath with low murmur').[26] The hymnic section that follows (*Mos.* 23-6) echoes *Georgics* 2.173-4 (*salve, magna parens frugum ... / magna virum*, 'Greetings, great mother of crops, great mother of men'), and Ausonius imitates Vergil's use of repetition (*amnis ... laudate ... laudate ... amnis ... consite ... consite ... amnis*) – though *Mosella* 381 is more closely constructed on the Vergilian model. *Mosella* 26 (*... amnis viridissime, ripas*, 'river most green ... banks') adds river-description detail from *Georgics* 3.144 (*viridissima gramine ripa*, 'the bank most green with grass'), with *amnis* echoing the sound of *gramine*. This concentrated allusion imports a Vergilian natural world into the *Mosella*. There is more than descriptive coincidence here. The Mosel region is textually transformed. Ausonius' descriptive narrative links it, here by implicit analogy, to the supreme model, the Italy of the *Georgics*.

This allusive concentration is really only matched in the concluding part of the *Mosella*. But there are other Vergilian clusters, of which the most striking is the virtuoso recasting of the section on the vine in *Georgics* 2.89-108, especially 97-108, in Ausonius' section on fish in *Mosella* 77-149.[27] The motif of the varieties that cannot be numbered or named is common to *Georgics* 2.103-4 and *Mosella* 77-80. There is common vocabulary in both passages: *contende*, 'compete with' (*Geo.* 2.96) and *contendere* (*Mos.* 117) – underlining the rivalry theme; *durare*, 'last' (*Geo.* 2.100) and *duraturus* (*Mos.* 87); a similar use of future participles (*temptatura ... vincturaque*, 'sure to trouble ... and to try', *Georgics* 2.94 and *duraturus ... nociturus*, 'sure to last ... to harm', *Mos.* 87-9); and the use of the same transitional formula at *Geo.* 2.101-2 (*non ego te ... / transierim*, 'I could not pass you over') and *Mosella* 97-8 (*nec te ... transierim*). Once the relation of the *Mosella* passage to the *Georgics* is realised, we can appreciate the verbal and rhetorical tour de force that links these disparate narratives.

There may be a reminiscence of *Aeneid* 6.800 (*et septemgemini turbant trepida ostia Nili*, 'and the mouths of the sevenfold Nile surge fearfully') at *Mosella* 92 (*qua bis terna fremunt scopulosis ostia pilis*, 'where the mouths roar at the six rocklike piers'), where the confluence of the Saar and Mosel is described. A more certain linking of Saar and Nile is at *Mosella* 367-8 *Saravus / tota veste vocat*, 'the Saar calls, with robe spread out', which is informed by *Aeneid* 8.711-12 *Nilum / ... tota veste vocantem*, 'the Nile calling with robe spread out': this is another instance of the motif already noted – the eulogising of all that is splendid in the region by comparison with supreme models in the wider world, and, importantly, in Vergil's text.

A detail of the Trojans rowing up the Tiber, the phrase *viridisque secant placido aequore silvas* ('and they cut through the green woods on the calm surface', *Aen.* 8.96), understood by Servius ad loc. to refer to the reflected woods in the water, is magnificently developed at *Mosella* 189-99, but Ausonius is probably also influenced by descriptions of reflections in Statius.[28] The fact that this has become a descriptive topos by Ausonius' day arguably weakens the specific link with Vergil's phrase: but the atmosphere of this part of *Aeneid* 8 – the magical journey through a river

9. sunt etiam Musis sua ludicra: *Vergil in Ausonius*

waterworld – undoubtedly informs this passage. Ausonius brilliantly uses verbal repetition to represent reflection at *Mosella* 198-9: *qua sese amni confundit imago / collis et umbrarum confinia conserit amnis*, 'where the reflection of the hill blends with the river and the river joins the bordering shadows'.[29] Vergilian water imagery influences the description of the Rhine at *Mosella* 418-19: *caeruleos ... sinus hyaloque virentem / ... peplum* ('azure folds and robe green as glass'). Here the use of Vergil's coinage of the latinised Greek word for glass, *hyalus*, otherwise found only in late Latin (Prudentius *Peristephanon* 12.53, describing mosaics, is another instance), undoubtedly alludes to the underwater world of Cyrene and her fellow-nymphs in *Georgics* 4, where the nymphs spin glass-green wool (*... vellera ... / ... hyali saturo fucata colore*, 'fleeces dyed the colour of glass', *Geo.* 4.334-5). Ausonius evokes this underwater world, not merely by using the word *hyalus*, but by embedding it in a reference to the robe of the river-god of the Rhine that alludes to the spinning of wool for garments in Vergil.

Vergil's narratives of the Cumae region are alluded to in various passages of the *Mosella*. The Cumae of *Aeneid* 3.442 (*divinosque lacus et Averna sonantia silvis*, 'the sacred lakes and Avernus' echoing woods') is echoed at *Mosella* 216 (*Euboicae ... per Averna sonantia cumbae*, 'Euboean boats on the echoing Avernus'), with strongly similar line endings. The Daedalus-Icarus theme of *Aeneid* 6.14-33, and the temple built by Daedalus at Cumae, is the context of *Mosella* 300-2, with 301-2 (*casus quem fingere in auro / conantem Icarios patrii pepulere dolores*, 'a father's grief frustrated him as he tried to fashion in gold the fall of Icarus') modelled on *Aeneid* 6.31-3 (*dolor ... / bis conatus erat casus effingere in auro, / bis patriae cecidere manus*, 'twice he tried to fashion in gold the fall; twice a father's hands failed'). At *Mosella* 345-8 the Mosel is described as a 'small-scale' (*exilia*) imitation of Baiae, and, even if the model here is Statius *Silvae* 1.5.60-2, what is significant is the linking – again – of the Mosel region and Campania.[30] The influence of *Aeneid* 6 is found again in the sound echo of *Aeneid* 6.327 *rauca fluenta*, 'hoarse-sounding waters' at *Mosella* 349 *glauca fluenta*, 'azure waters'; cf. *Mosella* 21 *amoena fluenta*, 'pleasant waters', but there is no necessary intertextual link to Vergil's Hades here, beyond the verbal reminiscence.[31]

At *Mosella* 381 (*salve, magne parens frugumque virumque, Mosella*, 'greetings, Mosel, great parent of crops and men') the hymnic mode (with *te* anaphora in 382-3) signals the start of the concluding part of the poem, but also reiterates the allusion to the *laudes Italiae* of *Georgics* 2 that dominated *Mosella* 20-3, with close echoing of *Georgics* 2.173 (*salve, magna parens frugum, Saturnia tellus*, 'greetings, great parent of crops, Saturnian land'). The themes of *Mosella* 381-8 reflect those of *Georgics* 2.167-74:[32] the *clari proceres* ('famous nobility') of *Mosella* 382 correspond to the named Roman heroes, from the Decii to Augustus, in Vergil; the *bello exercita pubes* ('youth trained in war', *Mosella* 382) corresponds to the *genus acre virum* ('energetic breed of men', *Geo.* 2.167), again with Vergil naming specific peoples. But *Mosella* 383 singles out the *facundia* ('eloquence') of the region, echoing a theme beloved of panegyric – Gallic eloquence. Ausonius the rhetor sets the record straight, and defends the much maligned Gallo-Romans.[33] A new Latin eloquence has developed in Gaul, and the theme is embedded in an intertext with Vergil's eulogy of Italy. The comparison motif is reinforced. Ausonius is not attempting to outdo Vergil,[34] but Gaul is 'repositioned' as a true representative of Rome and its values: *Mosella* 384-5 asserts that *mores et laetum fronte severa / ingenium natura tuis concessit alumnis* ('nature has given to your children morals and a cheerful character with a grave appearance').[35]

The themes of praise, autobiographical *sphragis*, and *recusatio* come together at *Mosella* 392-3, with its citation of a phrase of Vergil's *sphragis* (*Geo.* 4.559-66), *ignobilis oti* ('inglorious leisure'),[36] bringing the achievement of the *Mosella* and that of the *Georgics* into proximity. The Vergilian *sphragis* also informs *Mosella* 438-44, from the *haec ego* of 438 (similar beginning at *Geo.* 4.559) to *audax* at 443 (as at *Geo.* 4.565). Ausonius names himself at *Mosella* 440, as Vergil does at *Geo.* 4.563. At this stage of the poem Ausonius also situates it generically: *Mosella* 443-4 asserts that *exigua fide concino ... / ... tenui libamine Musae* ('I sing to humble strings ... a slight offering of poetry'). The reference may be to poetry like Vergil's *Eclogues*, where *tenuis* ('slight') is a technical term for a particular type of poetry;[37] but it can also refer to the *Georgics* (e.g. *Geo.* 4.6), and it is in keeping with the *recusatio* element of *Mosella* 392-417, which anticipates major panegyric, in a section that has the same thematic function as Vergil's proem in *Geo.* 3.10-39.

As in the opening part of the poem, Vergilian allusions in concentrated form dominate the conclusion of the *Mosella*. Again, the *laudes Italiae* of *Georgics* 2 is prominent. At *Mosella* 454-8 the repeated *addam urbes ... addam ... addam* ('I shall tell in addition of cities ... and I shall tell ...') echoes *adde ... urbes* (*Geo.* 2.155). And *Georgics* 2.157 (*fluminaque antiquos subterlabentia muros*, 'rivers flowing under ancient walls') is reflected in *Mosella* 454-5 (*urbes, tacito quas subterlaberis alveo, / moeniaque antiquis te prospectantia muris*, 'cities under which you glide in your hushed channel, and forts that look on to you with ancient walls'). But *addam urbes* in the proem to *Georgics* 3 (3.30) is also part of Ausonius' context. Vergilianisms enrich his text here: *Mosella* 460 is a Vergilian hexameter cited in its entirety (= *Aen.* 8.63, where it refers to the Tiber: Ausonius is again linking Gaul with Italy), as well as characteristically enclosing a line with two participles in the same case (cf. *Mos.* 393; and e.g. in Vergil, *Geo.* 4.501, *Aen.* 6.657). And *hominumque boumque labores* ('the

9. sunt etiam Musis sua ludicra: Vergil in Ausonius

work of men and cattle') at *Mosella* 459 is from *Georgics* 1.118. Finally, there is a cluster of Vergilian phrases and words at *Mosella* 466-9.[38]

If Aeneas in Hades is the principal intertext of the opening lines of the poem, as Ausonius makes his way from the Nahe to the Mosel, the celebration of the natural world (*naturae mirabor opus*, 'I shall wonder at nature's work', *Mos.* 51) that is at the heart of the *Mosella* is fused with Vergil's praise of the countryside of Italy in the *Georgics* – the dominant intertext of the early part of the praises of the Mosel and of the poem's later sections. It is clear from the above analysis that we cannot reduce this interplay of texts to mere rhetorical and stylistic emulation: the presence of Vergil's text in Ausonius' poem is part of the *Mosella*'s meaning. We have seen that this presence is wide-ranging, reflecting the scope of Vergil's three works (though the presence of the *Eclogues* in the *Mosella* is the least developed of the three).[39] The allusions to the *Aeneid* focus chiefly on *Aeneid* 6, and here the intertext develops the themes of the narrator as epic persona, of the journey through a dark and perilous region to a revelation of a bright and brilliant world (Elysium-Mosel), and of a privileged Italian landscape – Campania – recreated in Gaul. By implication, the *Aeneid* intertext also imports an imperial, neo-Augustan colouring into the world of the Mosel, a place at once of peace and of war: though a eulogistic passage like *Mosella* 420-6 owes as much, if not more, to the proem of *Georgics* 3 as it does to Vergilian epic.

At the same time, the Vergilian dimension must be understood in the context of the *Mosella* as a whole. Recent scholarship has uncovered important intertextuality with Statius in Ausonius' poem: no full interpretation of the poem can ignore this dimension. Scholars are too anxious to find a single key to the poem's meaning, whether it be the interplay of ambivalently true and false images (*Mos.* 239), or the theme of boundaries and their violation, or praise of a natural world that cannot be undermined by human violence, with humans removed to the periphery of that world.[40] All these interpretations have the merit of taking the poem seriously and being attentive to its subtleties. It is beyond the scope of this chapter to offer a full interpretation of the *Mosella*. But the Vergilian dimension suggests that, if we uncover Ausonius' interpretation of the *Georgics*, in particular, we shall understand Ausonius better. In the light of recent scholarship, we can no longer assume that Vergil's poem of the countryside implies a uniformly benevolent relationship between humans and the natural world, or that Vergil is indifferent to the beauty of natural landscapes, independently of their human exploiters. The tension between the intrusive cultural invasion of nature that farming entails and the pristine natural environment is strong in Vergil, writing in the immediate aftermath of civil war.[41] There is no reason to doubt that Ausonius understood this tension, or that he found in Vergil a model vision of a natural world resistant to, but not unaffected by, human aggression. For these reasons, the *Georgics* could become a template for the *Mosella*. It is, of course, true that the poetic sequel that Ausonius imagines in his *recusatio* is not the kind of imperial panegyric that Vergil imagines in the proem to *Georgics* 3, even if Ausonius also envisages praising a good political leader. Peace and plenty will be his principal themes (fortresses become granaries, *Mos.* 457), and the natural world will continue to be the focus of Ausonius' poetry, and the means of praise (*Mos.* 438-68). But this complex of themes also has its counterpart in the *Georgics*.[42] Moreover, Ausonius' critique of the art and technology praised in Statius' villa poetry brings him closer to Vergil and the moralising tone of Augustan poetry, rather than distancing him from it. The damage done by humans to nature is undoubtedly a central theme of his poem, but it is a theme that cannot, and need not, be divorced from his Vergilian readings.

The *Mosella* is the artistic climax of Ausonius' poetry, and also the most sophisticated example of his Vergilianism. The variety and range of his interplay with Vergil is characteristic of a poem that defies unitary interpretation. In that respect, the *Mosella* displays in microcosm the variety and range, from comic to serious, from meditative to parodic, of Ausonius' engagement with the *divinus vates* ('divine poet', *Ephem.* 8.22).[43]

Notes

1. For Ausonius' career see Kaster (1988) 247-9; Sivan (1993). Correspondence with Paulinus: *Ep*. 17-24.

2. Green (1999) – the OCT – is now the standard edition, and its page numbers and ordering and sequence of Ausonius' works are followed in this chapter; Green (1991) provides an extended and masterly commentary. Prete (1978) is less reliable than Green, but includes wide-ranging references to antecedents. Evelyn White (1919, 1921) provides the only adequate English translation (and I acknowledge its help with the translations provided in this chapter), but it is seriously outdated. I acknowledge gratefully the Vergilian citations and allusions identified by Green and Prete, as well as by Hosius (1926); Posani (1962); Green (1977); Kay (2001); and, for the *Mosella*, above all Görler (1969): I do not claim to identify significant new Vergilian allusions, but I have more and different things to say about them than my predecessors. Consoli (1995) is disappointing, drawing a simplistic distinction between intertextuality and originality in Ausonius. Hinds (1998) is a brilliant programmatic work for all future studies of allusion and intertextuality in Latin poetry: his reconstruction of authorial intention has influenced me here. – References to *Eclogues* and *Ecl.* are to Vergil's book, and not to Ausonius' collection of poems (on the calendar and other miscellaneous topics) of the same title.

3. Cf. *Ep*. 12, p. 232.22. In *Epigr*. 75.8 *Aen*. 4.415 *ne quid inexpertum frustra moritura relinquat* ('that she might not leave anything untried, and face her death in vain'), on Dido's despairing love, is cited verbatim (a rare full-line citation outside the *cento*) in an obscene context, (a use of Vergil already established in

9. sunt etiam Musis sua ludicra: *Vergil in Ausonius*

Petronius 132.11: see Kay [2001] 221-2). Dido in the underworld (*Aen.* 6.454) lies behind the witty account of a patient's revenge on his doctor at *Epigr.* 79.3.

4. Cf. *Ludus Septem Sapientum* 9-10, where *Geo.* 3.186 and 208 relate the breaking of horses metaphorically to the poet's dealing with criticism and praise.

5. Cf. Clausen (1994) 48-9.

6. *Parent.* 9.7-9 echoes Dido's grief for Sychaeus (*Aen.* 4.17) and Juno's anguish at the Trojans' progress (*Aen.* 10.507), the latter allusion reminding us that the striking phrase in isolation, rather than the context, can often generate an allusion.

7. See Green (1991) 286.

8. Vergil in Paulinus, Poem 11: Roberts (1985). For the correspondence between Ausonius and Paulinus see Witke (1971) 3-74; Trout (1999) 78-89; Conybeare (2000) 147-57.

9. Note the coincidence of word-position: *virginitatis amorem* at line end in both instances; *colit* before caesura in Vergil, *coluit* at line end in Ausonius.

10. *Ephem.* 3.19-20, 34-5, 85, echoing respectively *Aen.* 7.578 and 1.8, *Geo.* 2.58, and *Aen.* 5.140-1, if *aethera* is read at *Ephem.* 3.85 with Green.

11. On the *interpretatio Christiana* of Vergil's fourth *Eclogue* see Benko (1980).

12. Cf. *manes* at *Prof.* 3.13, where *Aen.* 6.743 may again be alluded to: *manes* here certainly does not have the meanings ('souls of the dead', 'shade of the individual dead') that it usually has in *Prof.*; see Green (1991) 336.

13. There may be Christian echoes here of Perpetua's dreams in *Passio sanctarum Perpetuae et Felicitatis*: Green (1991) 263. Dreams and visions in late Latin literature: Amat (1985).

14. The words *angusti ... tecti* are placed in the same line position as in Vergil – before caesura and at line end – by Ausonius.

15. Theodosius' letter is reprinted in Green (1991) 707.

16. Green (1991) 240.

17. Note the use of Vergil's words in the same line position.

18. Gratian's archery is attested elsewhere in Ausonius: Green (1991) 533 refers to *Epigr.* 2 and 6. Gratian as sportsman-fighter: *Grat. Act.* 64.

19. Cf. *Pan. Lat.* XI(3).14.2 on Maximian, cited by Green (1991) 540. On use of this tag in Latin panegyric see Rees (2002) 16-17, 88 and above, Chapter 2.

20. Note that *et tandem ... oris* are in the same framing position in the line in both Vergil and Ausonius.

21. Note how Ausonius' *mutua* echoes the sound of Ovid's *muta*; cf. Ovid, *Met.* 4.433 (of an underworld river) *per muta silentia sedes*.

22. Cf. *Aen.* 1.164-5; 7.565-6; 8.95-9, 597-9; 9.86-7, 381-3; 11.522-5; (Görler (1969) 99 n.3).

23. Görler (1969) 87 with n. 2 refers to depictions of extreme contrasts in journey literature (Horace *Ser.* 1.5 is the obvious example): but there is more than that in play in *Mos.*

24. For the use of the phrase by Silius, Martial and Juvenal see Hosius (1926) 30.

25. Cf. Horace *Ser.* 1.5.26: *impositum saxis late candentibus Anxur*.

26. For *rumor* see Vergil *Aen.* 8.90 with Fordyce (1977) ad loc.

27. See Görler in Lossau (1991) 175.

28. Cf. Wilson (1995), and, for the Statius passages, Green (1991) 485.

29. On the technique of prepositional repetition see Wills (1996) 437-8.

30. The 'little Troy' of *Aen.* 3.349-50, which Helenus shows to Aeneas and his fellow-Trojans, may have had some influence here.

31. Link to Vergil's Hades: Görler (1969) 103: but see Green (1991) 500.
32. Cf. Görler (1969) 108.
33. Cf. Green (1991) 504.
34. As Görler (1969) 108-9 suggests.
35. Cf. Green (1991) 504 for *mores laeti* in *Ordo* 37 and *laetitia* in *Prof.* and *Parent. laetus* is a favourite word in Vergil's *Georgics*: for its meanings there see Mynors (1990) 230.
36. Cf. also *Praef.* 5.15.
37. Cf. *mollia ... carmina ... / ... tenuique ... subtemine*, *Mos.* 396-7; *tenui ... camenae*, *Mos.* 474. For *tenuis* as a poetic concept in Vergil's *Ecl.* see Clausen (1994) xxv, 175; cf. *Ecl.* 1.2; 6.8.
38. Cf. Green (1991) 513.
39. See Green above, Chapter 1.
40. Ambivalent images: Fontaine (1977); boundaries and violation: Roberts (1984); a natural world with humans removed to the periphery: Newlands (1988), and, to a lesser extent, Green (1989). Kenney (1984) strikes a judicious balance in discussing Ausonius' debt to Statius. Roberts (1989) is a remarkable analysis of the miniaturist element in late Latin poetry, including *Mos*.
41. See especially Thomas (1982) 35-69, (1988) 1.179-90; Mynors (1990) 29-30, 268-70, 319. On nature and landscape in the context of Vergil's poetry see Jenkyns (1998).
42. See especially *Geo*. 2.458-540 with 1.493-7. Conversely, civil strife is reflected in neglect of the land: *Geo*. 1.506-8. Shanzer (1998) 292-6 discusses the linking of political and nature themes in propaganda contexts in Claudian, Ammianus, Symmachus and *Mos*.
43. For Servius on *Aen*. 3.463 Vergil is *poeta divinus*.

10

Claudian, Vergil and the Two Battles of Frigidus

Catherine Ware

This chapter is an attempt to solve a literary puzzle: Claudian's description of the Battle of Frigidus. The details of the battle itself are straightforward.[1] Arbogast, *magister militum* and Frank, elevated his puppet Eugenius to the purple. He had the support of Nicomachus Flavianus, praetorian prefect of Italy and a member of a prominent pagan senatorial family. In September 394, Arbogast's army marched as far as the Alps. Their actions on the journey were self-consciously ideological. Statues were erected to Jupiter along the route while the soldiers carried images of Hercules: these imperial symbols indicated that under Eugenius the traditional pagan *mos maiorum* would be restored. The rebels met Theodosius' army at the river Frigidus. The Christian emperor Theodosius spent the night before battle in watchful prayer *corpore humi fusus, mente caelo fixus* ('his body lying on the ground, his mind fixed on heaven').[2] Theodosius was victorious and as a joke (*hilariter*), distributed the golden thunderbolts among his men.[3] He forgave the families of his enemies and allowed them to convert to Christianity. Under the circumstances, it is not surprising that the battle should have been hailed instantly as the final triumph of Christianity over paganism.[4]

The imperial victory was naturally lauded by the court poet and Claudian gives the battle prominence in two poems, his panegyrics on Honorius' third consulship (in 396) and fourth consulship (in 398):[5] the success of the panegyric of 396 is indicated by the fact that Augustine and Orosius quote Claudian in their description of the victory. (Orosius was working from Augustine's version). Both omit the same line (96-7) and attribute the victory to the Christian God:

> o nimium dilecte deo, cui militat aether,
> et coniurati veniunt ad classica venti!

> O well beloved of God, for whom heaven fights,
> and the winds come as allies to your trumpet call!⁶

Here lies the puzzle. In Claudian's account, Frigidus is won because Aeolus fights on the emperor's side, and his battle-scene appears to be a reworking of Vergil's storm in the *Aeneid*. Christianity has no place in the description of the battle. Whether Claudian himself was pagan or not is irrelevant: this was the last victory of a devoutly Christian emperor and was widely recognised as a specifically Christian victory, yet in two panegyrics Claudian describes the occasion in Vergilian terms and his poems were successful. Why was a Vergilian, pagan interpretation of an uncompromisingly Christian victory so acceptable to the Christian court?

The answer lies in politics. As Cameron has demonstrated, Claudian used his poetry to support the politics of his patron Stilicho, the regent of the emperor Honorius and *magister utriusque militiae*.⁷ Levy posed the practical question: with what segments of the public did Stilicho's regime stand in special need of the work of a publicist?⁸ His conclusion was that 'the one group with which it was both feasible and possibly advantageous for Claudian's pen to support Stilicho's sword was the pagan aristocracy of the old capital'.⁹ This was the group most resistant to the ascendancy of Stilicho, who after the death of Theodosius was regent in the West but was both Christian and Vandal. Bypassing Stilicho's religion and parentage therefore, Claudian praises him for the possession of the cardinal virtues (*Stil.* 2.6-49), his likeness to the heroes of ancient Rome (*VI Cons.* 489-90) and his reverence for the *mos maiorum*. In short, he makes Stilicho into a fully fledged Roman of old in his character and actions.

Although Levy was specifically concerned with the role of Stilicho in Claudian's work, his conclusion is equally valid when considering the panegyrics on the young emperor Honorius: Claudian had to convince the pagan aristocracy of Rome that Honorius was the right and proper person for the office and therefore his portrayal of Honorius' father, Theodosius the Great, also had to be carefully drawn for it was on his father's merits that Honorius had succeeded. Their family was honourable enough: Theodosius came from Spain, which allowed Claudian to associate him with Trajan (*IV Cons.* 18-20), and he was the son of a famous general whose military victories the poet praises (and whose disgrace and execution he omits). Theodosius' election as Augustus after the death of Valens in 378, Claudian describes as a tribute to his virtues (*IV Cons.* 47-8). Although the emperor was Christian, even militantly so, Claudian does not mention it as the reminder would have done him no service with the pagan section of the audience. Instead, he concentrates on Theodosius' prowess in battle, his good government and his virtues. Theodosius' merits were enough to secure the purple for him, but more was needed to secure Honorius'

10. Claudian, Vergil and the Two Battles of Frigidus

position in the minds of the old aristocracy. It was necessary to mark Theodosius and Honorius as Roman through and through, imbued with Roman ideals and ready to uphold Roman standards.

Part of Claudian's technique was to employ the iconography of *imperium*. The pagan gods of Rome were seen as inseparable from Rome's world domination throughout Roman history. Unlike Christianity, traditional Roman religion was not doctrinal and was intimately related to social hierarchies and government. For centuries, emperors had been associated with Jupiter or Hercules, and it was understood that they would become gods after death. The ancient divinities and their mythology were part of Roman literature, architecture, ritual and art. They were part of the essence of Rome and signified *Romanitas* rather than paganism. When Eugenius and Arbogast marched under the images of Jupiter and Hercules, they were marching under the traditional images of rulership. This was in part a challenge to Theodosius' Christianity but more essentially an assertion that their claim was valid: they were Romans. As panegyrist of the emperor, this iconography was also available to Claudian and he reclaimed the imagery, drawing parallels between Theodosius and Jupiter, Theodosius and Mars, Honorius and Bacchus. In his first court panegyric Claudian describes Theodosius in the aftermath of Frigidus (*Prob. et Olyb.* 73-99). He is resting, like Mars after a battle, and his relaxation offers Roma the opportunity to beg him for a boon. As would be the case throughout Claudian's work, the emperor's religion is unstated because to the poet it is irrelevant: what matters is the emperor's relationship with Rome. The popularity of Claudian's work proves that these images did not impute paganism to a most pious emperor but rather emphasised his authority. Like Arbogast and Eugenius, Claudian too could insist that the *mos maiorum* would be upheld.

It was not enough to rely on mythological imagery however, such allusions being poetic flourishes rather than ideological arguments. To persuade his listeners that Theodosius and Honorius were true Romans of Rome, Claudian drew upon the literature of the past and wrote of Honorius and Theodosius as though they were characters of epic, self-consciously influenced by the noble deeds of the past and believing themselves to be destined to continue this great tradition. In order to endow the imperial family with Roman *mores*, Claudian turned naturally to Vergil, using his work, as it were, as a stamp of *Romanitas*. Unlike most epic writers (and Claudian certainly believed himself to be one), Claudian did not concern himself with details of battle but concentrated instead on what he perceived to be the overall significance of the event and frequently turned to the work of other poets to emphasise this significance. By alluding to earlier epic works, Claudian could create an instantly recognisable background which would give weight to the situations he described. No poet could give greater weight than Vergil. The battle of Frigidus is central to the panegyrics on Honorius' third and fourth consulship, each retelling having a different focus but both based on Vergilian texts and each intended to present the victors, Theodosius and Honorius, as Vergilian heroes, upholders of the Vergilian tradition, their relationship to Claudian in direct succession to the relationship between Vergil and Augustus.

Claudian and Vergil

From its publication, the *Aeneid* had been recognised as having given expression to the identity of Rome, covering its entire history from the fall of Troy to the *imperium sine fine* ('government without limit') promised by Jupiter (*Aen.* 1.279), limitless in time and space. To claim that all subsequent epic writers were profoundly influenced by the *Aeneid* would be to misstate the case: it would be more accurate to state that all subsequent epics were derived from the *Aeneid*. Since the *Aeneid* covered all of Roman time from its pre-foundation history to the foretelling of the kings, civil, wars, principate and the crucial phrase, 'without limit', then all epics which dealt with Rome were, by definition, set somewhere within the compass of the *Aeneid*.[10] All poets recognised this and, knowing that every line of Vergil was familiar to an educated Roman, poets drew on Vergil's work, always aware of the resonances. When poets described a storm, they did so in the knowledge that the storm would be understood against the background of the storm in the *Aeneid*; so too descriptions of the Underworld or of a council of the gods would necessarily be seen as imitations of or deviations from the Vergilian original.

As an epic writer whose task it was to praise the emperor, Claudian saw himself as the direct successor of Vergil with very similar concerns.[11] Like Vergil, he was an epic poet writing in praise of the emperor. The *Aeneid* dealt with the establishment of Rome under the government of the Julian family and encompassed that family history from Anchises and Aeneas to Augustus: Claudian's works take the *imperium sine fine* of the *Aeneid* several generations further to Augustus' descendants, Theodosius and Honorius. By this reasoning then, the changes which had taken place in the Roman empire from the time of Augustus to the late fourth century were far less important than the similarities: the Roman empire was still the Roman empire, it was still ruled by the descendants of Aeneas and Augustus and celebrated by Claudian, that latter-day Vergil.

The enemies of Aeneas also had their descendants and Claudian describes them in terms which would have been familiar to Vergil. The obstacles which faced Aeneas, as varied as the storm of Aeolus, the love of Dido and the enmity of Turnus, are identical in being described as the product of *furor*,[12] that insane force derived from Juno's hatred of the

10. Claudian, Vergil and the Two Battles of Frigidus

Trojans, which works to hinder Aeneas. To Vergil, anyone who threatened the evolving establishment of Rome was driven by *furor* and this topos occurs repeatedly in later epic. To Lucan, *furor* drove Caesar: when he marched towards Rome, a Fury was seen before the city, shaking her burning torch (1.572-4). As the successors of Dido and ancient enemies of Rome, the Carthaginians were naturally inspired by *furor* and Silius describes Hannibal as being governed partly by *patrius furor* (1.71) as Hamilcar had been nourished by fury (*Pun.* 1.79). Each age found its own definition for *furor*, whether the Fury inspired Turnus or Caesar or Hannibal.

To Claudian, the particular relevance of *furor* can be found in Juno's words to Allecto:

> tu potes unanimos armare in proelia fratres
> atque odiis versare domos (*Aen.* 7.335-6)

> you can set single-minded brothers to battle
> and overthrow families with hatred

The words could apply directly to the empire in the late fourth century. On his death in 395, Theodosius had left the empire to his two sons Arcadius in the East and Honorius in the West. Claudian insisted on the unity of the brothers, the *concordia fratrum* (*Gild.* 4) but his reference to *unanimi fratres* ('unanimous brothers', *III Cons.* 189) and its echo of *Aeneid* 7.335 only emphasises the fragility of their unity. So too, relying on his audience's knowledge of Juno's *furor*, can Claudian attack Eutropius:

> geminam quid dividis aulam
> conarisque pios odiis committere fratres? (*In Eutrop.* 1.281-2)

> Why do you separate the twin empires
> and try to make enemies of loving brothers?

Supporting his patron Stilicho, who claimed that the care of the entire empire had been left to his regency, Claudian insisted that all opponents of this claim challenged the *concordia* of the empire and were inspired by *furor*.[13] Among the *furor*-driven, therefore, were Arcadius' ministers Rufinus and Eutropius, as well as the external enemies Gildo and Alaric, and – of course – the rebels Eugenius and Arbogast.

To combat the powers of *furor*, Claudian's heroes are naturally endowed with the *pietas* to be expected in the descendants of Aeneas (*In Eutrop.* 1.281-2) as well as the other virtues which made Rome great. Theodosius is described as having restored the golden age and brought back *Concor-*

dia, Virtus, Fides and *Pietas* (*Ruf.* 1.52-3). One may assume that Honorius will inherit these virtues but lest there be any doubt, the panegyric on his fourth consulship is devoted to a lengthy speech in which Theodosius describes qualities necessary to rule Rome. The speech is not simply a discourse on kingship but is intended to invoke literary echoes in the mind of the listener: his speech suggesting Anchises' words to Aeneas and the parade of heroes in the sixth book of the *Aeneid*, thereby associating the earliest and latest rulers of Rome with advice on rulership and examples culled from the great heroes of Rome. Nor is it any coincidence that the speech is placed after Theodosius' victory at Frigidus.

The Battle of Frigidus. *IV Cons.*

The main body of the panegyric on Honorius' fourth consulship is concerned with Theodosius' speech on kingship but unless it is looked at in its context within the poem, the reader loses much of Claudian's intention. The various episodes of the poem – Theodosius' victories, the inauguration of Honorius as Augustus, the lecture on good government – are described in Vergilian terms and each scene is intended to add weight to the next. From this point of view, the whole poem is designed to impress the listeners that Theodosius and Honorius are the successors of Aeneas – not just literally, as the rulers of Rome, but in spirit as the upholders of the virtues which he embodied and which his father Anchises proclaimed: a knowledge of Anchises' words in *Aeneid* 6 is central to the understanding of Claudian's poem.

The panegyric opens with praise of the military success of the family of Honorius: his grandfather and, more particularly, his father. Theodosius is portrayed as the only man who could save the empire: a lone man against hordes of barbarians (*IV Cons.* 56-8). He defeated the external enemies but two usurpers arose, Maximus and Eugenius. Although these rebellions were separated by five years, Claudian makes the usurpers partners in evil (*IV Cons.* 75), describing them as twin tyrants (72) united in their execution by the sword (84-6). Evidently, by suppressing the individuality of the usurpers and their separate rebellions, the poet's aim is to highlight the victor and, in particular, his behaviour towards the vanquished:

> non insultare iacenti
> malebat: mitis precibus, pietatis abundans,
> poenae parcus erat (*IV Cons.* 112-14)

He did not choose to abuse the fallen:

10. Claudian, Vergil and the Two Battles of Frigidus

> he was open to prayers, generous of piety
> and sparing of punishment.

About to play the role of Anchises to his son, Theodosius is now a living example of Anchises' closing words to Aeneas:

> parcere subiectis et debellare superbos. (*Aen.* 6.853)
>
> to spare the fallen and make war on the proud.

Clearly, his opponents could count as *superbos*:

> qui modo tam densas nutu movere cohortes,
> in quos iam dubius sese libraverat orbis. (*IV Cons.* 87-8)
>
> Who recently moved close packed cohorts at a nod
> into whose power a tottering world had swung.

Theodosius had very properly made war on them but was sparing of punishment when the war was over. The reference to Vergil is pointed, even without the phrase *pietatis abundans* ('generous of piety'). There is even a suggestion of the death of Turnus in the defeat of the usurpers. Aeneas had killed Turnus in revenge for the slaying of Pallas:

> 'Pallas te hoc vulnere, Pallas
> immolat et poenam scelerato ex sanguine sumit.'
> hoc dicens ferrum adverso sub pectore condit
> fervidus; ast illi solvuntur frigore membra
> vitaque cum gemitu fugit indignata sub umbras. (*Aen.* 12.948-52)
>
> 'Pallas sacrifices you with this wound,
> Pallas exacts the punishment from your evil blood.'
> So saying, burning with anger, he buried the sword in his enemy's breast;
> but Turnus' limbs relaxed with cold
> and his life, unworthy, fled with a groan to the shadows.

Likewise Theodosius has pursued his opponents in order to avenge their victims, the emperors Gratian and Valentinian II, and is described as the avenger (*IV Cons.* 94, 109). The result is that *Augustas par victima mitigat umbras* ('an equal sacrifice balanced the imperial deaths', *IV Cons.* 95). The shadows, *umbras*, which end the line and book in Vergil and line and section in Claudian are obvious verbal parallels, but Claudian's use of *victima* ('victim') echoes the sacrificial note of *immolat* ('sacrifices', 949).[14]

The abrupt ending of the *Aeneid* has led to much discussion as to Aeneas' motives but in the panegyric there is no sense that Theodosius may have acted rashly. Instead, *illi iustitiam confirmavere triumphi* ('these triumphs established justice', *IV Cons.* 98). Claudian may have merged two wars and suppressed details of the actual fighting but the audience would have recognised the final battle as Frigidus and would have understood the religious significance of the victory. Eugenius, Christian though he was, may have guaranteed the restoration of the old ways but Claudian relies on Vergil to prove that he was no real Roman after all but a *tyrannus* ('tyrant', *IV Cons* 72), one of the proud whom it was the duty of a real Roman to destroy. The war with Maximus and the victory at Frigidus here serve to depict Theodosius as a Roman who has taken Anchises' words to heart. He may be Christian, but Claudian implies he is Roman above all. When Honorius later promises that he will not be unworthy of his father (*IV Cons.* 354-5) he is promising that he will not fall short of the Vergilian ideal which Theodosius embodies.

The omen which attended Honorius' elevation to Augustus confirmed the Vergilian allusion. On a dark day, a star shone brightly: Claudian is doubtful as to whom this star represented but its meaning is clear:

> adparet quid signa ferant. ventura potestas
> claruit Ascanio, subita cum luce comarum
> innocuus flagraret apex Phrygioque volutus
> vertice fatalis redimiret tempora candor. (*IV Cons.* 192-5)

> It was clear what the signs meant. His coming power
> illuminated Ascanius when the top of his head
> burned harmlessly with the sudden light and the
> brightness of destiny swirled round the Trojan head
> and wreathed his temples.

When this omen occurs in the *Aeneid*, those who witness it react realistically and fearfully, trying to put out the fire with water (*Aen.* 2.685-6). Anchises prays to the gods to reveal the significance of the portent and a comet appears whose meaning he interprets. Claudian reverses the Vergilian episode: in the *Aeneid*, the wreath of fire led to the comet while in Claudian's poem, the appearance of the star only reminds the poet of the fire. The lesson is the same, however: Honorius and Ascanius are destined for greatness. Ascanius' family may have been in doubt as to the relevance of the omen but Claudian firmly informs his listeners that the star which attended the new emperor was the light of power: *imperii lux illa fuit* and that it was an omen, *praesagus* (*IV Cons.* 182). By introducing the image of Ascanius, the listener is convinced of this prophetic star, even though no such corona appeared around Honorius' head. It is enough that the literary association is made and that Honorius and Ascanius, the future

10. Claudian, Vergil and the Two Battles of Frigidus

rulers of Rome, are united in the line which stretched from Anchises through Aeneas and Ascanius to Honorius.

They are further united in the speech of Theodosius. From the outset, Theodosius is at pains to enforce the idea that the ruler of Rome is of a different kind from any other ruler. Although in procession, Arcadius and Honorius appear identical (*IV Cons.* 206-11), Honorius is now singled out as the future ruler of the West as Theodosius advises him that, unlike the effeminate rulers of the East, the Roman emperor must rely on *virtus* rather than *sanguis*, merit instead of blood (*IV Cons.* 220). He must learn to govern himself before he can govern others and, in particular, *sis pius in primis* ('above all, be dutiful', *IV Cons.* 276).

Advising Honorius to turn to literature for his examples, Theodosius suggests:

> nec desinat umquam
> tecum Graia loqui, tecum Romana vetustas. (*IV Cons.* 398-9)

> never cease to study the antiquity of Greece and Rome.

It is evident what particular piece of Roman antiquity he has in mind as he paraphrases Vergil's parade of heroes from the sixth book of the *Aeneid*.

> [quis reliquat] ... parvoque potentem
> Fabricium vel te sulco, Serrane, serentem?
> quo fessum rapitis, Fabii? (*Aen.* 6.843-5)

> who could pass over Fabricius,
> powerful with few possessions or you, Serranus, ploughing your furrow?
> where do you rush me, wearied, Fabii?

Casting himself as a latter-day Anchises, Theodosius offers up again the familiar examples:

> pauper erat Curius, reges cum vinceret armis,
> pauper Fabricius, Pyrrhi cum sperneret aurum;
> sordida dictator flexit Serranus aratra. (*IV Cons.* 413-15)[15]

> Curius was a poor man when he conquered kings in battle,
> Fabricius was poor, when he rejected the gold of Pyrrhus,
> Serranus as a dictator turned his lowly plough.

Claudian is here deliberately playing with time and with the epic characters. To Theodosius, these are examples from history while to Anchises they are visions of the future. As he recalls these names to his son, the living Theodosius echoes the dead Anchises but the panegyric is actually being recited several years after the death of the emperor (17 January 395) and so both speeches really come from the Underworld. Honorius, as listener and son of the speaker plays Aeneas – having previously been cast as Ascanius – but as emperor, he is also the successor of Augustus, the restorer of the golden age and a living extension of the parade of heroes. Both Anchises and Theodosius look to the same past from their different temporal perspectives but Theodosius looks no further forward into the future than his brief prophecy regarding Honorius *fas sit promittere patri: / tantus eris* ('let it be right for a father to promise: you shall be great', *IV Cons.* 378-9). The listener is left to make the connection that Honorius, representing Aeneas/Ascanius/Augustus is part of *omnis Iuli / progenies magnum caeli ventura sub axem* ('the whole race of Iulus about to come beneath the great sky, *Aen.* 6.789-90).

Throughout the panegyric, then, the listener is directed to Vergil. The aim of the panegyric was to prove to the pagan Roman aristocracy that the young Honorius was a truly Roman ruler; by relying on his audience's knowledge of Vergil, Claudian associates the young emperor with Ascanius, marked by heaven as a ruler, with Aeneas, the epitome of *pietas*, and through the parade of heroes, with all the great figures of Roman history. That catalogue culminated in Augustus: the fourth-century audience is to understand that Theodosius and Honorius are his successors. With this weight of allusive proof, Claudian can assert of a fourteen-year-old who had visited Rome once as a small child:

> quae denique Romae
> cura tibi! quam fixa manet reverentia patrum! (*IV Cons.* 503-4)

> What care for Rome you then showed!
> how well-established was the respect you showed for the senators!

By inserting Vergilian panegyric on Augustus into his own panegyric on Honorius and by focussing on Theodosius' Vergilian qualities, Claudian succeeded in marking the Christian victory of Frigidus as a truly Roman triumph. It has become a latter-day *exemplum* of *pietas* destined to take its place in the catalogue of *exempla*, whether described by Theodosius or Anchises. This poem, intent only on establishing Theodosius as a Vergilian hero, seems remarkable for its lack of historical information, but in fact Claudian was building on his earlier more detailed depiction of Frigidus. In the panegyric on Honorius' third consulship, two years before, Claudian had established the Frigidus as a Vergilian battlefield, and, as in the later poem, used Vergilian allusion to turn a pagan-Christian conflict into a triumph of the Roman *mos maiorum* of Theodosius and Honorius.

10. Claudian, Vergil and the Two Battles of Frigidus

The battle of Frigidus: *III Cons.*

interea turbata fides. civilia rursus
bella tonant dubiumque quatit discordia mundum.
pro crimen superum, longi pro dedecus aevi:
barbarus Hesperias exul possederat urbes
sceptraque deiecto dederat Romana clienti ... (*III Cons.* 63-7)

ille vetat rerumque tibi commendat habenas
et sacro meritos ornat diademate crines.
tantaque se rudibus pietas ostendit in annis,
sic aetas animo cessit, quererentur ut omnes
imperium tibi sero datum. victoria velox
auspiciis effecta tuis. pugnastis uterque:
tu fatis genitorque manu. te propter et Alpes
invadi faciles cauto nec profuit hosti
munitis haesisse locis: spes inrita valli
concidit et scopulis patuerunt claustra revulsis.
te propter gelidis Aquilo de monte procellis
obruit adversas acies revolutaque tela
vertit in auctores et turbine reppulit hastas
o nimium dilecte deo, cui fundit ab antris
Aeolus armatas hiemes, cui militat aether
et coniurati veniunt ad classica venti. (*III Cons.* 83-98)

Meanwhile loyalty was thrown into confusion. Again civil wars
thundered and discord shook a wavering world.
O crime of the gods, o disgrace throughout long ages:
a barbarian exile had taken possession of Italian cities
and had given the command of Rome to a low retainer ...

He refused and gave command of the state to you
and adorned your worthy head with the holy diadem.
So much piety did you display in your young years,
so did your spirit outstrip your age, that all complained
that power was given to you too late.
Swift victory was accomplished
under your auspices. Both of you fought:
you used your destiny, and your father his arm. Because of you
the Alps were easily entered nor did it profit the wary enemy
that he clung to fortified places: the empty hope
in the walls fell away and when rocks were torn away their
    barriers lay open.
Because of you, the North wind overthrew the enemy lines
with icy mountain storms and turning the weapons round

> hurled them back upon their owners and drove back the spears
>   in a whirlwind:
> o well-beloved of god, for whom Aeolus pours from his caves
> the armed storms, for whom the heaven fights
> and the winds come as allies to your trumpet call.

The battle of Frigidus had occurred only some sixteen months before Claudian described it in his panegyric on Honorius' third consulship and was therefore fresh in the minds of the audience. They did not need to be reminded of the statues of Jupiter set up in the Alps or that Eugenius had been supported by the aristocratic Nicomachus Flavianus. Whether the Roman senatorial aristocracy had supported Eugenius or not was irrelevant: they had remained pagans despite Theodosius' Christianity and now were presented with his eleven-year-old son. One might expect Claudian to gloss over the events of the rebellion – after all, this was a panegyric on Honorius, not Theodosius, and the boy could not have been involved. Instead, Claudian makes Frigidus central to the poem and uses the victory to persuade his audience of two points: that Honorius was capable of being a successful and victorious emperor and that he was more truly Roman than those who attempted to usurp his father's position.

To present Honorius as a military victor, Claudian first gives him the expected education. It is clear that although born in the purple, Honorius is a hero at heart, trained as a hero should be to endure heat and cold, to swim torrents, climb mountains, run over plains and master the use of all weapons (44-50). When Theodosius returns from battle, dusty and bloodstained, the infant Honorius rejoices to embrace his father – superior in courage to the son of Hector who howled at the sight of his father's armour (29-32). In endurance and training, Honorius is the equal of Achilles (60-2). The lines on birth and education may be staples of panegyric but the references to Hector and Achilles, to the glorious deeds of Honorius' father and grandfather give the poem an epic resonance and prepare the audience for the coming battle.

It comes abruptly. Having finished with Honorius' birth and education, Claudian swiftly changes the scene with *interea* ('meanwhile'). This is a formula frequently used as the first word of a new book of an epic or to introduce a new episode within the action.[16] Only 211 lines long, this panegyric can be at most a mini-epic: the use of *interea* gives pace and urgency to the poem. The following words mark the passage as fully epic in theme: *turbata fides* ('confused allegiance') and *civilia bella* ('civil wars') (62-3).

Within the passage all elements of epic are present, from the outbreak of war: *civilia ... bella tonant* (63-4) through the mustering of the armies by Theodosius (69-72) to the epic simile of the lion cub longing for his first

10. Claudian, Vergil and the Two Battles of Frigidus

kill (77-82) to the battle itself which begins with its conclusion – *victoria velox* ('swift victory', 87) and ends with the topos of the river choked with corpses (99-101). The lines are redolent with allusions to earlier poets and offer a layered history of Roman wars. The generic epic *interea* is followed by *turbata fides* which suggests the opening to the third book of Silius' *Punica*: *postquam rupta fides Tyriis* ('after Carthaginian loyalty had been broken', *Pun.* 3.1). However, the impression that Claudian is describing Rome's ancient enemy is quickly overshadowed by the specific *civilia bella* with its connotations of Lucan's *bella ... plus quam civilia* ('wars more serious than civil wars', 1.1). *turbata fides*, then, is even more serious when applied to internal rebellion and the *discordia* which is produced in Claudian's lines strikes closer to the heart of the Roman empire. The verb *tonant* may be said to prefigure both the actual and the metaphorical storm. Within two lines, Claudian has established an epic scene and, pausing only to liken Honorius to a savage lion cub thirsting for blood, he proceeds to battle.[17]

As in the wars between Theodosius and the usurpers, Maximus and Eugenius, what is important is victory and Claudian awards swift victory to his heroes. However, his emphasis in this poem is not on Theodosius' prowess and clemency but on the fact that victory was achieved equally by himself and his son: *pugnastis uterque: / tu fatis, genitorque manu* ('You each fought, you with your fates and your father with his hand', 88-9). *victoria velox* is given not after battle (the details of fighting are given later) but after Honorius' coronation and his assumption of *imperium* (87) as though his elevation were a trigger of victory. In fact, the repetition of *te propter* (89, 93) suggests that Honorius had more to do with the success than did his father: his influence opens up the Alps to his father's armies and brings the north wind against their enemies. Both Theodosius and Aeolus are presented as fighting commanders but it is their superior, Honorius, who causes the war to be won. Theodosius forbade him to take part in battle but Claudian demonstrates that this was not necessary: Honorius is too great an emperor to need weapons: simply because he is an emperor, the gods fight for him.[18] When Arbogast finally enacts righteous judgement on himself, the union of Theodosius and Honorius is given shape in the two swords with which Arbogast commits suicide:

> at ferus inventor scelerum traiecerat altum
> non uno mucrone latus, duplexque tepebat
> ensis. (102-4)

> But the evil founder of crime pierced his side deep
> with no single sword, and a double blade
> grew hot.

In this portrayal of Frigidus, details of the battle are relevant since they serve to introduce Aeolus and the Vergilian allusion. A storm had indeed arisen and had blown their weapons back on the enemy which turned the tide of battle and gave victory to the emperor. To Orosius and Augustine it was the work of the Christian god, but the image was familiar to Claudian from classical sources. On at least two occasions, Aeolus had fought against Rome, firstly inspired by the *furor*-driven Juno to attack Aeneas as he sailed from Troy:

> haec ubi dicta, cavum conversa cuspide montem
> impulit in latus; ac venti velut agmine facto,
> qua data porta, ruunt et terras turbine perflant.
> incubuere mari, totumque a sedibus imis
> una Eurusque Notusque ruunt creberque procellis ...
> intonuere poli, et crebris micat ignibus aether. (*Aen.* 1.81-5, 90)

> So saying, he [Aeolus] drove his spear into the side of
> a hollow mountain, and the winds, as though forming a battle column,
> where their exit was made, rushed forth and blew over the lands like a whirlwind.
> They burdened the sea and from the depths of their seats
> together rushed out in close packed storms, the East wind and the South ...
> the heavens thundered and the sky flashed with frequent fire.

Vergil had portrayed the storm in military language: now Claudian took the military winds and gave them a real battle to fight. The parallels of *procellis* (93) and *aether* (97) and their identical positioning in the line, the echoes of *venti* (98), *monte/montem* (93) and *turbine* (95), the details of the spears being driven back: all these clearly mark Claudian's lines as an evocation of Vergil and establish a link between Honorius and Aeneas. In the *Aeneid*, Aeolus was acting against the will of Jupiter and was attempting to thwart the destiny of Rome. By contrast, Honorius is *o nimium dilecte deo* (96), the darling of the gods, the one for whom they fight. There is no opposition from Juno, and Aeolus is free to ally himself with the right side, sending his winds to act as *coniurati* (98). Frigidus gives Aeolus his chance to make amends for his actions in the *Aeneid* and he takes it.

Silius had also reworked the Vergilian storm for his portrayal of the battle of Cannae, the catastrophic defeat of the Romans by Hannibal. In the *Punica*, Juno again persuades Aeolus to release the winds with the result that the missiles of the Romans are blown back behind them while those of the Carthaginians are given extra strength (*Pun.* 9.491-510). Claudian's Frigidus, while shaped by Vergil's storm, is in theme a retelling of Cannae: there are no verbal parallels but the details of battle are the same, particularly if the opening *turbata fides* (63) has suggested Silius'

10. Claudian, Vergil and the Two Battles of Frigidus

rupta fides (*Pun.* 3.1). Claudian's lines are in effect a rewriting of Cannae: Claudian transforms the greatest Carthaginian victory which was won with divine intervention into a Roman victory.[19] The spears have been redirected once more, as it were, and are at last being blown against the enemies of Rome. The well-read audience may also remember Jupiter's reaction to Hannibal's savagery at Cannae:

> venit hora diesque,
> qua nullas umquam transisse optaverit Alpes. (*Pun.* 9.549-50)

The day and the hour shall come when
he shall wish that he never had crossed the Alps.

Like Hannibal, Eugenius and Arbogast paid for their temerity in crossing the Alps. They may have set up effigies of Jupiter and Hercules but Claudian implies, they are closer in spirit to the Carthaginians.

Further evidence comes from the emphatic repetition of *te propter* (89, 93). Although the Vergilian storm is the dominant and most obvious allusion within the passage, the most striking verbal allusion comes from the fourth book of the *Aeneid*. The repeated *te propter* occurs in Dido's speech:

> te propter Libycae gentes Nomadumque tyranni
> odere, infensi Tyrii; te propter eundem
> exstinctus pudor et, qua sola sidera adibam,
> fama prior. (*Aen.* 4.320-3)

> Because of you the Libyan peoples and the rulers of the Numidians
> hate me, the Tyrians are hostile; because of you my honour and earlier
>   reputation,
> by which alone I approached the stars, are destroyed.

The echo creates a contrast between the sorrowing Dido, the originator of Carthaginian hatred for Rome, and the victorious Honorius who defeats the heirs of Dido's hostility. In hindsight, the opening *turbata fides* can now be seen as reaching back through Silius' Carthaginians to Vergil's Dido: *fides* was a word frequently applied to her love before it became transformed into the untrustworthiness of the Carthaginians, the *Punica fides* ('Carthaginian treachery').[20] The same book of the *Aeneid* links Dido with Claudian's description of Arbogast. Giving power to Eugenius, he is described as a foreigner with his dependent:

> barbarus Hesperias exul possederat urbes
> *sceptra*que deiecto *dederat* Romana clienti. (*III Cons.* 66-7)

> A barbarian exile had taken possession of Italian cities
> and had given the command of Rome to a low retainer.

The words recall Dido's investiture of Aeneas,

> infelix Dido, nunc te facta impia tangunt?
> tum decuit, cum *sceptra dabas*. en dextra fidesque ... (*Aen.* 4.595-6)

> Unhappy Dido, is it now that your wicked deeds affect you?
> It should have been then when you were handing over your power.
> Behold his right hand and loyalty ...

her *impia facta* implicitly attributed to Arbogast. All is reversed. Claudian has rewritten literary history so that Dido's defeat has become Honorius' victory, Frigidus has become a second and successful Cannae and those who claimed to be Roman – Eugenius and Arbogast – are suggested to be closer to the Carthaginians, inheritors of Dido's enmity, breakers of faith with Rome, essentially alien and hostile.[21]

*

In conclusion, it is evident why the battle of Frigidus was central to Claudian's portrayal of the two emperors, Theodosius and Honorius. The victory was too important to be ignored by a panegyrist, but it was a victory which would seem to do little to help the victors with their most critical subjects, the old pagan aristocracy of Rome. Claudian's answer was to ignore the Christian overtones of the battle. Omitting any religious significance of Jupiter and Hercules, the symbols of the rebels, he concentrated on what these gods truly represented: the essence and tradition of Roman government and this he claimed for the emperors. In the two panegyrics on Honorius, Claudian uses Vergil the most Roman of all poets to attack the claims of the usurpers, never overtly challenging their claim to re-establish the old ways but rather repeatedly demonstrating that Theodosius and Honorius were in character and action descended from the Vergilian depiction of Aeneas and Anchises. At the same time, he weakens the rebels' claim of *Romanitas*, linking them instead with the Carthaginians and relying on Vergilian allusion to show that their claim was empty: although they pretended to be Romans they were in essence *barbari*, the enemies of Rome.[22]

Notes

1. For the historical background, see Williams and Friell (1994) 127-36.
2. Orosius *Hist.* 7.35.14.
3. Augustine *De civ. D.* 5.26.

10. Claudian, Vergil and the Two Battles of Frigidus

4. e.g. Ambrose *Ex. Psal.* 36.25.2-4.

5. Abbreviated respectively to *III Cons.* and *IV Cons.* Other abbreviations are as follows: *In Eutropium = Eut.*; *Panegyric for the consuls Probinus and Olybrius = Prob. et Olyb.*; *In Rufinum = Ruf.*; *De bello Gildonico = Gild.*; *De consulatu Stilichonis = Stil.*; *De bello Gothico = Goth. pr.*; *Panegyric on the sixth consulship of Honorius = VI Cons.*

6. *III Cons.* 96, 98; Augustine *De civ. D.* 5.26; Orosius *Hist.* 7.35.21. 96-7 reads *cui fundit ab antris / Aeolus armatas hiemes* ('for whom Aeolus pours from his caves the armed storms').

7. Cameron (1970).

8. Levy (1958) 338.

9. Levy (1958) 339.

10. Hardie (1993) 12.

11. Note the pride with which he refers to his statue (*Goth. pr.* 8) inscribed with the claim that he had united 'a Homer's music with a Vergil's mind' (*CIL* vi.1710).

12. For example, *Aen.* 1.107; 4.68-9; 12.680. For a discussion of *furor*, see Herschkowitz (1998).

13. For the opposition of *concordia/discordia* see Cairns (1989) 85-108.

14. The allusion might also suggest a pun to the educated reader who would associate Vergil's *frigore* ('cold') with the present circumstances of the river Frigidus; Vergil himself here plays with the contrast between *fervidus* ('burning') and *frigore* ('cold') and in *Aeneid* 9.414-15, inverts the concept of icy river and warm blood: *volvitur ille vomens calidum de pectore flumen / frigidus et longis singultibus ilia pulsat* ('he rolls over, vomiting a hot river from his breast, and icy-cold he shakes his chest with long sobs') while Claudian offers a variation in *III Cons.* 99-100: *Frigidus amnis / mutatis fumavit aquis* ('the icy river smoked with new waters').

15. Possibly as an echo of Anchises' description of the transmigration of souls, Claudian incorporates a philosophical section into Theodosius' speech which describes the natures of the souls and the humours and, like the Vergilian model, derives from Plato.

16. *Aen.* 5.1, 10.1, 11.1, Valerius Flaccus *Argo.* 2.1, Silius *Pun.* 7.1, Statius *Theb.* 2.1.

17. The image is taken from Statius *Achilleid* 1.858-63.

18. A similar point is made in *Gild.* when Stilicho argues that Honorius' presence in the battle would give too much honour to the Moor and remarks, probably with greater truth than was intended that *plus nominis horror / quam tuus ensis aget* (384-5).

19. For similar 'rewriting' of history see Dewar (1994) 356.

20. For Dido's genuine *fides* see *Aen.* 4.12, 373, 552, 597; 6.459; its transformation into *Punica perfidia* had become a byword by the time of Hasdrubal, the father of Hannibal (Livy 21.4).

21. One might argue for a further Vergilian reference associating the *barbarus* Arbogast with the *barbarus* who threatens Meliboeus' fields in *Ecl.* 1: any suggestion that their lands might be under attack would surely speak directly to the pagan land-owning aristocracy of Rome!

22. I am grateful to Damien Nelis, TCD, David Scourfield, Maynooth, NUI, and Diarmuid Scully, UCC, for their most helpful suggestions; also to the Irish Research Council for the Humanities and Social Sciences for financial support during my studies.

11

'The Plato of Poets': Vergil in the *Historia Augusta*

Daniel den Hengst

The collection of biographies known as the *Historia Augusta* (*HA*) contains the lives of the emperors Hadrian to Diocletian (117-284). They have come down to us under the names of six different *scriptores,* Aelius Spartianus, Iulius Capitolinus, Aelius Lampridius, Vulcacius Gallicanus, Trebellius Pollio and Flavius Vopiscus. As we find in the text a number of dedications to Diocletian and Constantine, the collection presents itself as written in the beginning of the fourth century. In a magisterial article, Dessau (1889) demonstrated that the *HA* contains passages that point to the end rather than the beginning of the fourth century as the time of composition, and that it is the work not of six different biographers but of one author writing under six pseudonyms. This is at present the *communis opinio* among students of the *HA*, to which I subscribe. For that reason I refer to the 'author' of the *HA*, and not to the six different *scriptores*.[1]

It will become clear that, in the *HA*, references to and quotations from Vergil are unevenly distributed, and that this distribution is related to the complicated genesis of this heterogeneous collection. The reader of the *HA* cannot fail to notice that there are striking differences in style and composition (not corresponding with the names of the traditional *scriptores*!) in particular between the lives of the great emperors of the second century, up to and including Caracalla, the so-called 'primary lives' ('*Hauptviten*'), and those of princes and usurpers of the same period, the 'secondary lives' ('*Nebenviten*'). It is also evident that many of the typical traits of these secondary lives are shared by the lives that go under the names of Trebellius Pollio and Vopiscus (Gallienus – Numerianus). For the primary lives the author obviously had an excellent source at his disposal; in the secondary lives and the lives that go under the name of Pollio and Vopiscus he relies to a large extent on his own *inventio*. Attention therefore has to be given to the context in which we find reminiscences or quotations from Vergil, in order to decide whether the author had found them in his

11. 'The Plato of Poets': Vergil in the Historia Augusta

sources or added them as an embellishment of his text or for special emphasis.

Explicit references to Vergil

In the life of the exemplary emperor Alexander Severus we read that he had a portrait of Vergil in one of his two private sanctuaries: *Vergilium autem Platonem poetarum vocabat*[2] *eiusque imaginem cum Ciceronis simulacro in secundo larario habebat, ubi et Achillis et magnorum virorum* ('He used to call Vergil the Plato of poets and he kept his portrait, together with a likeness of Cicero, in his second sanctuary of the Lares, where he also had portraits of Achilles and the great heroes', *AS* 31.4).[3] This respect for the poet as a repository of wisdom is typical of the nostalgic admiration of classical literature in late antiquity, exemplified by Macrobius, in whose works Vergil, *quem constat erroris ignarum* ('who was, as everyone knows, never mistaken', *somn.* 2.8.8) is celebrated as a sage rather than an artist. In the *HA* serious study of Vergil and other classical authors is a characteristic of a good emperor.[4] In this respect the elder Gordian resembled Alexander Severus: *hac enim vita venerabilis, cum Platone semper, cum Aristotele, cum Tullio, cum Vergilio ceterisque veteribus agens* ('worthy of respect as such a life had made him, he passed his days with Plato and Aristotle, Cicero and Vergil and the other ancient authors', *Gd.* 7.1). This emperor is even reported to have written an epic poem himself in thirty books on the Antonini as a young boy (*puerulus*).[5] By contrast, a light-hearted prince like Aelius, Hadrian's adopted son, studied Apicius and Ovid's *Amores* and called Martial *suum Vergilium* ('his own Vergil', *Ael.* 5.9).

Vergil is mentioned by name only four more times in the *HA*.[6] The first instance is what one would expect in a biography, a remark on the literary taste of the emperor, in the style of Suetonius.[7] In the archaising fashion of his contemporaries Hadrian 'preferred Ennius to Vergil, Cato to Cicero and Coelius to Sallust' (*H.* 16.6). The remaining three are more typical for the *HA*. In the *vita Severi* 21.2 Vergil is mentioned in a digression on the sons of great men, rulers and writers: *iam vero quid de Homero, Demosthene, Vergilio, Crispo et Terentio, Plauto ceterisque aliis loquar?* ('what shall I say of Homer, Demosthenes, Vergil, Crispus, Terentius, Plautus and such as they?'). This is part of a notorious insertion by the author into the main body of the life, which underlines the necessity to look at the distribution of the references to Vergil over the *Historia Augusta* as a whole. Secondly, in *Alexander Severus* 14.5 we are told that Alexander Severus, at the instance of his father, turned away from philosophy and music to other arts. Which arts were meant, is made clear by the *sortes Vergilii* he was honoured with. They are among the most famous verses of the *Aeneid*: *excudent alii ... / tu regere imperio populos, Romane memento / hae tibi erunt artes* ('Others, doubt not, shall beat out ... you, Roman, be sure to rule the world, be these your arts', 6.847-52). This raises the question of the *sortes Vergilianae* (or *Vergilii*), an expression found only in the *HA*, although the practice of consulting poets for divinatory purposes, *rhapsodomanteia*, is also known from other sources. Finally, in *Maximinus* 27.4 we are informed that Fabillus, the teacher of Maximinus iunior, translated *Aeneid* 8.589-91 into Greek verses. Translations from Latin to Greek and vice versa are a recurrent feature in the *HA*, which deserves special attention.

Sortes Vergilianae

'The random consultation for mantic purposes of a poet or other revered author' is Pease's definition of the technique called *rhapsodomanteia*.[8] To this end especially Homer, Vergil and the Bible were consulted. The practice is best known from Augustine, who quotes a respected medical doctor as saying *de paginis poetae cuiuspiam longe aliud canentis atque intendentis, cum forte quis consulit, mirabiliter consonus negotio saepe versus exiret* ('although the poet had been thinking, as he wrote, of some quite different matter, it often happened that the reader placed his finger on a verse which had a remarkable bearing on his problem', *Conf.* 4.3.5, tr. Pine-Coffin). Augustine disapproved of the use of the Bible for such trivial purposes, although he preferred it to pagan forms of divination: *hi vero, qui de paginis evangelicis sortes legunt, etsi optandum est, ut hoc potius faciant, quam ad daemonia consulenda concurrant, tamen etiam ista mihi displicet consuetudo, ad negotia saecularia et ad vitae huius vanitatem propter aliam vitam loquentia oracula divina velle convertere* ('as to those who take *sortes* from the pages of the evangelists, although it is preferable for them to do this rather than to consult the heathen gods, still I disapprove of that practice, to try to adapt to worldly affairs and the vanity of this life the words of God that are spoken in view of another life', *Ep.* 55.20, my translation).[9] It is not just the trivial character of the information required that is condemned by Augustine, but more generally the fact that a meaning is elicited from lines taken out of context that was not intended by the author. This point is made more clearly in *De Civitate Dei*: *ne more centonum ad rem quam volumus tamquam versiculos decerpere videamur, velut de grandi carmine, quod non de re illa, sed de alia longeque diversa reperiatur esse conscriptum* ('Otherwise I fear that I might seem to be gathering individual verses on the topic in hand, in the technique of the *centos*, when one makes selections from a long poem not written on the same subject, but on another and totally different one', 17.15).[10] This is what the consultation of texts for divinatory purposes and the composition

11. 'The Plato of Poets': Vergil in the Historia Augusta

of *centos* have in common: lines and verses are taken out of context and given an entirely new meaning never envisaged by the original author. Both procedures are found in the *HA*.

Different ways of consulting *sortes* are on record. At the shrine of Fortuna Primigenia at Praeneste, which is mentioned in *Alexander Severus* 4.6, lots were drawn from a box (*arca*) by a young child.[11] In other instances the lots were shaken in a receptacle until one of them fell out.[12] Another method, not mentioned in the *HA*, is the *apertio libri*, the random opening of a book, most famously attested in the *'Tolle, lege'* episode in Augustine *Confessions* 8.12.29.[13] Yet another method is known from the so-called *sortes Astrampsychi*.[14] There we find a list of questions with a number attached to each of them. This number led the consultant indirectly to a list of responses from which he could choose his answer.

The *sortes Vergilianae* are mentioned for the first time in *Hadrian* 2.8: Hadrian, anxious to know if he was still Trajan's favourite for the succession, consulted the *sortes*. He received the following oracle:

> quis procul ille autem ramis insignis olivae
> sacra ferens? nosco crines incanaque menta
> regis Romani, primum qui legibus urbem
> fundabit, Curibus parvis et paupere terra
> missus in imperium magnum, cui deinde subibit.

> But who is he apart, crowned with sprays of olive
> offering sacrifice? I recognise the hoary hair and beard
> of that king of Rome who will make the infant city
> secure on a basis of laws, called from the needy land
> of lowly Cures to sovereign might. (*Aen.* 6. 808-12)[15]

The manner in which Hadrian consulted the *sortes* is not specified, neither is the location where the consultation took place. Taken literally, the formula *sors excidit* ('the lot fell out') following the quotation suggests that lots were shaken in a receptacle, until one of them was thrown out. The author would have us believe that the lines from Anchises' great speech in book 6 of the *Aeneid*, the 'Heldenschau', in which king Numa is introduced, were written on such a lot. This seems highly unlikely and it is preferable to interpret the words less literally in the sense of *sors contigit* ('the lot was granted to him'). The author proceeds: *quam alii ex Sibyllinis versibus ei provenisse dicunt* ('others, however, declare that this prophecy came to him from the Sibylline verses'). Again, taken literally, this would mean that the passage from Vergil was found in the Sibylline verses. Such a fantastic notion would not be beyond the power of invention of the author, as is proved by *Pescennius Niger* 8.6, where a line from Vergil is passed off as a translation of an oracle delivered in Greek by the Pythia. But a less literal

175

interpretation of the phrase would be that, according to some, Hadrian found the prediction of his future reign not in Vergil, but in the Sibylline books.[16] The *Oracula Sibyllina* do indeed contain a number of references to this emperor, in which, moreover, he is described as 'silver-haired' (*arguroukranos*) which tallies with Vergil's *incanaque menta*, 'his hoary beard'.[17] Still, the connection between Vergil and the Sibylline verses deserves special attention. The association of ideas may have been inspired by the central role played by the Sibyl in book 6, from which the quotation was taken, or from the *Cumaeum carmen* of the fourth *Eclogue*. According to Lactantius and Augustine, the prophecy in this poem had simply been taken over by Vergil from the Sibylline verses. Lactantius remarks after a lengthy quotation from the fourth *Eclogue*: *quae poeta secundum Cymaeae Sibyllae carmina prolocutus est* ('the poet has spoken these words in accordance with the verses of the Cumaean Sibyl', *Div. inst.* 7.24.12). Augustine was of the same opinion: *quod ex Cymaeo, id est Sibyllino carmine se fassus est transtulisse Vergilius* ('Vergil has openly declared that he had taken this prophecy from the Cumaean, i.e. the Sibyl's song', *Ep.* 258.5).[18] This may seem to be a far cry from the text under consideration, but, as we will see, there may be more similarities with Christian authors in the context of the *sortes*.

The quotation from Vergil is inserted into a highly informative section of the life of Hadrian, where the author closely follows his source, commonly identified as Marius Maximus.[19] The question whether the author adopted the quotation from this source does not admit of an easy answer. As Zoepffel observes, the sentence preceding it seems to imply that Hadrian was worried about Trajan's feelings toward him, so that the consultation of an oracle in any form would follow naturally.[20] On the other hand, the alternative of the Sibylline verses and the unattested Apollonius Syrus Platonicus are clearly in the style of the author as we know it from the secondary lives and the lives in the last part of the *HA*. For the moment I would prefer to see in this passage an embellishment by the author of his source, to which he returns in §10 (*denique statim suffragante Sura ad amicitiam Traiani pleniorem redit*, 'finally, through the good offices of Sura, he was instantly restored to a friendship with Trajan that was closer than ever'). The return may be marked by the words *ut Marius Maximus dicit* ('as Marius Maximus tells us').

Quotations in the secondary lives: *Aelius, Pescennius Niger, Clodius Albinus*

Vergil is introduced again in the life of Aelius, Hadrian's intended successor. It is one of the 'secondary lives', which differ from the main lives of the great emperors of the second century in that the author has little informa-

11. 'The Plato of Poets': Vergil in the Historia Augusta

tion to offer and therefore resorts to different forms of *mythistoria* in the form of prefaces, dedications, fake documents and programmatic statements. In *Aelius* 4 we are told that Hadrian, an expert astrologer, who knew that Aelius did not have long to live, used to say about him:

> ostendent terris hunc tantum fata neque ultra
> esse sinent.
quos versus cum aliquando in hortulo spatians cantitaret, atque adesset unus ex litteratis, quorum Hadrianus speciosa societate gaudebat, velletque addere
> nimium vobis Romana propago
> visa potens, superi[ori], propria haec si dona fuissent
Hadrianus dixisse fertur 'hos versus vita non capit Veri', illud addens:
> manibus date lilia plenis;
> purpureos spargam flores animamque nepotis
> his saltem accumulem donis et fungar inani
> munere

'only a glimpse of him will fate give earth, nor suffer him to stay' (*Aen.* 6.869-70). And once when Hadrian was singing (or 'reciting') these verses while strolling about in his garden, one of the literary men, in whose brilliant company he delighted, happened to be present and proceeded to add, 'Too powerful, O gods above, you deemed the Roman people, had these gifts of yours been lasting' (*Aen.* 6.870-1). Thereupon the emperor remarked, it is said: 'the life of Verus will not admit of these lines,' and added: 'Grant me to scatter in handfuls lilies of purple blossom, to heap at least these gifts on my descendant's shade and perform an unavailing duty' (*Aen.* 6.883-6).

Again the author uses the 'Heldenschau' for his own ends. The seemingly otiose detail that Hadrian sung these verses while walking in his garden deserves special attention. It calls to mind the most famous instance of *sortilegium* in classical literature, the *Tolle, lege* episode in Augustine's *Confessions* 8. That scene is also set in a garden: *hortulus quidam erat hospitii nostri ... abscessi ergo in hortum et Alypius pedem post pedem* ('there was a small garden attached to the house where we lodged .... So I went out into the garden and Alypius followed at my heels', 8.8.19). His friend Alypius, who accompanied him may without exaggeration be called one of the *litterati* in Augustine's circle of friends. Just as Hadrian is singing the verses from the *Aeneid*, Augustine hears *vocem de vicina domo cum cantu dicentis et crebro repetentis quasi pueri aut puellae, nescio* ('a voice from a nearby house, as if it had been of a boy or girl, I cannot say, in a sing-song voice saying and often repeating' etc.). Moreover, just as the *litteratus* in Hadrian's company continues the quotation by Hadrian, Alypius sees a personal relevance in the verse in Paul's Epistle to the Romans (13.14) that comes immediately after the verse that led to

177

Augustine's conversion. It would be rash to assert on the basis of these similarities between the two episodes that the author of the *HA* had the story of Augustine's conversion in mind when he wrote this passage. The warning at the end of Syme's *Ammianus and the Historia Augusta* must always be kept in mind: 'To be much in the company of the *Historia Augusta* is to risk the fatal exhilaration that befell the guests of Africanus, *poculis amplioribus madefacti*.'[21] Still, in view of the mounting evidence that the author was familiar with Christian literature, especially the work of Jerome,[22] correspondences like these should be registered carefully. Isolated instances may not carry conviction; taken together they provide cumulative evidence that cannot be ignored.

The next flight of fancy to be admired is in chapter 8 of the Life of Pescennius Niger, again one of the secondary lives. Pescennius is one of the two rivals of Septimius Severus, the other one being Clodius Albinus. The priest of Apollo at Delphi, when asked who would be the next emperor gave the following answer:

> fundetur sanguis albi nigrique animantis
> imperium mundi Poena reget urbe profectus.

> both of the Black and the White shall the life-blood be shed;
> empire over the world shall be held by the native of Carthage.

As Dessau saw, the second verse with its prediction of Severus' victory is modelled upon *Aeneid* 1.340: *imperium Dido Tyria regit urbe profecta* ('Dido, who came from the city of Tyre, wields the sceptre').[23] The author takes the liberty to adapt Vergil's text to his own purposes. This is continued in the next oracle. The priest responded in the following words to the question how long Severus' reign would last (in Greek, as we are explicitly told: *respondisse Graeco versu dicitur*):

> bis denis Italum conscendit navibus aequor
> si tamen una ratis transiliet pelagus

> in twice ten ships he will cleave the Italian waters
> if only one of his barques will bound over the sea.

Dessau duly noted that the first line, with its prediction of Severus' twenty-year reign, was based on *Aeneid* 1.381: *bis denis Phrygium conscendi navibus aequor* ('with twice ten ships I embarked on the Phrygian sea'). He might have added that the second line is a variation on Horace *Odes* 1.3.23-4: *si tamen impiae / non tangenda rates transiliunt vada* ('If in spite of him the impious ships dash across the depths he meant not to

11. 'The Plato of Poets': Vergil in the Historia Augusta

be touched').[24] This is the first specimen of centonisation and the only example of contamination with other poets. The whole procedure calls to mind the scornful passage in Cicero *De divinatione* 2.116:

> quis enim est qui credat Apollinis ex oraculo Pyrrho esse responsum:
>   Aio te, Aeacida, Romanos vincere posse?
> Primum Latine Apollo numquam locutus est; deinde ista sors inaudita Graecis est; praeterea Pyrrhi temporibus iam Apollo versus facere desierat.

> Who would believe that Apollo's oracle gave the following response to Pyrrhus:
>   'O son of Aeacus, my prediction is that you the Roman army will defeat.'
> In the first place Apollo never spoke in Latin; second, that oracle is unknown to the Greeks; third, in the days of Pyrrhus Apollo had already ceased making verses.

The companion piece to the *Pescennius Niger* is *Clodius Albinus*. The author does not have much real information about this usurper, so he has recourse to his usual tricks, fake documents, an address to the emperor – Constantine this time – and *omina*. In *Clodius Albinus* 5.1 we read that Albinus was a bellicose and arrogant general:

> nam fertur in scholis saepissime cantasse inter puerolos
>   arma amens capio, nec sat rationis in armis
> repetens
>   arma amens capio

> for at school, it is said, he used often to recite to the children:
>   'Frantic I seize arms: yet little purpose is there in arms.'
> And he repeated again and again the words
>   'Frantic I seize arms.' (*Aen.* 2.314).

One of the predictions of his reign is described as follows: Clodius went to the temple of Apollo in Cumae to consult the god about his fate:

> cum illic sortem de fato suo tolleret, his versibus eidem dicitur esse responsum:
>   hic rem Romanam magno turbante tumultu
>   sistet eques, sternet Poenos Gallumque rebellem

> when he made inquiry of the oracle there concerning his fate, he received a response, it is said, in the following lines:
>   'When the Roman state is reeling under a brutal shock,
>   he will steady it, will ride down Carthaginians and the insurgent Gaul'
> (*Aen.* 6.857-8)

The technical expression *sortem tollere* is used incorrectly here. Drawing lots was not the procedure followed at Cumae, but in the temple of Fortuna at Praeneste, as described in Cicero *De divinatione* 2.86: *sortis, quae hodie Fortunae monitu tolluntur* ('At the present time, the lots are taken from the receptacle, if Fortuna directs.').[25] For the use of epic verse by an oracle, we find striking parallels in Cassius Dio, who tells us that Caracalla, when still an ordinary citizen, received an oracle in the sanctuary of Baäl-Zeus at Apamea predicting his future reign in verses taken from the *Iliad* (79.8.6). The same happened later in the same shrine to Macrinus.[26]

Opilius Macrinus and Diadumenianus

The life of the emperor Macrinus opens with a programmatic preface in which the author states his intention to write the lives of little-known rulers: *vitae illorum principum seu tyrannorum sive Caesarum, qui non diu imperarunt* ('The lives of such emperors, usurpers or Caesars, as held their throne for no long time'). The reliable source which he had followed for the great emperors of the second century had clearly run out and the preface marks the beginning of a new section of the *HA*. The life of the short-lived emperor Macrinus contains two short poems that have been translated, clumsily as the author says himself, into Greek. There are also two lines from Vergil, sung by the people when Macrinus' son Diadumenianus entered the circus in honour of his beauty and at the same time to discredit his father (*OM* 12.7):

> egregius forma iuvenis,
> cui pater haud Mezentius esset.

> A youth of passing beauty,
> not deserving to have as his father Mezentius,

another example of centonisation, in which *Aeneid* 6. 861 (*egregium forma iuvenem*, about Marcellus) is joined to 7.654 (about Lausus).

In agreement with this announcement, the author provides a biography of Macrinus' son, whom he calls Diadumenus, although his real name was Diadumenianus. Hardly anything is known about this boy, who was killed at the age of ten, one month after he had been made an Augustus. The author manages to write a short life only by elaborating the theme of the *nomen Antoninorum*, the praise of the emperors who bore that name (which had been adopted by Diadumenianus) and by inserting speeches and letters. In one of these letters (*Dd*. 8.5-8) the young prince protests against the clemency of his father towards insurgents. He embellishes the letter with a quotation from Vergil:

11. 'The Plato of Poets': Vergil in the Historia Augusta

> si te nulla movet tantarum gloria rerum,
> Ascanium surgentem et spes heredis Iuli
> respice, cui regnum Italiae Romanaque tellus
> debetur

'If the glory of such a fortune does not stir you,
have regard for growing Ascanius, the promise of Iulus your heir,
to whom the kingdom of Italy and the Roman lands are due.' (*Aen.* 4. 272-6)[27]

The quotation is well chosen to convince Macrinus that the interest of his son must prevail over any inclination to clemency. According to some, we are informed, the letter was written, not by the young prince himself, but by one Caelianus, a former rhetor from Africa.

Alexander Severus

As we said at the beginning, the *HA* Alexander Severus is depicted as the ideal emperor. In chapter 4 the young emperor is described as beloved by all. He was called *pius, sanctus* and *utilis rei publicae*. When his life was threatened by his predecessor Heliogabalus, he received this oracle in the shrine of Fortuna in Praeneste:

> si qua fata aspera rumpas
> tu Marcellus eris.
>
> Could you but shatter the cruel barrier of fate!
> You are to be Marcellus. (*Aen.* 6.882-3)[28]

Again the oracle is taken from the 'Heldenschau', a passage which the author must have known by heart and to which he will return several times in the sequel.[29] As Marcellus forms the culmination of the 'Heldenschau', the quotation marks Alexander as the emperor par excellence.

Two long chapters (13-14) are devoted to his *omina imperii*. In chapter 14 we are told that both his mother and his father received unmistakable signs of the future greatness of their son. The author continues:

> ipse cum vatem consuleret de futuris, hos accepisse dicitur versus adhuc parvulus et primum quidem sortibus: *te manet imperium caeli terraeque intellectum est, quod inter divos etiam referetur. te manet imperium, quod tenet imperium*, ex quo intellectum est Romani illum imperii principem futurum; nam ubi est imperium nisi apud Romanos, quod tenet imperium? et haec quidem de Graecis versibus prodita. ... inlustratus est Vergilii sortibus huius modi:
> excudent alii spirantia mollius aera,

181

credo equidem, et vivos ducent de marmore vultus,
orabunt causas melius caelique meatus
describent radio et surgentia sidera dicent:
tu regere imperio populos, Romane, memento.
hae tibi erunt artes pacique imponere morem,
parcere subiectis et debellare superbos. (*Aen.* 6. 847-53)

And when Alexander himself consulted a prophet about his future, being still a small child, he received, it is said, the following verses, at first from the *sortes*: 'Thee doth empire await on earth and in heaven.' It was understood that he was even to have a place among the deified emperors; then came 'Thee doth empire await which rules an empire', by which it was understood that he should become ruler of the Roman empire; for where, save at Rome, is there imperial power that rules an empire? And these prophecies came to him in Greek verses. (...) He was honoured by verses from the *sortes Vergilianae*:
'Others, I doubt not, shall with softer mould beat out the breathing bronze, coax from the marble features to the life
plead causes with more eloquence and with a pointer trace
heaven's motions and predict the rising of the stars.
You, Roman, be sure to rule the world (be these your arts)
to crown peace with justice, to spare the vanquished and to crush the proud.'

The passage deserves to be quoted in full, because it is in many ways characteristic of the author's method. First we have two lines that are said to be translated from Greek, which is a sure sign that the author made them up himself.[30] The first one is an incomplete hexameter, in which the sixth foot is missing. Casaubonus duly supplied *marisque* ('and the sea'). But the point of the line is made as it stands, as the author explains himself: Alexander Severus will be deified after his death. The idea of a ruler who is promised a reign in heaven is of course familiar from the fourth *Eclogue* and the proemium to the *Georgics*, but it is not superfluous to note that *imperium caeli terraeque* is a unique phrase,[31] so that Straub's comparison with Matthew 28.18: *data mihi est omnis potestas in caelo et in terra* ('All power in heaven and earth was given to me') does not seem too fanciful. Those words were spoken by Christ after his Resurrection, just as Alexander will receive his *imperium caeli* after his death.[32] The next *sors* is in the form of a pentameter. The question is whether it is just a *lusus verborum* on two different meanings of the word *imperium*,[33] or another allusion to a biblical text, as Straub has argued. Before entering into his argument, we must again realise that the seemingly innocuous phrase *te manet imperium, quod tenet imperium* is highly unusual. The first *imperium* means 'imperial power', the second 'empire'. Now the expression *imperium tenere* is common enough with a personal agent as its subject,[34] but an abstract noun as subject of *tenere imperium* is again

11. 'The Plato of Poets': Vergil in the Historia Augusta

without parallel – reason enough to look closely at other cases in which *imperium* and *tenere* are linked. Straub has pointed to Christian speculations about II Thessalonians 2.6, in which the Apostle refers obscurely to τὸ κατέχον 'that which detains', which prevents the Antichrist from coming, after whom Christ will return for the Last Judgment. He quotes passages from Tertullian, Lactantius, Augustine and Jerome to show that they interpreted τὸ κατέχον as the *imperium Romanum* and translated κατέχειν with *detinere*, c.q. *tenere*.[35] The problem is, however, that in the text from the New Testament and in the interpretations by Latin Christian writers, the verb κατέχειν, c.q. *tenere/detinere* are used absolutely and that the Antichrist must be supplied as its object, whereas in the text under discussion *tenere* has *imperium* in the sense of 'empire' as its object. For that reason there is, in my opinion, no compelling reason to interpret *Alexander Severus* 14.4 as an allusion to these eschatological Christian views.

On the other hand, the insistence that by 'empire' the Roman empire must be meant is puzzling. It is unlikely that anyone in the early days of Alexander would have expected otherwise. In the period, however, in which the *HA* was given its final form, that is to say well after the battle of Adrianople, confidence had been shaken and the future of the empire did seem to be in danger.[36] In that context an assurance such as is given in the present holds a message for the contemporary reader not to despair of the situation. There is no alternative world power to take over from Rome and the end of Rome is not approaching. And here Vergil is introduced to drive the message home. The proud and classical assertion that it is Rome's mission to rule the world in what are probably the most quoted lines in the *Aeneid* crowns this passage that began with doggerel of the author's own making.

Again we are forced to think of Augustine, who on the first page of his *De civitate Dei* challenged Vergil's proud proclamation. *Rex enim et conditor civitatis huius ... in scriptura populi sui sententiam divinae legis aperuit, qua dictum est: Deus superbis resistit, humilibus autem dat gratiam* ('The king and founder of this City has in the scriptures of his people revealed this statement of the divine law, which says: "God resists the proud and gives grace to the humble" ').[37]

After Alexander

With the life of Alexander Severus the author seems to have used up the possibilities of this play with Vergil and we do not come across new types of imitation. In the lives of the two Maximini, the son is honoured with a quotation from Vergil in praise of his beauty (*Max.* 27.4), just as had been done in the life of Diadumenianus:

> qualis ubi Oceani perfusus Lucifer unda,
> extulit os sacrum caelo tenebrasque resolvit,
> talis erat iuvenis patrio sub nomine clarus.

> Like to the star of the morning when he, new-bathed in the Ocean,
> raises his holy face and scatters the darkness from heaven,
> So did the young man seem, fair-famed in the name of his father.

Here *Aeneid* 8. 589 and 591 are followed by a lame verse added by the author himself. We are told that the tutor of the young prince Fabillus, a Greek man of letters, translated these lines from Vergil into Greek verse. Translations such as these, most often from Greek into Latin, are an oddity in the *HA*. Repeatedly, the author himself criticises the poor quality of these translations.[38] In an earlier publication I compared the author in this respect to Ausonius, whose works contain a number of poems, marked *ex Graeco* ('from the Greek') in the manuscripts.[39] This time I would like to add that again in Augustine we find strikingly similar remarks. Even the criticism of the performance of the translator is there: *haec sane Erythraea sibylla quaedam de Christo manifesta conscripsit, quod etiam nos prius in latina lingua versibus male latinis et non stantibus legimus per nescio cuius interpretis imperitiam, sicut post cognovimus* ('This Erythraean Sibyl certainly wrote some passages that openly refer to Christ: these we read first in a Latin translation composed in verses of poor Latinity and not metrically sound, due to the ignorance of their anonymous translator, as we afterwards learned', *De civ. D.* 18.23).

The prophecy about Marcellus in the 'Heldenschau' (*Aen.* 6.869-71) seems to be the author's favourite passage. It is quoted once again in *Gd.* 20.5 about Gordianus Junior in a prediction by the Elder Gordian of the untimely death of his son, just as Hadrian had predicted the early death of Aelius. The first line of the prophecy is quoted a third time in the life of Claudius 10.6 about the short reign of that emperor's brother Quintillus. In the same chapter we find no fewer than three *sortes* given to Claudius. The first, in hendecasyllables, no doubt of the author's own making, predicts a brilliant future for Claudius' offspring. When the emperor inquired after the duration of his reign, he received the following oracle: *tertia dum Latio regnantem viderit aestas* ('until the third summer will have seen him as king in Latium', *Aen.* 1.265), which tallies exactly with the period of September 268 – September 270 during which he was Augustus. About his descendants he was told *his ego nec metas rerum nec tempora pono* ('Neither a goal nor a limit of time will I set for their power', *Aen.* 1.278), which was Baynes' main argument for his thesis that the *HA* was written to celebrate Julian the Apostate, the last emperor of the second Flavian dynasty.

11. 'The Plato of Poets': Vergil in the Historia Augusta

Finally, in the life of Tacitus (5.1) the aged senator is called upon by his fellow-senators to accept the throne. When he pleads to be excused on account of his old age he is put under pressure by acclamations such as these: *et Hadrianus ad imperium senex venit* and *et tu legisti: incanaque menta regis Romani*. The explicit mention of Hadrian and the quotation of the same verse from the 'Heldenschau' betrays the same hand we saw at work earlier in the life of Hadrian.

*

This is not a complete list of Virgilian reminiscences in the *HA*,[40] but the examples presented so far give a clear impression of the ways the author treated the sacred text of the *Aeneid*. The following general observations can be made. The range of the quotations is small. The 'Heldenschau' provides the bulk of the material. Quotations from this passage are found in all parts of the work, in most of which the author clearly does not follow his sources timidly, but indulges his personal whims. In all probability this is even the case in the otherwise reliable life of Hadrian. The resemblance to *Tacitus* 5.1 makes it practically certain that the quotation in *Hadrian* 2.8 was an addition by the author himself. So the use of verses from the *Aeneid* may be added to the list of devices that are dear to him, along with the prefaces, the fake documents and the programmatic statements.

The most important passage is the one in *Alexander Severus* in which the quotation from the 'Heldenschau' serves to inspire confidence in the future of Rome. In this respect the *HA* is diametrically opposed to Christian authors such as Lactantius and Augustine. It cannot be stated with absolute confidence that the author directly makes a stand against Christian views, but a number of resemblances between the *HA* and the *Tolle, lege* episode in Augustine's *Confessions* does suggest that the author of the *HA* was familiar with Augustine's work.

Notes

1. The best overview of the '*HA*-Forschung' is Chastagnol's (1994) 'Introduction Générale'. In English Syme (1968) and (1971) together with Barnes (1978) are the most important contributions. This is not the right place for a detailed discussion of the 'Autorfrage', but I want to specify my position at the outset as follows: in view of the heterogeneous character of the *HA* I would personally prefer to speak of the 'redactor' rather than the 'author' of the collection. I conform to the prevailing terminology not to distract attention from the main subject, the use made of Vergil in the *HA*. Lives are referred to by standard abbreviations.

2. I have found no exact parallel for this designation of Vergil, but ὦ σοφώτατε ποιητὰ Μάρων ('Maro, wisest of poets') in Constantine's *Oratio ad sanctorum coetum* 20 comes close. It is modelled on expressions concerning Plato himself, like

deus philosophorum, Homerus philosophorum ('the god, the Homer of philosophers'), for which see Pease (1955, 1958); Cic. *Nat. D.* 2.32.

3. Unless stated otherwise, the English translations are taken, with slight adaptations, from the Loeb editions.

4. More on this topic in Rösger (1976) 9-18.

5. *Gd.* 3.2 *scripsit praeterea, quemadmodum Vergilius Aeneidos et Statius Achilleidos et multi alii Alexandridos (Alexandriados?), ita etiam ille Antoniniados* ('Besides these, just as Vergil wrote an Aeneid, Statius an *Achilleïd* and many others *Alexandriads*, he wrote an *Antoniniad*'). In *ThLL* II 189.63 this term is mistaken for a genitive (sc. *carmen*). The author must have thought *Antoniniados* was a patronymic of the type *Memmiades*.

6. See the Index Nominum in Hohl's Teubner edition. Under the name of Vergil Hohl also gives the references to the *Aeneid*. The list is not complete. See also Velaza (1996) 305, who adds *Aen.* 1.381 (*PN* 8.6), but omits 7.654 (*OM* 12.9). Velaza has studied the text of the quotations in the *HA* from Vergil. He concludes that it is closest to F (Vaticanus Latinus 3225) and P (Vaticanus Palatinus Latinus 1631).

7. *Ciceroni Catonem, Vergilio Ennium, Sallustio Coelium praetulit, H.* 16.6.

8. (1920, 1923) on Cic. *Div.* 1.12; the note provides an excellent introduction to this form of divination. See further Bouché-Leclercq (1882) IV 145-59 and for modern literature De Kisch (1970) 324 n. 1, but above all Courcelle (1952) and (1963) 143-63. De Kisch does mention Courcelle's article *Divinatio* in *RAC*, but he seems to have missed Courcelle's fundamental studies on the '*Tolle, lege*' episode in *Conf.* Cf. Klingshirn (2002).

9. In Graham Greene's novel *Travels with My Aunt* the narrator, Henry Pulling, relates how his father used to consult the works of Sir Walter Scott for playing the *Sortes* – 'a game my mother considered a little blasphemous unless it was played with the Bible.' See Katz (1994) 258.

10. A similar criticism is voiced by Jerome in a letter to Paulinus of Nola, 53.7, where he speaks of people who *nec scire dignantur quid prophetae, quid apostoli senserint, sed ... ad voluntatem suam scripturam trahere repugnantem* ('who do not deign to know what the prophets and the apostles thought ... but adapt the bible against its intention to their own ends.' Jerome goes on to speak about *Homerocentones* and *Vergiliocentones*, my translation). Cf. Pollmann above.

11. Cic. *Div.* 2.86.

12. The procedure is already described in Homer (*Il.* 3.316, *Od.* 10.206-7). In the *HA* itself we find it in *Pr.* 8.4.

13. As Dessau (1892) 583 remarks in passing, this procedure is difficult to imagine with the *volumen*; a *codex* is much better suited to this purpose.

14. The *sortes Astrampsychi* are a collection of oracles probably dating from the third century. For a detailed description see Björck (1939).

15. In all probability the author regarded the quoted lines as a finished sentence, in which *cui* referred to *imperium* rather than to *regis Romani*. It is therefore misleading to end the quotation at *imperium magnum*, as Zoepffel (1978) does. Naturally, Hadrian interpreted the lines as a prediction of his future reign.

16. The literal interpretation is favoured by Dessau (1892) 582; Casaubonus in his note ad loc. in his Paris edition of 1603 prefers the latter interpretation.

17. e.g. *Orac. Sib.* 5.46-50, 8. 50-9, 12.163-75. See Callu (1992) ad loc. and in particular Zoepffel (1978) 394 n. 16 and 425-7.

18. Cf. also *Ep.* 104.11 *Nam utique hoc non a se ipso se dixisse Vergilius in eclogae ipsius quarto ferme versu indicat, ubi ait ... unde hoc a Cumaea Sibylla dictum esse incunctanter apparet* ('for no doubt Vergil himself indicates himself in

11. 'The Plato of Poets': Vergil in the Historia Augusta

about the fourth verse of his *Eclogue* that he has not sung these words by himself ... this proves plainly that this has been sung by the Cumaean Sibyl'). See Guillaumin (1978) 191 and Wlosok (1983) 71.

19. For recent literature on the vexed problem of Marius Maximus, see Paschoud (1994).

20. (1978) 293; unfortunately the sentence is incomplete. It is impossible to assess the extent of the lacuna.

21. (1968) 220.

22. Paschoud (2001) 179.

23. (1918) 391.

24. The interpretation of the line from Horace, more specifically of *tamen*, in the new context is far from clear. In Horace *tamen* expresses the contrast between the ordinance of Jupiter and the disobedience of men. In the oracle concocted by the author of the *HA tamen* can only be understood as a proviso: Severus' reign will last twenty years, provided he manages to bring one year to an end, i.e. provided he succeeds in disposing of his rivals. If this is what the author intended to say, he would have done better to change the perfect *conscendi* to the future *conscendet*, which is the reading of S. But it is entirely possible that he could not be bothered.

25. More examples in Courcelle (1952) 183 n. 55.

26. 79.40.4, 'upon his consulting the oracle of Zeus Belus the god had answered him: "Truly indeed, old man, young warriors sorely beset thee, spent is thy force, and grievous old age is coming upon thee." ' (*Il.* 8.102-3).

27. Line 273 is omitted in accordance with the primary mss.

28. Bouché-Leclercq IV, 153 must have had this passage in mind when he wrote: 'À un moment où l'*Énéide* passait moins pour un chef-d'oeuvre humain que pour un livre inspiré et où les sorts virgiliens étaient à la mode, la Fortune se servit, pour répondre des vers de Virgile.'

29. He evidently interprets the *si*-clause as conditional rather than as a wish, as it must certainly be taken in the original context. It is impossible to decide if this is how he read Vergil's text, or whether he adapts it to the new context: 'if you escape the threat from Heliogabalus, you will live to be a Marcellus.'

30. Casaubonus in the note ad loc. translated them back for the benefit of his readers, but as we have seen, the author does not hesitate to present quotations from Latin poets as translations. Apart from *PN* 8.6, discussed above, we have *OM* 14.2

centum nam moechos passa est centumque rogavit.

ipse etiam calvus moechus fuit, inde maritus

'Lovers a hundred she knew and a hundred were those whom she courted

Lover was also the bald head, who later was known as her husband'

in which we have a centonisation of Cat. 11.16-17 and Suet. *Caes.* 51. See also Straub (1963) 150, n. 70 and Baldwin (1978).

31. I found no parallel in the CD-Rom containing the *Bibliotheca Teubneriana* nor in the *ThLL* s.v. *imperium*.

32. For a full discussion see Straub (1963) 149-63.

33. So the *ThLL* VII 1.580.31.

34. e.g. Verg. *Aen.* 1.236 (*Romanos*) *qui mare, qui terras omnis dicione tenerent* ('[The Romans] who were to hold all sea and land under their sway')

35. e.g. Augustine *De civ. D.* 20.19.3 *non absurde de ipso Romano imperio creditur dictum* ('not without reason this is taken to refer to the Roman empire itself'), and Jerome *in Hiër.* 5, 27 (*CSEL* 59, 312) *eum qui tenet, Romanum imperium ostendit* ('He demonstrates Roman power who holds him').

36. For the impact of the battle of Adrianople and the anxiety of observers like Ambrose and Jerome see most recently Lenski (1997).

37. See MacCormack (1998) 200-2, whose translation is quoted here.

38. Very little has been written on this, admittedly inferior, poetry. See Baldwin (1978).

39. (1995)

40. Other undisputed instances are *AS* 41.1 – *Aen.* 1.655; *Gall.* 8.7 – *Aen.* 8.717; *Tac.* 24.3 – *Aen.* 6.365 (also in Eutropius); *Car.* 2.3 – *Aen.* 4.229; *Car.* 13.3 – *Aen.* 10.830.

12

The Truth about Vergil's Commentators

Charles Murgia

In the title, of course, I have my tongue in my cheek. Everyone who speaks or writes claims to tell the truth, yet what is said on any given subject varies widely, not only because of differences in knowledge, experience, and judgment of the speaker or writer, but because of differences in the questions which concern different critics, and of the kinds of answers which they take to satisfy those questions. The most obvious example from Servius' commentary on Vergil is his explanation of the two gates of dreams at *Aeneid* 6.893-6. There are two gates of sleep, Vergil tells us, one of horn, through which *verae umbrae* exit, the other of ivory, through which the shades send false dreams to the upper world. Through the latter gate, the gate of false dreams, Anchises sends Aeneas and the Sibyl out of the underworld (898). The implication, that Aeneas and the Sibyl are false dreams, has bothered, or at least attracted the attention, of critics ever since, especially those who have compared, as the ancient commentators did too, the corresponding passage in Homer. First of all, Servius does not reduce the question to one of Latin semantics: *verae umbrae* could, so far as the Latin goes, be taken to mean 'genuine ghosts' as against 'dreams', which are pretended ghosts. But the commentary tradition is aware of Penelope's description of the gates of true and false dreams in *Odyssey* 19.562-7, and Servius firmly asserts that by *umbrae verae* Vergil means *somnia vera*, 'true dreams'. That said, he has no problem. Poetically, he says, the meaning is obvious. Vergil wants us to understand that everything that he has said is false. End of poetic explanation.

Servius now passes on to give us the physiological explanation, which seeks to explain, not why Aeneas and the Sibyl leave through the gate of false dreams, but why the gate of false dreams is of ivory, and gate of true shades is of horn. So Servius does distinguish different levels of interpretation, but even his poetic explanation is understandable only in the light of an understanding of Servius' own concerns, and of the kind of question which he, as a *grammaticus*, asks of a poetic text.

For a modern literary critic, an explanation that the poet symbolically has revealed that everything that he has said is false is horrendously problematic: is it a proper function of serious poetry to lie, and then admit to the lie? A poet can undercut some of what he says, but can he undercut everything? A poet can speak differently with the symbolic meaning of his text than he appears to do in the surface meaning of his text, but can he deny even the symbolic meaning? Servius perceives none of the problems which a modern critic would have with a statement *falsa esse omnia quae dixit*, 'that everything that Vergil has said is false'. To determine Servius' meaning, one must first determine what it is that Servius believes Vergil has said; and that belief is in part determined by the questions which Servius asks of the text.

Servius composed probably in the early fifth century, perhaps in its first decade, shortly after Christianity had essentially triumphed over paganism.[1] The Roman religion was not, like the Christian religion, a body of beliefs, but its essential characteristic was sacrifice, and when in 391 the emperor Theodosius banned sacrifice, he rang the death knell for polytheistic religion, at least in Rome itself (the word *pagani* attests that pagan practices continued longer outside the City). Polytheistic beliefs could continue, but a Roman religion that could not be practised was not (in the same sense) a religion. The *grammatici* however viewed themselves as preservers of knowledge of antiquity. Vergil and other poets were available as source books from which, together with a long tradition of ancient comment, such knowledge could be extracted. Among the knowledge extracted from the texts and earlier commentaries was knowledge of Roman religion and ritual, which had always been assiduously noted by the *grammatici*; but in late antiquity more than ever, when Roman religion was under challenge, such knowledge needed to be noted for students in their middle teens who might never actually see such ritual performed.

Aelius Donatus probably taught about the time of Julian the Apostate, who died in 363.[2] So though the practice of Roman religion was allowed, and even in a state of revival, attempts to suppress it had already occurred and would occur again. Probably even if pagan religious practices were not under threat Donatus would have had an interest in noting them, as matters of importance for a living religion, but the religious turmoil of the time made preservation of such knowledge all the more important, and all the more dependent on the role of the *grammaticus*. But when Donatus described sacrifice and ritual, he did so in the present tense, as something which continued to be performed in his day.[3] When Servius borrowed these descriptions from Donatus, he usually changed Donatus' present tenses into past tenses, thereby indicating to us that they are things of the past in Servius' time. Nevertheless, Servius was not a Christian.[4] But, since he lived in an age in which what we refer to as paganism, or at least its

12. The Truth about Vergil's Commentators

rituals, had been banned and Christianity was demanding assent to its tenets, the determination of the truth about basic elements of religious belief, such as the existence of the gods and the immortality of the soul, was a pressing concern to him. And since the source of all knowledge was the text of Vergil as interpreted by the grammatical tradition, it was natural that Servius would look to Vergil as furnishing basic truths about the universe in which we live. Servius is careful to distinguish between *fabula* ('fable') and *vera historia* ('true history').[5] What poets present directly, complete with divine apparatus, is *fabula*, and not to be taken as factually true; but occasionally they allude to *historia*.

In *Aeneid* 6.893, when Servius says that Vergil wants us to understand that everything that he has said is false, Servius means nothing more than that there is no life after death, and there is no underworld. Aeneas never went down to the underworld: that is *fabula*. We find Servius expressing directly his attitude toward life after death in his comment on *Aeneid* 5.725 (where the ghost of Anchises speaks):

> **725.** CARE MAGIS pro 'carior'. bene autem addidit *dum vita manebat*: nulla enim est vita post mortem.

> **725.** MORE DEAR is used for 'dearer'. But he did well to add 'while my life remained': for there is no life after death.

Although I have tried to set Servius in the context of the time in which he wrote, I do not believe that there is much difference between the standards of judgment of Servius and of earlier *grammatici*. All operated in a traditional mode of thought, and if Servius wanted to preserve knowledge of ancient religion because its preservation might otherwise die out, earlier commentators equally wanted to preserve it for reasons suited to their own times.

One characteristic that informed the commentary tradition from the earliest times when we can contact it is the belief among the main stream of *grammatici* that the poet never erred. If there is anything which seems unjustified, the fault is with our understanding of antiquity, and not because the poet has done something wrong, or even innovated (which to the *grammaticus* is as good as doing something wrong). This view can be traced back at least to Valerius Probus, the last of the *grammatici* described by Suetonius in his *De grammaticis et rhetoribus*. Since Suetonius (24.4) claims that Probus published very few and slight works, but left a large forest of observations on ancient usage, there is no agreement whether Probus ever composed or published a commentary on Vergil (or possibly a collection of comments called *Silva*) or edited Vergil. First-rate scholars may be found on all possible sides of the issues.

Aulus Gellius cites Probus six times by name, but in all his citations Probus' testimony is presented as something that Gellius has heard. In the two that refer to Vergil (9.9.12 and 13.21.1) Gellius claims to know Probus' view from his students (*ex Valerii Probi discipulis*) and from a close friend of Probus (*ex familiari eius quodam*). This may be just verisimilitude. Actually the best evidence that suggests that Probus left a written commentary on Vergil comes from Gellius, 2.6[6] where Probus is not named by Gellius, but where the interpretation of Gellius 2.6.5 is attributed to Probus by Servius on *Eclogue* 6.76,[7] and Servius Auctus expanded Servius with words which agree closely with Gellius.[8] Again, on *Aeneid* 10.314, Servius Auctus agrees closely with the section of Gellius 2.6 (19-22) which comments on that line. The third comment in Gellius 2.6 (9-18) is on *Georgics* 3.4, a section for which Servius Auctus does not survive except through the diluted excerpts of the Vatican scholia. Servius' usual source was the commentary of Aelius Donatus, and since Servius elsewhere cites Probus and Donatus together (as on *Aen.* 6.177 *Probus et Donatus ... dixerunt*, on *Aen.* 7.543 *Probus, Asper, Donatus*), we should suppose that citations of Probus reach Servius through attributions in Donatus' commentary.

Donatus himself tells us that it was his practice to copy his sources verbatim,[9] and we can observe a similar practice in Servius Auctus, which is a probably seventh-century conflation of Servius with another ancient commentary, either the commentary of Aelius Donatus or a commentary which often copied Donatus verbatim. The Compiler, as I call the monk who made the conflation, copied Servius as far as Servius went, and then supplemented Servius with material from the other ancient commentary, making only minimal changes to facilitate connection and to reflect the status of the new commentary as a separate work. (For instance on *Aen.* 5.725, which I quoted earlier, the Compiler suppressed Servius' statement that there was no life after death.[10]) Servius, on the other hand, did not copy verbatim, but deliberately reworded what he found in Donatus or other sources, as we can observe by comparing Servius' life of Vergil with Donatus'.

On *Eclogue* 6.76, when Servius Auctus supplements Servius with words which agree closely with Gellius, the simplest explanation has both Servius and Servius Auctus deriving the comment from Donatus, and Donatus deriving it from Probus' comment on the line, which Gellius also copied verbatim. The first sentence of Gellius' chapter places us in the genre of commentaries: *nonnulli grammatici aetatis superioris, in quibus est Cornutus Annaeus ... qui commentaria in Vergilium composuerunt* ('Some *grammatici* of the previous age (among whom is Annaeus Cornutus) ... who have composed commentaries on Vergil'). The chapter is couched as a response to ancient commentators on Vergil, but most likely

12. The Truth about Vergil's Commentators

that response was itself lifted from a commentary which defended Vergil against the criticism of earlier *grammatici*. So Cornutus here falls in the category of detractors of Vergil (*obtrectatores* or *Vergiliomastiges*), mentioned by Servius (on *Aen.* 5.521 and *Ecl.* 2.23) and Donatus' *Life* (ch. 43), and against whom Asconius Pedianus is reported to have written a work (*Life* 46).

There is a clear shift in style when Gellius launches into the defence in section 5. *sed de verbo vexasse ita responderi posse credo* reads as if it is Gellius' own bridging filler, but what immediately follows reads like a direct quotation from a commentator: *vexasse grave verbum est factumque ab eo [videtur] quod est 'vehere', in quo inest vis iam quaedam alieni arbitrii; non enim sui potens est qui vehitur*. This (with the exception of *videtur*) reads with the style of a *grammaticus*, especially the *ab eo quod est* (which is among what Servius attributes to Probus, and which is a standard expression among the *grammatici* for introducing an etymology). Servius Auctus (quoted in n. 8) has added from Donatus the parts which Servius omitted, and his awkward *est enim* (which gets two *enim*s in successive clauses) results from the Compiler's makeshift way of combining the additional comment without duplicating anything that Servius had already paraphrased: Servius' *ab eo quod est veho* paraphrases *ab eo quod est vehere*, which in Donatus would have provided the antecedent for *in quo*, but is now too far removed to do so; therefore *in quo inest* of Probus/Gellius/Donatus has been supplanted with *est enim*. The comments in Gellius are all attached to a Vergilian lemma, in the sequence of texts of Vergil (*Ecl., Geo., Aen.*), or at least of the ancient commentaries on Vergil. Gellius seems to have combined comments from three separate parts of a running commentary. This seems to have been a variorum commentary: note for instance how two explanations of *inlaudati* are joined in section 15 by *altero modo 'inlaudatus' ita defenditur* ('*inlaudatus* is defended in another way as follows'), a mechanism in a variorum commentary for combining the comments of more than one commentator, and a good indication that Gellius is reproducing transmitted lore, not inventing his own explanations. Further, since Servius attributes to Probus the defence of *vexasse* by reference to *vehere*, and shares with Gellius the word *arbitrium* (not a natural word to connect with *vexare*), it is clear that Gellius did not originate the explanation of the word which he gives.

The evidence suggests as Gellius' source a commentator writing after Cornutus (and before Gellius). Probus fits. Since Probus is said to have published little himself but to have left a whole forest of comments, it is possible that the commentary of 'Probus' in question was not published by Probus himself, but by some student from his notes. Or the commentary in question may not even be a commentary that went under the name of

Probus, but one which introduced the explanation of *vexasse* with something such as *quod Probus ita defendit* ('which Probus defends as follows'); Gellius is careful when he begins each comment to obscure his borrowing (5 *ita responderi posse credo*, 9 *duo videntur responderi posse*), but his *ita defenditur* in 15 gives the game away, and suggests that the individual comments may have started with something such as 'So and so' *ita defendit*.

But the best reason for believing that the commentary went under the name of Probus himself is that Gellius does not attribute any of the comments to Probus. Probus was an authority worthy of naming if the source had named him. But it is standard policy not to name proximate sources except for refutation. So the commentary which is being used will have named Annaeus Cornutus as a foil for refutation, and Gellius transmits that name, but Probus' name is not invoked probably because it is Probus' work from which Gellius directly borrows. On the other hand, when Donatus excerpted Probus, he gave explicit credit (as was his custom), while Servius, in borrowing from Donatus, followed his own custom of crediting the ultimate source (Probus) while suppressing the proximate source (Donatus).

The fragment of Probus in Gellius and the Servian commentaries puts Probus in this instance on the side of defenders of Vergil, although we do have other fragments of Probus which show him critical. The urge to defend can be traced back further, to Hyginus, a freedman of Augustus, in the comment transmitted by Servius on *Aeneid* 12.120.

12.120 VELATI LINO atqui fetiales et pater patratus, per quos bella vel foedera confirmabantur, numquam utebantur vestibus lineis. unde dicimus errore factum, ut linea vestis contra morem adhiberetur ad foedera quae firma futura non erant. scimus enim hoc ubique servare Vergilium, ut rebus quibus denegaturus est exitum, det etiam infirma principia. sic in Thracia (3.21), civitatem condens Aeneas quam mox fuerat relicturus, contra morem Iovi de tauro sacrificavit. sic senatum ad privata Latinus convocat tecta (11.234), quando eius non erunt firma consilia. sic paulo post (12.247) in augurio liberatus cycnus in fluvium concidit, quia Turnum Rutuli, licet rupto foedere, liberare non poterunt. Caper tamen (40 K) et Hyginus (11 F) hoc loco dicunt lectionem esse corruptam: nam Vergilium ita reliquisse confirmant 'velati limo'. limus autem est vestis qua ab umbilico usque ad pedes teguntur pudenda poparum.

12.120 VEILED WITH LINEN and yet the *fetiales* and *pater patratus*, through whom wars or treaties were confirmed, never used linen clothing. As a result we say that it was done in error that a linen garment was employed contrary to usage for a treaty which was not going to hold. For we know that Vergil everywhere preserves the practice of giving weak beginnings as well to

12. The Truth about Vergil's Commentators

anything to which he is going to deny an end. So in Thrace, when founding a city which he was soon going to leave, Aeneas contrary to usage sacrificed to Jupiter with a bull. So Latinus calls the senate to a private home when his advice was not going to stand. So a little after in an augury a freed swan falls into water because the Rutulians, despite breaking the truce, will not be able to free Turnus. Nevertheless Caper and Hyginus say that in this passage the reading is corrupt: for they affirm that Vergil had left *velati limo*. A *limus* is a garment, streching from the navel to the feet, with which the private parts of *popae* are covered.

In the passage of Vergil, the Rutulians and Trojans are preparing to strike a treaty of peace. Some prepare altars, others were bringing water and fire, *velati lino et verbena tempora vincti*, as the MSS have it: 'hooded with linen and with their temples bound with *verbena*'. The line created a problem, because, as Servius tells us, the *fetiales* and *pater patratus*, who later were in charge of the ceremonies of peace and war, allegedly from the time of Numa, never wore linen. Evidently Vergil was subjected to criticism for this reading at an early date (the underlying assumption being that Vergil should provide accurate aetiology of Roman ritual). Servius gives a rather sophisticated interpretation: Vergil is not ignorant, but has deliberately injected a discordant element because the peace treaty was ill-fated.[11]

But Servius also reports a different interpretation of *Aeneid* 12.120 by Hyginus and Caper, that Vergil did not write *lino*, but *limo*.[12] The *limus* is a type of butcher's skirt worn by *popae*, the ministers who actually brought the animals for sacrifice, and performed the physical acts of sacrifice, such as wielding the axe. We have depictions of them in illustrated MSS of Vergil, stripped to the waist and wearing the skirt from waist to foot to catch the blood of sacrifice. The *popae* were in a very menial role: the priest did not wear a *limus*, and I would doubt very much if *fetiales* or *pater patratus* wore one. But our interest here is that once Hyginus had rescued Vergil from the charge of using the wrong cloth in a religious context, he evidently did not feel compelled to deal with the problems of the new reading. *velare* is the *vox propria* for covering one's head; the *vox propria* for wearing a *limus* is *cincti*. Although *velare* can also be used of covering other parts of the body, almost all of Vergil's uses refer to covering one's head, especially in sacred contexts.[13] So connected is *velare* with sacrifice that Lucretius was able to say *velatum saepe videri* ('often to be seen veiled') with the meaning 'often to be seen sacrificing' (5.1198). No one takes Lucretius to mean 'to be seen wearing a *limus*'. When no other part of the body is specified, *velatum* means 'with the head veiled'.[14]

The aetiology for sacrificial veiling is given in *Aeneid* 3.403-9, where Helenus advises Aeneas when he sacrifices to veil his lock with an *amictus* (that is, a cloak that can be drawn over the head). Servius rightly explains the purpose of the Roman practice was avoidance of any ill-omened sight.

In 3.543 Aeneas follows Helenus' advice, and he and his men veil their heads with a Phrygian *amictus*. In 8.33 the apparition of the Tiber was veiled with a linen *amictus*. The D comment on the line is *quod autem ait 'tenuis glauco velabat amictu carbasus' docet quaedam sacra pure a linteatis debere fieri. carbasus autem genus lini est* ('That he says 'a thin *carbasus* veiled him with a blue cloak' teaches that certain rites have to be performed purely by men clothed in linen. *carbasus* is a type of linen').[15] There is no recognition here of a problem with wearing linen at sacrifices. So in 12.120, the Trojans did not wear a butcher's skirt over their heads or even around their waist. It is much more likely that they hooded their heads to avoid any ill-omened sight, which would have prevented continuance of the ceremony.

A more prominent example of a commentator's feeling his duties acquitted when he has answered the first level of questioning is Servius' explanation of the beginning of the *Aeneid*. Many debate why Vergil began from *arma*, he says, but this is idleness, since everyone knows that he did not, but began with *ille ego qui quondam* ('I am he who once'). Servius thinks that he has answered the question, but he has simply dodged it. 'Why then did Vergil begin with *ille ego*?' most of us would ask. The commentator feels no need to explain, and is not even conscious that it would be much easier to explain why Vergil began with *arma* than it would be to explain why an epic poet would begin with *ille ego*; Servius has just claimed (*praef*. 101) *veteres incipiebant carmen a titulo carminis, ut puta 'arma virumque cano'* ('The ancient poets used to begin a poem with the title, as for example *I sing of arms and a man*').[16]

Again, in the *Georgics* ancient commentators had difficulty explaining the long excursus on Orpheus and Euridice and on Aristaeus. The commentators solved their problem in a typical way. Servius on *Georgics* 4.1 (and *Ecl.* 10.1): the excursus was not originally there, but the whole second half of book 4 contained praise of Gallus. The original question solved, no need was felt to answer why a poem on farming, dedicated to Augustus, should end with half a book praising Gallus, nor was any need felt to explain why it should be an excursus on Aristaeus that filled the space left by removing the praise.

In fairness to Servius, he was able to see through a similar approach to the unexplained when his range of experience permitted. So (*praef.* 89-96) he rejected the claim that there originally was no flashback in *Aeneid* 2-3, since he knew that flashbacks belonged to epic style. Servius did not lack intelligence so much as breadth of experience. Lacking experience of Hellenistic Greek poetry, he was susceptible to an external explanation of the excursus in *Georgics* 4 once he found it in his learned predecessors. I think that modern critics would find the excursus more easily explainable than what Servius believed to have been Vergil's original text. But it is

12. The Truth about Vergil's Commentators

important to recognise the intellectual environment in which stories such as the original ending of the *Georgics*, the original beginning of the *Aeneid*, the original sequence of *Aeneid* 1-4, and various learned variants in the texts develop and gain some degree of acceptance. Respect for the learning of the scholiastic tradition should be tempered with a highly developed sense of scepticism.

More than scepticism, but even scorn for the learning of the *grammaticus* was manifested in the second half of the fourth century by Tiberius Claudius Donatus, who wrote a rhetorical analysis of the *Aeneid*, insisting that Vergil should be interpreted not by the *grammaticus* but by the orator. Tiberius does everything the opposite of Aelius Donatus, insisting, in a long prefatory letter to his son, that he will be wordy, while Aelius Donatus, in a brief letter to Munatius, says that he will be brief, and will report even the words of his sources verbatim.[17] While Aelius Donatus presented a variorum commentary, culling the wisdom of a long tradition, Tiberius offers his own analyses, and has no tolerance for the claimed inside information of the *grammatici* (although it is clear that he knew and sometimes borrowed from them). So Tiberius has no hesitation in saying that the *Aeneid* properly starts in the seventh year of Aeneas' wanderings, lest it become repetitive when Dido, at the end of book 1, asks Aeneas to recount his adventures: *haec ergo quae posterioris temporis fuerunt posuit prima et in aliud tempus superiora distulit, ut in convivio Didonis narrarentur, ne, si prima ponerentur, odiosum foret haec eadem inquirente Didone repetere, quae vitandae prolixitatis causa semel dici convenerat* ('Therefore events which belonged to a later time he put first and delayed the previous to another time to be narrated in the banquet of Dido, lest, if they be put first, it would be tiresome to repeat, when Dido asked, events which it was better to say once to avoid being prolix', p. 6f. G).

Another rejection of the comment of Aelius Donatus can be reconstructed at *Aeneid* 1.4, *saevae memorem Iunonis ob iram*. There Tiberius comments: *non enim saevam potentem dixit, ut alii volunt, sed revera saevam, quae persequeretur innocentem et eum qui nihil admisisset et esset deorum omnium perindeque ipsius quoque Iunonis antistes et cultor* ('He has not meant by *saevam* "powerful", as others want, but genuinely "cruel", since she pursued an innocent man who had committed no wrong and who was a priest and worshipper of all the gods as well as of Juno herself'). Tiberius is having none of the attempt of *grammatici* to rescue Vergil's piety by claiming that *saeva* means *potens*. Now this diction comes from Aelius Donatus, as we can reconstruct in three ways.

First, Servius on the line so interprets: *cum a iuvando dicta sit Iuno, quaerunt multi cur eam dixerit 'saevam', et putant temporale est epitheton, quasi saeva circa Troianos, nescientes quod saevam dicebant veteres magnam, ut Ennius, 'induta fuit saeva stola'; item Vergilius, cum ubique pium indicat Aenean, ait 'maternis saevus in armis Aeneas', id est, 'magnus'.* ('Since the name Juno is formed from *iuvando* ("helping"), many ask why Vergil has called her *saeva*, and they think that it is a temporal epithet, on the grounds that she is cruel toward the Trojans, unaware that the ancients used *saeva* for *magna* ("great"), as Ennius, "she was clothed in a *saeva* stole"; again Vergil, although he everywhere indicates that Aeneas is *pius*, says "Aeneas *saevus* in his mother's armour", that is, "great".') The first part of Servius' comment is a rejection of Tiberius' explanation, while the interpretation that *saevam* means *magnam* is an adoption of the comment of Aelius Donatus, with a characteristic change of vocabulary.

But that *potens* was the diction used by Aelius Donatus can be established by comparing the other interpretations of *saeva* in the D comment of Servius Auctus. There is no D comment in Servius Auctus in *Aeneid* 1.4, but on *Aeneid* 1.138, where Servius explains SAEVVMQVE as *vel magnum, ut superius, vel vere saevum in ventos, quia minatur* ('Either *magnum*, as above, or genuinely cruel toward the winds, because he is making threats.') Servius Auctus adds (after *magnum*) *et potentem*.[18] Servius also explains SAEVVS by *magnus* at *Aeneid* 1.99, where D adds *vel fortis vel bellicosus* ('or brave or warlike').[19] So we find Servius' diction choosing *magnus* as the gloss, and the Compiler of Servius Auctus adding to Servius the diction which he found in the D commentary, in 1.138 *potens*, which has essentially the same meaning.

We have direct evidence that Donatus used *potens* as his gloss on *Aeneid* 1.4 in a glossary contained in the ninth-century MS Paris. Lat. 11308 (the same MS that transmits Donatus' letter to Munatius). This glossary on *Aeneid* 1-4, probably put together in the fifth century by excerpting Servius, Aelius Donatus, and other sources, glosses a high percentage of the words in *Aeneid* 1, and on line 4 has SAEUAE *potentis iratae* ('powerful', 'angry').[20]

The different modes of glossing *saeva* accorded by the *grammatici* and by Tiberius Claudius Donatus illustrate the penchant of the *grammaticus* to seize upon an explanation which allows him to demonstrate the value of his profession as transmitter of recherché knowledge, while Tiberius Claudius Donatus' scorn of this approach illustrates that even in late antiquity the approach was not universally valued.[21]

Notes

1. Cf. Introduction and Chapter 10 above.
2. Cf. Introduction above; Kaster (1988) 276.
3. See Murgia (1988) n. 5.
4. Although Servius euhemerises many of the ancient myths, and believed, for instance, that Saturn was a king who came to Latium as an exile (on *Aen.* 8.319), when he discusses minor divinities he expresses no scepticism about their reality, and feels no need to qualify references to nymphs and such with a *dicuntur* ('are

12. The Truth about Vergil's Commentators

said') or such (e.g. see his comments on Hamadryads at *Aen.* 3.34 and *Ecl.* 10.62). He was therefore, in belief, a polytheist, although even there he seems to accord credibility to the Stoic belief that the various divinities are but manifestations of a single god who was both male and female (cf. on *Aen.* 2.632; 4.638; 7.498).

5. See Dietz (1995).

6. *sed de uerbo 'vexasse' ita responderi posse credo: 'vexasse' graue verbum est factumque ab eo videtur, quod est 'vehere', in quo inest vis iam quaedam alieni arbitrii; non enim sui potens est, qui vehitur. 'vexare' autem, quod ex eo inclinatum est, vi atque motu procul dubio vastior est. Nam qui fertur et rapsatur atque huc atque illuc distrahitur, is vexari proprie dicitur* ('But I think that the response concerning the verb *vexasse* can be given as follows: *vexasse* is a weighty word, and seems to be formed from *vehere*, in which there is already a certain meaning of someone else's whim. For he who is carried is not in his own control. *vexare*, which is derived from it, is, without doubt, of a wider meaning and motion. For he who is carried and repeatedly snatched and pulled hither and thither is properly said to be harried.')

7. *quod Probus vult hac ratione defendere, dicens vexasse venire ab eo quod est veho, vecto, vexo, ut vexasse sit portasse, et sine dubio pro arbitrio suo evertisse* ('Which Probus wishes to defend in the following way, by saying that *vexasse* comes from *veho, vecto, vexo,* so that *vexasse* is to have carried, and, without doubt, to have overturned on her own whim') – the 'her' is Scylla who is claimed to have overturned Ulysses' ship; the verb *vexasse* actually means 'to have harried'.

8. [*'vexasse'*] *est enim vis quaedam alieni arbitrii; non enim sui potens est, qui vehitur. bene ergo inclinatum verbum est; nam qui fertur et raptatur et huc atque illuc distrahitur vexari proprie dicitur* ('For there is a certain meaning of someone else's whim. For he who is carried is not in his own control. Therefore the verb is well derived, since he who is carried and snatched and pulled hither and thither is properly said to be harried'). I have secluded *vexasse* at the beginning, which arose from a miscorrection of an omission: codex L omitted *venire ... evertisse*, the preceding line or two in Servius (quoted in the previous note), and the corrector inserted *vexasse venire ... evertisse* before *vexasse*, instead of *venire ... evertisse* after *vexasse*.

9. Donatus is quoted below, n. 17.

10. He has substituted the inane *ut ostendat vita fuisse cariorem* ('to show that he had been dearer than life').

11. A similar interpretation is offered by Servius on the sacrifice of a bull to Jupiter in *Aeneid* 3.21 – his comment on that line is cross-referenced in his comment on 12.120 – and by Macrobius, *committitur non ignorantia, sed ut locum monstro faceret secuturo* ('the mistake is made not out of ignorance but in order that he might allow for the prodigy that will follow', *Sat.* 3.10.7); the common source of Servius and Macrobius is probably the commentary of Aelius Donatus.

12. Unfortunately a lacuna after Macr. *Sat.* 3.12.10 prevents us from knowing which justification Macrobius would have selected.

13. The Vergilian examples of veiling are at *Aen.* 3.174, 405, 545; 5.72, 134, 246, 366; 8.33, 277 (all explicitly or by implication of the head), 7.815 of the shoulders (*umeros*), and *Geo.* 3.383 *velatur corpora*. In *Aen.* 2.249, 3.549, 7.154, 11.101 the reference is to ritual ornamentation, in 10.205 to a fringed river.

14. The English word 'veiled' has a similar range: certainly capable of being used of veiling other parts of the body when the part is specified, but normally indicating the veiling of the face when there is no other part specified: so I noticed in the Leeds City Art Gallery a statue of a 'Veiled Venus' (by Kuhne Beveridge and

her mother Ella von Werde), who is naked except for a veil over her face; perhaps the title is a deliberate pun, but it at least illustrates the most common usage of the word 'veiled'.

15. The 'D comment' is a term given to the non-Servian ancient comment in Servius Auctus, which is generally believed to derive (whether directly or indirectly) from the commentary of Aelius Donatus.

16. Servius gets things backwards: the ancients referred to poems by their opening; so Propertius and Ovid call the *Aeneid arma*. But Servius shows no awareness of the contradiction with his very next words. Did he really believe that Vergil intended his poem to be known as the 'I am he who'?

17. Donatus' letter to Munatius is published from its sole source, codex Paris. Lat. 11308, by Brummer (1912) vii. It was later republished by Hardie (1954). See introduction above. The relevant sentence is *cum enim liceret usquequaque nostra interponere, maluimus optima fide, quorum res p<raeval>uerant, eorum etiam verba servare* ('For though we could everywhere have interposed our own words, we have preferred to preserve with the greatest fidelity even the words of those whose interpretations had prevailed'). Where I have printed *praevaluerant,* the codex has *puerant.* Hardie read Woelfflin's conjecture *fuerant* ('they had been') and Morel conjectured *placuerant* ('had pleased me'). But the authors' interpretations and data did not cease being theirs when Donatus excerpted them, nor did they cease to please him (as the pluperfect implies). But what most influences me is the fact that with either *fuerant* or *placuerant* the clausula would be almost the only one in the letter to lack the accentual requirement of the three main forms of the *cursus mixtus,* which the studies of Oberhelman and Hall (1984, 1985, 1988a, 1988b) showed to be common from the third to fifth centuries. If one wanted to read *fuerant,* one could opt for *res fuerant* followed by an appropriate participle, but I do not see a reason for the pluperfect in the periphrastic construction. The conjectured *praeualuerant* would have been corrupted to *puerant* from failure to notice the line above *p* (the abbreviation for *prae*), and the scribe's eye skipping from one *u* to the other, the latter perhaps aided by a slight misspelling for *-ual-,* namely *uel*, abbreviated by *u* with a superscribed line (therefore *puuerant* > *puerant*).

18. The Harvard Edition incorrectly prints the Servius Auctus reading for Servius; but *et potentem* is in only C, the codex of Servius Auctus.

19. Even this gloss of D, *fortis*, seems to have been known to Tiberius Claudius Donatus through Aelius Donatus: so on *Aen.* 11.290, Tiberius refers back to *Aen.* 1.99 and adds *illic quippe 'saevum' non 'fortem' dixit, ut alii volunt, sed 'nulli hosti parcentem'* ('there he has not meant by *saevum* "brave", as others want, but "sparing no enemy" '). So the evidence is that on *Aen.* 1.4 and 1.138 Aelius Donatus interpreted *saevus* as meaning *potens*, and at 1.99 as meaning *fortis*, and in at least two of the passages Tiberius rejected the interpretation, while showing no knowledge of Servius' diction, *magnus*. On *Aen.* 12.107 (which Servius has cited at *Aen.* 1.4 as an example of the meaning *magnus*) there is an interesting reversal, in which Servius glosses *saevus* with *fortis*, and Servius Auctus adds *vel magnus*.

20. The gloss *iratae* also goes back to Aelius Donatus, as we can see in the comment on *Aen.* 11.910 SAEVVM, where, to Servius' comment, D adds *an iratum?* Codex Paris. Lat. 11308 and its glossary are briefly described in my Prolegomena (1975) 26-32.

21. A version of this chapter was delivered in October of 1990 at the Leeds International Latin Seminar under the title 'The Truth about Vergil and his Commentators'.

Epilogue

Danuta Shanzer

If one were to pick the author who most influenced Latin literature, it would be Vergil. He rapidly became classic, achieving status as a school author unusually early, and maintaining his appeal throughout the second century.[1] Although Latin literature declined during the dark years of the third century, Roger Rees starts us off with a telling vignette that illustrates the real currency of the bard: Vergil on the edge of the empire adorning the coinage of a third-century British usurper.[2] The fourth century saw a true *aetas Vergiliana*, documented in the fine studies in this book. The period covered by this volume is a cohesive and meaningful unit with real 'befores' and 'afters', and a rich and varied literary history in many genres.

The poet's fate was magnificently documented in Comparetti's classic *Vergil in the Middle Ages* (1872).[3] But times and critical theories have changed, and there is a clear need for a new look at this old question. While one cannot fault Comparetti's learning and indeed one is frequently annoyed (or should it be ashamed?) to find some choice nugget one thought one's own anticipated in an obscure footnote of his,[4] one is even more constantly and annoyingly reminded of his classicist's snobbery towards later Latinity, 'rudeness', 'barbarity', to say nothing of most Christian writers.[5] So there is every need for a 'sympathetic reading'[6] of the reception of Vergil in the later Roman empire.

Tradition hands on. An author in the process of tradition was both a rolling snowball gathering accretions and a pebble worn smooth in the welter of the centuries. A classical author travelled by word of mouth and in copies of books whose text was transferred from one exemplar to another. Words were lost, gained, and altered. This constituted transmission, and Vergil's was extensive in all ways. Even if our great Vergilian manuscripts perished, we would be able to reconstitute a considerable portion of his text from the indirect tradition, scrawls on Pompeian walls,[7] pen trials on papyrus,[8] or integral passages quoted *in extenso* by ancient critics.[9]

Book and text were transmitted, but the poet was too. Image made a man in every sense. Even notorious homosexuals, for example, adorned their libraries with statues of stern philosophers.[10] And 'to be a "classic" in the Roman sense implied by Varro's *Imagines* meant to hold a place in a gallery of portraits visited by educated people across the empire.'[11] Vergil sat stiffly, young and unbearded, the 'virgin,' in a manuscript;[12] his image was adorned with a laudatory epigram quoting his own verse in a fifth-century Gallic library.[13] Very special authors evoked belated correspondence from their fans: Petrarch, for example, wrote to Cicero.[14] But Vergil did better. No bronze or man-sized marble statue has survived, nor indeed any recognisable Vergilian physical 'type,' it is true.[15] But already in the late fifth to early sixth centuries we see him, not as a talking book, but incarnate in conversation with Fulgentius the Mythographer. Crude and unsympathetic as the authoritative frowning brow,[16] and didactic raised fingers may be,[17] they anticipate the sympathetic ghost of Vergil who would lead Dante through his *Inferno*.[18]

A poet's trajectory: genre to genre

The author of the *Aeneid* was special, unlike even the divine Homer. Three genres made a man in Vergil: pastoral, didactic and epic. These, the constituents of the *Rota Vergiliana*, were seen to circumscribe the development of the *vates* and his *aetates*.[19] A fine[20] anonymous poet interpolated a lead-in to the *Aeneid*:

> ille ego *qui quondam* gracili modulatus avena
> *carmen* et egressus silvis vicina coegi
> ut quamvis avido parerent arva colono,
> gratum opus agricolis: at nunc horrentia Martis[21]

I am *he who once* he had made music (*verse*) on the slender reed, and after leaving the woods, forced the nearby fields to obey the tenant-farmer, however greedy, a work pleasing to farmers, but now the fierce <arms> of Mars <I sing and the man>

Long afterwards (AD 524), awaiting execution at the hands of Theoderic the Ostrogoth, Boethius, perhaps the last documented truly classical reader of Rome's poet, alluded to this canonical poetic progression at the opening of his *Consolation of Philosophy* (1.M.1.1-4)

> *carmina qui quondam* studio florente peregi
> flebilis, heu, maestos cogor inire modos!
> Ecce mihi lacerae dictant scribenda Camenae
> et veris elegi fletibus ora rigant.

I who once wrote *verses* in my flourishing youth, alas am now forced to start sad measures! Lo, Muses in mourning dictate what I must write and my face is wet with true tears of elegy.

Epilogue

These lines reveal a sandwiched allusion both to the interpolated proem to the *Aeneid* and to the end of the fourth *Georgic* (4.565-6):

> *carmina qui* lusi pastorum audaxque iuventa,
> Tityre, te patulae cecini sub tegmine fagi.

> *I who* disported myself with shepherd-*verses* and bold in my youth, sang you, Tityrus, beneath the cover of the broad beech.

Boethius thus created an authenticating seal, a poetic transition of genre, a homage to Vergil, and what an independent source reveals to be an allusion to lost juvenilia of his own, a pastoral (*carmen bucolicum*).[22] Like Ovid he made a false start, and stopped a foot short with an elegiac bump, not however to write love-elegy, but to pen the true elegiac tears of exile and eventual death.[23]

Not all progressions in the Vergilian genres were as rigid as what we see in the dense allusions of the *Consolation of Philosophy*. Indeed, a delightful distinction of later Roman writers was their willingness to mix genres. In this volume Michael Roberts lays out the serious and formal generic mixture of the *Aeneid* and the *Georgics* in Juvencus' paraphrase of Matthew. The *gesta Christi* provide contrast imitation to arms and the man, while the four-book format formally echoes the *Georgics*, as does the envoi to the work. Biblical pastoral and agricultural metaphors can be integrated smoothly into what Roberts charmingly calls 'the Georgics and Bucolics of the soul'.[24]

Roger Green traces more complicated generic encapsulations in later Roman pastoral, from the mini-*Georgic* in Calpurnius 5 to the didactic-hymnic combination in Nemesianus 3. The experiment is carried even further in Endelechius' *On the death of the cattle*. Its metre is Horatian; contents and form are both Vergilian. Three bucolic characters converse, and *Eclogue* 1.6-7 is evoked, when one asks what god has rescued Tityrus from disaster.[25] But his question *quis deus?* does not evoke just the *Eclogues*; we also hear *Georgics* 4, 'What god, Muses, has devised this art for us?'[26] The loss in Endelechius was not land (as in *Eclogue* 1), but cattle, who succumb to a plague. While *Georgics* 4.538-43 had prescribed the sacrifice of four bulls and four heifers to restore Aristaeus' bees, for Endelechius 'No altar is wet with blood, nor is the disease of cattle repelled by slaughter'.[27] No Vergilian witch-doctor mummery was required to restore the kine. Christ's *signum* alone branded on the cattle causes the plague to pass over, and the flocks to survive, a new and bloodless Christian *bugonia*.

Many of the contributions here in many ways address the great chiasmus, *interpretatio Vergiliana* of the Bible and *interpretatio biblica* of

Vergil, but three explore Vergil's role in contemporary politics. A different sort of ornamental miscegenation was happening in prose. Roger Rees's is the starting point because it (like Roberts's and Green's) investigates miscegenation, this time of media, not genres. He shows how poetic citations crept into oratory in the imperial period, and especially into panegyric. To flaunt Vergil was to fly the flag and talk the talk. The Gallic panegyrists showed *Romanitas* and proclaimed their loyalty to the emperor through their networks of allusions. The strong were worthy of Vergil, and at the beginning of the fourth century Constantine emerged as a new Aeneas in the Battle of the Milvian Bridge. The poet here has a clear political function.

Vergil would continue to adorn famous victories and military moments. Truly important events might be praised many times by different voices, sometimes in both prose and verse. For example, in 395 Paulinus of Nola wrote a (now lost) prose panegyric of Theodosius.[28] And like his Gallic predecessors, the pagan poet Claudian sang praises too,[29] but in verse. Catherine Ware dissects his two accounts of Theodosius' victory at the Frigidus (394). She shows how after the great Theodosius' death a network of Vergilian allusions served to market the young and feeble Honorius to the pagan senators of Rome as a new Ascanius and new Aeneas.

Politics of allusion likewise underlie Roy Gibson's study of Avienus. Roberts examined the place of Vergil in biblical paraphrase. Gibson carefully documents the marked introduction of Vergil into another sort of paraphrase, namely a translation from the Greek, where the Roman master had no place. Some of Avienus' Vergilian amplifications are purely rhetorical, but many deliberately replace Homeric material in his model, Dionysius' *Periegesis*. Gibson shows that Avienus routinely writes out or deflates Homer and Troy, but that at the same time even in the most panegyric purple patches reveals an empire reduced to North and West, no longer the former four proud compass points.[30] Most surprisingly of all Rome is erased. Even though in other authors the fairest of cities might be reduced to one line among other cities of the empire, her status nonetheless shone supreme *vis-à-vis* Antioch, Trier, etc.[31] Perhaps Avienus, a pagan denizen of Etruscan Volsinii, did indeed reject a city that was, as Prudentius would put it, 'already given over to Christ'.[32]

Centonisation was the most extreme form of literary spoliation. Karla Pollmann compares and contrasts the *Nuptial cento* of Ausonius and the biblical *cento* of Proba. The one degrades Vergil (all in good fun, of course), while the other revalues him to show that he sang the deeds of Christ. And both in their own ways exhibit links to the exegetic tradition. The golden bough (*Aen.* 6.405) had long been identified as a cacemphaton, and would continue its unseemly career even in Christian poets[33] and eventually in a centonic epithalamium for a barbarian written in North Africa under the Vandals.[34]

'What has Athens to do with Jerusalem?' cried Tertullian, opposing Christianity to classical culture,[35] and Jerome's nightmare of being beaten for being a Ciceronian rather than a Christian is an old chestnut.[36] Less entertaining, but equally important are those careful studies of patristic authors that tell us whether they put their money where their mouths were: did they or did they not give up their bad old classical habits?[37] Jerome, dream notwithstanding, was a tergiversator,[38] who defended himself against the charge of further pagan reading pagan by invoking quotations long-embedded in his consciousness.[39] Augustine, after the agonisings of the *Confessions*, seems largely to have lived up to his ideals.[40] Ivor Davidson examines Ambrose's use of Vergil to unearth yet a different situation. This was no tortured relationship, but a deep and calm companionship, evident in all of Ambrose's works. There was 'insouciant reminiscence,' but there were also heretics as Vergilian monsters, and the harmonious world of the bees. Exegetes of Matthew 13.3-8 (the Parable of the Sower) saw in the differing yields (hundred-fold, sixty-fold, and thirty-fold) virgins, widows and wives.[41] Ambrose turned to the *Georgics* to expound the best crop-rotation for the virginal body.

C.S. Lewis once remarked that nothing would have pleased medieval scholars more than the card index.[42] We can now update that remark to substitute hypertext. Vergil's branch became a great tree of links out to our fourth-century authors. And the text of a poet such as Prudentius would have links on innumerable words leading back to the author of the *Aeneid*. The positive appropriation of Vergil to forge a Christian ideology of Rome has been studied extensively in Prudentius, and we have seen an untroubled relationship in the work of Ambrose too.[43] Here Charles Witke concentrates instead on colonisation, translation and destabilisation. Even short and, in some cases, comparatively colourless phrases, such as *furor impius* ('impious madness', *Aen.* 1.294), *cernere erat* ('one could see', *Aen.* 6.596 and *Aen.* 8.676), *fugite, o miseri* ('Flee, o wretches!', *Aen.* 3.639) and *fletibus ora rigabat* ('He wet his face with tears', *Aen.* 6.699) are interpreted as intentional links. The dismembered body of Hippolytus evokes the body of monstrous Tityos, spread over nine acres in a rather different way. Heresy, in this case Novatianism, becomes a Cyclopic monster.[44] And contrast imitation rules as the persecutor issues forth from Rome to condemn Hippolytus at Ostia, in what Witke sees as a reversal of Aeneas' historic voyage from Ostia to Rome.

Vergil saw the 'tears of things' (*semper Vergilius, semper dolens*, dare one say?), and fourth-century writers were as sensitive as modern scholars from Harvard to this aspect of his poetry in, for example, a lament for an untimely death.[45] Gerard O'Daly shows us carefully how Vergil was used in pathetic moments by Ausonius, be it the demise of a colleague or a damaged friendship evoked as a pastoral love. But the mixture of personal and the political ever present in Vergil must needs affect his imitators. O'Daly makes a point that should be connected both to Rees's contribution and to Gibson's: that Ausonius, *Gallus scribens Gallis*, repositions Gaul by applying panegyrical motifs from the *Georgics* to create a new *laudes Galliarum*. The move inevitably de-centres Rome.

Any reader with a text in front of them that is not an autograph at some point must decide whether it is authentic and correct as transmitted. Then comes the problem of exegesis. But no reader can ever fully disengage themselves from the inherent circularity of deciding whether an author wrote what they think the author wrote on the basis of assumptions about what the author says elsewhere (if there are *comparanda*) or what the reader (for whatever reason) thinks the author ought to be saying. Ancient textual and literary critics trained on poets, particularly Homer and (in the Latin-speaking world) Vergil. Just as 'every boy and every gal that's born into the world alive is either a little Liberal or else a little Conservative', so too the temperaments of textual critics are divided. They come either conservative or conjectural. The former are defence-lawyers who like to give whatever happens to be on the page the benefit of the doubt and to consider it innocent until proven guilty; the latter prosecute and are prepared to get in under the hood and tinker. A brilliant Latin textual critic gives the following formulation: 'It could be said, for example, that the conjectural critic, even when he goes astray is at least urging his fellow scholars to be sceptical, to doubt, to think; while he who defends the text must necessarily appeal to the desire, too deeply seated in most men, to accept a comfortable assurance, to believe that all is for the best in the best of all possible manuscripts, and to shun the stony road of thought.'[46] Two of our contributions are concerned not with the implicit exegesis of Vergil that is inherent in all intertextuality,[47] but with explicit interpretation of, and scholarship on, the Vergilian text.

No book on Vergil in the fourth century would be complete without a study of the great Vergilian commentators Valerius Probus, Aelius Donatus, Tiberius Claudius Donatus, and Servius.[48] And we are fortunate to have as our guide one of the editors of the Harvard Edition of Servius. The grammarians, Vergil-defenders or *Vergiliomastiges*, were learned men, aware that a reading could be corrupt. While this contribution may seem to be primarily about commentators and their (often to modern readers) devious thought-processes, it is really about religious antiquities and the transmission of pagan religious conservatism through the medium of the Vergilian text. Murgia gives fine examples of how defensive conservatism about the poet's image plays out in the commentators' treatment of the text. For a correct[49] reading *lino* ('linen') is suggested *limo* ('butcher's apron') even though *Aeneid* 12.120 clearly refers to something that covers the head. The motivation? An assumption that Vergil is correct on all matters of religious practice and linen was allegedly not worn by priests. Juno (*Aen.* 1.4) must be *saeva* in the sense of 'great' or 'powerful,' for otherwise Vergil would be guilty of impiously predicating an evil quality of a goddess.

This latter point, namely what divinities could and could not do, makes a nice transition to Richard Lim's contribution on how the inherent conservatism of scholarship on Vergil, namely its willingness to defend not just the poet, but, whenever possible, the text in the commentator's manuscript influenced Augustine. The sinner turned saint, a man who came to Carthage burning, enjoyed an Aenean trajectory,[50] abandoning Carthage and a woman who loved too much for Rome and a brilliant career.[51] He would eventually (AD 397/402) castigate himself for weeping for Dido.[52] But at Cassiciacum he was prepared to use the Vergilian Proteus as an image of the Truth,[53] and to set a line of the *Aeneid* for his son Adeodatus to explicate in the *De magistro*.[54]

Lim suggests that in the period before Augustine's ordination in Hippo (386-91) the generally conservative grammatical exegetical tradition on Vergil ('explain anything that's there') directly and positively influenced the development of his anti-Manichean exegetical theory. The Manichees had employed the critical scalpel to hew away all of the Old Testament as unbefitting a well-behaved and omnipotent God and Christian *mores*. Augustine in *De utilitate credendi* 1.7 attacks their biblical criticism and paranoid theory of interpolation, suggesting at 6.13 that the reader who is over-quick in condemning the author is not a good audience for any text. He argues from the authority and patience granted Vergil by his interpreters to the respect the Manichees should similarly accord Scripture. He eventually drew distinctions between credulity and suspicion, excessive curiosity and diligence, to conclude that belief (*credere* or *fides*) is quite different from credulity.

Augustine had been badly disappointed in his first serious Manichee, the much-anticipated Faustus. Far from being superbly educated in all the *disciplinae*, he had mastered only grammar and that in 'the most customary fashion'.[55] What is interesting about his tractate to Honoratus is that this (ex-pagan) Manichee, a friend of Augustine's youth,[56] enjoyed a much higher level of education, if the quantity of classical allusion in the text is anything to go by.[57] By the time he tried to bring Honoratus around, however, Augustine's relationship with Vergil was on the turn, for the poet seems to be more of a tool, an argumentation-point, or a stick to beat the Manichees with than a lofty bard loved and appreciated.[58] Augustine even suggests that Vergil could have written lecherous little verses.[59] The prominence of Vergil and the argumentation from ancient grammatical exegesis (tendentiously, one suspects, presented as more conservative than it really was)[60] may have more to do with Honoratus and a desire to flatter him than with Augustine.[61] One might hazard a guess that the two had been adolescent 'companions-in-Vergil.' Augustine, after all, addressed his friend as *mea maxima cura*, 'the object of my special solicitude', echoing *Aeneid* 1.678.[62]

We have seen the literary use through allusion and scholarly exegesis of the Vergilian text. We have had a brief glance at the poet's violation and also sacralisation in *centos*. We end with a study that pulls all of these strands together. Daniel den Hengst examines the use of Vergil in the *Historia Augusta*. This collection of imperial biographies is bogus in many different ways. It is the work not of many named, but one unnamed author, and it dates not to the time of Constantine,[63] but in all probability to the late fourth century. Den Hengst shows us first that the passages used (above all the parade of heroes of *Aeneid* 6) and the manner of their spoliation (and indeed centonisation) point to a single author. More interestingly the *Historia Augusta* is the first text to attest the *sortes Vergilianae*, a practice attributed to the time of Hadrian.[64] Den Hengst suggests that the *sortes Vergilianae* and also the fabricated oracles based on Vergilian lines in the pro-pagan work could constitute competition for Christian *sortes biblicae*. He draws our attention to a possible parallel to Augustine's famous biblical sortition in *Confessions* 8 in *HA Aelius* 4. A Vergilian line intoned by Hadrian as he walked in his garden was prophetically capped by another party present. Thus here again Vergil may be invoked as the pagan cultural counterweight to the Bible.

If one had time enough innumerable other byways could be followed. One might speculate further about Vergil's influence in the Greek East.[65] One might try to pursue traces of lost philosophical *quaestiones* on Vergil.[66] One might essay a general comparison between the readings of Vergil attested in the fourth century and those in the fifth. This latter approach would have permitted consideration both of Augustine's *City of God* and also of Macrobius' *Commentary on the Dream of Scipio* and *Saturnalia*. The latter work is a particularly important document in the creation of the image of Vergil as universal sage. Might we find a gradual defusing of the dichotomy between Christianity and classical culture? If we took the story later and to Italy we would find ourselves in the world of Ennodius (AD 474-521) who continued to keep Vergil alive. After he became an ecclesiastic, he repented of his youthful obsession with secular verse and membership in the *grex poetarum* in his autobiographical *Eucharisticon*.[67] Should we be surprised that the paragraph begins *ille ego qui*?[68] That when an evanescent or erotic poem caused him to mingle with the choirs of angels and when he wrote fine verses himself in metrical form, like Vergil's Daphnis, he used to see beneath his feet whatever was covered by the

Epilogue

turning heaven?[69] And that when his fiancée converted to the monastic life first, 'a woman became the leader of a renowned title?'[70]

Eventually, if we moved to Africa, we would encounter Fulgentius, with whom we are almost over the border into the early Middle Ages.[71] The *Aeneid* is interpreted as an allegorical depiction of the life of Man. Juno, the goddess of childbirth, precipitates the storm, which signifies the dangers of birth. The surviving ships are said to be seven, because the number is associated with birth.[72] Venus appears in disguise because the newborn does not recognise his mother. Achates, Aeneas' trusty companion, is associated with sadness, for children cry and scarcely begin to smile by the fifth month.[73] And the music and food at the end of *Aeneid* 1 are appropriate for the child who wants no more than to be delighted by sounds and satiated with food. After this intriguing beginning (with curious parallels to the development of the child in Augustine *Confessions* 1), virtually complete ellipsis of the *fabulae* in *Aeneid* 2 and 3,[74] and extensive development of *Aeneid* 6 (invariably the most interesting book),[75] the treatise tails off into nothing. 'Vergil' abandons even authorial book-distinctions after book 9.[76] We feel we have been left wandering in a dark wood of Greco-Latin etymology applied to the names in Vergil.[77]

Gregory of Tours (d. 594) makes a good end for even the longest and most generously construed *Spätantike*. And a sad scholarly controversy heralds the advent of a Dark Age in Francia: how much of the *Aeneid* did the Bishop of Tours know and did he know it directly or through intermediaries? Scholars have constructed tables of his *Aeneid* citations[78] to show that they go no further than book 8.[79] They have gone to extremes to argue that his Vergilian learning is just borrowed feathers.[80] They have even argued about what time of life he acquired his Vergil.[81] But these are the voices of the detractors. Gregory longed to have his own prose paraphrased in verse,[82] he had a close friendship with Venantius Fortunatus,[83] he executed his own prose paraphrases of Christian poetry (e.g. Prudentius, Paulinus of Nola, and Paulinus of Périgueux)[84] and criticised his own barbarian monarch's poetic efforts.[85] Gregory was a master story-teller, and constant phrases of 'epic allure'[86] or demonstrable epic derivation enliven both his history[87] and his hagiography. How likely is it that someone with these ambitions and connections, who demonstrably knows Vergil would not have read the whole *Aeneid*? The issue is, however, not so much *what*, but *how*. And it is here that Gregory fails in comparison to a master-poet and *uomo di cultura* such as Ausonius. His forty plus Vergilian citations rarely engage the source-text in any substantive literary fashion, either through evocation of original context or through polemical allusion. Nor does any focussed image of Gregory's Vergil emerge. Instead the greatest Roman poet is largely being used as ornamentation, wall-paper, or occasionally mood-music.[88] But perhaps we should be cheered that this, after, all was still a world where one Gogo, an official of King Sigibert's would modestly disclaim the *eloquentia Maroniana* to praise his *dux*, Chamingus.[89] What happened afterwards is a long story for subsequent volumes.

Notes

1. Goold (1970) 162-3. Q. Caecilius Epirota added him to the curriculum in 26 BC.
2. Rees, above pp. 1-2.
3. Now with a new introduction, Comparetti (1997).
4. *pereant qui ante nos nostra!*
5. A sampling might include Comparetti (1997, 112) on Fulgentius: 'It is hard to conceive how any sane man can seriously have undertaken such a work, and harder still to believe that other sane men should have accepted it as an object for serious consideration.' At p. 86 'There were a few fanatics ...' At pp. 87-8 'The greatest enemies of profane studies were the authors of the Lives of the Saints ... the great mass of them were uncultivated and ignorant.' At p. 69 'To this period of decadence ...' At p. 53 'The idea of such "Centos" could only have arisen among people who had learnt Vergil mechanically and did not know of any better use to which to put all these verses with which they had loaded their brains.'
6. See Chapter 7 above.
7. Comparetti (1997) 26-7.
8. *P. Tebtunis* 686 cites *Geo.* 4.1-2 (six times) paired with accounts. See Grenfell, Hunt et al. (1902) 333-4.
9. Gellius *NA* 17.10 on Aetna in Pindar, *Pyth.* 1 and *Aen.* 3.570.
10. Cf. Juv. *Sat.* 2.6-8, *si quis Aristotelen similem vel Pittacon emit/ et iubet archetypos pluteum servare Cleanthas/fronti nulla fides ...*, 'If anyone buys a similar Aristotle or Pittacos and orders his wall-bracket to guard original busts of Cleanthes, the façade is completely untrustworthy.'
11. Vessey (2001) 294.
12. Brandt (1927) suggested that the *ille ego* lines might originally have appeared beneath an author portrait prefacing a MS of the *Aeneid*. He compared epigraphical *carmina* beginning with the same formula that were inscribed on statues and also Martial 14.186.2, *ipsius vultus prima tabella gerit* ('The first illustration bears his (Vergil's) countenance'). For a damaged example in the Vatican Vergil, see Wright (1993) 60-1, 79. For a full-length portrait, see the Codex Romanus in Heintze (1991) 99.
13. See *Epistula Rustici ad Eucherium* in *CSEL* 31.197-8 for an image of Vergil: *nam cum supra memoratae aedis ordinator ac dominus inter expressas lapillis aut ceris discoloribus formatas effigies vel oratorum vel etiam poetarum specialia singulorum autotypis epigrammata subdidisset, ubi ad praeiudicati eloquii venit poetam hoc modo orsus est: 'Vergilium vatem melius sua carmina laudant,/ in freta dum fluvii current, dum montibus umbrae/ lustrabunt convexa, polus dum sidera pascet,/ semper honos, nomenque tuum laudesque manebunt'* ('Since among the images of orators and poets fashioned in mosaic or in many-coloured wax, the builder and master of this building [sc. the library] had added special epigrams to the portraits, when he came to the poet of the clearly attested eloquence, he began thus: "His own poems praise the poet Vergil better:/ As long as rivers flow down to the sea,/ Shadows range the curves of the mountains,/ While the pole feeds the stars,/ Your honour, name and praises will last forever" ').
14. *Fam.* 24.3 and 4.

Epilogue

15. Heintze (1991).

16. Fulgentius *Virgiliana Continentia* p. 86.6-7 Helm, *contracto rugis multiplicibus supercilio*.

17. Ibid. p. 86.20-1, *erectis in iotam duobus digitis tertium pollicem comprimens*.

18. Consider Vergil's acknowledgement of his own paganism. See *Virgiliana Continentia*, p. 103.9.

19. *Rota Vergilii* in *EV* 4, 586-7.

20. Goold (1970) 128: 'Of course the lines (which, let us confess, are superb) were never written by Vergil.' For cogent arguments against their authenticity, see Brandt (1927).

21. Donatus *Vita Vergiliana* p. 10.165-9 Brummer; Conington (1863) 30-1.

22. Esener (1877) 4 *condidit et carmen bucolicum* ('He composed a bucolic poem too').

23. See *Am.* 1.1.1-4: 'I was preparing to publish Arms and violent wars in a solemn measure ... part of the verse was shorter: Cupid is said to have laughed and stolen one foot' (*arma gravi numero violentaque bella parabam* (again an allusion to *Aen.* 1.1)/ *edere, materia conveniente modis/ pars erat inferior versus; risisse Cupido/ dicitur atque unum surripuisse pedem*). Also *Am.* 3.1.8 for a prosopopoieia of Elegy, who limped, her feet of unequal length.

24. Chapter 3 above. Gregory of Tours, also a 'Georgius,' will note of a young nun called Georgia who lived in the country (*Gloria Confessorum* 33) 'It is quite right that she was called "Georgia" for she so exercised her mind in the cultivation of her spirit that after acquiring the produce of the sixtyfold fruit of virginity, she was honoured with celestial exequies when she left this world' (*Unde non immerito Georgia nuncupata, quae sic exercuit mentem cultura spiritali, ut, adepto virginitatis sexagisimi fructus [ut] proventu, egrediens e saeculo caelestibus honoraretur exsequiis*).

25. Endelechius 101.

26. *Geo.* 4.315, *quis deus hanc, Musae, quis nobis extudit artem?*

27. 117-18, *non ullis madida est ara cruoribus/ nec morbus pecudum caede repellitur*.

28. For Paulinus' prose panegyric of Theodosius, see Paul. Nol. *Ep.* 28.6; Jer. *Ep.* 58.8, and Gennadius *Vir. ill.* 49, *et ad Theodosium imperatorem ante episcopatum prosa panegyricum 'super victoria tyrannorum' eo maxime quod fide et oratione plus quam armis vicerit* ('And before his episcopate <he wrote> a panegyric in prose to Theodosius on his victory over the usurpers, saying he conquered more by faith and prayer than by force of arms'). One notes the contrast to Claudian's presentation, where prayer and faith are significantly omitted.

29. Or more accurately served as Stilicho's 'spin-doctor'.

30. For similar shrinking in geographic propaganda, see Shanzer (1998) 302.

31. Ausonius *Ordo nobilium urbium* 1 devotes one line to her.

32. Prudentius *Per.* 2.1. Pagan priests were brought to Rome from Etruria in 408 to help drive out the Visigoths. See Zosimus 5.41. Endelechius 105 notes the dominion of Christ in great cities.

33. Prud. *Contra Symmachum* 1.115.

34. Luxorius *Carm.* 91.64-6, ed. Rosenblum, *illum turbat amor; ramum qui veste latebat/ eripit a femine et flagranti fervidus infert./ it cruor inque humeros cervix conlapsa recumbit* ('Love incites him. He whips from his groin the branch that was hidden in his clothing and applies it to <her> afire. The blood issues forth and her neck bends relaxed on her shoulders').

35. *De praescr. haeret.* 7.

36. *Ep.* 22.30.
37. Hagendahl (1958) 97.
38. Hagendahl (1958) 97-328.
39. *In Gal.* 3, pp. 485-6 (*PL* 26.399D): 'And if any quotation from <pagan authors> creeps in while I speak, I remember it, as if through the cloudy film of an ancient dream', *et si quid forte inde dum loquimur, obrepit, quasi antiqui per nebulam somnii recordamur.*
40. Hagendahl (1967).
41. Jer. *Ep.* 48.2.
42. Lewis (1964) 10.
43. e.g. Buccheit (1966) and Palmer (1989) 98-139.
44. Cf. Chapter 6 above.
45. See Chapter 6 above.
46. Willis (1972) 12.
47. Rees points out, for example, that the panegyric intertextualities he studies clearly favour a triumphalist rather than subversive reading of the *Aeneid*.
48. The latter's *floruit* fell, however, in the early fifth century. See Cameron (1966).
49. *pace* Mynors.
50. *Conf.* 1.13.22, p. 17.17 Skutella: 'That Aeneas at some point came to Carthage', *Aenean aliquando Carthaginem venisse poeta dicit*, and *Conf.* 3.1.1, p. 36.25 Skutella: 'I came to Carthage', *veni Carthaginem*.
51. *Conf.* 5.8.15.
52. *Conf.* 1.13.20.
53. *Contra academicos* 2.10 on which see Shanzer (1991) 131-4.
54. See pp. 115-16 above.
55. See *Conf.* 5.3.3, 5.3.6, and 5.6.11 for the stages of his disillusionment.
56. *De utilitate credendi* 1.1, *ab ineunte adolescentia ... flagravimus*, and 6.13, *nobis tunc pueris*.
57. e.g. Allusions to Vergil, Lucretius and Epicurus at *De utilitate credendi* 4.10; to Archimedes, Aristotle, and Epicurus at 6.13, to Vergil at 6.13; to Caecilius, Erucius, Cicero, Asper, Cornutus, Donatus at 7.17. For his prosopography, see Decret (1978). At *Retract.* 14.1 Augustine says that Honoratus mocked the Catholic discipline of faith that ordered men to believe rather than be taught what was true through reason.
58. e.g. the tone of *De utilitate credendi* 13: 'innumerable questions by which grammarians are accustomed to be agitated and upset.'
59. *De utilitate credendi* 7.17: 'Do you not see that men try to interpret the Catamite of the *Eclogues* (Alexis) for whom the hard shepherd melted (with a double entendre on "ejaculated") and the boy Alexis to whom Plato is even said to have written an amatory poem as signifying something important which has escaped the judgement of the inexperienced, when without the slightest sacrilege the prolific poet might be seen as having published lecherous little verses?', *nonne cernis, ut Catamitum Bucolicorum cui pastor durus effluxit, conentur homines interpretari, et Alexim puerum, in quem Plato etiam carmen amatorium fecisse dicitur, nescio quid magnum significare, sed imperitorum iudicium fugere affirment; cum sine ullo sacrilegio poeta uberrimus videri possit libidinosas cantiunculas edidisse?* For epigrams ascribed to Plato, see Diogenes Laertius 3.29-32. See Ludwig (1963).
60. There is less evidence for critical signs in the Latin tradition than in the Greek, but there is certainly evidence of their use both to criticise the style of the

original and to note possible interpolations. See Jocelyn (1985). In specific connection with Vergil one notes, for example, the controversy over the end of the fourth *Georgic* and the Helen Episode.

61. The classical paraphernalia is confined to the opening of the treatise, up to 7.17.
62. *De utilitate credendi* 1.3.
63. *contra* see Lippold and Waldherr (1998).
64. Comparetti (1997) 48-9. *HA Hadrian* 2.8.
65. Starting with the translations in Constantine's *Oratio ad Sanctos* 19-21.
66. For some bibliography on this question see Shanzer (1986a) 189.
67. *Opusc.* 5; 438 Vogel.
68. *Opusc.* 5; 438.5 Vogel.
69. 438.6 Vogel: *sub pedibus meis subiectum quidquid caeli tegitur axe cernebam*, imitating *Ecl.* 5.57: *sub pedibus videt nubes et sidera Daphnis* ('Daphnis sees clouds and stars beneath his feet').
70. See *Aen.* 1.364: *dux femina facti* ('a woman was the leader of the enterprise') evoked in 438.27 Vogel: *et fieret praeclari dux femina tituli*.
71. For a *terminus post quem* after Corippus, see Hays (2002) 202n.12.
72. Seven is normally a prime or virginal number. See Martianus Capella 7.738, p. 266.17 Willis.
73. p. 93.4 Helm. One must also consider *Ecl.* 4.60: 'Begin, little boy, to recognise your mother with a smile.' Also August. *Conf.* 1.6.8: 'Later I began to smile too.'
74. p. 93.20 Helm.
75. pp. 95.14-103.14 Helm.
76. Last on p. 105.12 Helm.
77. Fulgentius *Virgiliana Continentia* p. 91.11 Helm provides the following etymology of Aeolus: 'For "Eolus" in Greek is like "eon-olus", that is to say "the destruction of the world".'
78. Kurth (1919) 15-21.
79. Ibid.
80. Lorenzo (1982).
81. Kurth (1919) 26-7 argues for early acquisition of 1-8 and a later encounter with 9-12, which were never properly assimilated.
82. *DLH* 10.31.
83. Fortunatus dedicated his collected poetry to Gregory, see *Carm. praef. MGH AA* 4.1, pp. 1-2. Gregory even requested Sapphics of Fortunatus. See Fortunatus *C.* 9.6. For Fortunatus' Vergilian citations, see Manitius in *Fortunati Opera pedestria, MGH AA* 4.2, pp. 132-7.
84. *GM* 40, *GM* 103, and *VSM* 1.2.
85. *DLH* 6.46.
86. D'Hérouville (1911) 802 of *DLH* 5 *Praef. dicturus bella regum*.
87. Meyers (1994).
88. Dido's tears colour both the weeping ghost of the confessor Maura and a female paralytic healed by Martin. See *GC* 18: *haec effata genas lacrimis rigabat obortis*, *VSM* 4.30: *haec effata genas lacrimis rigabat ubertim*, and *Aen.* 4.30: *sic effata sinum lacrimis implevit obortis*.
89. *Epp. Austras.* 13.5.

Bibliography

Adams, J.N. (1981) 'Ausonius' *cento nuptialis* 101-131', *SIFC* 53, 199-215
Adkin, N. (1998) 'Il canto delle Sirene in Ambrogio, Gerolamo e altri Padri della Chiesa', in Pizzolato, L.F. and Rizzi, M. (eds), 673-95
Alfonsi, L. (1965) 'L'ecphrasis ambrogiana del libro delle api vergiliano', *Vetera Christianorum* 2, 129-38
Allgeier, A. (1930) 'Der Einfluß des Manichäismus auf die exegetische Fragestellung bei Augustin: Ein Beitrag zur Geschichte von Augustins theologischer Entwicklung', in Grabmann, M. and Maubach, J. (eds), *Aurelius Augustinus: Die Festschrift des Görresgesellschaft zum 1500. Todestage des heiligen Augustinus* (Cologne), 1-13
Amat, J. (1985) *Songes et visions: l'au-delà dans la littérature latine tardive* (Paris)
Baldwin, B. (1978) 'Verses in the *Historia Augusta*', *BICS* 25, 50-8
―――― (1982) 'Vergil in Byzantium', *A&A* 28, 81-93
Barnes, T.D. (1978) *The Sources of the Historia Augusta* (Brussels)
―――― (1981) *Constantine and Eusebius* (Cambridge, Mass.)
―――― (1982) *The New Empire of Diocletian and Constantine* (Cambridge, Mass.)
Barnes, W.R. (1995) 'Vergil: the literary impact', in Horsfall (ed.) 257-92
Batty, R. (2000) 'Mela's Phoenician geography', *JRS* 90, 70-94
Baynes, N. (1926) *The Historia Augusta, its Date and Purpose* (Oxford)
Bédoyère, G. de la (1998) 'Carausius and the marks RSR and INPCDA', *NC* 158, 79-88
Benko, S. (1980) 'Virgil's Fourth *Eclogue* in Christian interpretation', *ANRW* 31.1, 646-705
Bergmann, I. (1926), *Aurelii Prudentii Clementis Carmina. CSEL* 61 (Vienna)
Bernhardy, G. (1828) *Geographi Graeci Minores I: Dionysius Periegetes* (Leipzig; repr. Olms 1974)
Bertonière, G. (1985) *The Cult Center of the Martyr Hippolytus on the Via Tiburtina*. British Academy in Rome International Series 260 (Oxford)
Biermann, M. (1995) *Die Leichenrede des Ambrosius von Mailand. Rhetorik, Predigt, Politik* (Stuttgart)
Binns, J.W. (1974) (ed.), *Latin Literature of the Fourth Century* (London)
Björck, G. (1939) 'Heidnische und Christliche Orakel mit fertigen Antworten', *SO* 19, 86-98
Bloch, H. (1963) 'The pagan revival in the West at the end of the fourth century', in Momigliano, A. (ed.), *The Conflict Between Paganism and Christianity in the Fourth Century* (Oxford)
Blockley, R.C. (1992) *East Roman Foreign Policy: Formation and Conduct from Diocletian to Anastasius. ARCA* 30 (Leeds)
Bochet, I. (2001) 'L'unité de *De utilitate credendi* d'Augustin', in Van Oort, J., Wermelinger, O. and Wurst, G. (eds), 24-42
Bonamente, G. (1988) 'Scriptores Historiae Augustae', *EV* 4, 734-7
Borrell Vidal, E. (1991) *Las palpebras de Virgilio en Juvenco* (Barcelona)
Børtnes, J. (2000) 'Eros transformed: same-sex love and divine desire. Reflections on the erotic vocabulary in St Gregory of Nazianzus's speech on St Basil the Great', in Hägg, T. and Rousseau, P. (eds), *Greek Biography and Panegyric in Late Antiquity*. Transformation of the Classical Heritage 31 (Berkeley), 180-93

Bibliography

Bouché-Leclercq, A. (1879-1882), *Histoire de la divination dans l'antiquité* (Paris), 4 vols
Bowersock, G. (2002) 'Philosophy in the Second Sophistic', in Clark, G. and Rajak, T. (eds), *Philosophy and Power in the Greco-Roman World: Essays in Honour of Miriam Griffin* (Oxford), 157-70
Brandt, E. (1927) 'Zum *Aeneis* Prooemium', *Philologus* 83, 331-5
Brenk, F.E. (1999) *Clothed in Purple Light: Studies in Vergil and in Latin Literature* (Stuttgart)
Brown, P. (1967) *Augustine of Hippo* (London)
―――― (1969) 'The diffusion of Manichaeism in the Roman empire', *JRS* 59, 92-103
―――― (1988) *The Body and Society: Men, Women and Sexual Renunciation in Early Christianity* (New York)
―――― (1992) *Power and Persuasion in Late Antiquity: Towards a Christian Empire* (Madison)
―――― (1996) *The Rise of Western Christendom* (Cambridge, Mass.)
Bruère, R.T. (1954) 'Tacitus and Pliny's *Panegyricus*', *CPh* 49, 161-79
Brummer, J. (1912) *Vitae Vergilianae* (Leipzig)
Bücheler, F. and Riese, A. (1894) (eds), *Anthologia Latina Pars Prior* (Leipzig)
Buchheit, V. (1966) 'Christliche Romideologie im Laurentius-Hymnus des Prudentius', in *Polychronion: Festschrift Franz Dölger* (Heidelberg), 121-49
―――― (1972) *Der Anspruch des Dichters in Vergils Georgika: Dichtertum und Heilsweg* (Darmstadt)
―――― (1988) 'Vergildeutung im *Cento* Probae', *Grazer Beiträge* 15, 161-76
Cairns, F. (1972) *Generic Composition in Greek and Roman Poetry* (Edinburgh)
―――― (1989) *Virgil's Augustan Epic* (Cambridge)
Callu, J.P. (1992) *Histoire Auguste I.1, Introduction Générale* (Paris)
Cameron, Alan (1966) 'The date and identity of Macrobius', *JRS* 56, 25-38
―――― (1970) *Claudian: Poetry and Propaganda at the Court of Honorius* (Oxford)
―――― (1977) 'Paganism and literature in late fourth century Rome', in Fuhrmann, M. (ed.), *Christianisme et formes littéraires de l'antiquité tardive en Occident. Fondation Hardt Entretiens sur l'antiquité classique* 23 (Geneva), 1-30
―――― (1984) 'The Latin revival of the fourth century', in Treadgold, W. (ed.), *Renaissances before the Renaissance: Cultural Revivals of Late Antiquity and the Middle Ages* (Stanford), 42-58
―――― (1995) 'Avienus or Avienius?', *ZPE* 108, 252-62
Cameron, Averil (1991) *Christianity and the Rhetoric of Empire: The Development of Christian Discourse* (Berkeley)
―――― (1993) *The Later Roman Empire* (London)
Casey, P.J. (1994) *Carausius and Allectus: The British Usurpers* (London)
Chadwick, H. (1991) *Saint Augustine. Confessions* (Oxford)
Champlin, E. (1978) 'The life and times of Calpurnius Siculus', *JRS* 68, 95-110
Charles, Sister (1968) 'The classical Latin quotations in the letters of St Ambrose', *G&R* 15, 186-97
Charlet, J.-L. (1980) *L'Influence d'Ausone sur la poésie de Prudence* (Aix-en-Provence)
―――― (1988) 'Prudenzio', *EV* 4, 335-6
Chastagnol, A. (1994) *Histoire Auguste. Les empereurs Romains des IIe et IIIe siècles* (Paris)
Chin, C.M. (2002) 'Christians and the Roman classroom: memory, grammar and rhetoric in *Confessions* 10', *Augustinian Studies* 33, 161-82

Bibliography

Clark, E.A. and Hatch, D. (1981) *The Golden Bough, The Oaken Cross. The Vergilian Cento of Faltonia Betitia Proba* (California)
Clausen, W.V. (1994) *Virgil. Eclogues* (Oxford)
Cock, M. (1971) 'A propos de la tradition manuscrite du *Carmen de mortibus boum* d'Endélechius', *Latomus* 30, 156-60
Coleman, R. (1969) 'Pastoral', in Higginbotham, J. (ed.), *Greek and Latin Literature: A Comparative Study* (London)
—— (1977) *Vergil. Eclogues* (Cambridge)
Comparetti, D. (1872) *Virgilio nel Medio Aevo* (Livorno). English trans. by Benecke, E.F.M., *Vergil in the Middle Ages* (Hamden, Conn. 1966); reprinted with new introduction by Ziolowski, J.M. (Princeton 1997)
Conington, J. (1863) *P. Vergili Maronis Opera with a Commentary* (London)
Connors, C. (1998) *Petronius the Poet* (Cambridge)
Consoli, M.E. (1995) 'Intertestualità ed originalità nella *Mosella* di Ausonio', *RCCM* 37, 127-39
Consolo, G. (1955) 'Risonanze virgiliane nell' *Exameron* di S. Ambrogio', *Miscellanea di studi di letteratura cristiana antica* 5, 66-77
Conte, G.B. (1986) *The Rhetoric of Imitation: Genre and Poetic Memory in Virgil and Other Latin Poets* (Ithaca, NY)
Contiades-Tsitsoni, E. (1990) *Hymenaios und Epithalamion* (Stuttgart)
Conybeare, C. (2000) *Paulinus Noster: Self and Symbols in the Letters of Paulinus of Nola* (Oxford)
Courcelle, P. (1952) 'Source chrétienne et allusions païennes dans l'épisode du "Tolle, Lege" (Saint Augustin, *Confessiones*, VIII, 12,29)', *RHPhR* 32, 171-200
—— (1957a) 'Les exégèses chrétiennes de la quatrième églogue', *REA* 59, 294-319
—— (1957b) 'Divinatio', *RAC* 3, 1235-51
—— (1963) *Les Confessions de Saint Augustin dans la tradition littéraire. Antécédents et postérité* (Paris)
—— (1984) *Lecteurs païens et lecteurs chrétiens de l'Énéide* (Paris), 2 vols
Coyle, J.K. (2001) 'What did Augustine know about Manichaeism when he wrote his two treatises *De moribus?*', in Van Oort, J., Wermelinger, O. and Wurst, G. (eds), 43-66
Curran, J.R. (2000) *Pagan City and Christian Capital: Rome in the Fourth Century* (Oxford)
Davidson, I.J. (2002) *Ambrose: De officiis* (Oxford), 2 vols
Davis, R. (1989) *The Book of the Pontiffs to 715 AD* (Liverpool)
De Lubac, H. (1959) 'Exégèse médiévale. Les quatre sens de l'Écriture', *Théologie* 41.1.177-87 (Paris)
Decret, F. (1970) *Aspects du manichéisme dans l'Afrique Romaine. Les controverses de Fortunatus, Faustus et Felix avec saint Augustin* (Paris)
—— (1978) *L'Afrique manichéenne (IVe-Ve siècles). Étude historique et doctrinale. Études augustiniennes* (Paris)
Del Ton, I. (1970) 'Hexaemeron S. Ambrosii Vergilium sapit', *Latinitas* 18, 27-31
Dessau, H. (1889) 'Über Zeit und Persönlichkeit der Scriptores Historiae Augustae', *Hermes* 24, 337-92
—— (1892) 'Über die Scriptores Historiae Augustae', *Hermes* 27, 561-605
Dewar, M. (1994) 'Hannibal and Alaric in the later poems of Claudian', *Mnemosyne* 47, 349-72
D'Hérouville, P. (1911) 'La culture classique de Grégoire de Tours', *Études des pères de la compagnie de Jésus* 126, 787-804

Bibliography

Diederich, M.D. (1931) *Vergil in the Works of St. Ambrose*. Catholic University of America Patristic Studies 29 (Washington, DC)

Dietz, D.B. (1995) '*Historia* in the Commentary of Servius', *TAPA* 125, 61-97

Digeser, E.D. (2000) *The Making of a Christian Empire. Lactantius and Rome* (Ithaca, NY)

Diehle, A (1994) *Greek and Latin Literature of the Roman Empire*, trans. Malazein, M. (London)

Doignon, J. (1983) 'La tradition latine (Cicéron, Sénèque) de l'épisode des Sirènes entre les mains d'Ambroise de Milan', in *Hommages à Jean Cousin. Rencontres avec l'antiquité classique* (Paris), 271-8

Döpp, S. and Geerlings, W. (1998) (eds), *Lexikon der antiken christlichen Literatur* (Freiburg, 1998, English trans. 2000)

Drijvers, J.W. (1998) 'Ammianus Marcellinus on the geography of the Pontus Euxinus', *Histos* 2 http://www.dur.ac.uk/Classics/histos/1998/drijvers.html

Drinkwater, J.F. (1987) *The Gallic Empire: Separatism and Continuity in the North-Western Provinces of the Roman Empire AD 260-274. Historia Einzelschriften* 52 (Stuttgart)

Du Quesnay, I.M. le M. (1979) 'From Polyphemus to Corydon: Vergil, *Eclogue* 2 and the *Idylls* of Theocritus', in West, D. and Woodman T. (eds), *Creative Imitation and Latin Literature* (Cambridge) 35-69

Duff, J.W. and Duff, A.W. (1968) (eds), *Minor Latin Poets* (Harvard)

Durry, M. (1938) *Pline le Jeune. Panégyrique de Trajan* (Paris)

Eckmann, A. (1988) 'Quid sanctus Augustinus de poesis ui docuerit', *Vox Populi* 15, 811-16

Edden, V. (1974) 'Prudentius', in Binns, J.W. (ed.), 160-82

Ellspermann, G. (1949) *The Attitude of the Early Christian Latin Writers toward Pagan Literature and Learning* (Diss., Washington, DC)

Elsner, J. (2000a) 'From the culture of *spolia* to the cult of Relics: the Arch of Constantine and the genesis of late antique forms', *PBSR* 68, 149-84

―――― (2000b) 'The *Itinerarium Burdigalense*: politics and salvation in the geography of Constantine's empire', *JRS* 90, 181-95

Emerson, R.W. (1876) 'Plato; or, The Philosopher', in *The Complete Works of R.W.E.*, vol. 4 (Boston/New York), 39-79

Ermini, F. (1909) *Il Centone di Proba e la Poesia Centonaria Latina* (Rome)

Evelyn White, H.G. (1919, 1921) *Ausonius* (Cambridge, Mass.), 2 vols

Fear, A.T. (1994) '*Laus Neronis*: the seventh eclogue of Calpurnius Siculus', *Prometheus* 20, 269-77

Fedeli, P. (1989) 'Il *Panegirico* di Plinio nella critica moderna', *ANRW* II.33.1, 387-514

Ferrua, A. (1942) *Epigrammata Damasiana* (Rome)

Fontaine, J. (1977), 'Unité et diversité du mélange des genres et des tons chez quelques écrivains latins de la fin du IVe siècle: Ausone, Ambroise, Ammien', in Fuhrmann, M. (ed.), *Christianisme et formes littéraires de l'antiquité tardive en Occident. Fondation Hardt Entretiens sur l'antiquité classique* 23 (Geneva), 425-72

―――― (1984) 'La figure du prince dans la poésie latine chrétienne du Lactance à Prudence,' in *La poesia tardoantica: tra retorica, teologia e politica* (Messina) 103-32

Fontaine, J. and Perrin, M. (1978) (eds), *Lactance et son temps: recherches actuelles* (Paris)

Fordyce, C.J. (1977) *Vergil, Aeneid 7 and 8* (Oxford)

Fowler, D. (1997) 'On the shoulders of giants: intertextuality and Classical Studies', *MD* 39, 13-34
——— (2000) *Roman Constructions: Readings in Postmodern Latin* (Oxford)
Frend, W.H.C. (1953) 'The Gnostic-Manichaean tradition in Roman North Africa', *JEH* 4, 13-26
——— (1984) *The Rise of Christianity* (London)
Galletier, E. (1949, 1952, 1955) *Panégyriques latins* (Paris), 3 vols
Gamberini, F. (1983) *Stylistic Theory and Practice in the Younger Pliny* (Hildesheim)
Genette, G. (1982) *Palimpsestes. La littérature au second degré* (Paris)
Georgii, H. (1905-6) *Tiberi Claudi Donati ad Tiberium Claudium Maximum Donatianum filium suum Interpretationes Vergilianae* (Leipzig)
Gibson, R.K. (2003) *Ovid. Ars Amatoria 3* (Cambridge)
Gioseffi, M. (1998) 'Ambrogio, Virgilio e la tradizione di commento a Virgilio', in Pizzolato, L.F. and Rizzi, M. (eds), 603-31
Glover, T.R. (1901) *Life and Letters in the Fourth Century* (Cambridge)
Goold, G.P. (1970) 'Servius and the Helen Episode', *HSCP* 74, 101-68
Goulon, A. (1978) 'Les citations des poètes latins dans l'oeuvre de Lactance', in Fontaine, J. and Perrin, M. (eds), 107-56
Görler, W. (1969) 'Vergilzitate in Ausonius' *Mosella*', *Hermes* 97, 94-114; reprinted with addenda in Lossau, M.J. (1991), 146-75
Green, R.P.H. (1971) *The Poetry of Paulinus of Nola: A Study of his Latinity* (Brussels)
——— (1977) 'Ausonius' use of the classical Latin poets: some new examples and observations', *CQ* 27, 441-52
——— (1980) *Seven Versions of Carolingian Pastoral* (Reading)
——— (1984) '*Tityrus Lugens*', in Livingstone, E.A. (ed.), *Studia Patristica* vol. xv. *Papers Presented to the Seventh International Conference on Patristic Studies held in Oxford 1975* (Berlin), 75-8
——— (1989) 'Man and nature in Ausonius' Mosella', *ICS* 14, 303-15
——— (1991) *The Works of Ausonius* (Oxford)
——— (1993) 'The Christianity of Ausonius', in Livingstone, E.A. (ed.), *Studia Patristica* vol. xxviii. *Papers Presented at the Eleventh International Conference on Patristic Studies held in Oxford 1991* (Leuven), 39-48
——— (1995) 'Proba's *cento*: its date, purpose and reception', *CQ* 45, 551-63
——— (1997) 'Proba's introduction to her *cento*', *CQ* 47, 548-59
——— (1999) *Ausonii Opera* (Oxford)
Grenfell, B.P., Hunt, A.S. et al. (1902) *The Tebtunis Papyri* (London and New York)
Gruber, J. (1981) 'Einflüsse verschiedener Literaturgattungen auf die prosimetrischen Werke der Spätantike', *Würzburger Jahrbücher* 7, 209-21
Gualandri, I. (1982) 'Avieno e Dionisio il *Periegeta*. Per un riesame del problema', in *Studi in onore de Aristide Colonna* (Perugia), 151-65
Guarducci, M. (1991) *San Pietro e Sant' Ippolito, Storia di statue famose in Vaticano* (Rome)
Guillaumin, M-L. (1978) 'L'exploitation des *Oracles Sibyllins* par Lactance et par le *Discours à l'Assemblée des Saints*', in Fontaine, J. and Perrin, M. (eds), 185-202
Haarhoff, T. (1920) *The Schools of Gaul* (Oxford)
Hagendahl, H. (1947) 'Methods of citation in post-Classical Latin prose', *Eranos* 45, 114-28

Bibliography

——— (1958) *Latin Fathers and the Classics: A Study on the Apologists, Jerome and other Christian Writers* (Gothenburg)
——— (1967) *Augustine and the Latin Classics, Studia Graeca et Latina Gothoburgensia XX* (Gothenburg), 2 vols
Hahn, J. (1989) *Der Philosoph und die Gesellschaft. Selbstverständnis, öffentliches Auftreten und populäre Erwartungen in der hohen Kaiserzeit* (Stuttgart)
Hardie, C. (1954) *Vitae Vergilianae Antiquae* (Oxford)
Hardie, P.R. (1986) *Virgil's Aeneid: Cosmos and Imperium* (Oxford)
——— (1993) *The Epic Successors of Vergil* (Cambridge)
Hartel, G. and Kamptner, M. (1999) (eds), *Paulinus Nolanus Carmina, Indices et Addenda. CSEL* 30 (Vienna)
Hatfield, J.T. (1890) *A Study of Juvencus* (Bonn)
Haupt, M. (1854) *De Carminibus Bucolicis Calpurnii et Nemesiani* (Berlin and Leipzig) = *Opuscula* 1 (Leipzig, 1875), 358-406
Hays, B.G. (2002) 'The pseudo-Fulgentian *Super Thebaiden*', in Miller, J.F., Damon, C. and Myers, K.S. (eds), *Vertis in Usum. Studies in Honor of Edward Courtney* (Munich and Leipzig), 200-18
Hedrick, C., Jr. (2000) *History and Silence: Purge and Rehabilitation of Memory in Late Antiquity* (Austin, Texas)
Heikel, I.A. (1902) (ed.), *Die Griechischen Christlichen Schriftsteller der Ersten Drei Jahrhunderte, Eusebius* (Leipzig), vol. 1
Heintze, H. (1991) 'Virgilio: ritratti antichi', *EV* 5.2, 98-102
Hengst, D. den (1995) '*Graece hoc melius*. Een schelm in litteris', in Van Erp Taalman, A.M. and De Jong, I.J.F. (eds), *Schurken en Schelmen. Cultuurhistorische verkenningen rond de Middellandse Zee* (Amsterdam), 138-48
Herschkowitz, D. (1995) 'Pliny the Poet', *G&R* 42, 168-81
——— (1998) *The Madness of Epic: Reading Insanity from Homer to Statius* (Oxford)
Herzog, R. (1975) *Die Bibelepik der lateinischen Spätantike: Formgeschichte einer erbaulichen Gattung* (Munich)
——— and Schmidt, P.L. (1989) (eds), *Restauration und Erneuerung: Die lateinische Literatur von 284 bis 374 n. Chr. Handbuch der Altertumswissenschaft* 8.5 (Munich)
Highet, G. (1949) *The Classical Tradition: Greek and Roman Influences on Western Literature* (London)
Himmelmann-Wildschütz, N. (1972) 'Nemesians erste Ekloge', *RhM* 115, 342-56
Hinds, S. (1998) *Allusion and Intertext: Dynamics of Appropriation in Roman Poetry* (Cambridge)
Höhl, E. (1997) *Scriptores Historiae Augustae* (Leipzig), vol. 1
Horsfall, N. (1995) (ed.), *A Companion to the Study of Virgil. Mnemosyne Supplement* 151 (Leiden)
Hosius, C. (1926) *Die Moselgedichte des Decimus Magnus Ausonius und des Venantius Fortunatus*, 3rd edn. (Marburg); reprinted 1981 (Hildesheim and New York)
Huemer, J. (1891) (ed.), *Gai Vetti Aquilini Iuvenci Evangeliorum Libri Quattuor. CSEL* 24 (Vienna)
Ihm, M. (1890) 'Studia Ambrosiana', in Flecheisen, A. (ed.), *Jahrbücher für klassische Philologie*, Suppl. Bd. 17, 1-124
Jacob, C. (1990) *La Description de la terre habitée de Denys d'Alexandrie ou la leçon de géographie* (Paris)
——— (1991) 'La mise en scène du pouvoir impérial dans la *Description de la terre habitée* de Denys d'Alexandrie', *CCG* 2, 43-53

Bibliography

Jenkyns, R. (1989) 'Virgil and Arcadia', *JRS* 79, 26-39
———— (1992) 'Pastoral', in Jenkyns, R. (ed.), *The Legacy of Rome: A New Appraisal* (Oxford), 151-75
———— (1998) *Vergil's Experience: Nature and History, Times, Names and Places* (Oxford)
Jensen, A. (1991a) 'Die ersten Christinnen der Spätantike', in Straub, V. (ed.), *Auch wir sind die Kirche* (Munich), 35-58
———— (1991b) 'Faltonia Betitia Proba – eine Kirchenlehrerin der Spätantike', in Pissarek-Hudelist, H. and Schottroff, L. (eds), *Mit allen Sinnen glauben. Feministische Theologie unterwegs* (Gütersloh), 84-94
Jocelyn, H.D. (1985) 'The Annotations of M. Valerius Probus (II)', *CQ* 35, 149-61
Jones, A.H.M. (1964) *A History of the Later Roman Empire* (London), 3 vols
Jones, J.W. (1986) 'The allegorical tradition of the *Aeneid*', in Bernard, J.D. (ed.), *Vergil at 2000. Commemorative Essays on the Poet and His Influence* (New York), 107-32
Jülicher, A. (1963-76) (ed.), *Itala: Das neue Testament in altlateinischer Überlieferung* (2nd ed., Berlin), 4 vols
Kallendorf, C. (1989) *In Praise of Aeneas: Virgil and Epideictic Rhetoric in the Early Italian Renaissance* (Hanover and London)
Kartschoke, D. (1975) *Bibeldichtung. Studien zur Geschichte der epischen Bibelparaphrase von Juvencus bis Otfrid von Weißenburg* (Munich)
Kaster, R.A. (1988) *Guardians of Language: The Grammarian and Society in Late Antiquity.* Transformation of the Classical Heritage 11 (Berkeley)
Kastner, G.R. and Millin, A. (1981) 'Proba. Introduction', in Wilson-Kastner, P. (ed.), *A Lost Tradition: Women Writers of the Early Church* (Washington, DC), 33-44
Katz, Ph.B. (1994) 'The *sortes Vergilianae*: fact and fiction', *CML* 14, 245-58
Kay, N.M. (2001), *Ausonius: Epigrams* (London)
Kenney, E.J. (1984), 'The *Mosella* of Ausonius', *G&R* 31, 190-202
Keydell, R (1962). 'Epithalamium', in *RAC* 5, 927-43
Khan, Y. (2002) *A Commentary on Dionysius of Alexandria's Guide to the Inhabited World, verses 174-382* (Diss., London)
Kirsch, W. (1989) *Die lateinische Versepik des 4. Jahrhunderts* (Berlin)
Kisch, Y. de (1970) 'Les *sortes Vergilianae* dans *l'Histoire Auguste*', *MEFRA* 82, 320-62
Klingshirn, W. (2002) 'Defining the *sortes sanctorum*: Gibbon, Du Cange, and early Christian lot divination', *JECS* 10.1, 77-130
Klotz, A. (1911) 'Studien zu den *Panegyrici Latini*', *RhM* 66, 513-72
Korzeniewski, D. (1976) *Hirtengedichte aus spätrömischer und karolingischer Zeit* (Darmstadt)
Kunzmann, F. and Hoch, C. (1994) 'Cento', in *Historisches Wörterbuch der Rhetorik* 2, 148-57
Kurth, G. (1919) 'Grégoire de Tours et les études classiques au sixième siècle', *Études Franques* 1, 1-29
La Bonnardière, A.-M. (1986) *Saint Augustin et la Bible* (Paris)
La Roy Ladurie, E. (1980) *Montaillou: Cathars and Catholics in a French Village 1294-1324* (Harmondsworth)
Lassandro, D. (2000) *Sacratissimus Imperator. L'immagine del princeps nell' oratoria tardoantica. Quaderni di Invigilata Lucernis* 8 (Bari)
Lausberg, H. (1998) *Handbook of Literary Rhetoric: A Foundation of Literary Study* (Leiden; German original Munich, ^{2}1973)

Bibliography

Leeman, A.D. (1963) *Orationis Ratio: The Stylistic Theories and Practice of the Roman Orators, Historians and Philosophers* (Amsterdam), 2 vols
Leisch-Kiesl, M. (1992) *Eva als andere* (Cologne)
Lenski, N. (1997) 'Initium mali Romano imperio', *TAPA* 127, 129-68
Leue, G. (1884) 'Zeit und Heimath des Periegeten Dionysios', *Philologus* 42, 175-8
Levy, H.L. (1958) 'Themes of encomium and invective in Claudian', *TAPA* 89, 336-47
Lewis, C.S. (1964) *The Discarded Image* (Cambridge)
Liebeschuetz, J.H.G.W (1990) 'Religion in the *Panegyrici Latini*', in *From Diocletian to the Arab Conquest* (Aldershot) 389-98 reprinted from Paschke, F. (ed.), *Überlieferungsgeschichtliche Untersuchungen* (Berlin, 1981)
Lieu, S.N.C. (1985) *History of Manichaeism in the Later Roman Empire and Medieval China. A Historical Survey* (Manchester, 2nd ed. 1992)
Lim, R. (1992) 'Manichaeans and public disputation in late antiquity', *Recherches Augustiniennes* 26, 233-72
——— (1995) *Public Disputation, Power and Social Order in Late Antiquity*. Transformation of the Classical Heritage 23 (Berkeley)
Lippold, A. and Waldherr, G. (1998) *Die Historia Augusta: eine Sammlung römischer Kaiserbiographien aus der Zeit Konstantins* (Stuttgart)
Lorenzo, J. (1982) 'Ecos virgilianos en Gregorio de Tours y Jordanes', *Helmántica. Revista de humanidades clásicas* 33, 359-69
Lossau, M.J. (1991) (ed.), *Ausonius. Wege der Forschung* 652 (Darmstadt)
Lowe, E.A. (1950) *Codices Latini Antiquiores* (Oxford), vol. 5
Lubbe, W.J.G. (1955) *Incerti Panegyricus Constantino Augusto Dictus* (Leiden)
Ludwig, W. (1963) 'Plato's love epigrams', *GRBS* 4, 59-82
Lühken, M. (2002) *Christianorum Maro et Flaccus. Zur Vergil- und Horazrezeption des Prudentius*. Hypnomnemata 141 (Göttingen)
MacCormack, S. (1998) *The Shadows of Poetry: Vergil in the Mind of Augustine*. Transformation of the Classical Heritage 26 (Berkeley)
Madec, G. (1974) *Saint Ambroise et la philosophie* (Paris)
——— (1975) 'Analyse de *De magistro*', *REAug* 21, 63-71
——— (1993) (ed.), *Saint Augustin. Le maître: dialogue avec Adéodat; Le libre arbitre: dialogue avec Évodius* (Paris)
Maguiness, W.S. (1932) 'Some methods of the Latin panegyrists', *Hermathena* 47, 42-61
——— (1933) 'Locutions and formulae of the Latin panegyrists', *Hermathena* 48, 117-38
Mahoney, A. (1934) *Vergil in the Works of Prudentius* (Washington, DC)
Malamud, M.A. (1989) *A Poetics of Transformation: Prudentius and Classical Mythology* (Ithaca, NY)
Mandouze, A. (1982) (ed.), *Prosopographie Chrétienne du Bas-Empire I, Prosopographie de l'Afrique Chrétienne (303-533)* (Paris)
Marcotte, D. (2000). 'Aviénus, témoin de Julien pour une interprétation et une datation nouvelles de la *Descriptio Orbis Terrae*', *REL* 78, 195-211
Margoni-Kögler, M. (2001) 'Typologie in den christlichen Vergilcentonen', *Studia Patristica* 36, 140-52
Marinone, N. (1969/70) 'Per la cronologia di Servio', *AAT* 104, 181-211
Markus, R.A. (1974) 'Paganism, Christianity and the Latin Classics', in Binns, J.W. (ed.), 1-21
——— (1990) *The End of Ancient Christianity* (Cambridge)
Marshall, P.K. (1997) *Servius and Commentary on Virgil*. University of North Carolina at Asheville, Occasional Papers no. 5 (Pegasus Press)

Martindale, C. (1997) (ed.), *The Cambridge Companion to Vergil* (Cambridge)
Mathews, T.F. (1993) *The Clash of the Gods: A Reinterpretation of Early Christian Art* (Princeton)
Matthews, J. (1967) 'Continuity in a Roman family: the Rufii Festi of Volsinii', *Historia* 16, 484-508
――― (1970) 'The historical setting of the *Carmen contra paganos*', *Historia* 20, 464-79
――― (1975) *Western Aristocracies and Imperial Court AD 364-425* (Oxford)
McGill, S.C. (2001) *Vergilius Alter: Studies in the Vergilian Cento* (Diss., New Haven)
McLynn, N.B. (1994) *Ambrose of Milan: Church and Court in a Christian Capital.* Transformation of the Classical Heritage 22 (Berkeley)
McWilliam, J. (1990) 'The Cassiciacum autobiography', *Studia Patristica* 18, 14-43
Meagher, L. (1947) *Augustine. The Immortality of the Soul, the Magnitude of the Soul, on Music, the Advantage of Believing, On Faith in Things Unseen. Fathers of the Church 4* (New York)
Mesk, J. (1911) 'Zur Quellenanalyse des plinianischen Panegyricus', *WS* 33, 71-100
Meslin, M. (1964) 'Nationalisme, état et religions à la fin du IVe siècle', *Archives de sociologie des religions* 18, 3-20
――― (1967) *Les Ariens d'Occident, 335-430* (Paris)
Meyers, J. (1994) 'Les citations et réminiscences virgiliennes dans les Libri Historiarum de Grégoire de Tours', *Pallas* 41, 67-90
Millar, F. (1977, 1992²) *The Emperor in the Roman World, 31 BC – AD 337.* London
Mohrmann, C. (1958) *Études sur le Latin des Chrétiens* (Rome)
Mommsen, T. (1870) '*Carmen contra paganos*', *Hermes* 4, 350-63
Monteleone, C. (1975), *L'ecloga quarta da Virgilio a Costantino* (Manduria)
Moorhead, J. (1999) *Ambrose: Church and Society in the Late Roman World* (London and New York)
Morison, S. (1972) *Politics and Script* (Oxford)
Morton Braund, S. (1998) 'Praise and protreptic in early imperial panegyric: Cicero, Seneca, Pliny', in Whitby, M. (ed.), 53-76
Murgia, C.E. (1975) *Prolegomena to Servius 5 – the Manuscripts. University of California Publications: Classical Studies* 11 (Berkeley)
――― (1988) '*Aen.* 9.236 – an unrecognized Vergilian variation', *Hermes* 116, 493-99
Mynors, R.A.B. (1990) *Virgil. Georgics* (Oxford)
Naumann, H. (1981) 'Suetonius' *Life of Vergil*; the present state of the question', *HSCP* 85, 185-7
Nazzaro, A.V. (1976) 'La I Ecloga virgiliana nella lettura di Ambrogio', in Lazzati, G. (ed.), *Ambrosius Episcopus. Atti del congresso internazionale di studi ambrosiani nel XVI centenario della elevazione di sant'Ambrogio alla cattedra episcopale, Milano, 2-7 decembre 1974* (Milan), 2 vols: 2: 312-24
――― (1988) 'Il mondo bucolico virgiliano nella catechesi di Ambrogio', in Felici, S. (ed.), *Crescita dell'uomo nella catechesi dei Padri: età postnicena. Convegno di studio e aggiornamento, Facoltà di Lettere cristiane e classiche (Pontificium Institutum Altioris Latinitatis), Roma, 20-21 marzo 1987* (Rome), 105-28
Nettleship, H. (1879) *The Ancient Lives of Virgil* (Oxford)
Newlands, C. (1988), '*Naturae mirabor opus*: Ausonius' challenge to Statius in the Mosella', *TAPA* 118, 403-19
Nicholson, O. (1999) '*Civitas quae adhuc sustentat omnia*; Lactantius and the City of Rome', in Klingshirn, W.E. and Vessey, M. (eds), *The Limits of Ancient*

Bibliography

Christianity. Essays on Late Antique Thought and Culture in Honor of R.A. Markus (Ann Arbor), 7-25
Nisbet, R.G.M. and Hubbard, M. (1970) *A Commentary on Horace Odes Book 1* (Oxford)
Nixon, C.E.V. (1990) 'The use of the past by the Gallic panegyrists', in Clarke, G. (ed.), *Reading the Past in Late Antiquity* (New South Wales), 1-36
Nixon, C.E.V. and Rodgers, B.S. (1994) *In Praise of Later Roman Emperors; The Panegyrici Latini*. Transformation of the Classical Heritage 21 (Berkeley)
Nodes, D.J. (1993) *Doctrine and Exegesis in Biblical Latin Poetry* (Leeds)
O'Daly, G. (1999) *Augustine's City of God. A Reader's Guide* (Oxford)
O' Donnell, J. (1980) 'Augustine's classical readings', *Recherches Augustiniennes* 15, 144-75
—— (1992) *Augustine. Confessions* (Oxford)
Oberhelman, S.M. (1988a) 'The cursus in late imperial Latin prose: a reconsideration of methodology', *CPh* 83, 136-149
—— (1988b) 'The history and development of the *cursus mixtus* in Latin literature', *CQ* 38, 228-42
Oberhelman, S.M. and Hall, R.G. (1984) 'A new statistical analysis of accentual prose rhythms in imperial Latin authors', *CPh* 79, 114-30
—— (1985) 'Meter in accentual clausulae of late imperial Latin prose', *CPh* 80, 214-27
Ogilvie, R.M. (1978) *The Library of Lactantius* (Oxford)
Opelt, I. (1970) 'Prudenz und Horaz', in Wimmel, W. (ed.), *Forschungen zur römischen Literatur: Festschrift Karl Büchner* (Wiesbaden)
—— (1976) 'Zwei weitere Elemente klassischer Literatur in Ambrosius' Schrift *De fide*', *RhM* 119, 288
Pabst, A. (1989) *Quintus Aurelius Symmachus: Reden. Texte zur Forschung* Band 53 (Darmstadt)
Pace, N. (1998) 'Il canto delle Sirene in Ambrogio, Gerolamo e altri Padri della Chiesa', in Pizzolato, L.F. and Rizzi, M. (eds), 673-95
Palmer, A.-M. (1989) *Prudentius on the Martyrs* (Oxford)
Paschoud, F. (1967) *Roma Aeterna. Études sur le patriotisme romain dans l'Occident latin à l'époque des grandes invasions* (Rome)
—— (1994) 'Propos sceptiques et iconoclastes sur Marius Maximus', *HA Colloquium Genevense* (Bari), 241-54
—— (2001) *Histoire Auguste* (Paris), 2 vols
Paterson, A. (1988) *Pastoral and Ideology: Virgil to Valéry* (Oxford)
Pease, A.S. (1920, 1923) (ed.) *Cicero, de divinatione* (Illinois), 2 vols
—— (1955, 1958) (ed.) *Cicero, de natura deorum* (Cambridge, Mass.), 2 vols
Pelland, G. (1972) *Cinq études d'Augustin sur le début de la Genèse* (Paris)
Petschenig, M. (1891) Review of Huemer (1891), *Berliner philologische Wochenschrift* 11, 137-44
Pichon, R. (1906) 'L'origine du recueil des *Panegyrici Latini*', *REA* 8, 229-49
Pizzolato, L.F. and Rizzi, M. (1998) (eds), *Nec timeo mori. Atti del Congresso internazionale di studi ambrosiani nel XVI centenario della morte di sant' Ambrogio, Milano, 4-11 aprile 1997* (Milan)
Poinsotte, J.-M. (1986) 'Les juifs dans les centons latins chrétiens', *Recherches Augustiniennes* 21, 85-116
Pollmann, K. (1996) *Doctrina christiana* (Fribourg)
—— (1997) 'Jesus Christus und Dionysos. Überlegungen zu dem Euripides-Cento Christus patiens', *Jahrbuch der österreichischen Byzantinistik* 47, 87-106

Bibliography

――― (2001) 'The transformation of the epic genre in Christian late antiquity', *Studia Patristica* 36, 61-75
――― (2002) 'Philologie und Poesie. Zu einigen Problemen der Textgestaltung', in *CSEL* 16', in Primmer, A. et al. (eds), *Textsorten und Textkritik* (Vienna), 211-30
Posani, M.R. (1962) 'Reminiscenze di poeti latini nella *Mosella* di Ausonio', *SIFC* 34, 31-69
Prete, S. (1978) *Decimi Magni Ausonii Burdigalensis Opuscula* (Leipzig)
Radice, B. (1968) 'Pliny and the *Panegyricus*', *G&R* 15, 166-72
Randers-Pehrson, J.D. (1983) *Barbarians and Romans: The Birth Struggle of Europe AD 400-700* (London and Canberra)
Rees, R.D. (2002) *Layers of Loyalty in Latin Panegyric 289-307* (Oxford)
Reeve, M.D. (1996-7) 'A rejuvenated snake', *Acta Ant. Hung.* 37, 245-58
Ries, J. (1961) 'La Bible chez saint Augustin et chez les manichéens', *REAug* 7, 238-9
Riha, K. (1971) *Cross-Reading und Cross-Talking: Zitat-Collagen als poetische und satirische Technik* (Stuttgart)
Roberts, M. (1984) 'The *Mosella* of Ausonius: an interpretation', *TAPA* 114, 343-53
――― (1985a) *Biblical Epic and Rhetorical Paraphrase in Late Antiquity. ARCA* 16 (Liverpool)
――― (1985b) 'Paulinus Poem 11, Virgil's First *Eclogue*, and the Limits of *Amicitia*', *TAPA* 115, 271-82
――― (1989) *The Jeweled Style: Poetry and Poetics in Late Antiquity* (Ithaca, NY)
――― (1993) *Poetry and the Cult of the Martyrs: The Liber Peristephanon of Prudentius* (Ann Arbor)
――― (1995) 'Martin meets Maximus: the meaning of a late Roman banquet', *REAug* 41, 91-111
――― (2001) 'Rome personified, Rome epitomised', *AJP* 122, 533-65
Romano, D. (1961) 'Licenzio poeta. Sulla posizione di Agostino verso la poesia', *Nuovo Didaskaleion* 11, 1-22
Rosenmeyer, T.G. (1969) *The Green Cabinet: Theocritus and the Pastoral Lyric* (California; repr. London, 2004)
Rösger, A. (1976) *Herrschererziehung in der Historia Augusta* (Bonn)
Röttger, W. (1996) *Studien zur Lichtmotivik bei Iuvencus. JbAC, Ergänzungsband* 24 (Münster)
Rougé, J. (1966) (ed.) *Expositio Totius Mundi et Gentium. Sources chrétiennes* 124 (Paris)
Russell, D. (1998) 'The panegyrists and their teachers', in Whitby, M. (ed.), 17-50
Russell, R.P. (1967) *Saint Augustine, The Teacher, the Free Choice of the Will, Grace and Free Will. Fathers of the Church* 59 (Washington, DC)
Saccone, M.S. (1985) *Le Interpretationes Vergilianae di Tiberio Claudio Donato. Studi e Testi dell' Antichita* 17 (Naples)
Sánchez Salor, E. (1991) 'Hin zu einer Poetik des Ausonius', in Lossau, M.J. (ed.), *Ausonius* (Darmstadt), 112-45
Santini, C. (1992) 'Il prologo della *Descriptio orbis terrae* di Rufio Festo Avieno', in Santini, C. and Scivoletto, N. (eds), *Prefazioni, prologhi, proemi di opere tecnico-scientifico latine II* (Rome), 949-95
Sarris, P. (2002) 'The eastern Roman empire from Constantine to Heraclius (306-641)', in Mango, C. (ed.), *The Oxford History of Byzantium* (Oxford), 19-59
Scarcia, R. (1998) 'Due effetti virgiliani in Ambrogio', in Pizzolato, L.F. and Rizzi, M. (eds), 751-2

Bibliography

Schelkle, K.H. (1939) *Virgil in der Deutung Augustins. Tübinger Beiträge zur Altertumswissenschaft* 32 (Stuttgart and Berlin)
Schenkle, C. (1881) 'Lectiones panegyricae', *WS* 3, 118-30
—— (1888) *Poetae Christiani Minores. CSEL* 16 (Vienna), 499-639
—— (1896) (ed.), *Sancti Ambrosii opera. CSEL* 32.1 (Vienna)
Schetter, W. (1975) 'Nemesians Bucolica und die Anfänge der spätlateinsichen Dichtung', in Gnilka, C. and Schetter, W. (eds), *Studien zur Literatur der Spätantike* (Bonn), 1-43
Schmid, W. (1953) 'Tityrus Christianus', *RhM* 96, 101-65
—— (1954) 'Bukolik', in Klauser, T. (ed.), *RAC* 2 (Stuttgart), 786-801
—— (1962) 'Endelechius', in Klauser, T. (ed.), *RAC* 5 (Stuttgart), 1-3
Schwan, C. (1937) *Vergil bei Prudentius* (Leipzig)
Schwartz, J. (1985) 'Reminiscences vergiliennes dans quelques Vitae de *l'Histoire Auguste*', *BHAC* 1982-3, 331-7
Shanzer, D. (1986a) *A Philosophical and Literary Commentary on Martianus Capella's De nuptiis Philologiae et Mercurii, book 1* (Berkeley)
—— (1986b) 'The anonymous *Carmen contra Paganos* and the date and identity of the centonist Proba', *REAug* 32, 232-48
—— (1989) 'The date and composition of Prudentius' *Contra Orationem Symmachi Libri*', *RFIC* 117, 442-62
—— (1991) 'Licentius's verse epistle to Augustine', *REAug* 37, 110-43
—— (1994) 'The date and identity of the centonist Proba', *Recherches Augustiniennes* 27, 74-96
—— (1998) 'The date and literary context of Ausonius' "Mosella": Ausonius, Symmachus, and the *Mosella*', in Knox, P. and Foss, C. (eds), *Style and Tradition: Studies in Honor of Wendell Clausen* (Stuttgart and Leipzig), 284-305
Shiel, N. (1972-3) 'A "quotation" from the *Aeneid* on the coinage of Carausius', *PVS* 12, 51-3
Shumacher, W. (1960) 'Prudentius an der Via Tiburtina', *Spanische Forschungen der Görresgesellschaft, Erste Reihe: Gesammelte Aufsätze zur Kulturgeschichte Spaniens* 16, 1-15
Sivan, H. (1993) *Ausonius of Bordeaux: Genesis of a Gallic Aristocracy* (London and New York)
Sixt, G. (1892) 'Des Prudentius' Abhängigheit von Seneca und Lukan', *Philologus* 51, 501-6
Skutsch, O. (1985) *The Annales of Ennius* (Oxford)
Slavitt, D. (1998) *Ausonius: Three Amusements* (Philadelphia)
Smolak, K. (1989) 'Nemesianus', in Herzog, R. (ed.), 313-14
—— (1999) 'Die Bibelepik als "verfehlte Gattung" ', *Wiener humanistische Blätter* 41, 7-24
Sotinel, C. (2000) 'La mémoire de la ville: Aquilée et son passé à la fin de l'Antiquité', in Sot, M. (ed.), *La mémoire de l'Antiquité tardive et le haut Moyen Âge* (Paris), 25-36
Stanton, G.R. (1973) 'Sophists and philosophers: problems of classification', *AJPh* 94, 350-64
Starr, R.J. (1992) 'An epic of praise: Tiberius Claudius Donatus and Vergil's *Aeneid*', *CA* 11, 159-74
—— (2001) 'The flexibility of literary meaning and the role of the reader in Roman antiquity', *Latomus* 60, 433-45
Stock, B. (1996) *Augustine the Reader: Meditation, Self-Knowledge and the Ethics of Interpretation* (Cambridge, Mass.)

Bibliography

Straub, J. (1963) *Heidnische Geschichtsapologetik in der christlichen Spätantike* (Bonn)
Suster, G. (1890) 'De Plinio Ciceronis imitatore', *RFIC* 18, 74-86
Syme, R. (1968) *Ammianus and the Historia Augusta* (Oxford)
—— (1971) *Emperors and Biography: Studies in the Historia Augusta* (Oxford)
Terzaghi, N. (1949) 'Tre fonti secondarie del *Panegirico* di Plinio', *Maia* 2, 121-7
Teske, R. (1991) *Saint Augustine. On Genesis. Two Books on Genesis against the Manichaeans and On the Literal Interpretation of Genesis: An Unfinished Book. The Fathers of the Church Series* 84 (Washington, DC)
—— (1992) 'Origen's and St Augustine's first commentaries on Genesis', in Daly, J.R. (ed.), *Origeniana Quinta* (Leuven), 179-85
Testini, R. (1977) 'Di alcune testimonanze relative a Ippolito', *Ricerche su Ippolito. Studio Ephemeridis Augustianum* 13 (Rome), 45-65
Theodorakopoulos, E. (1997) 'Closure: the book of Virgil', in Martindale, C. (ed.), 155-65.
Thilo, G. et Hagen, H. (1881) (eds), *Servii Grammatici qui feruntur in Vergilii carmina commentarii* (Leipzig)
Thilo, G. (1887) (ed.), *Servii Grammatici qui feruntur in Vergilii Bucolica et Georgica Commentarii* (Leipzig)
Thraede, K. (1962) 'Epos', *RAC* 5, 983-1042
Thomas, R.F. (1982) *Lands and Peoples in Roman Poetry: The Ethnographical Tradition. PCPS* Suppl. 7 (Cambridge)
—— (1988) *Vergil. Georgics* (Cambridge), 2 vols
Treggiari, S. (1991) *Roman Marriage* (Oxford)
Trout, D.E. (1999) *Paulinus of Nola: Life, Letters, and Poems.* Transformation of the Classical Heritage 27 (Berkeley)
Upson, H.R. (1943) 'Medieval lives of Vergil', *CPh* 38, 103-11
Usener, H. (1877) *Anecdoton Holderi: ein Beitrag zur Geschichte Roms in Ostgothischer Zeit* (Bonn)
Van der Nat, P.G. (1977) 'Zu den Voraussetzungen der christlichen lateinischen Literatur: Die Zeugnisse von Minucius Felix und Laktanz', in Fuhrmann, M. (ed.), *Christianisme et formes littéraires de l'antiquité tardive en Occident. Fondation Hardt Entretiens sur l'antiquité classique* 23 (Geneva), 191-234
Van Oort, J. (1997) 'Manichaeism and anti-Manichaeism in Augustine's *Confessiones*', in Cirillo, L. and Van Tongerloo, A. (eds), *Atti del Terzo Congresso Internazionale di Studi 'Manichaeismo e Oriente cristiano antico' Arcavacata di Rende-Amantea, 31 Agosto – 5 Settembre, 1993*, Manichaean Studies III (Louvain/Naples)
Van Oort, J., Wermelinger, O. and Wurst, G. (2001) (eds), *Augustine and Manichaeism in the Latin West. Proceedings of the Fribourg-Utrecht International Symposium of IAMS* (Leiden)
Velaza, J. (1996) 'El texto de Virgilio en la *Historia Augusta*', HA *Colloquium Barcinonense* (Bari), 298-306
Verdière, R. (1966) 'La Bucolique post-virgilienne', *Eos* 56, 161-85
—— (1974) *Prolegomènes à Nemesianus* (Leiden)
Vereeke, E. (1975) 'Le Corpus des Panégyriques latins de l'époque tardive: Problèmes d'imitation', *AntCl* 44, 141-60
Vessey, M.M. (2001) 'The *Epistula Rustici ad Eucherium*', in Mathisen, R.W. and Shanzer, D.R. (eds), *Society and Culture in Late Antique Gaul: Revisiting the Sources* (Aldershot), 278-97
Volphilhac, P. (1975) (ed.), *Némésien. Oeuvres* (Paris)

Bibliography

Von Albrecht, M. (1997) *History of Roman Literature* (Leiden), 2 vols
Walker, J. (2000) *Rhetoric and Poetics in Antiquity* (Oxford)
Walter, B. (1972) *Der Ertrag der Auseinandersetzung mit den Manichäern für das hermeneutische Problem bei Augustin* (Munich), 2 vols
Walter, H. (1988) *Studien zur Hirtendichtung Nemesians. Palingenesia* 26 (Stuttgart)
Webb, R. (1997) 'Poetry and rhetoric', in Porter, S.E. (ed.), *Handbook of Classical Rhetoric in the Hellenistic Period 330 BC – AD 400* (Leiden), 339-69
Weber, D. (1998) (ed.), *Sancti Augustini Opera: De Genesi contra Manichaeos. CSEL* 91 (Vienna)
—— (2001) 'Augustinus, *De Genesi contra Manichaeos*. Zu Augustins Darstellung und Widerlegung der manichäischen Kritik am biblischen Schöpfungsbericht,' in Van Oort, J., Wermelinger, O. and Wurst, G. (eds), 298-306
Wenning, G. (1990) 'Der Einfluß des Manichäismus und des Ambrosius auf die Hermeneutik Augustins', *REAug* 36, 80-90
Weyman, C. (1897) 'De Ambrosio Vergilii imitatore', *Literarisches Zentralblatt* 687-91, 1691
—— (1926) *Beiträge zur Geschichte der Christlich-Lateinischen Poesie* (Munich)
Whitby, M. (1998) (ed.), *The Propaganda of Power: The Role of Panegyric in Late Antiquity. Mnemosyne Supplement* 183 (Leiden)
White, C. (2000) *Early Christian Latin Poets* (Harmondworth)
Widmann, H. (1906) *De Gaio Vettio Aquilino Iuvenco carminis evangelici poeta et Vergili imitatore* (Breslau)
Williams, D.H. (1995) *Ambrose of Milan and the End of the Nicene-Arian Conflicts* (Oxford)
Williams, H.J. (1986) *The Eclogues and Cynegetica of Nemesianus* (Leiden)
Williams, R.D. (1967) 'The purpose of the *Aeneid*', *Antichthon* 1, 29-41
Williams, R.D and Pattie, T.S. (1982), *Vergil: His Poetry through the Ages* (London)
Williams, S. (1985) *Diocletian and the Roman Recovery* (London)
Williams, S. and Friell, G. (1994) *Theodosius: The Empire at Bay* (London)
Willis, J.A. (1972) *Latin Textual Criticism* (Urbana)
Wills, J. (1996) *Repetition in Latin Poetry: Figures of Allusion* (Oxford)
Wilson, A.M. (1995), 'Ekphrasis in Ausonius and Prudentius', in Innes, D., Hine, H. and Pelling, C. (eds), *Ethics and Rhetoric: Classical Essays for Donald Russell on his Seventy-Fifth Birthday* (Oxford), 149-59
Witke, C. (1968) 'Prudentius and the tradition of Latin poetry', *TAPA* 99, 509-25
—— (1971) *Numen Litterarum: The Old and the New in Latin Poetry from Constantine to Gregory the Great. Mittellateinische Studien und Texte* 5 (Leiden and Cologne)
Wlosok, A. (1983) 'Zwei Beispiele frühchristlicher "Vergilrezeption" ', in Pöschl, V. (ed.), *2000 Jahre Vergil. Ein Symposon* (Wolfenbüttel), 63-86
Woestijne, P. van de (1961) (ed.) *La Descriptio Orbis Terrae d'Avienus* (Brugge)
Woolf, G. (1998) *Becoming Roman: The Origins of Provincial Civilization in Gaul* (Cambridge)
Wright, D. (1993) *The Vatican Vergil: A Masterpiece of Late Antique Art* (Berkeley)
Zanker, P. (1988) *The Power of Images in the Age of Augustus,* trans. Schapiro, A. (Ann Arbor)
Zehnacker, H. (1989) 'D'Aratos à Aviénus: astronomie et idéologie', *ICS* 14, 317-29
Ziolkowski, T. (1993) *Vergil and the Moderns* (Princeton)
Zoepffel, R. (1978) 'Hadrian und Numa', *Chiron* 8, 391-427

Index Locorum

References to the pages of this book are in bold type.

AMBROSE
De Abraham 1.68, **103**; 1.82, **110**; 2.4, **110**
Apologia prophetae David 33-4, **110**
De bono mortis 45, **110**; 51, **110**
De fide 1-2, **100-1**; 1.46, **101**; 3-5, **102**; 3.3, **102**; 3.4, **102**, **110**; 3.4-6, **102**
De officiis 1.31, **110**; 1.43-4, **110**; 1.79-80, **110**; 1.92, **110**; 1.94, **110**; 1.108, **110**; 1.121, **103**; 1.126, **110**; 1.132-5, **110**; 1.141, **110**; 1.144, **99**; 1.177, **103**, **110**; 1.180, **110**; 1.203, **111**; 1.208, **99**; 2.6, **110**; 2.48, **110**; 3.2, **110**; 3.80, **110**; 3.92, **110**
De viduis 31, **107**
De virginibus 3.16-17, **106**
Epistulae 7[37] 28, **110**
Epistulae extra collectionem 11[51].3, **110**
Exaemeron 1.28, **105**; 3.23, **105**; 5.66-72, **104**
De excessu fratris 1.30-3, **107**; 1.42, **110**; 2.127-8, **107-8**; 2.129, **108**; 2.131, **108**
Explanatio Psalmorum 43.17, **110**; 43.75, **110**; 43.80, **110**
Expositio evangelii secundum Lucam 4.2-3, **110**; 7:49, **103**; 7.127-8, **106**; 10.10, **31**
Expositio Psalmi CXVIII 2.13, **110**; 18.4, **110**
Hymn 3 [*Deus creator omnium*] 2-3, **109**; 11, **109**
De Iacob et vita beata 2.39, **111**; 2.56, **103**
De interpellatione Job et David 4.36, **111**
De Nabuthae historia 56, **103**
De Noe et Arca 24, **110**

De obitu Valentiniani 3, **108**; 56, **109**; 78, **109**
De paenitentia 2.1, **110**
De spiritu sancto 2 prol. 13, **103**; 2.36, **102**

AMMIANUS MARCELLINUS
22.8.1-48, **63**; 25.4, **15**

APOLLONIUS
Argonautica 1.1-2, **68**

ARISTOPHANES
Frogs 1238ff., **80**

ARISTOTLE
Rhetorica 1.iii.1-3, **44**

AUGUSTINE
De civitate Dei 1, **183**; 1.3, **93**; 1.17-18, **125**; 1.22, **125**; 1.26, **125**; 5.26, **170-1**; 11, **126**; 17.15, **174**; 18.14, **125**; 18.23, **184**; 20.19.3, **187**
Confessiones 1-2, **126**; 1.6.8, **213**; 1.13.20-3, **110**; 1.13.20, **212**; 1.13.22, **212**; 1.17.27-18.28, **110**; 1.27, **113-14**; 3.1.1, **212**; 3.11, **117-18**, **126**; 4.3.5, **125**, **174**; 4.14.21, **125**; 5.3.3, **212**; 5.3.6, **212**; 5.6.11, **212**; 5.8.15, **212**; 7.9.15, **110**; 8.8.19, **177**; 8.12.29, **175**
Contra academicos 2.4.10, **125**; 2.10, **212**
Contra felicem 2.1, **126**
De catechizandis rudibus 6.10.20, **125**
De doctrina Christiana 2.40.144-7, **110**
De genesi ad litteram imperfectus liber **126**
De genesi contra Manichaeos **126**; 1.1, **126**; 2.2, **126**
De magistro 1.2, **115**; 1.46, **126**
De ordine 1.5.12, **95**; 1.7.24, **95**; 1.8.26, **125**

229

Index Locorum

De utilitate credendi 1.1, **212**; 1.3, **213**; 1.7, **207**; 2, **126**; 4, **125**; 4.10, **212**; 5, **126**; 6.13, **207**, **212**; 7.17, **212**; 10, **120**; 11, **120**; 13, **121-2**, **212**; 17, **121**
Epistulae 7.2.4, **126**; 55.20, **174**; 104.11, **186-7**; 258.5, **176**
Retractationes 1.10.1, **126**; 1.11, **126**; 2.34, **126**; 14.1, **212**
Sermo 241.5.5, **15**
Soliloquies 2.11.19, **125**; 2.15.29, **126**

AULUS GELLIUS
Noctes Atticae 2.6, **192**; 2.6.5, **192**; 2.6.9-18, **192**; 2.6.19-22, **192**; 9.9.12, **192**; 13.21.1, **192**; 17.10, **210**

AUSONIUS
Caesares 1.3-5, **16**
cento nuptialis **141**; *Pref.*, 80-1, **142**; 25-6, **83**; 33-56, **85**; 57-66, **85**; 67-79, **86**; 69, **85**; 70-8, **85**; 70-2, **86**; 73, **85**; 75-6, **83**, **86**; 77, **86**; 78-9, **86**; 97-8, **83**; 105, **86**; 107, **92**; 110, **86**; 118, **87**; 119, **87**; 121, **87**; 122-3, **87**; 126, **87**
Cupido cruciatus 1, **142**; 37-9, **142**; 101-3, **142**
Ephemeris 3.19-20, **153**; 3.28, **144**; 3.34-5, **153**; 3.41, **144**; 3.57, **144**; 3.85, **153**; 8.22-6, **145**; 8.22, **152**; 8.37, **145**
Epigrammata 2, **153**; 6, **153**; 75.8, **152**; 79.3, **153**; 137.1, **93**
Epistulae 2.62-72, **22**; 12, **152**; 17-24, **152**; 23.20, **144**; 24.124, **144**
Genethliacos 26-7, **143**
Gratiarum actio 34, **44**; 1.5, **45**; 5, **45**, **146**; 64, **153**; 65, **45**, **146**
Ludus septem sapientium 9-10, **153**
Mosella 76, **141**; 1, **146**; 3, **146**; 4, **146**; 5, **146**; 10, **147**; 12-13, **147**; 14-17, **147**; 14-15, **147**; 15, **147**; 20-3, **149**; 20, **147**; 21, **149**; 22, **147**; 23-6, **147**; 26, **148**; 51, **151**; 77-149, **148**; 77-80, **148**; 87-9, **148**; 87, **148**; 92, **148**; 97-8, **148**; 117, **148**; 189-99, **148**; 198-9, **149**; 216, **149**; 239, **151**; 300-2, **149**; 301-2, **149**; 345-8, **149**; 349, **149**; 367-8, **148**; 381, **149**; 382-3, **149**; 382, **150**; 383, **150**; 384-5, **150**; 392-417, **150**; 392-3, **150**; 393, **150**; 396-7, **154**; 418-19, **149**; 420-6, **151**; 438-68, **152**; 438-44, **150**; 438, **150**; 440, **150**; 443-4, **150**; 443, **150**; 454-8, **150**; 454-5, **150**; 457, **152**; 459, **150**; 460, **150**; 466-9, **151**; 474, **154**
Ordo Urbium Nobilium 1, **211**; 37, **154**; 163, **146**
Parentalia 9.7-9, **153**; 9.24, **143**; 6.11, **143**; 23.15-16, **143**; 26.3-4, **144**
Pater ad filium 11-15, **143**
Praefationes Variae 3.21, **145**; 5.15, **154**
Precationes Variae 1.12-17, **145**; 1.14-15, **145**
Professores 3.13, **153**; 6.36-7, **143**; 21.6-8, **142**; 24.11-2, **143**
Protrepticus ad Nepotem 1, **141**; 21, **142**; 29-30, **142**; 44, **142**; 57, **142**; 75-6, **142**

AVIENUS
Descriptio orbis terrarum 1-10, **64**; 1-5, **67**; 4, **77**; 6-7, **67**; 7, **65**; 114-17, **66**; 115, **66**; 141, **77**; 183, **65**; 198ff., **77**; 249-56, **77**; 257-62, **64-5**; 287-8, **71**; 290, **71**; 302-12, **72**; 303ff., **65**; 359ff., **75**; 368-9, **77**; 374-80, **77**; 425ff., **77**; 494-5, **74**; 494, **77**; 498-500, **70**; 540ff., **77**; 585, **77**; 603ff., **76**; 608-9, **69**; 625-9, **69**; 648ff., **77**; 655ff., **77**; 662-5, **77**; 689ff., **77**; 723-9, **70**; 752, **77**; 801ff., **77**; 811-16, **65**; 918, **77**; 921-2, **77**; 936, **77**; 937-40, **77**; 942, **65**; 948, **77**; 953ff., **77**; 960ff., **77**; 977ff., **77**; 985-6, **70**; 1003, **77**; 1032ff., **77**; 1077-93, **76**; 1216ff., **77**; 1247-8, **74**
Ora maritima **62**
Phaenomena **62**; 67-70, **77**; 172-3, **64**

BIBLE
Acts 17.28, **102**
Canticum Canticorum 2.1, **111**; 4.12, **106**
Genesis 1:2, **105**; 1:9, **105**; 34, **103**
Hebrews 13:4, **107**
Isaiah 11:2-3, **103**

Index Locorum

John 2:1-11, **51**; 4:46-54, **51**;
  6:16-21, **89**; 6:18ff., **90**; 6:19, **90**;
  11:38, **55**
Judges 16:19-21, **103**
I Kings 17, **103**
Luke 12:27, **106**
II Maccabees 7, **103**
Mark 6:45-54, **89-90**
Matthew 2:9, **53**; 8:26-7, **95**; 9:36,
  57; 13:3-8, **205**; 14:6-11, **51**;
  14:19, **52**; 14:22-33, **89**; 14:26, **90**;
  14:28-31, **90**; 17:5, **53**, **55**; 22:1-4,
  51; 27:60, **56**; 27:66, **56**; 28:18, **182**
Psalms 133:2, **109**
Romans 5:12, **89**; 13:14, **177**
II Thessalonians 2.6, **183**
I Timothy 1.19, **101**
BOETHIUS
  Consolation of Philosophy
  1.M.1.1-4, **202**
CALPURNIUS
  Eclogues 1, **19**, **21**; 1.20-32, **30-1**;
  2.1, **20**; 2, **21**; 2.68-9, **27**; 3.1, **26**;
  4, **19**, **21**; 5.2, **20-1**; 7, **21**
CATULLUS
  1.1-2, **82**; 11.16-17, **187**; 11.21-4, **84**,
  143; 16.5-6, **90**; 61.121, **94**;
  64.321-2, **94**
CICERO
  De divinatione 1.12, **186**; 2.86, **180**,
  186; 2.116, **179**
  De natura deorum 2.32, **186**
  De oratore 3.39, **33**; 153, **33**
  Pro Marcello 44
CLAUDIAN
  De tertio consulatu Honorii 29-32,
  166; 44-50, **166**; 60-2, **166**; 62-3,
  166; 63-7, **165**; 63, **168**; 63-4, **166**;
  66-7, **169**; 69-72, **166**; 77-82, **167**;
  83-98, **165**; 87, **167**; 88-9, **167**; 89,
  167, **169**; 93, **167-9**; 95, **168**; 96,
  155-6, **168**; 97, **168**; 98, **155-6**,
  168; 99-100, **171**; 99-101, **167**;
  102-4, **167**; 189, **159**
  De quarto consulatu Honorii 18-20,
  156; 47-8, **156**; 56-8, **160**; 72, **160**,
  162; 75, **160**; 84-6, **160**; 87-8, **161**;
  94, **161**; 95, **161**; 98, **162**; 109,
  161; 112-14, **160-1**; 182, **162**;
  192-5, **162**; 206-11, **163**; 220, **163**;
  276, **163**; 354-5, **162**; 378-9, **164**;
  398-9, **163**; 413-15, **163**; 489-90,
  156; 503-4, **164**
  De sexto consulatu Honorii 489-90,
  156
  De bello Gothico praef. 8, **171**
  De bello Gildonico 4, **159**; 384-5, **171**
  In Eutropium 1.281-2, **159**
  In consulatum Probini et Olybrii
  73-99, **157**; 160-3, **73**
  In Rufinum 1.52-3, **159-60**
  De consulatu Stilichonis 2.6-49, **156**
CONSTANTINE
  Oration to the Saints, **22**; 20, **185**
DIO CASSIUS
  67.4.6, **77**; 79.8.6, **180**; 79.40.4, **187**
DIOGENES LAERTIUS
  3.29-32, **212**
DIOMEDES
  Ars 2, **86**
DIONYSIUS
  Periegesis **62**; 1-4, **68**; 77-8, **66**;
  112-34, **62**; 140-1, **77**; 154-5, **63**;
  167-9, **77**; 197, **71**; 205-10, **72**;
  207, **73**; 239ff., **75**; 249-50, **77**;
  254-9, **77**; 290ff., **77**; 351-6, **70**,
  74; 360, **70**; 390ff., **77**; 425, **77**;
  447-8, **69**; 461-4, **69**; 473ff., **63**;
  483ff., **77**; 487ff., **77**; 494-5, **77**;
  513-32, **62**; 516ff., **77**; 541-8, **70**;
  580, **63**; 619, **65**; 707-17, **63**; 719,
  63; 753ff., **77**; 758ff., **77**; 775ff.,
  77; 788ff., **77**; 807ff., **77**; 815-19,
  70; 869ff., **77**; 1020ff., **77**; 1051-2,
  74
DONATUS
  Life of Vergil 1-16, **12**; 3, **14**; 17-34,
  13-14; 25, **14**; 37-8, **16**; 39, **14**;
  43-6, **14**, **193**
EINSIEDELN ECLOGUES
  2, **26**
ENDELECHIUS
  De mortibus boum 1-32, **23-4**; 13,
  27; 19, **28**; 21-8, **27**; 21-4, **23**; 21,
  26; 28, **26**; 35-6, **27**; 47, **28**; 51, **26**;
  53-6, **27**; 65, **26**; 80, **28**; 85-8, **26**;
  97-132, **24-5**; 99, **28**; 101, **211**;
  105, **211**; 116, **28**; 117-18, **211**;
  123-4, **28**
ENNODIUS
  Opuscula 5, **213**

Index Locorum

EPIGRAMMA PAULINI
   6-7, **29**; 26-9, **29**; 55, **29**
EUSEBIUS
   Historia Ecclesiastica 10.5.2-14, **15**
EXPOSITIO TOTIUS MUNDI ET GENTIUM
   64, **68**, 23, **75**; 32, **75**; 42, **71**; 52, **71**;
   54, **75**; 55, **71**, **75**; 61, **71**; 63, **71**
FULGENTIUS
   Virgiliana Continentia, **213**
GENNADIUS
   Viri illustres 49, **211**
GREGORY OF NAZIANZEN
   Orationes 2.9, **30**
GREGORY OF TOURS
   Decem libri historiarum 5 praef.,
      213; 6.46, **213**; 10.31, **213**
   In gloria confessorum 18, **213**; 33,
      211
   In gloria martyrum 40, **213**; 103,
      213
   De virtutibus Sancti Martini 1.2,
      213; 4.30, **213**
HERODOTUS
   4.173, **77**; 4.177, **72**
HESIOD
   Opera et dies 678ff., **76**
HISTORIA AUGUSTA
   Aelius 4, **177**, **208**; 5.9, **173**
   Alexander Severus 4, **181**; 4.6, **175**;
      13-14, **181**; 14.4, **183**; 14.5, **173**;
      31.4, **173**; 41.1, **188**
   Carus 2.3, **188**; 11.2, **18**; 13.3, **188**
   Claudius 10.6, **184**
   Clodius Albinus 5.1, **179**
   Diadumenianus 8.5-8, **180**
   Gallienus 8.7, **188**
   Gordian 3.2, **186**; 7.1, **173**; 20.5, **184**
   Hadrian 2.8, **175**, **213**; 2.10, **176**;
      16.6, **173**, **186**
   Maximinus 27.4, **174**, **183**
   Opilius Macrinus 1, **180**; 12.7, **180**;
      12.9, **186**; 14.2, **187**
   Pescennius Niger 8.6, **175**, **177**, **186**,
      187
   Probus 2.7, **15**; 8.4, **186**
   Severus 21.2, **173**
   Tacitus 5.1, **185**; 24.3, **188**
HOMER
   Iliad 3.316, **186**; 8.102-3, **187**;
      8.306-7, **84**
   Odyssey 4.364ff., **77**; 10.1-2, **69**;

      10.195, **68**; 10.206-7, **186**;
      12.39-54, **110**; 19.562-7, **189**
HORACE
   Odes 1.3, **95**; 1.3.23-4, **178**; 4.5.5, **2**
   Sermones 1.5, **153**; 1.5.26, **153**;
      1.9.1, **146**; 1.10.44, **145**
ISOCRATES
   Evagoras **34**
JEROME
   Epistulae 21.13.9, **31**; 22, **97**; 22.30,
      15, **110**, **211**; 48.2, **212**; 53.7, **31**,
      61, **95**, **186**; 58.8, **211**; 70, **110**;
      70.5, **59**
   In epistulam ad Galatianos 3, **211**
   In Hieremiam prophetam 5.27, **187**
   De viris illustribus 84, **59**
JOHN CHRYSOSTOM
   Contra Judaeos et Gentiles 9, **32**
JULIAN
   Misopogon **76**
JUVENAL
   2.6-8, **210**; 11.180-1, **142**
JUVENCUS
   Evangeliorum libri, praef. 6-24, **48**;
      praef. 6, **48**; *praef.* 19, **48**; *praef.*
      27, **48**; 1.106, **60**; 1.148, **60**;
      1.243-5, **53**; 1.343, **61**; 1.759, **61**;
      2.33, **60**; 2.53, **52**; 2.55, **53**;
      2.142-3, **51**; 2.143-4, **52**; 2.161,
      61; 2.211, **61**; 2.342, **60**; 2.342-3,
      51; 2.346, **61**; 2.368-9, **55**; 2.384,
      60; 2.423-7, **57-8**; 2.505, **61**;
      2.652, **61**; 2.702, **61**; 3.7, **61**;
      3.83-4, **52**; 3.87, **52**; 3.102-4, **90**;
      3.104-6, **90**; 3.110-23, **90**; 3.115,
      50; 3.330-1, **55**; 3.333, **53**; 3.486,
      60; 3.592, **61**; 3.693-5, **61**; 3.743,
      60; 3.753, **60**; 4.170-1, **61**; 4.368,
      60; 4.372-3, **55**; 4.377, **50**; 4.568,
      54; 4.574, **61**; 4.588, **54**; 4.630, **50**;
      4.707, **50**; 4.724, **56**; 4.725, **56**;
      4.734, **51**; 4.741, **56**; 4.772-3, **54**;
      4.804-5, **49**; 4.806-8, **49**; 4.806,
      48; 4.809-11, **49**
LACTANTIUS
   De ave phoenice **59**
   De mortibus persecutorum 48, **15**
   Divinae Institutiones 1.1.10, **47**;
      1.11.30, **47**; 1.11.34, **47**; 5.1.15,
      47; 5.10.2-9, **60**; 7.24.12, **95**, **176**

Index Locorum

LIVY
   Ab urbe condita 21.4, **171**; 42.12.4, **94**
LUCAN
   Bellum civile 1.1, **167**; 1.572-4, **159**; 2.585, **65**
LUCIAN
   Symposium 17, **93**
LUCRETIUS
   De rerum natura 1.4, **77**; 1.197-9, **79**; 1.823-7, **79**; 1.912-14, **79**; 1.921ff., **65**; 2.62-6, **111**; 2.355-66, **28**, **32**; 2.688-9, **79**; 2.1013-22, **79**; 5.1198, **195**; 6.495-7, **111**; 6.738-9, **111**
LUXORIUS
   91.64-6, **211**
MACROBIUS
   Saturnalia 1.24.5, **93**; 3.10.7, **199**; 3.12.10, **199**; 4.1.1, **93**; 4.5.2, **87**; 5.2.14, **93**; 6.6.17, **87**
   Somnium Scipionis 2.8.8, **173**
MARTIAL
   12.67, **142**; 12.67. 4-5, **142-3**, 14.186.2, **210**
MARTIANUS CAPELLA
   De nuptiis Philologiae et Mercurii 5.518, **84**; 7.738, **213**
MENANDER RHETOR
   Basilikos logos 369, **45**; 374, **45**
NEMESIANUS
   Cynegetica 63-75, **18**
   Eclogues 1.1-8, **19**; 1.17-18, **19**; 1.48, **19**, **31**; 1.49-55, **19**; 1.83-6, **19**; 2.1, **20**; 2.15, **31**; 2.34-5, **27**; 2.41, **20**; 2.60, **20**; 2.78, **20**; 3.2, **20**; 3.61-2, **21**; 4, **21**; 4.12, **27**; 4.13, **31**; 4.62, **22**
ORACULA SIBYLLINA
   5.46-50, **186**; 8.50-9, **186**; 12.163-75, **186**
OROSIUS
   Historiae 1.18, **93**; 7.35.21, **155**, **171**
OVID
   Amores 1.1.1-4, **211**; 3.1.8, **211**
   Ars Amatoria 3.149-52, **77**
   Fasti 5.259-60, **140**
   Metamorphoses 4.134-5, **31**; 4.433, **153**; 7.785, **65**; 10.53-4, **147**; 11.417-18, **31**; 14.80, **142**
   Epistulae ex Ponto 4.4.35-42, **44**

PACATUS see *PANEGYRICI LATINI* II(12)
PALLADIUS
   Apology 81-7, **101**
PANEGYRICI LATINI
   II(12)1.3-5, **45**; II(12)1.5, **36**; II(12)4.4, **45**; II(12)17.2, **45**; II(12)39.1, **36**; II(12)44.5, **45**
   III(11)28.5, **36**
   IV(10)7.1, **40**; IV(10)7.4, **41**; IV(10)18.2, **41**; IV(10)19.3, **41**; IV(10)26.1-2, **41**; IV(10)29.5, **41**; IV(10)30.1-4, **40**; IV(10)30.4, **40**; IV(10)31.3, **42**; IV(10)33.5, **41**; IV(10)36.5, **41**; 37.5, **46**
   VII(6)12.6-7, **39**; VII(6)14.1, **39**
   VIII(4)14.2, **36**
   IX(5)7.3, **37**
   X(2)1.3, **36**; X(2)2.5, **36**; X(2)11.3, **36**
   XI(3)2.3, **38**; XI(3)3.6, **38**; XI(3)4.2, **38**; XI(3)14.2, **45**, **153**; XI(3)14.2-3, **38**; XI(3)16.3, **37**; XI(3)17.1, **38**
   XII(9)1.2, **45**; XII(9)4.4, **41**; XII(9)9.4, **41**; XII(9)9.5, **41**; XII(9)11.2-4, **40**; XII(9)11.2, **41**; XII(9)12.3, **45**, **46**; XII(9)12.4, **40**; XII(9)14.2, **40**; XII(9)16.5, **40**; XII(9)17.2, **40**, **46**; XII(9)17.3, **40**; XII(9)18.2, **40**; 19.5, **36**; XII(9)21.5, **40**; XII(9)26.1, **41**
PAULINUS OF NOLA
   Epistulae 11, **144**; 28.6, **211**
PETRONIUS
   Satyricon 129.1, **83**; 132.9-10, **94**; 132.11, **83**, **153**; 132.12, **83**
PINDAR
   Pythian 1, **210**
PLINY
   Epistulae 1.20, **44**; 2.1, **44**; 2.5, **44**; 3.13, 18, **34**, **44**, **45**; 5.20, **44**; 6.27.1, **44**; 7.9, **44**; 9.26, **44**
   Panegyricus 33-4, **44**; 15.4, **44**; 90.3, **44**
PROBA
   cento 9, **88**; 12, **88**; 23, **88**; 50-1, **88**; 316, **88**; 317-32, **89**; 317-18, **88**; 319-22, **88**; 334, **89**; 340, **88**; 345, **89**; 348, **89**; 409, **89**; 414, **88**; 418, **89**; 447, **88**; 472, **89**; 531-44, **89**; 545-61, **90**; 545, **90**; 546, **90**; 547-9, **90**; 550-1, **90**; 552-5, **90**;

Index Locorum

556, **90**; 558, **90**; 559, **90**; 560-1,
  90; 600-24, **89**; 618, **92**; 666, **89**
PROPERTIUS
  carmina 2.34.65, **14**
PRUDENTIUS
  Contra orationem Symmachi 1.115,
    211; 1.550, **140**
  Peristephanon 2.1, **211**; 8, **140**;
    11.1-22, **129-30**; 11.1-5, **138**; 11.1,
    133; 11.5-6, **131-2**; 11.7, **138**;
    11.18, **130**; 11.25, **132**; 11.28, **132**;
    11.31-2, **133**; 11.39-48, **133**;
    11.40, **133**; 11.42, **133**; 11.45, **133**;
    11.47, **133**; 11.110, **133**; 11.123ff.,
    134; 11.125, **134**; 11.127, **134**;
    11.131, **134**; 11.147-52, **134**;
    11.151, **134**; 11.185ff., **135**;
    11.191ff., **135**; 11.194, **135-6**;
    11.196, **135**; 11.199-210, **135**,
    140; 11.213, **136**, **140**; 11.215ff.,
    140; 11.215, **137**; 11.229-30, **137**;
    11.231, **139**; 11.239-46, **138-9**;
    12.53, **149**
QUINTILIAN
  Institutio oratoria 1.8.9, **93**;
    1.8.10-12, **33**; 3.4.15-16,
    44;10.1.27, **33**; 10.2.21, **33**
SENECA
  Ad Polybium de consolatione 8.2, **93**
  De clementia **44**
  Oedipus 269, **65**
SENECA THE ELDER
  Controversiae suasoriae 3.7, **82**
SERVIUS
  Ad Aeneidem: praef. 89-96, **196**;
    praef. 101, **196**; 1.4, **197-8**; 1.99,
    198; 1.138, **198**; 1.159, **86**; 2.19,
    87; 2.632, **199**; 3.21, **199**; 3.34,
    199; 3.463, **154**; 4.638, **199**; 5.521,
    193; 5.725, **191**, **192**; 6.177, **192**;
    6. 237, **56**; 6.322, **60**; 7.498, **199**;
    7.543, **192**; 10.272, **76**; 10.314,
    192; 11.817, **87**; 11.910, **200**;
    12.107, **200**; 12.120, **194-5**
  Ad Eclogas proem **15**; 1, **16**; 2, **16**;
    2.23, **193**; 6.76, **192**; 10.1, **196**;
    10.27, **87**; 10.62, **199**
  Ad Georgica 4.1, **196**
SILIUS ITALICUS
  Punica 1.71, **159**; 1.79, **159**; 3.1,

167, **169**; 7.1, **171**; 9.491-510,
  168; 9.549-50, **169**
STATIUS
  Achilleid 1.858-63, **171**
  Silvae 1 praef. , **93**; 1.5.60-2, **149**;
    2.1.114, **142**; 4.1, **44**;
  Thebaid 2.1, **171**; 4.819, **111**
SUETONIUS
  Caesar 51, **187**
  De grammaticis et rhetoribus 24.4,
    191
SYMMACHUS
  Orationes **34-5**; 1.4, **36-7**; 2.26, **37**;
    3.9, **37**, **45**
TACITUS
  Dialogus 20.5-6, **33**
TERENCE
  Phormio 39-40, **94**
TERTULLIAN
  Ad Nationes 2.9.12-4, **60**
  De praescriptione haereticorum 7,
    211; 39, **94**; 39.5, **92**
THEOCRITUS
  Idylls 11.34, **27**
THEODOSIAN CODE
  16.10.10, **15**
TIBERIUS CLAUDIUS DONATUS
  Ad Aeneidem 1.4, **197**; 2.52, **87**;
    4.690-1, **87**; 11.290, **200**
TIBULLUS
  2.4.13, **59**
VALERIUS FLACCUS
  Argonautica 2.1, **171**
VERGIL
  Aeneid: Prologue, **202**; 1.4, **200**,
    207; 1.8, **153**; 1.33, **41**; 1.38, **113**;
    1.52ff., **69**; 1.60ff., **69**; 1.74-5, **86**;
    1.99, **200**; 1.107, **171**; 1.138, **200**;
    1.143, **46**; 1.159, **86**; 1.164-5, **153**;
    1.167, **29**; 1.225, **45**; 1.234, **45**;
    1.236, **187**; 1.249, **50**; 1.254, **46**;
    1.265, **184**; 1.278, **184**; 1.279, **158**;
    1.291ff., **131**; 1.294-6, **42**; 1.294,
    205; 1.330, **86**; 1.340, **178**; 1.364,
    213; 1.365-6, **71**; 1.380, **77**; 1.381,
    178, **186**; 1.416ff., **77**; 1.432-3,
    111; 1.435, **111**; 1.492, **77**; 1.543,
    41; 1.545, **46**; 1.637-8, **60**; 1.655,
    188; 1.664, **61**; 1.678, **208**;
    1.706-8, **52**; 1.724, **60**; 2.14, **60**;
    2.52, **87**; 2.53, **87**; 2.57, **54**; 2.62,

Index Locorum

60; 2.64, 54; 2.132, 55; 2.204, 41; 2.249, 199; 2.274-6, 111; 2.283, 1; 2.288, 46; 2.305-7, 46; 2.313, 46; 2.314, 179; 2.321, 61; 2.353, 46; 2.360, 46; 2.408, 46; 2.413, 85; 2.496-9, 46; 2.576, 50; 2.621, 46; 2.659, 115; 2.685-6, 162; 2.692-8, 53; 2.779, 140; 3.102, 50; 3.112, 111; 3.174, 199; 3.195, 111; 3.244, 110; 3.268, 101; 3.349-50, 153; 3.403-9, 195; 3.405, 199; 3.424, 101; 3.431-2, 101; 3.442, 149; 3.493, 86; 3.507, 146; 3.543, 196; 3.545, 199; 3.549, 199; 3.556, 46; 3.570, 210; 3.639, 132, 205; 3.642, 111; 3.656-7, 111; 3.665, 90; 3.692-715, 101; 3.714, 146; 4.12, 171; 4.13, 46; 4.17, 153; 4.30, 213; 4.41, 45, 146; 4.53, 76; 4.68-9, 171; 4.172, 111; 4.229, 188; 4.249, 142; 4.272-6, 181; 4.320-3, 169; 4.373, 171; 4.382, 86; 4.415, 152; 4.552, 171; 4.555, 60; 4.595-6, 170; 4.597, 171; 4.690-1, 87; 5.1, 171; 5.72, 199; 5.134, 199; 5.139, 46; 5.140-1, 153; 5.176, 90; 5.237, 111; 5.246, 199; 5.366, 199; 5.408, 56; 5.537, 140; 5.854-71, 39; 5.859, 45; 5.860, 45; 5.867, 45; 6.2, 147; 6.14-33, 149; 6.14-19, 108; 6.31-3, 149; 6.42, 55; 6.46, 77; 6.86, 145; 6.87, 46; 6.122, 87; 6.123, 66; 6.157-8, 41; 6.159, 50; 6.164-5, 14; 6.237, 56; 6.255, 61; 6.258, 61; 6.273-81, 46; 6.282-4, 145; 6.288, 61; 6.314, 46; 6.322, 53; 6.325, 146; 6.327, 149; 6.365, 188; 6.405, 204; 6.406, 86; 6.408, 61; 6.413, 90; 6.430, 61; 6.454, 153; 6.459, 171; 6.469-70, 83; 6.471, 84; 6.486, 61; 6.555-70, 46; 6.576, 101; 6.595, 134; 6.596, 205; 6.616, 56; 6.626, 61; 6.640-1, 55, 147; 6.646, 103; 6.657, 150; 6.662, 48; 6.673, 111; 6.684-5, 52; 6.687, 1; 6.696, 61; 6.699ff., 136; 6.701, 136; 6.724-6, 46, 102; 6.726-7, 45; 6.739, 144; 6.743, 144, 153; 6.756-9, 111; 6.760-87, 135; 6.789-90, 164; 6.800, 148; 6.803, 45; 6.808-12, 175; 6.828, 60; 6.830, 45; 6.843-5, 163; 6.847-53, 181-2; 6.847-52, 174; 6.851-3, 44, 95; 6.851, 95, 145; 6.852, 39; 6.853, 42, 161; 6.857-8, 179; 6.861, 180; 6.869-71, 184; 6.869-70, 143; 6.870-1, 177; 6.872-3, 108; 6.882-3, 181; 6.883-6, 111, 177; 6.884, 14; 6.893-6, 145, 189; 6.898, 189; 7.15-20, 108; 7.27, 46; 7.30ff., 140; 7.37-40, 111; 7.66, 92; 7.147, 60; 7.154, 199; 7.279, 111; 7.324-31, 46; 7.335-6, 159; 7.558, 140; 7.565-6, 153; 7.578, 153; 7.654, 180, 186; 7.658, 101; 7.660, 60; 7.749, 111; 7.771, 60; 7.815, 199; 8.31-78, 46; 8.33, 196, 199; 8.63, 150; 8.86-9, 46; 8.90, 153; 8.95-9, 153; 8.96, 148; 8.107-8, 111; 8.176, 52; 8.188, 46; 8.277, 199; 8.314-36, 67; 8.319, 198; 8.332, 46; 8.364, 46; 8.366, 145; 8.367ff., 44; 8.411-13, 107; 8.500, 86; 8.526, 46; 8.538-40, 46; 8.540, 77; 8.548-9, 46; 8.581, 53; 8.589-91, 174; 8.589, 184; 8.591, 184; 8.597-9, 153; 8.676, 140, 205; 8.691, 77; 8.711-12, 148; 8.717, 188; 8.726-8, 73; 9.40ff., 138; 9.59-61, 138; 9.86-7, 153; 9.124-5, 46; 9.181, 143; 9.381-3, 153; 9.414-15, 171; 9.435-6, 143; 9.436, 83; 9.446, 86, 111; 9.449, 145; 9.486-7, 111; 9.503, 46; 9.598-620, 67; 9.603, 77; 9.613, 111; 9.812, 41; 10.1, 171; 10.100, 90; 10.103, 46; 10.159-60, 46; 10.189-93, 108; 10.205, 199; 10.237, 46; 10.310, 46; 10.362-3, 46; 10.437, 140; 10.507, 143, 153; 10.592-3, 46; 10.607, 86; 10.621, 140; 10.674, 46; 10.829-30, 46; 10.830, 188; 11.1, 171; 11.62-3, 143; 11.101, 199; 11.158-9, 107; 11.176, 54; 11.187, 147; 11.192, 46; 11.372, 146; 11.393-4, 46; 11.435ff., 140; 11.522-5, 153; 11.583-4, 144; 11.686-9, 46; 11.804, 87; 11.817, 87; 12.35-6, 46; 12.120, 196, 207; 12.162,

Index Locorum

144;12.413, **111**; 12.440, **142**; 12.680, **171**; 12.791, **140**; 12.846, **46**; 12.948-52, **161**; 12.949, **161**
Appendix Vergiliana **13**
Culex **13**; 12, **59**
Eclogues 1, **20, 171**; 1.2, **154**; 1.6-7, **203**; 1.18, **27**; 1.27, **27**; 1.43-5, **143**; 1.45, **110**; 1.58, **31**; 1.71, **29**; 1.82, **147**; 2.1, **20**; 2.13, **19**; 2.20, **103**; 2.21, **27**; 2.70, **29**, **61**; 3, **21**; 3.60, **38**, **146**; 3.83, **83**, **84**; 3.99, **111**; 3.100, **32**; 4, **21, 22, 23, 37, 89, 99, 176**; 4.4, **99**; 4.6, **45**; 4.6-7, **1, 15**; 4.7, **95**; 4.17, **144**; 4.18-20, **95**; 4.21-45, **95**; 4.23, **95**; 4.28-30, **45**; 4.28, **95**; 4.33, **61**; 4.39, **111**; 4.46-7, **86**; 4.49, **46**; 4.60, **213**; 5, **20**; 5.10, **30**; 5.12, **30**; 5.13-14, **30**; 5.16, **83**; 5.24-8, **31**; 5.34, **143**; 5.37, **61**; 5.57, **213**; 6.8, **145, 154**; 6.15, **21**; 6.48-51, **108**; 6.74-5, **101**; 7, **19, 21**; 7.9, **32**; 7.43, **143**; 7.69, **20**; 8, **21, 29**; 8.29, **86**; 8.30, **86, 94**; 8.32, **86**; 8.64, **86**; 8.87, **143**; 8.108, **144**; 9, **26-7, 29**; 10.16, **31**; 10.27, **87**; 10.44-5, **46**; 10.70-2, **18**; 10.75, **29**
Georgics 1.1-5, **67**; 1.1, **58**, **111**; 1.14-15, **58**; 1.69, **61**; 1.82, **111**; 1.118, **151**; 1.122, **46**; 1.157, **61**; 1.165, **142**; 1.168, **49**; 1.211, **46**; 1.298, **61**; 1.493-7, **154**; 1.506-8, **154**; 1.508, **40**; 2, **21**; 2.58, **153**; 2.89-108, **148**; 2.94, **148**; 2.96, **148**; 2.97-108, **148**; 2.100, **148**; 2.101-2, **148**; 2.103-8, **65-6**; 2.103-4, **148**; 2.120-1, **77**; 2.136-76, **67**; 2.146-7, **110**; 2.149ff., **78**; 2.155, **150**; 2.156, **147**; 2.157, **147**, **150**; 2.161ff., **78**; 2.167-74, **149**; 2.167, **150**; 2.173-4, **147**; 2.173, **149**; 2.223, **111**; 2.283, **46**; 2.356-7, **111**; 2.458-540, **154**; 2.534, **74**; 2.540, **77**; 3.4, **192**; 3.10-39, **150**; 3.30, **150**; 3.144, **148**; 3.186, **153**; 3.207-8, **142**; 3.208, **153**; 3.339-83, **67**; 3.352-5, **77**; 3.382, **45**; 3.383, **199**; 3.440-556, **26**; 3.455, **26**; 3.463, **77**; 3.469, **26**; 3.470-1, **26**; 3.498, **26**; 3.518, **28**; 4.1-2, **210**; 4.6, **150**; 4.19-23, **111**; 4.71, **46**; 4.109, **111**; 4.116-48, **67**; 4.149-227, **103**; 4.149-50, **103**; 4.153-4, **111**; 4.154, **88**; 4.155, **111**; 4.158-67, **111**; 4.159-64, **111**; 4.161, **111**; 4.168, **111**; 4.169, **111**; 4.184, **111**; 4.198, **111**; 4.200-1, **111**; 4.201, **111**; 4.208, **110**; 4.210-12, **111**; 4.212-18, **111**; 4.214, **111**; 4.236-8, **111**; 4.250, **111**; 4.262, **105**; 4.282, **88**; 4.315, **211**; 4.334-5, **149**; 4.340, **86**; 4.380, **86**; 4.501, **150**; 4.521, **77**; 4.538-43, **203**; 4.559-66, **150**; 4.559, **48**, **150**; 4.560-2, **48**; 4.562, **49**; 4.563, **150**; 4.565-6, **203**; 4.565, **150**

ZONARAS
Ann. 13.23, **93**
ZOSIMUS
5.41, **211**

General Index

This index is generally historical and geographical in scope.
For specific textual references or authors, see the Index Locorum.

Achaia, 62
Adrianople, Battle of, 4, 100, 183
Aelius, 173, 176-7, 184
Africa, 18, 20, 62, 71-3, 107
Alexander Severus, 173, 181, 183
Allectus, 1, 35
allusion, see intertextuality
Ambrose, 4, 10, 23, 97-111
Antioch, 4
Ammianus Marcellinus, 5, 63
Arbogast, 155, 159, 167, 169-70
Arcadius, 3, 5
Arius, Arianism, 3, 100-1
Athanasius, 4
Augustine, 5, 8, 10, 97, 112-27, 168, 174
Augustus, 2, 13-14, 21, 39, 42-3, 164
Ausonius, 5, 8-9, 22-3, 80-7, 129, 141-54
Avienus, 5, 62-78

biography, 8, 11-14, 172-88
Boethius, 202-3

Calpurnius, 18-21
Caracalla, 172
Carausius, 1, 6, 35
Carthage, 6, 114, 116, 168-70
Cassiciacum, 112-13, 114-16
Cato, 173
cento, 8, 79-95
Christianity, Christians, Christian, 3, 5, 23-30, 87-90, 114-16, 144
  conversion, 114, 116
  Gospels, 47-61
  martyrs, 128-40
  toleration, 3
Cicero, 9, 33, 35-6, 43, 98, 173, 202
Claudian, 4, 5, 6-7, 9, 22, 73, 155-71
Constans, 2
Constantine, 2, 4, 22, 39, 41-2, 48, 179

Constantine II, 2
Constantinople, 4
Constantius, 1
Constantius II, 2
Crispus, 47

Dante, 202
Diadumenianus, 180, 183
didactic, 7, 49, 57-8, 62-78
Diocletian, 1-3, 35, 38, 172
Dionysius, 62-3
Donatus, Aelius, 11-14, 123, 190, 192-4, 197-8

Endelechius, 23-8
Ennius, 37, 51, 173
epic, 47-9, 91, 158, 167
Eugenius, 9, 155, 162, 166-7
Eusebius, 3-4

Firmicus Maternus, 5
Frigidus, Battle of, 10, 155-6, 160-70
Fulgentius, 209

Gaul, 5, 23, 34, 35, 150-1
Gratian, 3, 34, 35, 37, 100, 141, 145-6, 161
Gregory of Nazianzen, 23
Gregory of Tours, 209

Hadrian, 172, 175-7, 184
Heliogabalus, 181
Hippolytus, St, 9, 128-40
Homer, 47, 68-71, 79, 132-3, 174, 189
Honorius, 3, 5, 155-70

intertextuality, allusion, 6-7, 49-51
Italy, 74-5, 150

Jerome, 11, 23, 47, 59, 97, 124
Jerusalem, 205

General Index

Julian, 3, 36, 184, 190
Juvencus, 5, 6, 7, 22, 47-61, 141

Lactantius, 5
Lewis, C.S., 205
Licinius, 3

Macrinus, 180-1
Macrobius, 123, 173, 208
Magnus Maximus, 35, 160, 167
Manichaeans, 10, 113, 116-19
Marius Maximus, 176
Maxentius, 2, 39, 40, 42
Maximian, 1, 35, 38, 39
Milan, 4

narrative, 47, 58
Nemesianus, 5, 18-22, 141
Nicaea, 3
Nicomachus Flavianus, 166
Nicomedia, 4

Palladius, 101-2
panegyric, 7-8, 33-46, 152, 160-70
pastoral, 7, 17-32
pathos, 143
Paulinus of Nola, 5, 22, 129, 141, 204
Persia, 4
Pescennius Niger, 178
Petrarch, 202
Pliny the Younger, 33-4, 36, 43

Praeneste, 175, 181
Proba, 8, 22, 87-90
Prudentius, 7, 9, 22, 128-40

Rome, 2, 4, 21, 62, 74-5, 114, 133-8
   Altar of Victory, 3
   Lateran Basilica, 3
   Milvian Bridge, 2, 8, 39
   Via Tiburtina, 9, 135

Sallust, 173
Servius, 10-11, 43, 123, 189-200
sortes Vergilianae, 8, 87, 173-6
Spain, 5, 128, 156
Stilicho, 155-6, 159
Suetonius, 12, 173, 191
Symmachus, 3, 5, 36-7

Tetrarchy, 2, 4
Theocritus, 17
Theodoric, 202
Theodosius, 3, 4, 5, 9, 128, 145, 155-8
Tiberius Claudius Donatus, 11, 43, 197-8
Trajan, 34
Trier, 2, 4, 35, 39
Troy, 1, 50, 70-1

Valens, 3
Valentinian, 3, 36, 141
Valentinian II, 3, 108, 161